EDUCATION POLICY
FOR THE 21ST CENTURY

CHICAGO ASSEMBLY BOOKS

Creating Jobs, Creating Workers: Economic Development and Employment in Metropolitan Chicago (1990)

Paying for Health Care: Public Policy Choices for Illinois (1992)

Affordable Housing and Public Policy: Strategies for Metropolitan Chicago (1993)

Crime, Communities, and Public Policy (1995)

Dilemmas of Fiscal Reform: Paying for State and Local Government in Illinois (1996)

Families, Poverty, and Welfare Reform: Confronting a New Policy Era (1999)

Education Policy for the 21st Century: Challenges and Opportunities in Standards-Based Reform (2001)

Education Policy for the 21st Century

Challenges and Opportunities in Standards-Based Reform

Edited by

Lawrence B. Joseph

A Chicago Assembly Book

Center for Urban Research and Policy Studies
Irving B. Harris Graduate School
    of Public Policy Studies
The University of Chicago

Distributed by University of Illinois Press

Copyright © 2001 by the University of Chicago. All rights reserved.

ISBN 0-9626755-6-3 (paper)

Published by:

        Center for Urban Research and Policy Studies
        Irving B. Harris Graduate School of Public Policy Studies
        The University of Chicago
        1155 East 60th Street
        Chicago, IL 60637

Distributed by:

        University of Illinois Press
        1325 South Oak Street
        Champaign, IL 61820

CONTENTS

TABLES

Lawrence B. Joseph

Melissa Roderick

Contents

G. Alfred Hess, Jr.

John Q. Easton and Sandra L. Storey

PREFACE:
THE CHICAGO ASSEMBLY

The Chicago Assembly is designed to illuminate critical public policy issues facing Chicago and the broader metropolitan region of northeastern Illinois. The major objectives of the Chicago Assembly are to focus attention and stimulate informed discussion on significant policy issues in the Chicago region; to educate government officials, community and civic leadership, and the general citizenry regarding the factual background and the range of policy options in each issue area; to facilitate more effective communication among decision-makers from the public, private, and non-profit sectors, as well as from city, suburban, and statewide entities; and to raise the level and quality of public policy discourse in metropolitan Chicago on a continuing basis.

Each Chicago Assembly program focuses on a public policy issue that has critical importance for the Chicago area, as well as broader national implications. In preparation for each assembly, the project commissions a set of background papers and commentaries written by leading public policy experts. The background material is distributed to participants in advance of the assembly itself, which includes prominent representatives from government, business, labor, civic groups, community-based organizations, advocacy groups, and academia. The Chicago Assembly is a working, participatory enterprise, where regional leaders gather for an intensive two-day period to deliberate about fundamental issues *and* to reach some conclusions. Each Chicago Assembly produces a written report, containing findings and recommendations, that is endorsed by participants at a concluding plenary session. The final report is an integrated document reflecting major points of agreement and disagreement among participants. Shortly after the assembly, the report is released for general distribution throughout the Chicago metropolitan area. Subsequently, the Chicago Assembly publishes a book containing the background papers, commentaries, and final report.

This book is a product of the seventh Chicago Assembly, "Education Reform for the 21st Century," which was held in January 1998 at Hickory Ridge Conference Center in Lisle, Illinois.

The Chicago Assembly is made possible by ongoing support from the M. R. Bauer Foundation and the Irving B. Harris Graduate School of Public Policy Studies.

Laurence E. Lynn, Jr.

Sydney Stein, Jr., Professor of Public Management
Director, Center for Urban Research and Policy Studies
Irving B. Harris Graduate School of Public Policy Studies
The University of Chicago

ACKNOWLEDGMENTS

The essays in this book are revised and updated versions of papers that were originally prepared for the Chicago Assembly on "Education Reform for the 21st Century." Major funding for the Chicago Assembly program on education reform was provided by the M. R. Bauer Foundation, with additional support from the Chicago Tribune Foundation and the Steans Initiative for Urban Policy Development.

The Chicago Assembly Report was developed with the help of a drafting committee consisting of facilitators and recorders: John Ayers, Suzanne Bassi, Larry Bennett, Joyce Hollingsworth, James Nowlan, Renae Ogletree, Sylvia Puente, and Wim Wiewel. Reva Nelson and Martha Ross wrote the initial draft of the report. Erin Krasik, Jennifer Matjasko, Audra Millen, and Jodie Zalk provided additional staff support. The concluding plenary session at the Chicago Assembly was chaired by Larry Lynn.

Barbara Ray once again served with distinction as copy editor for this volume. Katherine Beacham, Brandy Jones, Steven Merriett, and Shana Whitehead assisted in preparing tables, checking references, and proofreading.

L.J.

NOTES ON CONTRIBUTORS

John Q. Easton is deputy director of the Consortium on Chicago School Research at the University of Chicago. He was formerly director of the Department of Research, Analysis, and Assessment for the Chicago Public Schools, as well as director of research for the Chicago Panel on School Policy. **Sandra L. Storey** is a senior research analyst with the Chicago Public Schools.

G. Alfred Hess, Jr., is research professor in the School of Education and Social Policy and director of the Center for Urban School Policy at Northwestern University. He was formerly executive director of the Chicago Panel on Public School Policy and Finance. His publications include *Restructuring Urban Schools: A Chicago Perspective* (Teachers College Press, 1995).

Lawrence B. Joseph is senior research associate in the School of Social Service Administration and the Irving B. Harris Graduate School of Public Policy Studies at the University of Chicago. He is associate director of the Center for Urban Research and Policy Studies, program director of the Chicago Assembly, and editor of Chicago Assembly books.

Richard D. Laine is director of education policy and initiatives with the Illinois Business Roundtable. He was formerly associate superintendent for policy, planning, and resource management at the Illinois State Board of Education.

Valerie E. Lee is professor in the School of Education at the University of Michigan. Her publications include *Catholic Schools and the Common Good* (co-author with Anthony S. Bryk and Peter B. Holland; Harvard University Press, 1993) and *Restructuring High Schools for Equity and Excellence: What Works* (with Julia B. Smith; Teachers College Press, 2001).

Dan A. Lewis is professor in the School of Education and Social Policy and faculty fellow with the Institute for Policy Research at Northwestern University. He is also a faculty affiliate of the Northwestern University / University of Chicago Joint Center for

Poverty Research. His publications include *Race and Educational Reform in the American Metropolis* (State University of New York Press, 1995)

Laurence E. Lynn, Jr., is the Sydney Stein, Jr., Professor of Public Management in the School of Social Service Administration and the Irving B. Harris Graduate School of Public Policy Studies at the University of Chicago. He is also director of the Harris School's Center for Urban Research and Policy Studies. His publications include *Improving Governance: A New Logic for Empirical Research* (Georgetown University Press, 2001).

Diane Massell is a senior research associate with Consortium for Policy Research in Education (CPRE) at the University of Michigan. She is co-principal investigator of CPRE's study of education reform policy. Her publications include *State Strategies for Building Capacity in Education: Progress and Continuing Challenges* (CPRE, 1998).

Dea Meyer is vice president of the Civic Committee of the Commercial Club of Chicago. In 1995-96, she was chief of staff for the Governor's Commission on Education Funding for the State of Illinois. She has also served as a member of the School Designation Task Force of the Illinois State Board of Education.

Charles M. Payne is professor in the Department of History and in the African and African-American Studies Program at Duke University. His publications include *Getting What We Ask For: The Ambiguity of Success and Failure in Urban Education* (Greenwood Press, 1984). He has been the director of a six-year ethnographic study of the Chicago implementation of the Comer School Development Process.

Lawrence O. Picus is professor and chair of the Division of Administration and Policy in the Rossier School of Education at the University of Southern California. He is also director of the Center for Research in Education Finance. He is co-author, with Allan R. Odden, of *School Finance: A Policy Perspective* (McGraw-Hill, 2nd edition, 2000) and co-editor, with James L. Wattenbarger, of *Where Does the Money Go? Resource Allocation in Elementary and Secondary Schools* (Corwin Press, 1996).

Melissa Roderick is associate professor in the School of Social Service Administration at the University of Chicago. She is also a director of the Consortium on Chicago School Research. She is the lead author of several Consortium reports, including *Ending Social Promotion: Results from the First Two Years* (1999) and *Changing Standards, Changing Relationships: Building Family-School Relationships to Promote Achievement in High Schools* (1998).

William Sander is professor of economics at DePaul University. His publications include *Catholic Schools: Private and Social Effects* (Kluwer Academic Publishers, 2001). **William Testa** is vice president and director of regional programs in the Research Department at the Federal Reserve Bank of Chicago. He has written widely in the areas of economic development programs, the Midwest economy, and state-local public finance.

Jerome Stermer is president of Voices for Illinois Children, a nonpartisan citizen advocacy group based in Chicago. The organization's activities include "Start Early: Learning Begins at Birth," a statewide public education campaign targeting young, at-risk parents. Voices also publishes *Illinois Kids Count*, an annual report on the state of children and families in Illinois.

Maris A. Vinovskis is the Bentley Professor of History and professor of public policy at the University of Michigan. He is also a senior research scientist with the Center for Political Studies in the Institute for Social Research. His publications include *History and Educational Policymaking* (Yale University Press, 1999).

Kenneth K. Wong is associate professor in the Department of Education and the College at the University of Chicago. He is the principal author of a series of reports on integrated governance in the Chicago public schools. His publications also include *Funding Public Schools: Politics and Policies* (University Press of Kansas, 1999).

INTRODUCTION

Lawrence B. Joseph

Public education in the United States has long been viewed as a panacea for a variety of social problems. This faith in the power of education has been associated historically with two core American values: "equality" and "achievement." Education has been viewed as a means for reconciling these competing values. At the same time, different periods in the history of American education have put different degrees of emphasis on equality and achievement.[1] The "common school" movement of the 1830s and 1840s viewed education as a moral and political force. Free public schools, attended by the children of the rich and poor alike, were agencies of democratic citizenship and social cohesion. Horace Mann, leader of the common school movement, saw the public school as both the "great equalizer" and the "balance wheel of the social machinery." It never worked exactly that way, of course. Many children attended private schools, while Native Americans and African-Americans typically attended either separate schools or no schools at all. Nonetheless, it was assumed that the existence of free public schools would somehow compensate for economic sources of inequality and that a common educational experience for all children would have the effect of widening the range of their opportunities. Moreover, exposure of children of diverse backgrounds to a common curriculum in a common school would strengthen community ties and produce a responsible citizenry.[2]

Beginning in the late 19th century, the nation experienced profound changes stemming from immigration, urbanization, and industrialization. Public schools assumed growing importance as "Americanizing" agents, although the center of attention became the high school rather than the common school of the pre-Civil-War period. It was thought that a high school

---

[1] See Welter, 1962; Perkinson, 1968; Lipset, 1973, pp. 1-3.

[2] See Coleman, 1968; Cremin, 1964; Wiebe, 1969; Curti, 1959.

education would enable lower-class children (especially children from immigrant families) to attain an honorable place in the expanding industrial order. At the same time, the social meaning and purpose of education began to shift toward more emphasis on competitive success and the material value of schooling. As early as 1915, statistical studies began to appear that tried to show that educating the lower classes would improve their economic status. With expanding industrialization, the view of public schools as the "great equalizer" was supplanted by the public school as the "great selector." Equal opportunity became a fair chance to compete for the best places in the occupational hierarchy. Moreover, with the expansion of high school enrollment, the standard classical, college preparatory curriculum no longer seemed to fit the needs of the new majority of students. The common school view of education for democratic citizenship was supplemented and overshadowed by a curriculum supposedly tailored to students with different abilities, interests, and post-high-school destinations.[3]

At mid-century, public education was increasingly seen as the promoter of the rise of the talented individual and as a training and selection mechanism for society's labor force.[4] In addition, the social meaning of high school had changed, as graduating, not just attending, became the expectation. The proportion of 14-to-17-year-olds who were enrolled in secondary school increased from 51 percent in 1929-30 to 76 percent in 1949-50. Over the same time period, the proportion of 17-year-olds who were high school graduates increased from 29 percent to 59 percent (see Table 1). With high school enrollment becoming nearly universal, there was emerging concern about weakening academic standards and declining educational quality.[5] During the 1950s, especially in the post-Sputnik years, heightened emphasis was put on cognitive skills and academic achievement. At the federal level, this was exemplified by the National Defense Education Act of 1958, which provided federal funding to improve teaching in science, mathematics,

---

[3] See Curti, 1959; Perkinson, 1968; Coleman, 1968; Cohen and Neufeld, 1981, pp. 71-74; Tyack and Cuban, 1995, pp. 16-22.

[4] See, e.g., Wiebe, 1969; Perkinson, 1968, pp. 146-153.

[5] See Cohen and Neufeld, 1981, pp. 75-78; Trow, 1961.

and foreign languages at the elementary, secondary, and post-secondary levels.[6] At the outset of the 1960s, John Gardner, president of the Carnegie Corporation—and soon to be secretary of health, education, and welfare in the Kennedy administration—noted the unprecedented demand for men and women of high ability and advanced training. He observed that the chief vehicle for carrying on the talent hunt was the nation's educational system, which had become "an increasingly rugged sorting-out process" (Gardner, 1961, p. 66).

TABLE 1: Secondary School Enrollment and High School Graduates, 1899-1900 to 1998-1999

	Enrollment in grades 9-12 (1,000s)	Enrollment as pct. of 14-to-17-year-old population	High school graduates (1,000s)	High school graduates as pct. of 17-year-old population
1899-1900	630	10.2	95	6.4
1909-1910	1,032	14.3	156	8.8
1919-1920	2,414	31.2	311	16.8
1929-1930	4,741	50.7	667	29.0
1939-1940	7,059	72.6	1,221	50.8
1949-1950	6,397	76.1	1,200	59.0
1959-1960	9,306	83.4	1,858	69.5
1969-1970	14,337	92.2	2,889	76.9
1979-1980	14,916	89.8	3,043	71.4
1989-1990	12,583	93.0	2,586	73.8
1998-1999 (est.)	14,658	94.5	2,786	70.6

Source: NCES, 1999, Tables 57 and 104.

[6] See CQ, 1965, pp. 1200-1201; Kaestle and Smith, 1982, pp. 392-396.

THE PURSUIT OF EQUAL
EDUCATIONAL OPPORTUNITY

In 1954, the U.S. Supreme Court issued its landmark decision in *Brown v. Board of Education of Topeka, Kansas*. The court declared that government-imposed segregation of public schools violated the equal protection provisions of the Constitution. It was not until the mid-1960s, however, that equal educational opportunity became a prominent issue on the nation's policy agenda. The Civil Rights Act of 1964 authorized the attorney general to file lawsuits for the desegregation of public schools. The same legislation prohibited racial discrimination in any program or activity receiving federal assistance (CQ, 1965, pp. 1638-1639). The Economic Opportunity Act of 1964, which launched the "war on poverty," included a new Head Start preschool program for children from low-income families. The Elementary and Secondary Education Act (ESEA) of 1965 marked a major turning point in the federal government's role in education. Title I of ESEA focused on disadvantaged students in both urban and rural areas, with federal aid distributed (through state education agencies) to local school districts on the basis of the number of children from low-income families. School districts could use Title I funds for a broad range of purposes, provided that the programs were "designed to meet the special educational needs of educationally deprived children" (CQ, 1969, pp. 710-711).[7]

The Civil Rights Act of 1964 also required that the U.S. Commissioner of Education produce a report on the lack of equal opportunities in America's public education institutions. The result was the largest educational research project ever undertaken, covering nearly a million pupils in 4,000 public schools, along with their teachers and principals. The project report, *Equality of Educational Opportunity*, was released in 1966 and came to be identified with its lead author, James Coleman of Johns Hopkins University (Coleman et al., 1966). The most striking finding of the Coleman Report was that the substantial academic achievement gap between Blacks and Whites could not be explained by differences among schools as

---

[7] See also Kaestle and Smith, 1982, pp. 396-400; Tyack and Cuban, 1995, pp. 26-29. Some Title I funds could be used for low-income children in private schools.

measured by conventional indicators such as per-pupil expenditures, equipment, teacher-student ratios, libraries, curricula, and teachers' formal qualifications. A student's family background was found to be a much stronger determinant of achievement than any attributes of the school. For Black students, some teacher characteristics (e.g., verbal ability as measured by standardized tests) had moderate effects on achievement, but the single most influential school factor for Blacks was the socioeconomic composition of the student body.

The Coleman Report spawned a vast amount of research, analysis, and policy debate on the effects of schools on academic achievement and on the issue of equal educational opportunity for children of different racial groups and socioeconomic backgrounds.[8] An important contribution of the Coleman Report was drawing attention to the idea of equality of educational opportunity in the context of the effects of schooling. Coleman concluded that what was important was not simply to provide equal access to equal school facilities, but to equalize the life-chances of children from different social backgrounds. Equal opportunity implied equally effective schools, and schools were thus successful only insofar as they reduced the dependence of children's opportunities on their social origins (Coleman, 1966, 1968).

The concern with equality of educational opportunity continued through the 1970s, at least at the federal level. Funding for ESEA Title I, Head Start, and various school improvement programs more than doubled over the decade (see Table 2). In addition, the focus on improving educational opportunities for disadvantaged groups extended into new areas. In 1974, the U.S. Supreme Court issued a decision that required public schools to meet the needs of non-English-speaking children. Congress responded by expanding federal bilingual education programs, which had originated under ESEA Title VII in 1967, and establishing a new Office of Bilingual Education. Legislation enacted in 1975 required states to provide free and appropriate education for all handicapped children; it also mandated that, when appropriate, handicapped children be educated together with other children (CQ, 1977, pp. 382-392).

---

[8] See, e.g., HER, 1968; Mosteller and Moynihan, 1972; Jencks et al., 1972; HER, 1973; Levine and Bane, 1975.

TABLE 2:   Federal On-Budget Funds for Selected Education Programs, 1965-1999 (in $ millions)

	Compensatory education (ESEA Title I)	Head Start	Special education	School improve-ment*	Bilingual education
1965	-------	96.4	13.8	72.3	-----
1970	1,339.0	325.7	79.1	288.3	21.3
1975	1,874.4	403.9	151.2	700.5	92.7
1980	3,204.7	735.0	821.8	788.9	169.5
1985	4,206.8	1,075.1	1,018.0	526.4	157.5
1990	4,494.1	1,447.8	1,616.6	1,189.2	188.9
1995	6,808.0	3,534.0	3,177.0	1,397.0	225.0
1999 (est.)	6,687.4	4,660.0	4,263.8	1,453.6	385.2
Pct. change:					
1970-80	139.3	125.7	939.0	173.6	697.8
1980-90	40.2	97.0	96.7	50.7	11.4
1990-99	48.8	221.9	163.7	22.2	103.9

* Includes Professional Development Grants, Safe and Drug-Free Schools and Communities, Education for Homeless Children and Youth, Innovative Education Program Strategies, and other programs.

Source: NCES, 1999, Table 368.

THE EMERGENCE OF STANDARDS-BASED REFORM

A changing political climate, which included critical reaction to the alleged shortcomings or excesses of equity-driven education policies of the 1960s and 1970s, brought a major shift in emphasis away from equality and back toward achievement.[9]   In August 1981, Terrel Bell, secretary of education in the Reagan administration, appointed a commission to undertake a nation-wide study of the condition of education.   Bell had previously suggested establishing a presidential commission, but his pro-

[9] See Timpane, 1996, pp. 78-79.

posal was rejected by a White House that was committed to abolishing the Department of Education, which had been established near the end of the Carter administration (Bell, 1993). In April 1983, the National Commission on Excellence in Education released its report, *A Nation at Risk*. The report, which was much more negative than Bell himself had anticipated, declared that America's "once unchallenged preeminence in commerce, industry, science, and technological innovation is being overtaken by competitors throughout the world." One of the key causes and dimensions of this problem was the nation's schools. The educational foundations of American society were being eroded by "a rising tide of mediocrity that threatens our very future as a Nation and a people" (NCEE, 1983, p. 5). The commission cited evidence of declining scores on various standardized tests, poor performance by American students on international comparisons of achievement, and unacceptable levels of functional illiteracy. The nation's educational decline was attributed to inadequacies in curriculum content, in expectations for students, in use of time by schools and students, and in the academic preparation and professional working lives of teachers.

The findings and strong language of *A Nation at Risk* had a major impact on education policy agendas at the national, state, and local levels.[10] The report, as well as other critical commentaries on the condition of public education, generated a flurry of reform initiatives, especially in the states. These efforts typically involved more stringent regulation of educational inputs and processes—for example, mandatory courses for students, the length of the school day or school year, graduation requirements, and teacher certification. In Illinois, the General Assembly mandated minimum coursework for high school graduation, certification tests for prospective teachers, periodic evaluation of teachers and other school personnel, and staff development programs at the school district level.

The "educational excellence" movement generated its own critical reaction, which focused on its top-down, regulatory approach to reform. Proponents of "school restructuring" argued that genuine education reform required decentralizing decision-making to the school level, empowering teachers and

---

[10] After the release of *A Nation at Risk*, Secretary Bell heard no more about abolishing the Department of Education (Bell, 1993).

parents, and changing the governance and organization of schools, as well as transforming the process of teaching and learning.[11]   In Illinois, the bottom-up approach was exemplified in the Chicago School Reform Act of 1988, which created a decentralized system of local school councils (LSCs) consisting of teachers, parents, and community members.   The LSCs were given authority to hire and fire principals, determine school budgets, and formulate school improvement plans.

By the end of the 1980s, a new synthesis of top-down and bottom-up approaches to education reform had begun to emerge.   In September 1989, President Bush and the nation's governors gathered for an Education Summit in Charlottesville, Virginia.   At the close of the summit, they issued a "Jeffersonian compact" declaring that the time had come to establish a process for setting national performance goals in education. The summit also outlined some basic features of successful education reform:

- a system of accountability that focuses on results, rather than on compliance with rules and regulations;
- decentralization of authority and decision-making responsibility to the school site, so that educators are empowered to determine the means for achieving the goals and to be held accountable for accomplishing them;
- a rigorous program of instruction designed to ensure that every child can acquire the knowledge and skills required in an economy in which our citizens must be able to think for a living;
- an education system that develops first-rate teachers and creates a professional environment that provides real rewards for success with students, real consequences for failure, and the tools and flexibility required to get the job done; and
- active, sustained parental and business community involvement (*New York Times*, 1989).

The Charlottesville Education Summit had articulated a new policy consensus that came to be known as "standards-based" reform.   According to some formulations, standards-based reform required "systemic" reform, which should include a coher-

---

[11] See Elmore, 1990; Murphy 1992; Timpane, 1996, pp. 82-84.

ent, coordinated set of policies regarding academic content standards, performance standards, assessment tools, teacher preparation and professional development, and accountability for results.[12] Various manifestations of the standards-based movement emerged at the national, state, and local levels. The National Council on Education Standards and Testing, created by Congress in 1991, recommended the development of voluntary national content standards, a new system of state-level assessments, and a set of performance standards for school systems (NCEST, 1992).[13] The Goals 2000: Educate America Act of 1994, which was the centerpiece of the Clinton administration's education agenda, authorized a National Education Standards and Improvement Council (NESIC) to develop voluntary national standards. The legislation also established federal grants to the states for systemic education improvement plans to develop academic content and performance standards, assessments aligned with those standards, and mechanisms to hold schools accountable for improving student achievement.[14]

The movement for voluntary national standards was stalled by the new Republican majorities in Congress in 1995-96. For example, the NESIC, which had never actually been established, was abolished in 1996.[15] Many states, however, continued to pursue education reform initiatives that focused on standards, performance, and accountability. In Illinois, the Chicago School Reform Amendatory Act of 1995 reorganized the central administration of the city's school system and gave the new board and chief executive officer stronger tools for intervention in low-performing schools. In 1997, the Illinois State Board of Education (ISBE) adopted new "Illinois Learning

---

[12] See, e.g., Smith and O'Day, 1991b; O'Day and Smith, 1993; Jacobson and Berne, 1993. In some instances, the terms "restructuring" and "systemic reform" have been used interchangeably: "Restructuring refers to systemic change in which many pieces and levels of the education system and supporting systems . . . must be transformed and linked for the system to be effective" (NGA, 1991, p. 1).

[13] See also Ravitch, 1995, pp. 139-146.

[14] See Riley, 1995; Smith and Scoll, 1995.

[15] See McLaughlin and Shepard, 1995, pp. 1-4; Ravitch, 1995, pp. xvi-xvii.

Standards," which became the basis for redesigning the state's assessment program. ISBE also began to implement a performance-based accountability system linked to student achievement.

One by-product of debates over standards-based education reform has been the re-emergence of concerns about equality of opportunity. The standards-based movement has been criticized for failing to address the social and economic problems faced by public schools. However, for some proponents of standards-based reform, the principle of higher expectations for all students is a potential tool for achieving greater equity in the educational system.[16] The National Council on Education Standards and Testing advanced the notion of "school delivery standards" as a measure of whether schools were providing students with the opportunity to learn the material specified in academic content standards (NCEST, 1992, p. E-5). The Goals 2000: Educate America Act provided for the development of voluntary national opportunity-to-learn (OTL) standards regarding the resources, programs, and qualified teachers needed to enable all students to meet the expectations reflected in new performance standards. The idea of OTL standards generated strong opposition, especially from the nation's governors, who feared that even voluntary OTL standards would lead to unwarranted federal intrusion. OTL provisions in federal legislation were eliminated in 1996, and OTL standards have not been prominent items on state policy agendas.[17]

Regardless of the fate of opportunity-to-learn standards, one of greatest challenges of standards-based reform is improving educational outcomes for disadvantaged students. This issue is especially critical for states and communities with large and growing minority populations. Among midwestern states, Illinois has the highest proportion of both Black students and Hispanic students (see Table 3). In fall 1999, combined Black and Hispanic enrollment in public schools was 36 percent statewide, 47 percent in metropolitan Chicago, and 87 percent in the city of Chicago (see Table 4). National data show that the gap in

---

[16] See, e.g., O'Day and Smith, 1993; McLaughlin and Shepard, 1995, pp. 10-12, 42-48; Gordon, 1995; Timpane, 1996, pp. 84-85.

[17] See Elmore and Fuhrman, 1995; Porter, 1995; Ravitch, 1995, pp. 148-153; Massell, Kirst, and Hoppe, 1997.

educational outcomes between Black and White students has been reduced since the publication of the Coleman Report in 1966, but there is still a long way to go.[18] Pursuing the goals of achievement and equality remains a central challenge in standards-based education reform.

TABLE 3:   Enrollment in Public Elementary and Secondary Schools, Percentage Distribution by Race/Ethnicity, Fall 1997

	White	Black	Hispanic	Asian/ Pacific Islander	American Indian/ Alaskan Native
Alabama	61.7	36.0	0.8	0.7	0.8
Alaska	62.8	4.7	3.0	4.8	24.8
Arizona	56.0	4.4	30.8	1.8	7.0
Arkansas	73.1	23.5	2.2	0.8	0.4
California	38.8	8.8	40.5	11.1	0.9
Colorado	71.3	5.6	19.3	2.7	1.1
Connecticut	71.5	13.7	12.1	2.5	0.2
Delaware	63.2	30.1	4.6	1.9	0.2
Dist. of Columbia	4.0	87.0	7.5	1.5	*
Florida	56.2	25.4	16.4	1.8	0.2
Georgia	57.1	38.0	2.9	1.9	0.1
Hawaii	21.6	2.6	4.7	70.7	0.4
Idaho	87.6	0.7	9.2	1.2	1.3
Illinois	62.0	21.3	13.4	3.1	0.2
Indiana	85.1	11.3	2.6	0.8	0.2
Iowa	91.8	3.6	2.6	1.6	0.5
Kansas	81.3	8.6	7.0	2.0	1.1
Kentucky	88.6	10.3	0.5	0.5	0.1
Louisiana	50.2	46.7	1.2	1.3	0.6
Maine	97.1	0.9	0.5	0.9	0.6
Maryland	55.9	36.1	3.7	4.0	0.3
Massachusetts	77.5	8.5	9.7	4.1	0.2
Michigan	75.6	18.8	2.9	1.6	1.0
Minnesota	85.5	5.6	2.5	4.4	2.0

[18] See, e.g., Smith and O'Day, 1991a; Jencks and Phillips, 1998.

TABLE 3 (continued)

	White	Black	Hispanic	Asian/ Pacific Islander	American Indian/ Alaskan Native
Mississippi	47.8	51.0	0.4	0.6	0.1
Missouri	80.7	16.7	1.3	1.1	0.3
Montana	87.1	0.6	1.4	0.8	10.0
Nebraska	85.7	6.2	5.3	1.4	1.5
Nevada	63.2	9.7	20.5	4.8	1.9
New Hampshire	96.3	1.0	1.4	1.1	0.2
New Jersey	61.9	18.3	14.0	5.7	0.2
New Mexico	38.0	2.4	48.0	1.0	10.6
New York	55.9	20.4	17.8	5.4	0.5
North Carolina	63.2	31.0	2.7	1.6	1.5
North Dakota	88.9	0.9	1.1	0.8	8.3
Ohio	81.7	15.6	1.5	1.0	0.1
Oklahoma	68.1	10.6	4.5	1.3	15.5
Oregon	83.7	2.6	8.1	3.5	2.1
Pennsylvania	79.7	14.5	3.9	1.8	0.1
Rhode Island	77.2	7.5	11.5	3.4	0.5
South Carolina	55.7	42.3	1.0	0.8	0.2
South Dakota	82.9	1.0	0.9	0.8	14.4
Tennessee	74.0	23.7	1.1	1.0	0.1
Texas	45.0	14.4	37.9	2.4	0.3
Utah	88.7	0.8	6.5	2.5	1.5
Vermont	97.1	0.9	0.4	1.1	0.5
Virginia	65.5	27.0	3.6	3.6	0.2
Washington	76.8	4.9	8.6	6.9	2.8
West Virginia	95.1	4.1	0.5	0.3	0.1
Wisconsin	82.2	9.8	3.6	3.0	1.4
Wyoming	88.6	1.1	6.6	0.8	2.9
U.S. total	63.5	17.0	14.4	3.9	1.2

Note: U.S. total includes American Samoa, Guam, Northern Marianas, Puerto Rico, and Virgin Islands.

* Less than 0.05 percent.

Source: NCES, 1999, Table 45.

TABLE 4: Public School Enrollment in Illinois and Metropolitan Chicago by Race/Ethnicity, 1984 and 1999

	Fall 1984	Pct. distr.	Fall 1999	Pct. distr.
State of Illinois	1,835,355	100.0	2,027,600	100.0
White	1,248,175	68.0	1,229,943	60.7
Black	405,027	22.1	432,686	21.3
Hispanic	140,426	7.7	295,896	14.6
Asian	38,503	2.1	65,963	3.3
Metropolitan Chicago	1,102,730	100.0	1,295,004	100.0
White	606,233	55.0	622,980	48.1
Black	330,607	30.0	338,731	26.2
Hispanic	130,922	11.9	272,413	21.0
Asian	32,951	3.0	58,666	4.5
City of Chicago	431,226	100.0	431,750	100.0
White	63,430	14.7	42,970	10.0
Black	261,386	60.6	226,611	52.5
Hispanic	94,246	21.9	147,705	34.2
Asian	11,421	2.6	13,731	3.2
Suburban Cook County	322,181	100.0	368,661	100.0
White	249,495	77.4	215,303	58.4
Black	44,856	13.9	74,885	20.3
Hispanic	16,101	5.0	56,631	15.4
Asian	11,315	3.5	21,313	5.8
Collar counties*	348,343	100.0	494,593	100.0
White	293,308	84.2	364,707	73.7
Black	24,365	7.0	37,235	7.5
Hispanic	20,575	5.9	68,077	13.8
Asian	10,215	2.9	23,622	4.8
Downstate	732,625	100.0	732,596	100.0
White	641,942	87.6	606,963	82.9
Black	74,420	10.2	93,955	12.8
Hispanic	9,504	1.3	23,483	3.2
Asian	5,552	0.8	7,297	1.0

* DuPage, Kane, Lake, McHenry, and Will counties

Source: ISBE, 1985, 2000.

CHALLENGES AND OPPORTUNITIES

The chapters and critical commentaries in this volume are
revised and updated versions of papers originally prepared for
the seventh Chicago Assembly, "Education Reform for the 20th
Century." The lead chapter by Melissa Roderick examines
major educational trends and issues in metropolitan Chicago,
the state of Illinois, and the nation as a whole. Roderick
observes that the current emphasis on standards, performance,
and accountability is occurring at a time when student populations across the Chicago area are increasingly diverse. These
demographic changes mean that issues of diversity and equity
among racial and ethnic groups are no longer limited to public
schools in Chicago. Roderick goes on to discuss standards-
based reform in the context of several other important developments: changing expectations about early childhood education
and school readiness; trends in reading and mathematics
achievement as indicated by the National Assessment of Educational Progress, as well as by results of standardized tests in
Illinois and Chicago; and the increasing importance of educational attainment (i.e., level of schooling completed) for economic success.

G. Alfred Hess focuses on state education policy in Illinois.
He identifies four major problems that have been contesting for
primacy on the education reform agenda: improving low-
performing schools attended primarily by low-income and minority students; setting higher standards for and improving the
skills and capabilities of all students; overcoming inequities in
the distribution of educational resources; and operating the
public education system more efficiently and at lower cost to
taxpayers. Hess argues that efforts to solve these problems
must address four conundrums: how to shift from regulating
school inputs to improving educational outcomes; how to define
standards and measure performance; whether the goal of school
finance reform should be "equity" or "adequacy"; and how to
define and measure "efficiency" in the use of educational resources. The chapter concludes with an examination of policy
strategies for improving teacher quality, improving school performance, and successfully engaging students, especially those
in low-performing schools.

Diane Massell discusses the progress of standards-based,
systemic reform in the states, drawing largely from an eight-
state study conducted by the Consortium for Policy Research in

Education. She begins by explaining the background of the standards-based reform movement and then turns to identifying some of the key issues that have arisen in state efforts to develop and implement new curriculum standards, assessment tools, and performance-based accountability mechanisms. Massell concludes with a discussion of strategies for building the capacity needed to achieve higher standards. She argues that a critical aspect of any reform strategy is the extent to which policymakers address the needs of teachers and school administrators for the knowledge and skills, resources, and organizational capacity to meet the challenges of standards-based reform.

John Easton and Sandra Storey describe the development of standards-based accountability systems by both the Illinois State Board of Education and the Chicago Public Schools. The authors maintain that a system for holding schools accountable for student performance should have the following major components: a set of clearly defined academic content standards that specify what students should know and be able to do; assessment tools that are explicitly designed to measure student achievement in relation to the content standards; a set of statistical indicators that report how well students are performing; and standards for school performance, with rewards, sanctions, intervention, and support tied to how schools do in relation to performance standards. Easton and Storey also present a set of recommendations on the use of standards-based assessment results for educational accountability. These recommendations include designing assessments to encourage good teaching and holding schools accountable for *gains* in student learning.

The chapter by Lawrence Picus addresses the question of how money matters in improving student achievement. Picus reviews major statistical studies of the link between public school spending and educational outcomes, noting that there remains considerable disagreement over the impact of additional resources on student performance. He then summarizes another body of research that shows remarkable similarity in how school districts nationwide allocate their resources. Picus maintains that it is crucial that schools focus whatever resources they have on those factors that are most likely to affect student performance and improve student learning. He goes on to argue that improving student performance, with or without additional funds, requires four key ingredients: reallocation of existing resources, incentives for improved performance, a more market-

based budgeting environment, and developing the concept of
"venture capital" for school restructuring.

Charles Payne looks at building-level obstacles to urban
school reform. The first part of his chapter presents a typology
of impediments to change in urban public schools. These
include social infrastructure, building-level politics, instructional
capacity, environmental turbulence, and structure of support for
implementation. The typology is used to analyze the limitations
of several influential school reform models—in particular, James
Comer's "School Development Process" and Theodore Sizer's
"Coalition of Essential Schools." The second section of
Payne's chapter focuses in greater detail on the problem of
"social demoralization." In the worst inner-city schools, the
basic web of social relationships is likely to be severely damaged, making it impossible to effectively use financial and
technical resources even when they become available. Payne
shows how social demoralization and pervasive distrust repeatedly undermined reform efforts in one Chicago elementary
school, even though it was not among the worst schools in the
city. He concludes with a discussion of implications for school
reform and education policy.

Dan Lewis offers an interpretive essay on lessons to be
drawn from the experience of Chicago school reform, especially
the first wave of reform that brought radical decentralization of
power to local school councils. He begins by putting the Chicago School Reform Act of 1988 in historical context, tracing
the roots of this reform effort back to political conflicts around
school desegregation during the 1960s. He then explains how
the decentralized structure of authority created in 1988 generated pressures that led to recentralization in the second wave
of reform beginning in 1995. The remainder of Lewis's chapter focuses on lessons regarding school improvement, teacher
improvement, and student improvement in Chicago's public
schools. Lewis maintains that both reformers and researchers
have been preoccupied with issues of process and governance.
Education reform in the next decade, he argues, must focus
more clearly on student learning.

The book concludes with the Chicago Assembly Report on
"Education Reform for the 20th Century." The report reflects
the views of a broad and diverse group of participants, including leadership from state government, local school districts,
community and civic organizations, business, labor, professional
associations, advocacy groups, foundations, and universities.

Chicago Assembly participants engaged in two days of intensive discussion and deliberation on policy strategies for enhancing learning opportunities and improving educational outcomes for student populations in metropolitan Chicago.

The findings and recommendations of the Chicago Assembly Report reflect broad agreement on some of the major issues of achieving higher standards, enhancing accountability, and building capacity for reform. The report states that a central goal of education reform should be to assure that all students acquire the basic skills and higher-order skills to prepare for the 21st century. A major obstacle to achieving higher standards for all students in the Chicago metropolitan region is a "two-tiered" education system that produces widely disparate outcomes for advantaged and disadvantaged students. Effective educational accountability systems should involve multiple stakeholders, with primary focus on principals and teachers at the school level. Greater emphasis should be put on rewards and recognition for improvement, as well as appropriate intervention in low-performing schools. Building capacity to achieve higher standards should focus on strategies to improve the quality of teaching. Such efforts should include attracting and retaining talented teachers, strengthening incentives to improve teacher performance, and investing in effective professional development. In addition, educational partnerships, involving collaboration with a wide variety of stakeholders, can be important tools for expanding resources and building long-term support for school reform.

REFERENCES

Bell, Terrel H. (1993). "Reflections One Decade After *A Nation at Risk*," *Phi Delta Kappan*, April 1993, pp. 592-597.

Carter, Robert L. (1995). "The Unending Struggle for Equal Educational Opportunity," *Teachers College Record*, vol. 96, no. 4 (Summer 1995), pp. 619-626.

Cohen, David K., and Barbara Neufeld (1981). "The Failure of High Schools and the Progress of Education," *Daedalus*, Summer 1981, pp. 69-89.

Coleman, James S. (1966). "Equal Schools or Equal Students?" *The Public Interest*, Summer 1966, pp. 70-75.

Coleman, James S. (1968). "The Concept of Equality of Educational Opportunity," *Harvard Educational Review*, vol. 38, no. 1 (Winter 1968), pp. 7-22.

Coleman, James S., et al. (1966). *Equality of Educational Opportunity.* Washington, D.C.: U.S. Government Printing Office.

CQ (1965). *Congress and the Nation, 1945-1964.* Washington, D.C.: Congressional Quarterly Service.

_____ (1969). *Congress and the Nation, Volume II: 1965-1968.* Washington, D.C.: Congressional Quarterly Service.

_____ (1977). *Congress and the Nation, Volume IV: 1973-1976.* Washington, D.C.: Congressional Quarterly Service.

Cremin, Lawrence A. (1964). *The Transformation of the School: Progressivism in American Education, 1876-1957.* New York: Vintage.

Curti, Merle (1959). *The Social Ideas of American Educators.* Paterson, N.J.: Pageant Books.

Elmore, Richard F., and Associates (1990). *Restructuring Schools: The Next Generation of Educational Reform.* San Francisco: Jossey-Bass.

Elmore, Richard F., and Susan H. Fuhrman (1995). "Opportunity-to-Learn Standards and the State Role in Education," *Teachers College Record*, vol. 96, no. 3 (Spring 1995), pp. 432-457.

Gardner, John W. (1961). *Excellence: Can We Be Equal and Excellent Too?* New York: Harper and Row.

Gordon, Edmund W. (1995). "The Promise of Accountability and Standards in the Achievement of Equal Educational Opportunity," *Teachers College Record*, vol. 96, no. 4 (Summer 1995), pp. 751-756.

HER (1968). *Harvard Educational Review, Special Issue: Equal Educational Opportunity*, vol. 38, no. 1 (Winter 1968).

_____ (1973). *Perspectives on Inequality.* Harvard Educational Review, Reprint Series No. 8.

ISBE (1985). "1984-1985 Public School Fall Enrollment and Housing Report." Springfield: Illinois State Board of Education.

_____ (2000). "1999-2000 Public School Fall Enrollment and Housing Report." Springfield: Illinois State Board of Education.

Jacobson, Stephen L., and Robert Berne, eds. (1993). *Reforming Education: The Emerging Systemic Approach.* Thousand Oaks, Calif.: Corwin Press.

Jencks, Christopher, et al. (1972). *Inequality: A Reassessment of the Effect of Family and Schooling in America.* New York: Basic Books.

Jencks, Christopher, and Meredith Phillips, eds. (1998). *The Black-White Test Score Gap.* Washington, D.C.: Brookings Institution Press.

Kaestle, Carl F., and Marshall S. Smith (1982). "The Federal Role in Elementary and Secondary Education, 1940-1980," *Harvard Educational Review,* vol. 52, no. 4 (November 1982), pp. 384-408.

Levine, Donald M., and Mary Jo Bane, eds. (1975). *The "Inequality" Controversy: Schooling and Distributive Justice.* New York: Basic Books.

Lipset, Seymour Martin (1973). *The First New Nation: The United States in Historical and Comparative Perspective.* New York: W. W. Norton.

Massell, Diane, Michael Kirst, and Margaret Hoppe (1997). *Persistence and Change: Standards-Based Systemic Reform in Nine States.* CPRE Policy Brief. Philadelphia: Consortium for Policy Research in Education, Graduate School of Education, University of Pennsylvania.

McLaughlin, Milbrey W., and Lorrie A. Shepard, with Jennifer O'Day (1995). *Improving Education through Standards-Based Reform: A Report of the National Academy of Education Panel on Standards-Based Education Reform.* Stanford, Calif.: National Academy of Education.

Mosteller, Frederick, and Daniel P. Moynihan, eds. (1972). *On Equality of Educational Opportunity: Papers Deriving from the Harvard University Faculty Seminar on the Coleman Report.* New York: Vintage.

Murphy, Joseph (1992). "Restructuring America's Schools: An Overview." In Chester E. Finn and Theodor Rebarber, eds., *Education Reform in the '90s.* New York: Macmillan.

NCEE (1983). *A Nation at Risk: The Imperative for Educational Reform.* Report of the National Commission on Excellence in Education. Washington, D.C.: U.S. Department of Education.

NCES (1999). *Digest of Education Statistics, 1999.* Washington, D.C.: National Center for Education Statistics, U.S. Department of Education.

NCEST (1992). *Raising Standards for American Education: A Report to Congress, the Secretary of Education, the National Education Goals Panel, and the American People.* Washington, D.C.: National Council on Education Standards and Testing.

NGA (1991). *From Rhetoric to Action: State Progress in Restructuring the Education System.* Washington, D.C.: National Governors' Association.

New York Times (1989). "A Jeffersonian Compact: The Statement by the President and Governors," *New York Times,* October 1, 1989, sec. 4, p. 22.

O'Day, Jennifer A., and Marshall S. Smith (1993). "Systemic Reform and Educational Opportunity." In Susan H. Fuhrman, ed. *Designing Coherent Education Policy: Improving the System.* San Francisco: Jossey-Bass.

Perkinson, Henry J. (1968). *The Imperfect Panacea: American Faith in Education, 1865-1965.* New York: Random House.

Porter, Andrew (1995). "The Uses and Misuses of Opportunity-to-Learn Standards," *Educational Researcher,* January-February 1995, pp. 21-27.

Ravitch, Diane (1995). *National Standards in American Education: A Citizen's Guide.* Washington, D.C.: Brookings Institution Press.

Riley, Richard (1995). "Reflections on Goals 2000," *Teachers College Record,* vol. 96, no. 3 (Spring 1995), pp. 380-388.

Smith, Marshall S., and Jennifer O'Day (1991a). "Educational Equality: 1966 and Now." In Deborah A. Verstegen and James Gordon Ward, eds., *Spheres of Justice in Education: The 1990 American Education Finance Association Yearbook.* New York: Harper Business.

_____ (1991b). "Systemic School Reform." In Susan H. Fuhrman and Betty Malen, eds., *The Politics of Curriculum and Testing: The 1990 Yearbook of the Politics of Education Association.* New York: The Falmer Press.

Smith, Marshall S., and Brett W. Scoll (1995). "The Clinton Human Capital Agenda," *Teachers College Record,* vol. 96, no. 3 (Spring 1995), pp. 389-404.

Timpane, P. Michael (1996). "The Uncertain Progress of Education Reform, 1983-1994." In Edward F. Zigler, Sharon Lynn Kagan, and Nancy W. Hall, eds., *Children, Families, and Government: Preparing for the Twenty-First Century.* New York: Cambridge University Press.

Trow, Martin (1961). "The Second Transformation of American Secondary Education," *International Journal of Comparative Sociology*, vol. 2, pp. 144-166.

Tyack, David, and Larry Cuban (1995). *Tinkering Toward Utopia: A Century of Public School Reform.* Cambridge: Harvard University Press.

U.S. Department of Education (1996). *Goals 2000: Increasing Student Achievement Through State and Local Initiatives.* Report to the Congress, April 30, 1996. Washington, D.C.: U.S. Department of Education.

Welter, Rush (1962). *Popular Education and Democratic Thought in America.* New York: Columbia University Press.

Wiebe, Robert H. (1969). "The Social Functions of Public Education," *American Quarterly*, vol. 21 (Summer 1969), pp. 147-164.

EDUCATIONAL TRENDS AND ISSUES IN THE REGION, THE STATE, AND THE NATION

Melissa Roderick

The past two decades have been a time of increased state activism in education policy. In the wake of reaction to *A Nation at Risk*, the 1983 report of the National Commission on Excellence in Education, many states enacted reform initiatives aimed at setting higher standards and improving elementary and secondary education (see NCEE, 1983). Researchers have characterized these policy developments as falling into three waves of reform. The first wave focused on "inputs," such as higher standards for teachers, more course requirements for students, and funds for special programs or initiatives, such as preschool and dropout prevention. The second wave involved "bottom-up" reform and efforts to restructure the governance of schools to make them more flexible and innovative. The third wave, often characterized as "systemic" reform, moved more closely to a focus on curriculum and instruction by setting standards for what students should know, assessing performance through standardized tests, and holding schools accountable for performance outcomes (Massell and Fuhrman, 1994; Fuhrman, Elmore, and Massell, 1993; Smith and O'Day, 1991).

Each successive wave of reform has had a greater focus on trying to influence classroom processes and promoting change at the school level. What is equally important is that as these reforms evolved, they have reflected a growing consensus on three common themes: (1) a focus on improving standardized test scores as the primary measure of success; (2) the belief that schools are responsible for student performance and must be doing more for the students they serve; and (3) a belief that all students, if they are to succeed in a changing economy, must reach higher standards and begin to develop the problem-solving, conceptual, and analytic skills previously reserved for only the top students. As Fuhrman, Elmore, and Massell note:

The reforms of the 1980s focused educational policy on a very important goal: academic learning for all students, regardless of race, social class, or cultural background. It is now increasingly common to hear elected officials, members of the business community, and educators alike voice the expectation that all students will need a high level of understanding of academic subjects, a capacity for problem solving, and an ability to apply knowledge in concrete situations to function effectively in an increasingly demanding economy and society (Fuhrman, Elmore, and Massell, 1993, p. 8).

Education policy initiatives in Illinois have reflected these national trends. Since 1985, Illinois has emerged as one of the most activist states in attempting to raise test scores and, in particular, focusing attention on poorly performing schools and districts. In 1985, reflecting the initial policy emphasis on inputs, the state legislature passed an education reform package that was aimed at expanding educational opportunities for preschoolers, setting higher professional standards for teachers and administrators, and pressuring schools to improve test scores through the Illinois Goals Assessment Program (IGAP). In 1988, this reform act was followed by the first of two dramatic steps in restructuring the governance of the Chicago Public Schools (CPS). The 1988 Chicago School Reform Act decentralized budgetary and hiring decisions to local schools, which would be governed by parent- and community-dominated local school councils (Lynn, 1997; Sevener, 1991b). In 1995, the Chicago School Reform Amendatory Act gave the mayor wide authority in controlling public education and reorganizing the CPS central office. This legislation also consolidated governance arrangements within the central administration. These reforms gave the new chief executive officer broad authority to target poorly performing schools and design district-wide educational policy and accountability.

The new management team of the CPS quickly used its new power to initiate a third wave of reform in Illinois, setting minimum standards for students and schools and focusing resources and attention on poorly performing schools—with the threat of retention for students and "reconstitution" for schools if minimum standards were not met (Lynn, 1997). The Illinois State Board of Education also moved toward systemic reform in 1995 by issuing statewide curriculum standards for each grade level and placing poorly performing schools on an Academic Early Warning List.

In sum, Illinois and Chicago stand at the forefront on policy initiatives that focus attention on achievement at the school level, on holding schools accountable for what they produce for students, and on demanding higher standards for all students. This emerging policy focus comes at a time when student populations in metropolitan Chicago are increasingly diverse. How are public schools in the Chicago region faring in meeting this changing educational context, and what will shape the capacity of families and schools to respond to these new expectations? The purpose of this chapter is to examine these issues in the context of the changing demographics of the student population. It begins by examining trends in the demographic and geographic distribution of students in the six-county Chicago metropolitan area. The chapter then looks specifically at three developments in education that affect the policy issues that public schools in this region will face: changes in the nature of early childhood education and in educational expectations for young children, an emphasis on higher standards and achievement in elementary and secondary schools, and trends in educational attainment.

ENROLLMENT TRENDS

In the 1999-2000 school year, there were more than two million students in Illinois public elementary and secondary schools, an increase of 10.5 percent since 1984.[1] In addition, about 322,000 students attended private schools. This makes Illinois the fourth largest state school system in the country, behind California, New York, and Florida. The U.S. Department of Education has projected that the number of students attending Illinois public schools will continue to grow in the next century, increasing by 6.8 percent between 1997 and 2009. This growth rate is the highest among midwestern states and higher than the expected national growth rate of 3.9 percent (NCES, 1999c).

Illinois students are largely concentrated in the Chicago metropolitan area. In fall 1999, 64 percent of Illinois public school students were in the six-county metropolitan area, an

---

[1] Unless otherwise noted, all enrollment and demographic data for Illinois and metropolitan Chicago in this section come from the Illinois State Board of Education.

increase from 60 percent in 1984. About 20 percent of Illinois's public school students are in Chicago, which has the third largest local school system in the United States.

More than 80 percent of students in the six-county metropolitan area attend public schools. Table 1 shows student enrollment in public and private schools in metropolitan Chicago for 1980, 1990, and 1999. In all six counties, the public-private distribution of students has been relatively stable, although the proportion of students in private schools has been declining in the city of Chicago. Within the private school sector, approximately 80 percent of students attend religious schools (MCIC, 1997).

Greater Diversity

The most important demographic trend facing the region's public schools is the increasing diversity of student populations. Half of all public school students in the six-county region are members of minority groups. In the 1999-2000 school year, 48 percent of students enrolled in public elementary and secondary schools in the Chicago metropolitan area were White, 26 percent were African-American, 21 percent were Hispanic, and 4.5 percent were Asian. Table 2 shows changes in the racial composition and growth in enrollment in metropolitan Chicago and Illinois over a 15-year period. From 1984 to 1999, the number of Hispanic students in the Chicago region more than doubled, while the number of Asian students increased by 78 percent. Increases in the number of Hispanics accounted for nearly 75 percent of the growth in the region's elementary and secondary school enrollment. Increases in the number of Asian students comprised an additional 13 percent of enrollment growth.

A major reason for the growing diversity of the student population is immigration. The United States has been undergoing one of the most dramatic waves of immigration since the early 1900s, and Chicago is the nation's third largest gateway. In 1997, there were 1.1 million immigrants in Illinois, most of whom lived in the Chicago area. Immigrants from Latin America accounted for 44 percent of the state's foreign-born population (including 37% from Mexico). Another 28 percent of immigrants to Illinois came from Europe and 22 percent from Asian countries (U.S. Bureau of the Census, 1999).

TABLE 1: Student Enrollment in Public and Private Schools, Chicago Metropolitan Area

	1980 Total (1,000s)	Pct. public	Pct. private	1990 Total (1,000s)	Pct. public	Pct. private	1999 Total (1,000s)	Pct. public	Pct. private
Cook County	1,022.3	80.1	19.9	853.1	81.5	18.5	975.8	82.0	18.0
Chicago	583.0	77.4	22.6	492.2	79.5	20.5	525.2	82.2	17.8
Suburbs	439.3	83.6	16.4	360.9	84.2	15.8	450.5	81.8	18.2
DuPage County	136.6	85.7	14.3	129.1	86.6	13.4	178.9	85.9	14.1
Kane County	59.1	86.2	13.8	61.0	86.1	13.9	110.5	88.2	11.8
Lake County	92.3	88.4	11.6	89.0	88.9	11.1	138.3	88.7	11.3
McHenry County	32.5	91.0	9.0	33.5	91.9	8.1	47.9	90.1	9.9
Will County	72.1	86.7	13.3	69.8	87.2	12.8	88.2	88.0	12.0
Metro area	1,414.9	82.0	18.0	1,235.5	83.4	16.6	1,539.5	84.1	15.9
Statewide	2,242.8	85.4	14.6	1,951.2	86.2	13.8	2,351.5	86.2	13.8

Sources: U.S. Bureau of the Census; Illinois State Board of Education.

TABLE 2: Public School Enrollment in Illinois and Metropolitan Chicago
by Race/Ethnicity, 1984 and 1999

	Fall 1984	Fall 1999	Change	Pct. change
State of Illinois	1,835,355	2,027,600	192,245	10.5
White	1,248,175	1,229,943	-18,232	-1.5
Black	405,027	432,686	27,659	6.8
Hispanic	140,426	295,896	155,470	110.7
Asian	38,503	65,963	27,460	71.3
American Indian	2,224	3,112	888	39.9
Metro area	1,102,730	1,295,004	192,274	17.4
White	606,233	622,980	16,747	2.8
Black	330,607	338,731	8,124	2.5
Hispanic	130,922	272,413	141,491	108.1
Asian	32,951	58,666	25,715	78.0
American Indian	1,657	2,214	557	33.6
Chicago	431,226	431,750	524	0.1
White	63,430	42,970	-20,460	-32.3
Black	261,386	226,611	-34,775	-13.3
Hispanic	94,246	147,705	53,459	56.7
Asian	11,421	13,731	2,310	20.2
American Indian	743	733	-10	-1.3
Suburban Cook	322,181	368,661	46,480	14.4
White	249,495	215,303	-34,192	-13.7
Black	44,856	74,885	30,029	66.9
Hispanic	16,101	56,631	40,530	251.7
Asian	11,315	21,313	9,998	88.4
American Indian	414	529	115	27.8
DuPage County	111,678	153,564	41,886	37.5
White	100,107	119,342	19,235	19.2
Black	2,367	6,816	4,449	188.0
Hispanic	3,346	14,034	10,688	319.4
Asian	5,660	13,104	7,444	131.5
American Indian	198	268	70	35.4
Kane County	67,264	97,518	30,254	45.0
White	52,068	62,508	10,440	20.1
Black	5,368	7,456	2,088	38.9
Hispanic	8,121	24,083	15,962	196.6
Asian	1,636	3,265	1,629	99.6
American Indian	71	206	135	190.1

TABLE 2 (continued)

	Fall 1984	Fall 1999	Change	Pct. change
Lake County	82,473	122,741	40,268	48.8
White	68,564	87,226	18,662	27.2
Black	7,352	10,903	3,551	48.3
Hispanic	5,269	19,108	13,839	262.6
Asian	1,818	5,254	3,436	189.0
American Indian	110	250	140	127.3
McHenry County	26,666	43,121	16,455	61.7
White	25,815	39,026	13,211	51.2
Black	38	289	251	660.5
Hispanic	645	3,192	2,547	394.9
Asian	156	544	388	248.7
American Indian	12	70	58	483.3
Will County	60,262	77,649	17,387	28.9
White	46,754	56,605	9,851	21.1
Black	9,240	11,771	2,531	27.4
Hispanic	3,194	7,660	4,466	139.8
Asian	945	1,455	510	54.0
American Indian	109	158	49	45.0

Source: ISBE, 1985, 2000

The diversity of immigrants in the city of Chicago means that even among public school students who are considered White, a high proportion are immigrants. This can be illustrated by looking at the composition of the city's high school population. Table 3 shows the distribution of Chicago's entering ninth-graders in 1995 by parental language. In the 1995 class, 56 percent of entering ninth-graders were African-American, 20 percent were Hispanic, 3.5 percent were Asian, and 11 percent were White. Because of the high proportion of African-Americans, two-thirds of students had parents whose primary language was English. An additional 25 percent had

parents whose primary language was Spanish. The Asian population was comprised of 14 different language groups.

Immigration to Illinois may slow somewhat in the coming
decade. Even among the most conservative projections, however, continued immigration—combined with the fact that Mexican immigrants tend to be younger and have higher fertility
rates—means that these trends can be expected to continue.
The U.S. Census Bureau projects that by 2010, one in five
school-age children (ages 5-17) nationwide will be Hispanic
(U.S. Bureau of the Census, 2000).

Geographic Shifts

What is most important about these changing demographics is
that the growing diversity of the student body is not limited to
Chicago. Table 2 shows changes in the demographic composition, components of growth, and distribution of students in the
Chicago metropolitan area. These data show two significant
trends. The first trend is the exodus of students from Chicago.
From the 1984-85 to 1999-2000 school years, the number of
students in Chicago's public schools increased slightly, but the
number of non-Hispanic Whites, both immigrant and non-
immigrant, declined by more than 20,000, or by 32 percent.
During the same period, the number of African-American students attending Chicago public schools declined by nearly
35,000. As a result, the city's public schools are increasingly
Hispanic. In just this 15-year span, the proportion of students
who were Hispanic increased from 22 percent to 34 percent.
The exodus of both White and African-American students from
Chicago schools is largely a reflection of geographic mobility,
not a shift from public to private schools (Chicago Public
Schools et al., 1995). During this time, as shown in Table 2,
there were increases in the total numbers of both African-
American and White students in the region's public elementary
and secondary schools.

TABLE 3:   Home Language of Chicago Public School Students Entering
Ninth Grade, 1995-1996

	Number of students	Percentage distribution	Percentage distribution
Total	34,171	100.0	------
English	23,377	68.4	------
Non-English	10,794	31.6	100.0
Spanish	8,486	24.8	78.6
Polish	649	1.9	6.0
Cantonese (Chinese)	169	0.5	1.6
Arabic	163	0.5	1.5
Urdu	163	0.5	1.5
Pilipino (Tagalo)	128	0.4	1.2
Vietnamese	115	0.3	1.1
Assyrian (Akkadian)	106	0.3	1.0
Serbian/Croatian	92	0.3	0.9
Romanian	79	0.2	0.7
Cambodian (Khmer)	63	0.2	0.6
Guajarati	60	0.2	0.6
Korean	60	0.2	0.6
Greek	40	0.1	0.4
Russian	36	0.1	0.3
Italian	33	0.1	0.3
Hindi	22	<0.1	0.2
Haitian	21	<0.1	0.2
Algonquin	20	<0.1	0.2
Telugu	19	<0.1	0.2
Malayalam	17	<0.1	0.2
Creole	14	<0.1	0.1
French	13	<0.1	0.1
Hmong	10	<0.1	<0.1
Albanian	10	<0.1	<0.1
Mandarin (Chinese)	10	<0.1	<0.1
Japanese	7	<0.1	<0.1
Unknown or other language	189	0.6	1.8

Source: Chicago Public Schools.

The second key trend shown in Table 2 is the growth in
minority enrollment in suburban Cook County and the collar
counties. From fall 1984 to fall 1999, the number of African-
American students attending public schools in suburban Cook
County increased by 67 percent, or by 30,000. In DuPage
County, the number of African-American students nearly
tripled. Almost all of the collar counties experienced dramatic
increases in Hispanic and Asian students. Thus, most of the
growth in enrollment in suburban Cook County and the collar
counties during this period occurred because of growth in
minority enrollment. The proportion of minorities in elementary and secondary schools—Asian, African-American, and Hispanic—increased from 23 percent to 42 percent in suburban
Cook County, from 10 percent to 22 percent in DuPage
County, from 23 percent to 36 percent in Kane County, from
18 percent to 29 percent in Lake Country, 3 percent to 9 percent in McHenry County, and from 22 percent to 27 percent in
Will County.

These enrollment trends mean that issues of diversity and
equity across racial and ethnic groups are no longer limited to
Chicago. It also means that as schools pursue higher standards,
they must do so with the understanding that more students have
parents who face very real barriers to supporting their children's education, including language barriers, lack of knowledge of the U.S. education system, and low levels of educational attainment.

Greater racial diversity also brings greater economic diversity. From fall 1989 to fall 1999, the proportion of Illinois
public school children from low-income families rose from
28 percent to 37 percent. As seen in Table 4, more than one in
five students in suburban Cook County and in Kane County, as
well as one in six students in Lake and Will counties, are now
low-income.

Although student populations in Illinois are increasingly
diverse, teaching staffs outside Chicago are not. In 1993-94,
the percentage of public school teachers in Illinois who were
minority, 13.4 percent, was average for the nation. These
teachers were, however, heavily concentrated in only a few
schools. Data from the National Schools and Staffing Survey
show that in 1993-94, 57 percent of Illinois public schools had
less than 1 percent minority teachers, compared with 42 percent
of public schools nationwide (NCES, 1996). In 1999, 41 percent of classroom teachers in Chicago were Black, and 11 per-

cent were Hispanic. Elsewhere in the state, only 3.5 percent of teachers were Black, and 1.4 percent were Hispanic (ISBE, 1999).

The changing composition of the metropolitan area's student populations, in and of itself, introduces new challenges for public schools. These changes are particularly important in light of broader changes in American education and the demands placed on schools, a shift that is as alive in Illinois as in any state in the nation.

TABLE 4: Public School Students from Low-Income Families, Metropolitan Chicago, 1989 and 1999

	Fall 1989		Fall 1999	
	No. of low-income students	Pct. low-income	No. of low-income students	Pct. low-income
Chicago	268,897	65.8	366,057	84.8
Suburban Cook	37,540	12.0	83,707	22.7
DuPage County	3,686	3.1	9,035	5.9
Kane County	10,127	14.1	21,749	22.3
Lake County	10,232	11.6	20,322	16.6
McHenry County	1,477	5.1	3,138	7.3
Will County	9,013	15.1	13,906	17.9
Metro area	340,972	31.3	517,914	40.0
State	500,340	27.8	741,618	36.6

Source: ISBE, 1990, 2000.

EARLY CHILDHOOD EDUCATION

One of the most important developments in education over the past several decades has been the expansion of formal schooling to include kindergarten. In 1950, only about one-third of first-graders had attended kindergarten in the previous year. Kindergarten enrollment increased rapidly throughout the post-war years. From 1950 to 1960, the proportion of first-graders enrolled in kindergarten the previous year increased from 32 percent to 52 percent, and by 1970 it was 72 percent. Since 1970, kindergarten has become a universal experience for children. In 1980, over 92 percent of first-graders were enrolled in kindergarten the previous year, and by 1990 the participation rate had reached 99.6 percent (NCES, 1993, Table 10).

The growth of kindergarten both reflects and has contributed to several additional important developments in early childhood education: increases in preschool enrollment, a shift in the focus of early childhood education from social development to academic skills, and rising expectations of what constitutes "readiness" for school. As kindergarten enrollments have increased, so has the proportion of children in child care and pre-primary programs. In 1965, only 5 percent of three-year-olds and 16 percent of four-year-olds were enrolled in some kind of formal education setting that could be called a preprimary program. Enrollment of three-year-olds in preprimary programs increased to 27 percent in 1980 and to 38 percent in 1998. Preprimary enrollment among four-year-olds reached 46 percent in 1980 and 67 percent in 1998 (NCES, 1999a, Table 46).

One of the central components of the Illinois school reform act of 1985 was the provision of funds for local school districts to expand preprimary programs for low-income students. Reflecting this policy emphasis, as well as the increasing demand for preschool programs more generally, enrollment in pre-kindergarten programs in Illinois public schools has expanded rapidly. Table 5 shows enrollment changes in Illinois public kindergarten and preprimary programs from 1984 to 1999. In 1984, the number of children enrolled in prekindergarten programs in Chicago was approximately 24 percent of first-grade enrollment that year. Other than in Chicago, few counties in Illinois had significant preschool programs in the mid-1980s. By 1999, the number of children in public preschool in the Chicago metropolitan area had nearly tripled, with significant growth in every county.

TABLE 5: Public School Kindergarten and Prekindergarten (Pre-K) Enrollment in Illinois, 1984 and 1999

	Pre-K Fall 1984		Pre-K Fall 1999		Kindergarten Fall 1984		Kindergarten Fall 1999		Pct. change in enrollment	
	No.	As % of 1st grade	No.	As % of 1st grade	No.	As % of 1st grade	No.	As % of 1st grade	Pre-K and K	1st-8th
Statewide	11,717	8.4	46,833	28.9	138,618	98.8	149,840	92.3	30.8	14.3
Metro area	10,487	12.4	27,615	25.2	82,413	97.2	98,739	90.1	36.0	24.8
Chicago	9,195	24.2	18,451	44.8	33,337	87.6	35,221	85.4	26.2	3.9
Suburban Cook	1,216	5.8	5,187	18.4	21,995	105.8	25,642	91.1	32.8	25.3
DuPage County	23	0.3	1,117	9.4	8,464	106.1	11,117	93.8	44.1	49.6
Kane County	0	0.0	958	11.4	5,484	106.2	8,112	96.5	65.4	51.4
Lake County	53	0.9	996	9.7	6,492	104.8	9,544	93.0	61.0	58.6
McHenry County	0	0.0	318	9.4	2,064	104.8	3,214	94.9	71.1	78.2
Will County	0	0.0	588	9.3	4,577	99.6	5,889	92.7	41.5	36.0

Note: "As % of 1st grade" = enrollment as a percentage of first-grade enrollment that year. Enrollment in prekindergarten excludes special education and bilingual programs.

Source: ISBE, 1985, 2000.

Some supporters of the new emphasis on early childhood education have argued that funding for such programs has been inadequate. According to these critics, funding for early childhood programs in the 1985 law met less than one-third of the need (Sevener, 1991a). Indeed, although preschool programs such as Head Start are often touted as important, increases in preschool participation for disadvantaged children have lagged significantly behind their more advantaged counterparts. Most of the growth in formal school participation of prekindergarteners is among children from more highly educated and affluent families and is usually outside of the public schools.

In the early 1990s, the U.S. Department of Education began a nationwide household education survey that tracks preschool experiences of students over time. Table 6 shows enrollment trends in public or private nursery, prekindergarten, kindergarten, and Head Start programs for various categories of families. The data illustrate just how fast preprimary enrollments are growing. In just the short period between 1991 and 1996, the proportion of preschoolers enrolled in a formal education setting increased from 31 percent to 37 percent among three-year-olds and from 53 percent to 58 percent among four-year-olds. Much of this growth is among higher educated and more financially well-off families. In 1996, over half (55%) of three-year-olds and 75 percent of four-year-olds from families with incomes over $50,000 were enrolled in some kind of formal education setting, compared with only 26 percent of three-year-olds and 53 percent of four-year-olds from families with incomes of $10,000 or less. Perhaps reflecting the importance of Head Start in expanding early childhood opportunities and a focus on early childhood education in the African-American community, African-American three- and four-year-olds in this survey were not any less likely than White children in their age group to be enrolled in preschool. Hispanic children—particularly Hispanic children whose mother's primary language is Spanish—were substantially less likely to be enrolled in preschool. In addition, while the proportion of children from upper-income and more educated families enrolled in preschool increased throughout this short period, enrollment rates among poor, less-educated, and Hispanic families changed little.

TABLE 6: Percentage of Children Enrolled in Nursery, Prekindergarten, Kindergarten, and Head Start Programs, 1991 and 1996

	3-year-olds		4-year-olds		5-year-olds	
	1991	1996	1991	1996	1991	1996
Total	31.4	36.7	52.7	57.7	86.4	90.2
Race						
White	33.4	39.6	52.4	58.8	85.7	88.8
Black	31.6	40.5	57.4	67.8	92.3	94.1
Hispanic	19.8	21.1	47.5	45.3	85.3	90.4
Household income						
$10,000 or less	25.4	26.0	43.3	52.7	86.1	92.7
$10,001-20,000	23.2	28.0	45.0	45.3	84.6	87.6
$20,001-35,000	21.3	30.8	48.0	50.6	85.1	87.8
$35,001-50,000	33.4	42.2	52.3	58.2	87.3	89.7
$50,001 or more	52.9	55.0	74.8	75.8	89.0	92.8
Parental education						
Less than high school	17.3	22.0	33.1	47.3	85.5	90.3
High school or GED	23.0	28.9	40.8	47.3	84.8	89.9
Some college	31.0	34.5	56.3	59.8	87.7	88.6
4 years college	41.5	49.6	67.2	62.6	88.1	92.6
Graduate school	53.0	60.4	72.0	78.1	87.0	92.1
Mother's language						
English	32.3	39.0	53.0	59.7	86.5	89.8
Spanish	18.9	19.6	45.0	41.5	88.6	94.2
Other	37.1	37.1	50.0	55.3	84.1	80.4

Source: NCES, 1998.

There is an important need for research on the degree to which these gaps in preschool participation rates reflect a lack of access to early childhood programs, compared with differences in the home environments and parental expectations of children. There is much evidence that less-educated, poorer, and, in particular, Hispanic children are less likely to be in home environments in which parents engage with preschoolers in literacy activities and prepare their children for school by building skills—a gap that data from the Household Education Survey also document is widening over time (NCES, 1999b, Table 1; Delgado-Gaitan and Trueba, 1991). Although there are small differences in school participation in kindergarten (age 5), many advantaged families are responding to rising educational expectations for children and the need for child care by enrolling their children in preschool.

The issue of differential access to early childhood education will become particularly important in the decades ahead. Research on Head Start and preschool programs more generally have consistently demonstrated that participation in these programs promotes early school success, improves health and behavioral outcomes, reduces the likelihood of grade retention, and promotes literacy environments in the home.[2] The lower participation rate of the fastest-growing population in the Chicago area means that Hispanic children will be less likely to enter kindergarten with the behavioral experience of having been in formal school and with skills that lay the basis for early school success. In the National Household Education Survey, for example, Hispanic mothers were much less likely to report that their children had developed skills that display "readiness" for school. The 1999 survey indicated that only 14 percent of Hispanic children could identify all letters of the alphabet, compared with 25 percent of both African-American and non-Hispanic White children. Similarly, 41 percent of Hispanic preschoolers were able to count to 20 or higher, compared with 60 percent of both Black and White children (NCES, 1999b, Table 2).

The disparity in preschool participation rates by family income and education levels poses special problems for public schools in metropolitan Chicago. As more children enter

---

[2] See Currie and Thomas, 1997; Entwistle et al., 1997; Goldenberg et al., 1992; Reynolds et al., 1997; Reynolds and Wolfe, 1997.

school with higher levels of skill, students without those skills face greater risk of falling behind and being deemed "not ready for school." These trends raise some critical public policy questions: Should Illinois make preschool accessible to all families, or should public preschool be targeted to poor and at-risk children, assuming that more advantaged families will continue to buy such resources outside the formal educational system? How can Illinois develop and expand access to preschool programs for Hispanic and, especially, non-English-speaking parents? To what extent does the increasing disparity in the skills that students bring to school require public schools to develop effective early intervention programs and teacher training in the early grades to equip schools and teachers to better deal with diversity in skills and family needs within classrooms?

STANDARDS AND ACHIEVEMENT

Higher educational expectations for children at early ages is, in part, a reflection of a nationwide trend toward higher expectations for student performance at all levels of education. Most of the policy focus in Illinois since 1985 has been on establishing higher standards, as well as links between curriculum-based standards and assessment measures as a way of promoting school improvement and student achievement. This section focuses on trends in reading and mathematics achievement at three levels: nationwide achievement as measured by the National Assessment of Educational Progress (NAEP), statewide student performance on the Illinois Goals Assessment Program (IGAP), and Chicago results for the Iowa Tests of Basic Skills (ITBS) administered in the elementary school grades and the Tests of Achievement and Proficiency (TAP) administered to ninth- and eleventh-graders.

Different achievement tests use different approaches to measuring skills and emphasize different levels of skill (see Easton and Storey, 2001). The ITBS and TAP, which are used by the Chicago Public Schools, are intended to assess whether students are able to demonstrate skills deemed appropriate by educators for their grade level. These tests are useful for examining how students and school districts perform relative to national norms. However, if tests are redesigned to reflect specific academic content, they become less useful in measuring change over time. For example, in order to align its assessment system with new learning standards, Illinois replaced IGAP with the Illinois Standards Achievement Test (ISAT). Although some achievement tests are useful for cross-sectional comparison by reporting the proportion of students meeting current standards or falling into national quartiles, they are less useful in assessing progress over time.

Nationally, the most reliable and widely used test of academic achievement is the National Assessment of Educational Progress. Since the early 1970s, the NAEP has, at regular intervals, tested a national sample of students at ages 9, 13, and 17 in reading, mathematics, writing, science, and social studies. The NAEP is explicitly designed to measure progress over time, examine the proportion of students attaining specific skills at each grade, and provide reliable indicators of progress for racial and ethnic groups. Illinois is one of the few states in the nation that does not participate in the NAEP but has opted instead to use its own tests (first IGAP, now ISAT).

When looking at trends in reading and math scores on these four tests, three major trends emerge. First, math scores have been rising consistently for all groups, while reading scores have been flat or declining. Second, there has been substantial progress in reducing achievement gaps between Whites and African-Americans and between Whites and Hispanics. Third, there has been much more progress in raising the minimum level of basic skills in both reading and mathematics than in raising the proportion of students who are demonstrating higher levels of achievement for their grade, especially for Hispanics and African-Americans.

Trends in Mathematics and Reading Achievement

Tables 7, 8, and 9 show trends in the average reading and mathematics proficiency of students nationally, in Illinois, and in Chicago on each of these achievement indicators. The story of the 1980s and 1990s is one of rising mathematics proficiency, with few gains and, in some cases, significant declines in reading. Table 7 shows trends in the IGAP for the state of Illinois. At every grade level, mathematics scores increased substantially throughout the 1990s, while reading scores were flat or declining. Table 8 shows similar trends in the Chicago Public Schools. Throughout the 1990s, the median percentile rank of CPS students on the ITBS in grades 3, 6, and 8 and on the TAP in grades 9 and 11 increased significantly in math, but improvement in reading was much less consistent. Of particular concern in the statewide trends is the marked decline in reading achievement among eighth- and tenth-graders (see Table 7).[3]

Why have reading scores not improved, while math scores have increased so consistently? The key explanation may lie not in Chicago or in Illinois but with the larger reform movement in mathematics education. Much of the initial concern over declining test scores, stagnant skills, and competitiveness of American students in the 1980s was centered on mathematics. In 1989, the National Council of Teachers of Mathematics (NCTM) was the first discipline-based group to issue curriculum, teaching, and professional standards for elementary and secondary schools. The NCTM spurred a national reform movement in mathematics, which focused on investments in professional development and new curriculum development. A particularly important goal of the NCTM standards was to challenge teachers to rethink their expectations and strategies for average and low-ability students. There has been no comparable professional movement in reading, although many reform efforts lie in the dissemination of model practices, such as the Success for All reading program based at Johns Hopkins University.[4]

---

[3] It has been suggested that the IGAP, largely because of the inclusion of longer reading passages, was measuring something different from other tests. As noted later in this section, if more progress was being made in raising the level of basic skills than in moving mid-level students to higher levels of performance, such as the ability to read longer passages, then we might have expected a different trend in the IGAP. What is most important is that these different trends in reading and mathematics began prior to the 1990s and are reflected nationally in NAEP scores (see Table 9).

[4] Although the notion that rising mathematics scores reflect the national curriculum reform in mathematics is the most common explanation, it has not been systematically tested. An equally important hypothesis is that different trends in mathematics and reading reflect changes in the demographic composition of student populations.

TABLE 7: Trends in Reading and Mathematics Scale Scores, Illinois Goals
Assessment Program, Statewide Results

	3rd grade	6th grade	8th grade	10th grade
Reading				
1988	250	250	250	----
1989	254	249	255	----
1990	257	249	254	----
1991	249	253	254	----
1992	247	244	248	----
1993	254	267	265	250
1994	255	263	260	244
1995	247	260	246	237
1996	249	248	238	223
1997	246	227	227	208
1998	246	248	237	228
Change	-4	-2	-13	-22
Math				
1989	250	250	250	----
1990	249	252	248	----
1991	255	253	255	----
1992	261	251	250	----
1993	269	256	266	250
1994	271	263	273	254
1995	275	272	275	259
1996	287	278	282	262
1997	288	280	288	264
1998	287	282	290	264
Change	+ 37	+32	+40	+14

Source: Illinois State Board of Education.

TABLE 8:   Trends in Reading and Mathematics on Iowa Tests of Basic
Skills (ITBS) and Tests of Achievement and Proficiency (TAP), Selected
Grades, Chicago Public Schools

	3rd grade (ITBS)	6th grade (ITBS)	8th grade (ITBS)	9th grade (TAP)	11th grade (TAP)
Reading					
1990	24	27	37	36	29
1991	26	25	34	31	31
1992	26	25	29	23	30
1993	26	32	33	31	32
1994	24	30	33	25	29
1995	21	29	33	30	30
1996	24	32	36	23	27
1997	26	38	39	27	31
1998	26	36	39	33	33
1999	29	38	44	36	37
2000	29	40	44	41	32
Change	+5	+13	+7	+5	+3
Mathematics					
1990	23	28	30	20	22
1991	26	28	28	20	25
1992	26	26	30	18	25
1993	34	34	30	25	30
1994	30	31	30	22	22
1995	30	34	30	25	30
1996	34	34	32	22	33
1997	30	42	40	30	31
1998	43	42	38	33	30
1999	43	44	46	42	41
2000	47	53	44	43	34
Change	+24	+25	+14	+23	+11

Note: Scores indicate median percentile on national norms.

Source: Chicago Public Schools.

Rising Test Scores for African-Americans and Hispanics

Although overall trends in reading have been flat or declining, there has been substantial progress in closing the achievement gap between African-Americans and Whites and between Hispanics and Whites. As seen in Table 9, throughout the 1970s and into the 1990s, NAEP reading and mathematics scores have risen faster among Hispanics and African-Americans than among Whites. This is particularly true in mathematics and is most pronounced among older youth. Average mathematics scores for both African-Americans and Hispanics increased substantially over the past two decades, reducing the racial/ethnic gap in achievement. Progress has been greater for African-Americans than for Hispanics. Unfortunately, there are some signs that progress among Hispanics and African-Americans has been slowing. Between 1990 and 1996, the gap between Whites and Hispanics increased in reading at ages 13 and 17 and increased in mathematics at ages 9 and 13.

Improvements in mathematics performance among African-American and Hispanic students are even more pronounced if one looks at the proportion of students attaining minimum levels of basic skills. Table 10 shows trends in the 1990s in the proportion of students in the NAEP at various math proficiency levels. In just this short period, even as progress on mean scale scores was slowing, the proportion of African-Americans who were performing at a level that was basic or above for their grade increased from 19 percent to 32 percent among fourth-graders, from 22 percent to 28 percent among eighth-graders, and from 27 percent to 38 percent among twelfth-graders. The proportion of Hispanics who were performing at a level considered basic for their grade level rose from 31 percent to 41 percent among fourth-graders and from 36 percent to 50 percent among twelfth-graders. Similar trends are observed among Whites and among Asians and Pacific Islanders.

While the data in Table 10 show substantial progress in improving basic math skills among minority children, these data also demonstrate just how far behind African-American and Hispanic children remain compared with their counterparts. In 1996, the proportion of African-American children who were meeting minimum criteria for their grade was less than half that of Whites and Asians. The figures for Hispanic students were only marginally better.

TABLE 9: Trends in Reading and Mathematics by Race and Ethnicity on the National Assessment of Educational Progress (NAEP)

Average reading scale scores:

		White	Black	Hispanic	White/ Black gap	White/ Hispanic gap
Age 9:	1971	214	170	----	44	---
	1975	217	181	183	36	34
	1980	221	189	190	32	21
	1984	218	186	187	32	31
	1988	218	189	194	29	24
	1990	217	182	189	35	28
	1992	218	185	192	33	26
	1994	218	185	186	33	32
	1996	220	190	194	30	26
	Change	+6	+20	+11	-14	-8
Age 13:	1971	261	222	----	39	---
	1975	262	226	233	36	29
	1980	264	233	237	31	27
	1984	263	236	240	27	23
	1988	261	243	240	18	21
	1990	262	242	238	20	24
	1992	266	238	239	28	27
	1994	265	234	235	31	30
	1996	267	236	240	27	27
	Change	+6	+14	+7	-12	-2
Age 17:	1971	291	239	----	52	---
	1975	293	241	252	52	41
	1980	293	243	261	50	32
	1984	295	264	268	31	27
	1988	295	274	271	21	24
	1990	297	267	275	30	22
	1992	297	261	271	36	26
	1994	296	266	263	30	33
	1996	294	265	265	29	29
	Change	+3	+26	+13	-23	-12

TABLE 9 (continued)

Average mathematics scale scores:

		White	Black	Hispanic	White/ Black gap	White/ Hispanic gap
Age 9:	1973	225	190	202	35	23
	1978	224	192	203	32	21
	1982	224	195	204	29	20
	1986	227	202	205	25	22
	1990	235	208	214	27	21
	1992	235	208	212	27	23
	1994	237	212	210	25	27
	1996	237	212	215	25	22
	Change	+12	+22	+13	-10	-1
Age 13:	1973	274	228	239	46	35
	1978	272	230	238	42	34
	1982	274	240	252	34	22
	1986	274	249	254	25	20
	1990	276	249	255	27	21
	1992	279	250	259	29	20
	1994	281	252	256	29	25
	1996	281	252	256	29	25
	Change	+7	+24	+17	-17	-10
Age 17:	1973	310	270	277	40	33
	1978	306	268	276	38	40
	1982	304	272	277	32	27
	1986	308	279	283	29	25
	1990	310	289	284	22	26
	1992	312	286	292	26	20
	1994	312	286	291	26	21
	1996	313	286	292	27	21
	Change	+3	+16	+15	-13	-11

Source: NCES, 1997b, pp. 63-64, 113-114.

TABLE 10: Percentage of Students Meeting Mathematics Achievement Levels on the National Assessment of Educational Progress (NAEP), by Race/Ethnicity, 1990 and 1996

	White		Black		Hispanic		Asian/ Pacific Islander	
	1990	1996	1990	1996	1990	1996	1990	1996
Grade 4								
Below basic	41	24	81	68	69	59	35	27
Basic or above	59	76	19	32	31	41	65	73
Proficient or above	16	28	1	5	5	8	23	26
Advanced	2	3	0	0	0	0	3	5
Grade 8								
Below basic	39	26	78	72	68	61	*	*
Basic or above	61	74	22	28	32	39	*	*
Proficient or above	19	31	5	4	5	9	*	*
Advanced	3	5	0	0	0	1	*	*
Grade 12								
Below basic	34	21	73	62	64	50	25	19
Basic or above	66	79	27	38	36	50	75	81
Proficient or above	14	20	2	4	4	6	23	33
Advanced	2	2	0	0	0	0	5	7

* Reliable data not available.

Note: At grade 4, for example, students at the basic level should be able to estimate and use basic facts to perform simple computations with whole numbers, show some understanding of fractions and decimals, and solve simple real-world problems. Fourth-graders performing at the proficient levels should be able to use whole numbers to estimate, compute, and determine whether results are reasonable and should have a conceptual understanding of fractions and decimals.

Source: NCES, 1997a, p. 55.

What accounts for the gains among African-Americans and Hispanics in the 1970s and 1980s? The answer appears to be a mix of changes in family characteristics and a focus on improving basic skills for disadvantaged children. David Grissmer and his colleagues looked at this question by analyzing student achievement trends using data from several national tests, including the NAEP (Grissmer et al., 1994). Although the predominant view is that American families were changing in negative ways during the 1970s and 1980s, several important trends may have contributed to improvements in academic achievement. Among African-Americans and Whites, educational attainment increased significantly, family size declined, and family income remained stable. Each of these family characteristics is strongly associated with improved student performance. The largest negative changes were a decrease in the average age of mothers and an increase in the proportion of children in single-parent households—family characteristics that are associated with negative but smaller effects on achievement, controlling for income. Overall, family changes for African-Americans would suggest improvements in test scores.

Net changes in family characteristics for Hispanics, however, were less positive. Education levels of Hispanic mothers improved slightly, but progress lagged significantly behind other groups. In addition, resources within the home for Hispanic children declined, largely because of declines in income without reductions in family size. As Grissmer and his colleagues note: "Although both black and non-Hispanic white families registered large gains in parental education, reduced family size, and stable real family income, Hispanic families showed much smaller gains in parents' educational attainment, smaller reductions in family size, and declines in family income" (Grissmer et al., 1994, p. 106). Thus, the gains made by Hispanic students are particularly important. Grissmer and his colleagues found that the actual gains made by both African-Americans and Hispanics exceed those that would have been predicted by changing family characteristics alone. In essence, this analysis suggests that schools played an important role in reducing racial and ethnic gaps in school achievement during the 1970s and 1980s.

More Progress at the Bottom than at the Top

A consistent criticism of America's public schools has been that they fail to impart the more complex problem-solving, analytical, and communication skills that are needed in a rapidly changing economy. Trends in Table 10 show mixed evidence for this criticism. Between 1990 and 1996, most of the smaller racial/ethnic gap in math came from a higher proportion of students meeting minimum skill levels for their grade rather than a higher proportion demonstrating achievement considered "proficient." (This trend was also evident in reading.)[5] At the same time, achievement trends for Whites show an increasing proportion of students meeting proficient levels. For example, the proportion of White fourth-graders demonstrating math skills at the proficient level or above increased from 16 percent to 28 percent. These improvements among Whites, as well as among Asian and Pacific Island students, suggest that racial/ethnic gaps in math may be widening.

Similar improvements in math achievement are reflected in Chicago. From 1990 to 1999, the proportion of students with ITBS/TAP math scores in the lowest national quartile declined for every grade level (see Table 11). Unlike the national trends, however, improvements in math scores among Chicago students have been more evenly dispersed, with rising proportions of students placed in the top two quartiles. By contrast, trends in reading scores are very troubling. While there has been some progress in reducing the proportion of students in the bottom quartile, especially in the earlier grades, there has been little improvement (and a decline among ninth-graders) in the proportion of students in the top quartile in national norms.

------

[5] During the 1970s and 1980s, the proportion of Hispanic 17-year-olds who could demonstrate basic skills in math (multiplication and two-step reasoning) and reading (ability to interrelate ideas and make generalizations) increased substantially. Yet the proportion demonstrating ability to do college-level work (e.g., learning from specialized reading material and doing geometry and algebra) increased from only 1.2 percent to 2.4 percent in reading and from 1.4 percent to 1.9 percent in math. In 1989, the proportion of non-Hispanic White students at this level was about 8 percent.

TABLE 11: Proportion of Chicago Public School Students with Mathematics
and Reading Scores in National Quartiles on ITBS and TAP

	Mathematics			Reading		
	1990	1999	Change	1990	1999	Change
Grade 3 (ITBS)						
Bottom quartile	50.4	33.9	-16.5	53.8	40.0	-13.8
Second quartile	22.4	24.0	1.6	29.9	38.8	8.9
Third quartile	17.4	23.9	6.5	11.5	15.6	4.1
Top quartile	9.8	18.3	8.5	4.9	5.7	0.8
Grade 6 (ITBS)						
Bottom quartile	46.0	28.2	-17.8	47.7	33.1	-14.6
Second quartile	29.0	31.2	2.2	33.0	36.9	3.9
Third quartile	17.0	23.6	6.6	13.5	23.1	9.6
Top quartile	8.0	17.0	9.0	5.8	6.9	1.1
Grade 8 (ITBS)						
Bottom quartile	42.0	19.6	-22.4	36.0	22.5	-13.5
Second quartile	22.0	37.7	15.7	35.8	42.2	6.4
Third quartile	17.0	27.3	10.3	19.5	24.6	5.1
Top quartile	8.3	15.4	7.1	8.7	10.6	1.9
Grade 9 (TAP)						
Bottom quartile	52.0	33.2	-18.8	40.0	35.1	-4.9
Second quartile	28.0	25.4	-2.6	28.5	35.9	7.4
Third quartile	14.0	28.1	14.1	19.1	19.1	0.0
Top quartile	6.0	13.3	7.3	12.4	9.9	-2.5
Grade 11 (TAP)						
Bottom quartile	52.0	35.7	-16.3	41.0	31.6	-9.4
Second quartile	24.0	21.7	-2.3	32.5	33.4	0.9
Third quartile	14.0	25.1	11.1	16.5	19.8	3.3
Top quartile	9.4	17.5	8.1	10.0	15.1	5.1

ITBS = Iowa Tests of Basic Skills
TAP = Tests of Achievement and Proficiency

Source: Chicago Public Schools

Basic Skills and Academic Promotion in Chicago

These conclusions regarding basic skills are clearly applicable to the recent approach to improving student achievement in Chicago—an emphasis on time-on-task, movement toward "teacher-proof" curriculum methods that align teaching with skills measured on standardized tests, and across-the-board policies that set minimum standards that can be implemented in a large, complex system without a great deal of attention to teacher training and professional development. Given the poor performance of Chicago students and schools, such an emphasis may indeed be warranted.

Since 1995, Chicago has instituted several strategies to improve student performance, including the threat of grade retention for students as a means of spurring a focus on basic skills. Beginning in 1995-96, the CPS ended social promotion, linked promotion in grade to performance on standardized tests, and implemented core academic requirements for high school students. Students in grades 3, 6, 8, and 9 in the 1996-97 school year were to achieve minimum test scores in reading and math before being promoted to the next grade. Students who did not meet the standards were required to attend summer school and were given a chance to meet the standards at the end of the summer. In addition, ninth-graders were required to pass exit exams in core subjects and enroll in summer school for any core course that they failed.

As a result of this policy, Chicago mounted its Summer Bridge program, the largest summer school effort in the country. In 1997, one in 10 students in third, sixth, eighth, and ninth grades were in summer school for not meeting achievement standards. This effort was mounted on top of regular summer school, which served an additional 42,000 students. At the end of the summer, about 32,000 students who were in summer school because of low test scores were given a second chance at passing. Fifty-seven percent of sixth-graders, 44 percent of third-graders, and 65 percent of eighth-graders passed and were promoted to the next grade. Following the 1999-2000 school year, Summer Bridge enrolled about 25,000 students.

Chicago's academic promotion policy raises critical questions about the benefits and potential limitations of relying on strong incentives and high-stakes testing as a means of pursuing higher standards. Evaluation of this initiative has found significant short-term increases in achievement test scores during the year in which students faced the promotional gate, particularly in lower-performing schools (Jacob, Roderick, and Bryk, 2000). Achievement gains during the school year were notably larger for sixth-graders and eighth-graders than for third-graders. There is also evidence that Summer Bridge has produced substantial increases in test scores (Roderick, Jacob, and Bryk, 2001). These findings suggest that using incentives, setting minimum standards for promotion, and providing resources to support low-achieving students may be effective in raising performance in the short run, at least among older students (i.e., sixth- and eighth-graders). We do not yet know whether these gains can be sustained over time or the extent to which test score increases reflect real improvement in students' skills, rather than just students taking the test more seriously and teachers spending more time on preparing students for the test.

These short-term achievement gains have come with considerable expenditure of resources. Chicago has gone further than any other school system in attempting to combine high-stakes testing with second-chance approaches and extra instructional support both during the school year and in the summer. CPS has demonstrated that policies that rely on high-stakes testing require serious commitment to additional services for students and schools. Indeed, the success of the Summer Bridge program has led to the expansion of mandatory summer school to the first and second grades.

Despite evidence of progress, Chicago's efforts to pursue higher standards also present concerns over potential costs to students who do not meet the standards. The new promotion policy has not adequately addressed the needs of students with the lowest skills, particularly students who are retained. Achievement gains during the school year were smallest among students with the weakest skills; in mathematics, the promotion policy was associated with negative effects on achievement (Jacob, Roderick, and Bryk, 2000). Moreover, when these students were retained, they did very poorly their second time through the process. In the first two years of the new promotion policy, less than half of third- and sixth-graders who were retained were able to raise their test scores to the promotional cutoffs even after two years in the same grade and a second Summer Bridge. For retained eighth-graders, lack of progress is particularly disturbing because so many of these students eventually dropped out. Among eighth-graders who were retained or sent to transition centers, only one-third were able to raise their test scores to the minimum cutoff by the end of the next school year, and nearly 30 percent dropped out within two years (Roderick, Nagaoka, Bacon, and Easton, 2000).[6] These findings suggest that students who are unable to raise their test scores the first time around may have special problems that the CPS is not addressing by simply using incentives and providing extra instructional time. Moreover, a comparison of learning gains of retained students and previously socially promoted students found that retained students had relatively flat achievement trends both in the year prior to retention and after retention. Among sixth-graders, three-year learning gains were weaker than among previously socially promoted students, while among third-graders, achievement trends were similar for retained and socially promoted students. Thus, evaluation of Chicago's efforts to end social promotion indicates that this policy may produce short-term achievement gains for many students both during the school year prior to testing and over the summer. But for the lowest-performing students—particularly those who have been retained—high-stakes testing policy without effective diagnosis of and intervention for student problems does not seem to provide substantial benefits. When combined with the potential negative effects of retention on self-esteem, the policy may indeed be harmful in the long run.

Student Achievement Trends: A Mixed Picture

Trends in test scores in Chicago, in Illinois, and nationwide point to both the difficulties and complexities of trying to raise student achievement. Statewide and national achievement trends suggest a glass that is half full and half empty. On the one hand, a focus on test scores as a measure of student and school performance, an emphasis on basic skills, and renewed attention to urban public education may be making progress in raising minimum levels of achievement and closing the achievement gap for African-Americans and Hispanics. The most positive news is that trends in Chicago look better than state and national indicators, particularly in math. The recent focus on achievement and skills across the school year may produce even

---

[6] Transition centers are alternative schools for students who have not graduated from eighth grade by the time they reach age 15.

greater gains. If, however, one is interested more broadly in whether students are moving to higher-order thinking, problem-solving, and analytic skills, the results are far from sanguine. Over the past ten years, there has been little improvement in reading scores. Moreover, there is some evidence of a potential widening in the racial/ethnic gaps in achievement as the proportion of Whites who are demonstrating more advanced skills has been increasing, while improvement in African-American and Hispanic achievement has largely been garnered by improvements in basic skills.

TRENDS IN EDUCATIONAL ATTAINMENT

The reasons for such dramatic changes in educational expectations are varied and complex. They reflect broader developments in policy, in demographics, and in the economy. In the 1980s, the declining competitiveness of the U.S. economy led to a new emphasis on cross-national comparisons in student performance and the claim that American students simply could not compete with their international counterparts. Although all of these and other factors come into play, one of the most important trends driving policy debates in education has involved economic payoffs to skills and educational attainment. If there is one clear trend in the American economy, it is one of rising payoffs to skills and dramatic declines in the economic status of the non-college-bound, a trend that will continue in the decades ahead. Economists and policymakers are in agreement about the need to raise the skill levels and educational attainment of entering workers if America is to compete in a changing global economy and meet the challenges of technological change. Just as important, differences in the payoffs to skills and educational attainment are at the center of one of the most pressing social problems in America, the widening of the income distribution.

Every ethnic and racial group has been affected. Table 12 shows trends in the median real annual earnings of young adult workers, ages 25 to 34. From 1980 to 1998, real annual earnings for males declined for all but those who were college graduates. Overall trends in earnings were better among women, but still reflected marked differences by education level. Indeed, the most important trend in Table 12 is that the payoffs to education have increased dramatically. In 1998, the median earnings of young male college graduates were more than

50 percent higher than their counterparts who had only graduated from high school. For female college graduates, the corresponding payoff was 100 percent.

TABLE 12:   Median Annual Earnings (in Constant 1999 Dollars) of Wage
and Salary Workers, Ages 25-34, by Gender and Educational Attainment

	Grades 9-11	High school	Some college	Bachelor's or higher
Males				
1980	$22,822	$31,075	$32,390	$37,021
1990	18,033	25,420	29,091	37,532
1998	17,976	25,864	30,124	40,363
Pct. change 1980-98	-21.2	-16.8	-7.0	9.0
Ratio:				
1980	0.73	1.00	1.04	1.19
1990	0.71	1.00	1.14	1.48
1998	0.70	1.00	1.16	1.56
Females				
1980	$10,284	$15,943	$19,801	$24,243
1990	8,848	15,365	20,545	29,528
1998	10,638	15,356	20,074	30,774
Pct. change 1980-98	3.4	-3.7	1.4	26.9
Ratio:				
1980	0.65	1.00	1.24	1.52
1990	0.58	1.00	1.34	1.92
1998	0.69	1.00	1.31	2.00

Source: NCES, 2000, Tables 23-1, 23-2.

High School Completion and College Enrollment

Given the dramatic increases in the payoffs to college, one would expect that high school students would respond with increases in educational aspirations, high school completion, and college enrollment. Table 13 shows trends in the educational attainment of 25-to-29-year-olds from 1971 to 1999. The first notable trend is that African-Americans have been graduating from high school at greater rates, but high school completion rates among Hispanics have improved only moderately. In 1999, nearly 40 percent of Hispanics in this age group had not graduated from high school or obtained high school equivalency degrees, compared with only 7 percent of Whites and 11 percent of African-Americans. From 1971 to 1999, the proportion of African-Americans in this age group who had graduated from high school increased from 59 percent to 89 percent, while the proportion of Hispanics who graduated increased from 48 percent to 62 percent.[7] All groups have experienced declines in earnings for low-skilled workers and increases in the payoffs to college, but Hispanics have been more affected because so many more Hispanics have not graduated from high school.

The second notable trend is that neither Hispanics nor African-Americans are making progress in closing the gap in college completion, mainly because college attendance is not translating into four-year degrees. Although the proportion of Hispanic high school graduates with at least some college increased from 31 percent in 1971 to 51 percent in 1999, the proportion that completed a four-year college degree increased from 10.5 percent to only 14 percent. A similar lack of progress is evident in college completion rates among African-

---

[7] Some of the lower educational attainment and the lack of relative educational progress among Hispanics is because many Hispanic young adults are immigrants who never attended U.S. schools, a proportion that has clearly risen throughout the past two decades. Mary Frase has found that differences in the educational attainment of U.S. and non-U.S. educated youths explain some but not all of the lower educational attainment of Hispanic young adults. About one in five Hispanic young adults completed their education outside the United States. Even after excluding these late-age immigrants, the dropout rate among Hispanics is still more than twice as high as among Whites and 60 percent higher than that of African-Americans (Frase, 1996).

Americans: 11.5 percent in 1971 and 17 percent in 1999. In comparison, the college completion rate of White high school graduates increased from 23 percent to 36 percent over the same period. The result is that the racial gap in college completion has widened over the past several decades (see Table 13).

Why is increasing college enrollment not translating into increases in college completion among African-Americans and Hispanics? One reason is the type of institution that students attend. Hispanics and African-Americans are much more likely than Whites to attend two-year colleges and proprietary schools. In 1997, 42 percent of African-Americans and 56 percent of Hispanics in degree-granting institutions were enrolled in two-year programs, compared with 37 percent of Whites (NCES, 1999a, Table 209). Hispanic college students are also much more likely to enroll in private, for-profit institutions that "typically offer programs of short duration leading to a vocational certificate in fields such as cosmetology; administrative and secretarial programs; health-related programs such as physician assistant and practical nursing; and trade and industry programs leading to such jobs as mechanics and repairers" (NCES, 1995a, p. 16).

Although there are many factors shaping college choice and enrollment, one of the most important has been rising college costs combined with stagnant family incomes. Between 1980 and 1994, the cost of tuition, adjusted for inflation, rose by 79 percent at public two-year colleges and by 111 percent at public four-year colleges. During this period, the real value of the maximum federal Pell Grant, the primary source of college assistance for low-income students, declined (see Table 14). A review of studies of price sensitivity of college enrollment finds that "a $100-per-year difference in college tuition levels is associated with a 1.2 to 1.6 percent difference in college enrollment rates among 18- to 24-year-olds" (Council of Economic Advisers, 1996, p. 217).

TABLE 13:   Educational Attainment Levels of 25-to-29-Year-Olds by Race/Ethnicity, 1971 to 1999

	White*	Black*	Hispanic
Percentage with high school diploma or equivalent:			
1971	81.7	58.8	48.3
1980	89.2	76.7	57.9
1990	90.1	81.8	58.2
1999	93.0	88.7	61.6
Change, 1971-99	11.3	29.9	13.3
Percentage of high-school completers with some college:			
1971	44.0	30.9	30.6
1980	53.8	42.3	39.9
1990	53.6	44.1	40.1
1999	68.7	57.8	50.6
Change, 1971-99	24.7	26.9	20.0
Percentage of high-school completers with four or more years of college:			
1971	23.1	11.5	10.5
1980	28.0	15.0	13.2
1990	29.3	16.4	14.0
1999	36.1	16.9	14.4
Change, 1971-99	13.0	5.4	3.9

* Non-Hispanic

Source: NCES, 2000, Tables 38-1, 38-2, 38-3.

TABLE 14: Average Undergraduate Tuition and Fees at Public Institutions of Higher Education and Maximum Federal Pell Grants

	Nominal dollars			Real (1982-84) dollars**		
	Tuition and fees*		Maxi-mum Pell Grant	Tuition and fees		Maxi-mum Pell Grant
	4-year	2-year		4-year	2-year	
1980-81	804	391	1,750	928	452	2,021
1981-82	909	434	1,670	966	461	1,775
1982-83	1,031	473	1,800	1,050	482	1,833
1983-84	1,148	528	1,800	1,128	519	1,768
1984-85	1,228	584	1,900	1,161	552	1,796
1985-86	1,318	641	2,100	1,211	589	1,930
1986-87	1,414	660	2,100	1,272	594	1,888
1987-88	1,537	706	2,100	1,327	610	1,813
1988-89	1,646	730	2,200	1,358	602	1,815
1989-90	1,780	756	2,300	1,402	595	1,811
1990-91	1,888	824	2,300	1,410	615	1,718
1991-92	2,117	936	2,400	1,532	677	1,737
1992-93	2,349	1,025	2,400	1,648	719	1,684
1993-94	2,537	1,125	2,300	1,735	769	1,573
1994-95	2,681	1,192	2,300	1,783	793	1,529
1995-96	2,848	1,239	2,340	1,843	802	1,515
1996-97	2,987	1,276	2,470	1,880	803	1,554
1997-98	3,110	1,314	2,700	1,923	813	1,670
1998-99	3,226	1,328	3,000	1,961	807	1,824
Pct. change						
1980-94	233.5	204.9	31.4	92.0	75.5	-24.3
1994-98	20.3	11.4	30.4	10.0	1.9	19.3
1980-98	301.2	239.6	71.4	111.2	78.8	-9.8

* Tuition and required fees paid by full-time-equivalent students.

** Using the Consumer Price Index adjusted to a school-year basis (NCES, 1999a, Table 38).

Sources: NCES, 1999a, Table 317; U.S. Department of Education, 1998, 1999.

Higher Education in Illinois

These national trends pose significant issues for education policy in Illinois. In fall 1997, institutions of higher education in Illinois enrolled more than 720,000 students, including 74 percent in public institutions. A much higher proportion of Illinois postsecondary students are enrolled in two-year institutions than postsecondary students in the nation as a whole or in neighboring states. In 1997, about half of all postsecondary students in Illinois (47%) attended public two-year institutions, compared with 37 percent for the nation as a whole (NCES, 1999a, Table 199).

Although Illinois's two-year institutions are relatively affordable by national and midwestern standards, the state's four-year public institutions are expensive. In 1998-99, the average cost of tuition at a public two-year institution in Illinois was $1,423, close to the national average of $1,328. Tuition at Illinois two-year institutions was also lower than in Indiana ($2,135) and Wisconsin ($2,120). By contrast, the average in-state tuition and room and board at Illinois public four-year colleges was $8,812, compared with the national average of $8,018. Corresponding costs of attending a public four-year college were $8,574 in Indiana, $6,732 in Wisconsin, and $6,761 in Iowa (NCES, 1999a, Table 318). The affordability of public institutions is particularly important in determining the educational attainment of Illinois students because most (79%) of the state's college-bound high school graduates choose to attend Illinois colleges and universities. In addition, Illinois public institutions of higher education predominantly serve students from Illinois. In 1996, 90 percent of students who attended Illinois's public institutions of higher education were state residents (NCES, 1999a, Table 207).

Enrollment in Illinois public institutions of higher education has been relatively stable since the mid-1980s. From fall 1985 to fall 1997, total enrollment in public higher education increased by only 3 percent, compared with an 18 percent increase for the United States as a whole. Total fall enrollment in the state's public colleges and universities declined by 4 percent from 1990 to 1995 (NCES 1999a, Table 194).

Not surprisingly, enrollments in Illinois public universities and community colleges are significantly less diverse than the elementary and secondary school population (see Table 15). In fall 1998, 13 percent of students enrolled in four-year public

universities and 14 percent of those enrolled in public community colleges were African-American, compared with 21 percent
of public school students across the state.   Hispanics represented only 5.5 percent of students in public universities and
7 percent of students in community colleges, compared with
14 percent of the state's public school enrollment.

TABLE 15:   Enrollment in Illinois Universities, Colleges, and Public
     Schools, Fall 1998

	Public universities	Public community colleges*	Independent institutions	Public schools
White	131,789	155,553	132,087	1,235,033
Black	24,783	30,109	21,171	429,736
Hispanic	10,666	15,388	13,386	279,717
Asian	12,920	9,186	13,588	63,990
American Indian	537	727	665	3,054
Non-resident alien	8,154	750	9,560	--------
Unknown	4,699	1,253	7,068	--------
Total	193,548	212,966	197,525	2,011,530
Pct. distribution:				
White	68.1	73.0	66.9	61.4
Black	12.8	14.1	10.7	21.4
Hispanic	5.5	7.2	6.8	13.9
Asian	6.7	4.3	6.9	3.2
American Indian	0.3	0.3	0.3	0.2
Non-resident alien	4.2	0.4	4.8	----
Unknown	2.4	0.6	3.6	----
Total	100.0	100.0	100.0	100.0

* Pre-collegiate and continuing education programs excluded.

Sources: IBHE, 1999, Table II-8; ISBE, 1999.

Recent changes in federal tax policy may dramatically alter the issues faced and demands placed on Illinois's public two- and four-year colleges. The Balanced Budget Act of 1997 contained a host of measures to increase the affordability of college, including tuition tax credits of $1,500 for the first two years of college. There has been much debate on how these credits will shape overall demand for college enrollment, students' choice of two-year versus four-year institutions, and access to and participation in institutions of higher education for poorer and minority youths. Clearly, states such as Illinois, with an increasingly diverse student population and very large community college and two-year college enrollment, must carefully monitor and assess the impact of these tax credits.

High Schools: The Weak Link

While the evidence points to the importance of focusing on postsecondary institutions, improving educational attainment in Illinois must start by addressing poor performance in high schools. There is a strong evidence that the state's high schools are in deep trouble. For example, in 1997, the Illinois State Board of Education followed the example of Chicago and placed schools on an Academic Early Warning List based on poor average IGAP scores. Of the 125 "troubled schools" identified, 55 were high schools, despite the fact that there are many more elementary and middle schools than high schools in the state. Chicago high schools dominated the list, but they were not alone. Forty-one of the 55 high schools placed on the warning list were Chicago high schools. In 1999, there were 87 schools on the Academic Early Warning List, including 41 high schools (with 35 from Chicago).

The concentration of poor academic achievement at the high school level is just one of many indicators that high schools as institutions are lagging in their response to the expectation that all students need higher levels of skills and educational attainment if they are to be successful. Reports from the Consortium on Chicago School Research have documented that although there was some progress at the elementary school level during the first wave of Chicago school reform, high schools were left largely untouched (Sebring et al., 1995, 1996). For example, surveys found that high school teachers were significantly more negative than elementary school teachers about their capacity to reach students, the quality of their work relationships, the overall academic focus of their school, and the impact of reform. Similarly, research on student performance in Chicago has found that student performance and engagement drops dramatically as students enter high school (Sebring et al., 1996). National reports indicate that the problems of high schools are widespread and not limited to urban schools, although this is where problems are most evident. In 1996, a report by National Association of Secondary School Principals advocated a policy focus on evaluating the academic curriculum and structures of high schools. The report called for greater coherence in the academic curriculum, reduction in high school size to allow for greater personalization for students, and investments in professional development for teachers (NASSP, 1996).

Issues of high school reform have taken center stage in Chicago. In 1997, seven high schools were reconstituted based on poor performance. In fall 2000, five high schools were targeted for a new sanction called "intervention," a modified version of reconstitution. Two of the intervention schools had been reconstituted three years earlier. In addition to these strategies, the CPS has undertaken a series of initiatives aimed at turning around poorly performing high schools, raising academic standards, and providing more support for students. The High School Redesign initiative introduced a mandatory core curriculum for high school students and has moved to develop junior and senior academies that focus on the special support needs of students in the transition to high school.

Many of the standards-based reform efforts by the current CPS administration, such as ending social promotion and a focus on raising achievement, build on previous reforms and are consistent with larger reform foci in Illinois and nationally. This is not the case with the CPS high school initiative. There appears to be an implicit assumption in Illinois policy debates that setting higher standards will benefit all students and will improve graduation rates. Research on effective schools finds that when schools pursue higher academic standards and focus on learning, students will learn more and report high levels of engagement, with less variance in achievement by socioeconomic status (Lee and Smith, 1995). However, the conditions needed to support this focus on learning—such as establishing smaller schools, allowing teachers to develop and implement instructional programs, and fostering environments that promote communication and interaction between teachers and students—seldom exist in high schools (Lee et al., 1997; New-mann, Wehlage, and Lamborn, 1992). Also important is whether urban high schools are to develop the organizational structures that provide families and students the personal supports they need to identify road maps to college, obtain the preparation throughout high school for college admission, and maneuver the process of choosing among postsecondary educa-tion options. In essence, improving educational attainment and achievement in high schools requires equal policy attention to issues of opportunities for student development and supports for families in meeting changing educational needs.

What will be critical over the next several years is whether the CPS administration can garner the resources and cooperation of unions, teachers, parents, and the community necessary to sustain and build this reform effort and whether other school systems and the state will join this effort to focus resources and attention on structural problems in high schools. Attention to high school attainment and the quality of high school experi-ences of students will be particularly important if schools in the six-county metropolitan area are to adequately serve growing populations of Hispanic students.

Given the changing demographic characteristics of students in metropolitan Chicago, the trends discussed in this section are particularly disturbing. There has been little progress in high school completion among Hispanics, the fastest-growing ethnic group in Illinois. At a time of rising payoffs to college and increased demands for skilled workers, there is a growing dis-parity in college completion rates by income and between racial and ethnic groups. Moreover, high schools are increasingly the weak link in our educational system. Yet issues of college access and high school graduation rates are nearly absent from the core debates on improving Illinois public schools.

CONCLUSION

If there is one central theme in state policy in Illinois, it is holding schools accountable for student performance, regardless of the populations they serve, and a belief that higher achieve-ment for all students is a central objective of state policy. State and local education reform initiatives in Illinois can be charac-terized as having three strategies in pursuing that goal: (1) a focus on standardized test scores, rather than increases in educational attainment and participation, as the main focus of school reform and the primary measure of progress; (2) a reliance on negative incentives, such as threats of retention of students and reconstitution of schools; and (3) a focus, particularly in Chicago, on raising the bottom, that is, focusing resources and policy attention on poorly performing students and schools.

There may be good reasons for this policy emphasis. In Chicago, 30-40 percent of students at most grade levels still have reading test scores in the lowest national quartile. This focus on poorly performing students and schools comes at a time when test scores overall have been improving. The first wave of Chicago school reform allowed many schools to progress but also left some behind. The evidence presented in this chapter, however, suggests three important gaps in state and local reform initiatives: educational attainment and poor performance in high schools; the widening gap in preschool participation between poor and non-poor children; and the need for professional development and curriculum investments to help teachers and schools pursue new standards among more diverse populations.

The focus on test scores and achievement does not directly address one of the most important challenges facing Illinois schools as they enter the next century—the question of how to raise educational attainment, particularly among Hispanics. There is little evidence that increasing payoffs to skills and to higher educational attainment will wane in the next several decades. Yet, African-Americans and Hispanics have made little progress in closing the racial/ethnic gap in college completion. There is also a widening gap in high school graduation rates between Hispanics and other groups. Addressing this problem requires more policy attention to restructuring high school environments so that they are not simply triage institutions, but are places that work to engage adolescents, provide road maps to college and other postsecondary options, and provide the support and monitoring that students need to accomplish their goals.

It is a particularly important time to focus on high schools and postsecondary links in Illinois. Families and students are clearly aware of the changed economic landscape. National surveys over the past several decades show that high school seniors have dramatically increased their educational aspirations. In 1980, only 47 percent of Whites, 45 percent of Blacks, and 38 percent of Hispanics planned to continue their education the next year in a four-year or two-year academic program. Twelve years later, the figures were 67 percent for Whites, 62 percent for Blacks, and 66 percent for Hispanics (NCES, 1995b, Table 3.2). Moreover, changes in federal tax law will open the door to college for many students. The question is whether and how Illinois high schools, communities, and post-secondary institutions will manage these new resources for families in ways that lead to new opportunities for Illinois students. Finally, Chicago has taken a first step in addressing poor educational outcomes in high schools with its High School Redesign initiative. Initial implementation was somewhat piece-meal and was not accompanied by substantial investments in new resources, curriculum, and professional development. Nonetheless, Chicago is leading the way nationally in attempting to take on the problems of high schools. Again, the question is whether this Chicago initiative will receive the sustained external and internal support it needs and whether the policy problem of high schools will become a larger metropolitan and state educational policy issue.

Another important trend is the gap in preschool participation between poor and non-poor children and, in particular, between Hispanic and non-Hispanic children. Hispanic children are the least likely to participate in early childhood programs. The benefits of preschool participation for all students have been widely documented. Most important, the gap in preschool enrollment, combined with rising educational expectations for students at earlier ages, means that those children who are most likely to benefit from preschool participation are least likely to receive those services and are at risk of falling further behind their more advantaged counterparts. As with high schools, addressing this problem will require structural and programmatic changes to expand preschool opportunities and increase the accessibility of preschool to low-income families.

Finally, schools in the Chicago metropolitan area are riding a national trend toward higher performance in mathematics and trying to buck a national trend of flat to declining reading scores. Performance incentives are effective when teachers, schools, and communities have the resources to respond to incentives and when teachers and schools have the substantive knowledge and pedagogical skills needed to use existing resources. Over the past two decades, standards for what children should know and be able to do have increased at all grade levels. For example, at the high school level, we are asking teachers to teach differently and engage students who have historically not been well-served. It also involves asking these high schools to send more students to college and to offer a more academically oriented curriculum for all students. Changes in academic expectations that students gain greater levels of skills, take more rigorous courses, and pursue postsecondary options also raise the bar for parents to be involved and monitor their children's education. These changing expectations will require new investments in professional development and in program, curriculum, and organizational models that develop the resources and knowledge base to enable teachers and schools to pursue these goals.

Marshall Smith and Jennifer O'Day (1991) have argued for a three-part systemic strategy for raising achievement: aligning tests with standards, developing curriculum materials and standards that are aligned with those tests, and working with postsecondary training institutions and teacher development to provide training in using assessment and materials to develop new pedagogy. In Illinois, most of the policy focus has been on the first two of these strategies. Little has been done in the area of teacher training and development. The central question is whether Illinois can pursue higher achievement, particularly in reading, without pursuing this third educational strategy.

REFERENCES

Chicago Public Schools, Chicago Urban League, and the Latino Institute (1995). *Chicago's Public School Children and Their Environment.* Chicago: Chicago Public Schools, Office of Accountability, Department of Research, Analysis, and Assessment.

Council of Economic Advisers (1996). *Economic Report of the President.* Washington, D.C.: U.S. Government Printing Office.

Currie, Janet, and Duncan Thomas (1997). "Does Head Start Help Hispanic Children?" *Focus* (Institute for Research on Poverty, University of Wisconsin-Madison), vol. 19, no. 1 (Summer/Fall 1997), pp. 22-25.

Delgado-Gaitan, Concha, and Henry Trueba (1991). *Crossing Cultural Borders: Education for Immigrant Families in America.* London: Falmer Press.

Easton, John Q., and Sandra L. Story (2001). "Standards and Assessment in School Accountability Systems in Illinois." In this volume.

Entwistle, Doris S., Karl L. Alexander, and Linda Steffel Olson (1997). *Children, Schools, and Inequality.* Boulder, Colo.: Westview Press.

Frase, Mary (1996). *Dropout Rates in the United States: 1995.* Washington D.C.: National Center for Education Statistics, U.S. Department of Education.

Fuhrman, Susan H., Richard F. Elmore, and Diane Massell (1993). "School Reform in the United States: Putting It into Context." In Stephen L. Jacobson and Robert Berne, eds., *Reforming Education: The Emerging Systemic Approach.* Thousand Oaks, Calif.: Corwin Press.

Goldenberg, Claude, Leslie Reese, and Ronald Gallimore (1992). "Effects of Literacy Materials from School on Latino Children's Home Experiences and Early Reading Achievement," *American Journal of Education,* vol. 100, no. 4 (August 1992), pp. 497-536.

Grissmer, David W., Sheila Nataraj Kirby, Mark Berends, and Stephanie Williamson (1994). *Student Achievement and the Changing American Family.* Santa Monica, Calif.: RAND.

IBHE (1999). *1999 Data Book.* Springfield: Illinois Board of Higher Education.

ISBE (1985). "1984-1985 Public School Fall Enrollment and Housing Report." Springfield: Illinois State Board of Education.

_____ (1990). "1989-1990 Public School Fall Enrollment and Housing Report." Springfield: Illinois State Board of Education.

_____ (1999). "1999 Illinois School Report Card." Springfield: Illinois State Board of Education.

_____ (2000). "1999-2000 Public School Fall Enrollment and Housing Report." Springfield: Illinois State Board of Education.

Jacob, Brian, Melissa Roderick, and Anthony S. Bryk (2000). "The Impact of High Stakes Testing in Chicago on Student Achievement in Promotional Gate Grades." Paper prepared for the annual meeting of the Association for Public Policy Analysis and Management, November 2000.

Lee, Valerie E., and Julia B. Smith (1995). "Effects of High School Restructuring and Size on Gains in Achievement and Engagement for Early Secondary School Students," *Sociol-*

ogy of Education, vol. 68, no. 4 (October 1995), pp. 241-270.

Lee, Valerie E., Julia B. Smith, and Robert G. Croninger (1997). "How High School Organization Influences the Equitable Distribution of Learning in Mathematics and Science," *Sociology of Education*, vol. 70, no. 2 (April 1997), pp. 128-150.

Lynn, Laurence (1997). "Public Schools Reform: The Chicago Story." Address to the Superintendents Work Conference, "The School and Community." New York: Teachers College, Columbia University, July 16, 1997.

Massell, Diane, and Susan Fuhrman (1994). *Ten Years of State Education Reform, 1983-1993: Overview with Four Case Studies.* New Jersey: Consortium for Policy Research in Education, State University of New Jersey, Rutgers.

MCIC (1997). *1997 Metro Survey Report.* Chicago: Metropolitan Chicago Information Center.

NASSP (1996). *Breaking Ranks: Changing an American Institution.* Washington, D.C.: National Association of Secondary School Principals.

NCEE (1983). *A Nation at Risk: The Imperative for Educational Reform.* Report of the National Commission on Excellence in Education. Washington, D.C.: U.S. Government Printing Office.

NCES (1993). *120 Years of American Education: A Statistical Portrait.* Washington, D.C.: National Center for Education Statistics, U.S. Department of Education.

_____ (1995a). *Minority Undergraduate Participation in Postsecondary Education.* Washington, D.C.: National Center for Education Statistics, U.S. Department of Education.

_____ (1995b). *Trends among High School Seniors, 1972-1992.* Washington, D.C.: National Center for Education Statistics, U.S. Department of Education.

_____ (1996). *SASS by State, 1993-1994: School and Staffing Survey Selected Results* Washington, D.C.: National Center for Education Statistics, U.S. Department of Education.

_____ (1997a). *NAEP 1996 Mathematics Report Card for the Nation and the States: Findings from the National Assessment of Educational Progress.* Washington, D.C.: National Center for Education Statistics, U.S. Department of Education.

_____ (1997b). *NAEP 1996 Trends in Academic Progress.* Washington, D.C.: National Center for Education Statistics, U.S. Department of Education.

_____ (1998). *The Condition of Education, 1998.* Washington, D.C.: National Center for Education Statistics, U.S. Department of Education.

_____ (1999a). *Digest of Education Statistics, 1999.* Washington, D.C.: National Center for Education Statistics, U.S. Department of Education.

_____ (1999b). *Home Literacy Activities and Signs of Children's Emerging Literacy.* Statistical Brief. Washington, D.C.: National Center for Education Statistics, U.S. Department of Education.

_____ (1999c). *Projections of Education Statistics to 2009.* Washington, D.C.: National Center for Education Statistics, U.S. Department of Education.

_____ (2000). *The Condition of Education, 2000.* Washington, D.C.: National Center for Education Statistics, U.S. Department of Education.

Newmann, Fred M., Gary G. Wehlage, and Susie D. Lamborn (1992). "The Significance and Sources of Student Engagement." In Fred M. Newmann, ed., *Student Engagement and Achievement in American Secondary Schools.* New York: Teachers College Press.

Reynolds, Arthur J., Emily Mann, Wendy Miedel, and Paul Smokowski (1997). "The State of Early Childhood Intervention: Effectiveness, Myths and Realities, New Directions," *Focus* (Institute for Research on Poverty, University of Wisconsin-Madison), vol. 19, no. 1 (Summer/Fall 1997), pp. 5-11.

Reynolds, Arthur J., with Barbara Wolfe (1997). "School Achievement, Early Intervention, and Special Education: New Evidence from the Chicago Longitudinal Study," *Focus* (Institute for Research on Poverty, University of Wisconsin-Madison), vol. 19, no. 1 (Summer/Fall 1997), pp. 18-21.

Roderick, Melissa, Brian Jacob, and Anthony S. Bryk (2001, forthcoming). "Summer in the City: Achievement Gains in Chicago's Summer Bridge Program." In Geoffrey D. Borman and Matthew Boulay, eds., *Summer Learning: Research, Policies, and Programs.* Mahwan, N.J.: Lawrence Erlbaum Associates.

Roderick, Melissa, Jenny Nagaoka, Jen Bacon, and John Q. Easton (2000). *Update: Ending Social Promotion—Passing, Retention, and Achievement Trends among Promoted and Retained Students, 1995-1999.* Chicago: Consortium on Chicago School Research, University of Chicago.

Sebring, Penny A., Anthony S. Bryk, and John Q. Easton (1995). *Charting Reform in Chicago: Chicago Teachers Take Stock.* Chicago: Consortium on Chicago School Research, University of Chicago.

Sebring, Penny A., Anthony S. Bryk, Melissa Roderick, and Eric M. Camburn (1996). *Charting Reform in Chicago: The Students Speak.* Chicago: Consortium on Chicago School Research, University of Chicago.

Sevener, Donald (1991a). "Revisiting the 1985 Education Reforms: Is the 'Old School Bus' Running Better?" *Illinois Issues*, vol. 17, no. 5 (May 1991), pp. 14-16.

_____ (1991b) "The Makings of a Revolution in Education from the Bottom, Not Top," *Illinois Issues*, vol. 17, no. 6 (June 1991), pp. 10-13.

Smith, Marshall S., and Jennifer O'Day (1991). "Systemic School Reform." In Susan H. Fuhrman and Betty Malen, eds., *The Politics of Curriculum and Testing: The 1990 Yearbook of the Politics of Education Association.* New York: Falmer Press.

U.S. Bureau of the Census (1999). *Profile of the Foreign-Born Population in the United States: 1997.* Washington, D.C.: U.S. Bureau of the Census.

_____ (2000). "Projections of the Total Resident Population by 5-Year Age Groups, Race, and Hispanic Origin with Special Age Categories: Middle Series, 1999 to 2100." Washington, D.C.: U.S. Bureau of the Census.

U.S. Department of Education (1998). *Title IV/Federal Pell Grant Program End-of-Year Report, 1997-98.* Washington, D.C.: U.S. Department of Education.

_____ (1999). *Student Guide: 1999-2000 Federal Pell Grants.* Washington, D.C.: U.S. Department of Education.

COMMENTS: EARLY CHILDHOOD EDUCATION

Jerome Stermer

In her chapter on educational trends and issues, Melissa Roderick describes the encouraging across-the-board data on increased preschool participation among Illinois children. Her analysis of the growth in early education includes a crucial cautionary note and points to a more overarching concern that is sure to challenge policymakers, educators, and social service professionals during the coming years. In displaying the early childhood education trend data, Roderick points to the disparity in participation among children of less educated, lower-income parents.

Roderick's chapter challenges us to find a way to bring the best of early education into the mushrooming number of child care settings that are likely to be the early education opportunities for the largest number of Illinois's future students. Her analysis leads us to recognize that because of the central importance of school readiness, policymakers will be challenged to incorporate early childhood into the overall agenda for education reform.

EARLY CHILDHOOD EDUCATION AND CHILD CARE

In Illinois, as in other states, programs for young children are often described in three categories: prekindergarten programs funded by the state through public schools; Head Start programs funded by the federal government; and day care programs, sometimes publicly subsidized, for the children of parents who are working or in school. Although these categories are delineated by both funding source and, to some degree, by types of services offered to children and parents, it is important to view them as an entirety—as a loosely related system (or non-system) of services available to young children before they enter kindergarten. Each program can, and should, provide the kinds of age-appropriate early childhood experiences that help prepare children for the more formal school experience.

State Prekindergarten Programs

Illinois has provided national leadership in developing programs for young children at risk of academic failure. In 1985, as a part of a school reform debate, legislation was enacted to establish a public school prekindergarten program for at-risk children, making Illinois one of the first states in the nation to begin offering services to children under the age of five in public school settings. In fiscal year 1998, the state appropriated $123.4 million for the program, which served more than 45,000 children, ages 3, 4, and 5, across Illinois's 102 counties.

The state's prekindergarten legislation is designed with programmatic requirements that are generally recognized as important to overall success: strong local control, parental involvement, and the potential for delivery of programs in multiple settings. The grant-based program requires that school districts screen and enroll children based on locally established criteria for academic risk. Most school districts use classroom-based programs of two to three hours, five days per week, during the school year. Some districts also offer home-based services, and some pay for early childhood education in community day care centers. In Chicago, the public schools and some two dozen nonprofit community child care centers have formed partnerships that allow both the educational and day care needs of children to be met in full-day settings (eight to nine hours per day), thereby reducing stress for both children and parents, who too often must cope with a complex web of transportation and day care arrangements.

While all school districts in Illinois have recognized the developmental value of prekindergarten for their at-risk children and have launched prekindergarten initiatives with available state dollars, the Chicago public schools are unique in their aggressive use of both state and local funds to increase early childhood opportunities. Chicago schools CEO Paul Vallas has worked to add classroom opportunities for children on the waiting list for prekindergarten. In an unprecedented effort to maximize resources, the Chicago schools are using the classic model of 2½ hours of programming, but with many classrooms for three separate groups. One group of children comes in the morning, another in the early afternoon, and a third in the late afternoon. This design naturally makes the assumption that parents can personally care for their children during the rest of the day (when the children are not in school) or are able to make other arrangements for child care.

Head Start

The federally funded Head Start program operates in Illinois through grants to community organizations and school districts. Programming is similar to state-funded prekindergarten in that most children come to the program sites for 2½ to 3 hours per day. Most programs operate four days a week during the school year, with the fifth day devoted to home visits or staff training. Federal officials have put a new emphasis on younger children through an effort known as Early Head Start, a program for low-income families with infants and toddlers. Enrollment is limited to children from households at or below the federal poverty level, which overlaps with the state prekindergarten criteria of locally determined "at risk of educational failure." In many communities, the two programs compete for children. In Illinois, Head Start is comparable in both funding ($130 million) and enrollment (approximately 40,000) to the state prekindergarten program.

A comprehensive approach to early childhood development has been the focus of Head Start programming since it was first funded by the federal government more than 30 years ago. For a variety of political reasons, Head Start has never been seen as connected or integral to local public schools. In fact, the funding structure means that individual Head Start programs or groups of programs relate not to state governments but directly to the federal government. Hence, the programmatic developments attached to Head Start, which have most often represented the best and most advanced thinking in early childhood development circles, have taken place in the somewhat insular world of the Head Start community. The most recent expansion of Head Start programming funding encourages local programs to provide "wrap-around" services, which means that programs can use new funds to integrate child care into the Head Start programs, allowing children of working parents to stay all day at a single site.

Federal funding has been made available to enable state governments to bring together critical players at the statewide and local levels in Head Start Collaboration Projects. The Illinois project is a joint effort of the Illinois Head Start Association and the Governor's Office, with the aim of developing links between Head Start and other community programs that serve preschool-age children. This is a deliberate effort to coordinate prekindergarten and child care programs with Head Start to maximize resources and to ensure that the education and day care needs of low-income children are more successfully met.

Child Day Care

In growing numbers of families with preschool children, both parents are working outside the home, either part-time or full-time. The multiple forms of child care arrangements have become the subject of a complex and important discussion, which unfortunately focuses more on the availability of child care than on the quality of the care. A variety of studies fuel the arguments of child care advocates, who call for greater public investment in the quantity and quality of subsidized programs. Other studies lend support to the arguments of those who lament the dramatic change in contemporary lifestyles in an attempt to persuade more parents to stay home with their young children.

Public subsidies for child care in Illinois have grown rapidly since the 1960s, when federal and state dollars were first combined to support child care centers for low- and moderate-income parents. Centers received funding from the state and enrolled children from their waiting lists. Eligibility was based on family income, but there was no formal entitlement to child care assistance. In the early 1990s, the focus of eligibility shifted significantly to include current or past recipients of government cash assistance. The state has adopted a dual strategy of administration, with some funding going directly to child care centers and some being distributed to parents in the form of vouchers. Eligible parents can use their vouchers to purchase care from relatives, neighbors, more formal child care homes, or licensed child care centers.

In spring 1997, Governor Jim Edgar and the state legislature agreed with child care advocates on a compromise package that provided for a new "entitlement" to child care subsidies that was linked to household income rather than welfare status. Current policy provides subsidies on a sliding scale for all families whose household income is at or below 50 percent of the state's median. Parents choose providers within the restrictions of existing licensing policy, which means they can select a provider who is either licensed or exempt from licensing (e.g., a neighbor who cares for one or two children). Some of available funding was earmarked for quality enhancement; for example, programs that care for special-needs children or that provide off-hours care can apply for extra funding.

Because there are no important benchmarks for quality in the child care subsidy program in Illinois, some service providers are seriously affected by a variety of problems, such as low levels of training, high staff turnover rates, and the like. Some of these issues are being addressed by a new state program, Great START (Strategy to Attract and Retain Teachers), which was signed into law by Governor George Ryan in June 2000. Great START provides wage supplements and incentives to encourage increased professional preparation and improve staff retention among child care workers. Another problem is that some for-profit providers refuse to accept subsidized children because of the lower rates paid by the state. Although no reliable studies have been conducted to assess the quality of subsidized care in Illinois, a number of concerns have been raised that should lead educators interested in the school readiness of their future kindergartners to pay greater attention to child care programs.

Integrating Day Care and Prekindergarten

Although they enroll essentially the same kinds of children, it is difficult to compare subsidized day care with the state-funded prekindergarten program in Illinois because of the fundamental philosophical goals attached to each approach. Many policymakers consider subsidized day care to be about "babysitting," while they understand that the prekindergarten program is intrinsically related to school readiness. Fortunately, there is a growing understanding among a broad spectrum of policymakers, educators, and human services professionals that both child care and prekindergarten programs have a powerful impact on the long-term school careers of young children. During the past several years, advocates have gained ground in their quest to focus attention on the quality of child care programs.

Many parents have two major objectives for their youngsters in the preschool years. They want their children to have an enriching "nursery school" experience, and they need to arrange child care while they are at work. Nursery school is seen as the place where children have a more formal opportunity to interact with adults and other children in the important process of socialization. In addition, both parents and children expect that nursery schools will give children pre-reading, pre-writing, and pre-math experiences. Most nursery schools (including Head Start and state-funded prekindergarten programs) use materials and lesson plans that are appropriate for the early childhood years, but they do not take on day care responsibilities.

Many child care programs have the same kinds of materials and organized activities as nursery schools. The key difference is that child care programs must arrange to serve children for as many as eight or ten hours each day, while prekindergarten programs normally have children for only two or three hours during the day.

As more parents of very young children enter the workforce, more children will need both day care and prekindergarten programming. Until recently, most educators have been reluctant to enter policy discussions that were based on the assumption that schools not only would be responsible for the prekindergarten programs but would also organize multiple hours of child care for three-, four- and five-year-old children. They recognize that there is a dramatic difference in pay scales and professional status between prekindergarten teachers and child care providers. Although children and parents normally designate both groups as "teachers," there are many practical differences between the two, including professional training, years of experience, resources available, and professional recognition.

There is a powerful new logic that would encourage policymakers to look at ways to improve child care by integrating programming with the more well planned and financed prekindergarten programs. This would have the potential of improving the quality of the early childhood experiences (thus improving school readiness and school outcomes), and it would also enable programs to respond to the needs of parents by combining child care and prekindergarten in a single setting.

CONCLUSION

Early childhood education has not been a vital part of the debate about school reform in Illinois. New understanding about the multiple influences on school readiness has led many to conclude that preschool children must be given a center-stage role in the education reform agenda for the next decade. There is a new conviction that without dramatic expansions and real improvements in the quality of early childhood programming, the overarching goals of education reform cannot be achieved. As more children are given the nurture and supports of quality early childhood programs, they will be more adequately prepared for the learning challenges of formal schooling.

EDUCATION REFORM POLICY IN ILLINOIS: PROBLEMS, CONUNDRUMS, AND STRATEGIES

G. Alfred Hess, Jr.[*]

Public education in the Chicago region has fulfilled the 1968 Kerner Commission prediction: we have become two nations (at least, two education systems), separate and unequal (Kerner Commmission, 1968).[1] Chicago and a small number of suburban school districts educate the vast majority of the region's minority and low-income students. Student achievement in these districts is generally quite low. By contrast, school districts in the north and northwest suburbs have few minority or low-income children, have the highest resources per pupil in the state, and have achieved at the highest levels in the world on the Third International Mathematics and Science Study (TIMSS) tests.

Educational decision-making in the Chicago metropolitan area has no regional focus. Most major decisions are made either at the local school district level or at the state level. State-level decisions in Illinois generally make few distinctions between issues of metropolitan interest and those of the other 96 counties across the state. One notable exception has been the imposition of property tax caps only on the six counties in the Chicago region, which may signal a greater awareness of regional differences in decision-making. In education, there is literally a different set of rules for the city of Chicago (Article 34

[*] I would like to express my gratitude to Lawrence Joseph, Richard Laine, and James Spillane for their helpful critiques of earlier drafts of this chapter. I have taken many of their suggestions that have improved the final product, but I am responsible for the errors that may remain and for the opinions articulated.

[1] Kweisi Mfume has made a similar point in his recent autobiography: "For ours is a nation divided against itself . . . a nation of two societies, one black, one white, separate and unequal" (Mfume, 1997, p. 370).

in the state school code applies only to cities over 500,000 in
population). Thus, any analysis of state education policy must
examine the differing educational contexts to which it must
apply.

About 64 percent of the two million public school students
in Illinois attend schools in the six-county metropolitan region.
Table 1 shows that in fall 1999, the Chicago Public Schools
enrolled two-thirds of the region's African-American students
and 54 percent of Hispanic-American students; Chicago also
enrolled over 70 percent of the region's low-income students.
Schools in the five counties surrounding Cook enrolled 11 percent of the region's African-American students and 25 percent
of its Hispanic-American students; only 13 percent of low-
income students in the region lived in the collar counties.
Within Cook County, 77 districts had fewer than 3 percent
African-American students, while 20 districts (mostly in southern Cook) were majority African-American.

Typically, educational policy initiatives are considered in
isolation from one another, with fierce debates about the merits
or disadvantages of each individual item.[2]   In fact, each is
usually part of some larger fabric of policymaking, including
the perceived problem to be solved, the basic orientations of the
advocates, and the potential strategies within which the initiatives fit.   Instead of presenting a laundry list of policy
initiatives currently being debated, this chapter is organized
around what I perceive to be the major issues facing education
policymakers in Illinois as we enter the 21st century.   Individual reform initiatives are considered within these larger
contexts.

---

[2] Paul Hill and Mary Beth Celio have described seven major
"school reform" proposals in the national policy debate in a paper for
the Brookings Institution.   They examine the standards movement,
teacher professional development, new school designs, decentralization, charters, contracts, and vouchers.   The authors bemoan the pro-
pensity for proponents of these initiatives to ignore their interconnec-
tions and to downplay the required conditions for the initiatives to be
successful.   They point to Chicago as an urban school system that is
unique for combining several different initiatives (Hill and Celio,
1997).

TABLE 1: Public School Enrollment in Metropolitan Chicago, Fall 1999 (in 1,000s)

	All pupils	Pct.	Black	Pct.	Hispanic	Pct.	Low-income	Pct.
Cook County	800.4	61.8	301.5	89.0	204.3	75.0	449.8	86.8
Chicago	431.7	33.3	226.6	66.9	147.7	54.2	366.1	70.7
Suburbs	368.7	28.5	74.9	22.1	56.6	20.8	83.7	16.2
Collar counties	494.6	38.2	37.2	11.0	68.1	25.0	68.1	13.2
DuPage	153.6	11.9	6.8	2.0	14.0	5.2	9.0	1.7
Kane	97.5	7.5	7.5	2.2	24.1	8.8	21.7	4.2
Lake	122.7	9.5	10.9	3.2	19.1	7.0	20.3	3.9
McHenry	43.1	3.3	0.3	0.1	3.2	1.2	3.1	0.6
Will	77.6	6.0	11.8	3.5	7.7	2.8	13.9	2.7
Total	1.295.0	100.0	338.7	100.0	272.4	100.0	517.9	100.0

Source: ISBE, 2000.

A further complication in school reform debates is the differing orientations of academics and the policymaking community. Many academics focus on developing models of new practice and their implementation in compatible sites. Policymakers tend to look for ways to affect the vast majority of schools or school districts and are thus more aligned with the smaller research and practice community focused on policy design and implementation. Models from "ideal sites" convince academics of the relevance of their innovations, but the lack of large-scale replicability frequently makes the models seem irrelevant to policymakers. This problem for policymakers is deepened when independent confirmation of the claims of success is made impossible because the innovator has extended a promise of confidentiality to the pilot site. Meanwhile, academics point out the complex interrelationships within the educational enterprise that are usually not susceptible to singular "silver bullet" political solutions and note the unforeseen and unintended consequences of many past policy initiatives. Thus, a credibility gap tends to exist between academic "reformers" and members of the policymaking community.   This chapter will seek to explicate major current reform proposals facing Illinois policymakers in light of the concerns raised by academics.

THE POLICY ACTORS

Public elementary and secondary education was deemed important enough to merit a separate article in the 1970 Illinois Constitution. Article 10, Section 1, reads:

> A fundamental goal of the People of the State is the educational development of all persons to the limits of their capacities.

> The State shall provide for an efficient system of high quality public educational institutions and services.   Education in public schools through the secondary level shall be free. There may be such other free education as the General Assembly provides by law.

> The State has the primary responsibility for financing the system of public education.

The General Assembly and the Governor

The Illinois General Assembly and the Governor are charged with setting policy for operating a system of public elementary and secondary schools across the state.   The Illinois School Code incorporates the currently applicable sets of policies that prescribe how the state's public schools will be organized, funded, and operated.   Over the last 15 years, several major reforms of the school code have been adopted.   In 1985, the General Assembly, following in the footsteps of other states responding to the report of the National Commission on Excellence in Education (NCEE, 1983), enacted statewide reforms that called for a definition of state learning goals, instituted a system of state achievement testing, created a set of categorical program initiatives, encouraged the consolidation of school districts (later rescinded), and provided the first significant state support for preschool programs.

In 1988, at the urging of school reform activists and members of the Chicago business community, the General Assembly adopted the Chicago School Reform Act, which established the goal that Chicago students achieve at national norms, reallocated compensatory education funds to schools on the basis of low-income student enrollments, and established school-based decision-making that included the right to hire and fire a principal, to adopt a spending plan for a school's newly acquired discretionary funding, and to create and implement a school improvement plan. In 1995, the General Assembly amended the Chicago School Reform Act to grant direct responsibility for the school system to the city's mayor (through the direct appointment of members of the new Chicago School Reform Board of Trustees and of the top five managers of the system), constrain the influence of the system's unions, and greatly simplify management of the system's finances.

Over a 20-year period, the General Assembly allowed the increase in state funds per pupil to fall below the rate of inflation, thereby further shifting the proportion of funds supporting local schools away from the state treasury and onto school districts with vastly different capacities to assume the added financial burden. As a result, the degree of inequity in school funding had dramatically increased at the very time that the state began holding school districts accountable for the performance of their students. While there has been much talk about reforming school funding, the state successfully defended the current finance system in Illinois courts, and the General Assembly has twice managed to ignore the recommendations of blue ribbon commissions for finance reforms. Meanwhile, two successive governors were willing or unwitting accomplices in the actions and inaction of the General Assembly. In 1997, Illinois revised its school finance system, providing additional state funding, requiring additional funding from low-spending school districts, and targeting supplemental grants to school districts with 20 percent or more of their students from low-income households (while actually reducing total state support distributed on the basis of low-income enrollment). This legislation allowed policymakers to make false claims of having "solved" the inequity in school funding across the state (see Hess and Braskamp, 1997).

The State Board of Education

The Illinois State Board of Education (ISBE) was created to administer the state's responsibilities to provide a free public education to every child. The state constitution says that the ISBE "may establish goals, determine policies, provide for planning and evaluating education programs, and recommend financing." The ISBE describes its major functions as:

- establishing performance standards, assessments, and accountability mechanisms that improve teaching and learning;
- establishing appropriate governance and service structures to support innovation and high-quality teaching and learning;
- ensuring a strong learning foundation for students and creating a safe and secure learning environment in and around schools;
- providing adequate, equitable, and predictable funding;
- creating a professional development system that will enable school, district, regional, and agency staff to keep pace with current knowledge on improving teaching and learning;
- using technology effectively and appropriately to improve student learning, increase operational efficiency, and improve educational equity;
- maximizing children's opportunities for academic success through the development and enhancement of collaborative relationships (ISBE, 1997, p. 4).

Although major policy directions are set by the General Assembly in enacted legislation signed by the Governor, many of the specific policies that prescribe the operations of school districts and individual schools are incorporated in the regulations adopted by ISBE. In the late 1980s, the myriad of mandates and regulations was perceived to be counterproductive to improved school operations, and there has been some effort to remove unjustifiable requirements. A waiver process has been installed whereby individual school districts may petition to be released from other requirements. The ISBE remains one of the potent forces in setting school policy, both by its own regulations and by its advocacy for legislation considered by the General Assembly. Other groups of citizens, lobbying groups, and educational professionals have the ability to influence decisions of both the state board and the legislature.

WHAT PROBLEMS SHOULD
THE STATE SEEK TO SOLVE?

Public policy initiatives are usually adopted in response to some perceived problem. If competing policy initiatives are based on a similar perception of the problem to be solved, then a comparative analysis of their projected outcomes is possible. Frequently, however, competing policy initiatives are based on different perceptions of what problems need to be solved. The problems experienced in one part of the state are often different from those in another part of the state, with the result that different initiatives are supported by residents from different areas. In some instances, a proposed initiative would apply to all areas of the state, although the problems encountered in other areas are quite different from the problem the proposed initiative is designed to address.[3] An effort to reach agreement about the major problem that school reform is trying to solve would facilitate greater agreement about appropriate policy solutions. Four prominent problem statements contest for primacy in the debates about reforming education policy in Illinois at the start of the 21st century.

Improving Low-Performing Schools and School Districts

Many "school reform" initiatives are focused on improving low-performing schools and school districts. These proposals assume that low-performing schools and districts can be identified and their problems addressed by policy initiatives enacted by the state. However, the problem appears quite differently depending on whether the focus is on school districts or on individual schools.

---

[3] This issue was avoided in the Chicago School Reform Act of 1988, which was designed to attack the problem of uniform decisions imposed on the city's 550 different schools in ways that made tailoring educational approaches to different kinds of students nearly impossible. Mandating a similar school-based management system on suburban districts that contain only one school would likely be inappropriate. Because Chicago's schools are governed under a separate article in the school code, a reform initiative aimed at the state's largest city did not affect the governance of other, smaller districts.

Low-performing school districts are spread across the state of Illinois. For example, on the Illinois Goals Assessment Program (IGAP) test of eighth-grade reading in 1992-93, there were 31 districts with an average score of less than 225 (out of 500, with the statewide average just over 250). These 31 districts were located in 13 counties; 13 were in Cook County, three each were in Madison and St. Clair counties (across the river from St. Louis), and the rest spread from Alexander County at the southern tip of the state to Whiteside County in the northwest. Low-performing districts can be found in every part of the state. There is little reason to think the situation is much different at the start of the new century.

At the school level, however, low performance is much more geographically concentrated. On the IGAP test of eighth-grade math in 1992-93, there were 234 schools with average scores under 200 (again, out of 500 possible, with the statewide average above 250); 214 of these low-performing schools were located in Chicago, while only 20 were located elsewhere in the state. State policies designed to affect low-performing *school districts*, the state's traditional policy focus, would be much more diffusely targeted than policies designed to affect low-performing *schools*, which have only recently appeared on the state policy screen.

In fall 1997, ISBE released a list of some 125 schools being placed on an academic early warning list. The ISBE promised to provide external supervision and monitoring of these schools and to provide technical assistance to the staffs of these schools as they sought to change. Of these schools, 93 were in Chicago, one was in the suburbs, and 31 were located elsewhere across the state. In fact, the Chicago school district, which had already placed these and a number of other schools on "probation," provided the external monitoring and support to city schools, while the ISBE provided those resources only to the 32 schools outside Chicago. This division of responsibility reflects a historic pattern in Illinois, where the ISBE frequently focuses on all school districts except Chicago.

Low-performing schools and the districts in which they are located predominantly enroll low-income students. Only six of the 31 districts with low eighth-grade reading scores in 1992-93 enrolled fewer than 30 percent low-income students. Similarly, only nine of the 234 schools with low eighth-grade math scores enrolled fewer than half of their students from low-income families. Thus, whether at the district or school level, solving the problem of low student performance involves solving the problem of improving the achievement levels of low-income students, many of whom are African-American or Hispanic-American.

This problem is quite different from trying to improve the achievement of students in the Lincolnshire-Prairieview School District in Lake County, which had the highest average eighth-grade reading score in 1992-93. Only 1.8 percent of the school's students came from low-income families, and less than 3 percent were African-American or Hispanic-American. To improve the performance of low-performing schools and districts is primarily an issue of improving the educational opportunities for low-income and minority students in these mostly urban schools and of intensifying their engagement in schooling. This problem is quite different from the issues faced by affluent suburban schools.

Improving the Skills and Capabilities of All Students

While some policymakers and members of the public focus on improving low-performing schools, others are more interested in improving the skills and capabilities of all students in the state. Frequently, this more generalized improvement goal is articulated in terms of meeting the demands for a "high-skills" workforce. The demands of the workplace are used to justify calls for improving the achievement levels of students in the public schools across the state. References frequently have been made to the U.S. Department of Labor's SCANS Report (1992), which added skills in problem-solving, human interaction, and technology to a list of basic skills (reading, writing, and computation) that are needed in the high-skills marketplace. It is in response to such concerns, as well as others about the importance of critical thinking to the future of democracy, that academic school reformers have sought to design inquiry-based curricula that force students (and teachers) to wrestle with a deeper knowledge of subject disciplines and their use in solving problems, both technological and human. Implementing these far-ranging, "constructivist" curricular reforms is a far different kind of problem than raising the performance on conventional, basic-skills-oriented measures of low-performing schools and districts.[4]

However, there are many who dispute whether public schools should focus on producing these "higher" skills in all students. Some contend that the "high-skills" marketplace will not be available to all emerging adults and that, in fact, the labor market is more dumbbell-shaped than simply "high-skills" dominated, with as many jobs being "dumbed down" as those being upgraded (see, e.g., Hargreaves, 1997). Although not endorsed by Hargreaves, in this case, it would be inefficient to "overeducate" large numbers of workers who are destined to hold jobs in the lower end of the dumbbell-shaped job market. Other doubters think problem-solving and human interaction skills are simply a vehicle for public schools to intrude into the area of personal beliefs and morals and are inappropriate arenas for public instruction. Still others—for example, Diane Ravitch, former director of the Office of Education Research and Instruction in the U.S. Department of Education—worry that a focus on higher skills leads away from teaching important facts and knowledge in favor of a focus on processes (Ravitch, 1997).

Even if there were agreement among policymakers that all students should learn higher skills, state policy initiatives to achieve that end might be quite difficult to design. State policy tends to target all districts and all schools alike, but as we have already noted, school contexts across the state are quite different. For example, it is quite likely that there would be at least three different types of school district responses to policy initiatives based on a rhetoric of meeting the needs of a high-skills marketplace.

Among schools that traditionally produce college-bound high school graduates, it would not be unusual to encounter personnel who do not believe their school needs to improve. They do not see the relevance of school-to-work and other workforce-generated school reform strategies because they see their job as preparing students for entry into higher education, and they frequently judge their success in terms of the percentage of their graduates who enroll in the most prestigious colleges and universities. Frequently, such school personnel are very aware

---

[4] Constructivist curricula focus on helping students construct meaning from data and their own experiences.

of the current advantages they enjoy in resources (both financial and human) and the access they have to the higher education universe. They work assiduously to maintain those advantages. Reforms that might narrow the gap in achievement between their students and those of other districts or schools would seem to be both irrelevant and a potential threat to their own resources, through which they have been so successful.

A different reaction might be expected from districts and schools whose high school graduates enter directly into the job market or who take further training in vocational or technical schools in preparation for job entry. School-to-work policies that would enhance the success of their graduates in getting jobs might seem much more appropriate in such districts.

At the low end of the performance spectrum, schools and districts that are struggling just to get half of their students to graduate from high school might find "high-skills," workforce-oriented reform strategies somewhat irrelevant in light of their struggle to impart "basic skills." Such personnel would be far more cognizant of the "low skills" jobs many of their graduates end up taking; they also recognize the geographic and social distance that stands between their students and access to "high-skills" employment.

Thus, in the effort to improve the skills and capabilities of all students, a state policy initiative built on a "high-skills" workforce model might find itself dismissed by both high-performing and low-performing districts and acceptable only to the districts in which most students either directly enter the workforce or continue schooling for only a year or two before doing so.

Overcoming the Inequity in Educational Resources

The 14th Amendment to the U.S. Constitution, adopted shortly after the Civil War, guaranteed that all citizens should have equal protection under the law. The 1970 Illinois Constitution contains a similar guarantee. Its education article requires the state to maintain an efficient system of free public schools. The Illinois General Assembly has traditionally delegated that responsibility to local school districts, assisted by the State Board of Education. Since education is a constitutionally mandated state function, and the state and federal constitutions require all citizens to be treated equally by government, one would logically assume that means the state should provide an equal education to all of its citizens. In other states, most recently Missouri and Kentucky, the courts have required such equity. However, the Illinois Supreme Court repeatedly has ruled that it is not necessary for the state's students to be treated equally; it reaffirmed that stance as recently as October 1996. In short, a separate and unequal education is judicially and politically acceptable in Illinois.

The inequity in school district funding in Illinois is one of the worst among the 50 states. One common measure of equity, called the "federal range ratio," compares the districts at the 95th and 5th percentiles in revenues per pupil (excluding the extreme cases as outliers that affect few students). For the 1991-92 school year, the 95th-to-5th percentile ratio for high school districts in Illinois was 2.72 to 1; for elementary districts, it was 2.45 to 1; and for unit districts, it was 1.45 to 1. That means that affluent high school districts have nearly three times the dollars per pupil available as property-poor districts, and rich elementary districts have two and one-half times as much. The Coalition for Educational Rights Under the Law, a statewide coalition of advocacy groups, proposed achieving a ratio of no more than 1.5 to 1, a very undemanding equity requirement. (Minnesota maintains an equity ratio of 1.15 to 1.) A ratio of 1.5 to 1 would mean that a school district at the 95th percentile would have half again as much to spend as one at the 5th percentile (e.g., $7,500 per pupil vs. $5,000 per pupil). The lower equity ratio of unit districts (those providing education across the full range of kindergarten to grade 12) reveals the more poorly funded condition of those school districts. In fact, the *median* funding level for high school districts across the state in 1991-92 ($5,246 per pupil) was $1,000 higher than the *95th-percentile* funding for unit districts ($4,213 per pupil).

The 1997 state school finance revisions had no impact on inequitable funding among high school districts, had a small impact on elementary district inequity, and virtually no impact on the more narrow spread among unit district revenues. In FY 1999, the equity ratio among high school districts continued to be 2.75 to 1; among elementary districts, the ratio fell to 2.02 to 1; the ratio among unit districts was little changed at 1.41 to 1. The median revenue per pupil among high school districts was $8,284, which was about the same level as the 95th-percentile elementary district, which received $8,208, and significantly greater than the 95th-percentile unit district, which received only $6,125 (Braskamp, Hess, and Keels, forthcoming). Thus, unit districts, in which a large majority of the state's minority and low-income students are enrolled, continue to be significantly less well funded than most high school districts and than many elementary school districts.

The political rhetoric about funding equity in Illinois has traditionally been posed as a city-suburban controversy. However, rising property values during the 1980s in the Chicago region and the stability of property values in the 96 downstate counties have greatly shifted the locus of the inequity. In terms of property wealth per pupil, Chicago is a mid-level school district; its funding problems relate to the more severe educational disadvantages of its students. In school finance terms, this is known as a problem of vertical, not horizontal, equity. The major horizontal equity gap is between the affluent suburbs to the north and west of Chicago and the much poorer districts in the south suburbs and the 96 downstate counties.

Historically and currently, Illinois courts, politicians, and citizens have demonstrated that they have little interest in the notion of treating children equitably. In 1995, Governor Jim Edgar appointed a blue-ribbon commission, primarily composed of business leaders from Chicago with a sprinkling of downstate and civil rights representatives, to address this issue. The Ikenberry Commission, as it came to be known, produced a report that virtually ignored equity, either horizontal or vertical. The commission report, though bemoaning the existing inequity in funding, focused on raising the level of adequacy of funding provided across the state (an important issue, to be sure). It addressed the gap in spending between rich and poor districts only by providing more funds for low-spending districts, not by changing the basic financing system. This means the equity gap would begin to grow again, as property-rich districts raise their spending more quickly than the state raises its support for students in poorer districts. The commission also delinked the level of compensatory funding for low-income students from the higher foundation level it was advocating, leaving the amount to be allocated for such vertical equity to the whim of the legislature, which overturned a reform adopted in 1973. The report provided the foundation for some of the revisions adopted in 1997, with the minimal impact on equity noted above.

Since the report was issued in March 1996, the school funding "reform" debate has focused on minimal adequacy of funding, completely abandoning the criterion of equity, except as a rhetorical device. This is true both of equity in resources for students and equity of burden for taxpayers. (Tax rates for homeowners across the metropolitan region vary by as much as 700 percent between property-poor south suburban and property-rich north suburban districts.) For its part, the General Assembly quickly killed the commission's proposals in 1996.

Caught up in partisan wrangling in anticipation of the 1998 general elections, the General Assembly did enact a significant increase in the foundation level of support for school districts. Adopted during a special session of the legislature called in December 1997, the legislation raised the foundation level to $4,225, thus providing more resources to the most poorly funded school districts. The bill also addressed a disproportionate revenue advantage previously enjoyed by high school districts by eliminating differences in pupil weighting by grade. This provision had little impact for the first three years, during which school districts were guaranteed not to lose funding. After that, the inequity between rich and poor high school districts would be likely to increase, as poor high school districts would qualify for less state aid, while districts with a richer property value base would continue to expand revenues. Overall, raising the bottom (i.e., the foundation level) reduced equity gaps somewhat among elementary districts, but had little effect on inequities among high school or unit districts. However, because there was no fundamental restructuring of the school finance scheme, the inequities are likely to increase over time as property-wealthy districts expand their revenues more quickly than the state increases funding for the poorest districts (see Hess and Braskamp, 1998).

Other midwestern states have more aggressively addressed the inequitable distribution of property wealth across their states. As noted above, the equity ratio in Minnesota is under 1.15 to 1. Several years ago, Michigan cut school property taxes on homeowners by more than 80 percent and essentially imposed a statewide tax on non-homestead property. It raised statewide sales and cigarette taxes to both make up the difference and raise the minimum funding per pupil to nearly $6,000 (in Illinois, it is now just over $4,000 per pupil). In Ohio, the courts have ruled the state's funding system unconstitutional, and the legislature is considering a new system. In Kentucky, a finance suit resulted in a Supreme Court ruling that the whole school code was unconstitutional, leading to the adoption of the Kentucky Education Reform Act, which both dramatically equalized school district funding and fostered widespread improvement efforts. In Illinois, despite the 1997 increase in the foundation level, many advocates still see school funding reform, a correction of a major inconsistency in the input regulation strategy, as the focal point for educational reform.

Maintaining the Current System at Lower Cost

A fourth option addresses a problem not directly connected to seeking to reform—or improve—education in the state but focuses instead on lowering the cost of providing a public education to the state's children without regard for improving student achievement. Much of the rhetoric about "reform" has been about ways to hold down the costs of public schooling. Attention has been paid to enhancing management of the schooling enterprise at all levels, to introducing paperwork reduction technology and speeding up the response time of the state (or district) "to its customers," to reducing the bargaining capacity of organized employees, and to limiting the revenue increases available to school districts to the rate of inflation. Deciding that greater efficiency is the problem to be solved avoids the problem of how to improve student achievement and frees policymakers from potentially divisive political decisions.

During the last 15 years, there has been much discussion of inefficiency in the delivery of all government services. In the statewide school reform enacted in 1985, legislators sought to address this concern by mandating a process of school district consolidation, thereby reducing the number and increasing the average size of districts across the state. Consolidation stirred up such a firestorm of protest in the affected school districts that the General Assembly was forced to rescind this provision of the reform law in 1986. Thus, the initial framing of the question of inefficiency was in terms of the number of school districts and the presumed efficiencies that could be accomplished by combining districts and thereby firing unneeded and duplicative bureaucratic staff in district offices. Yet, at the same time, the General Assembly expanded the responsibilities, and thereby the size, of the state education bureaucracy. In addition, it created an overlapping jurisdiction by adding a competing level of regional service centers to the intermediate administrative level of county school superintendents—a new inefficiency only now being eliminated a decade later. The legislature's efforts to bring efficiency to public schooling fell far short of creating an efficient administrative system.

Explicit policy-driven consolidation efforts have encountered popular resistance based on the desire to preserve local autonomy in educational decision-making. However, economic pressures have resulted in voluntary consolidations that have reduced the number of school districts in Illinois by more than 100 during the past decade. There are now just over 900 school districts in the state.

Before Illinoisans latch onto one or another of the currently popular school reform policy initiatives, it would be helpful if they came to some agreement about which problem or problems they are trying to solve. I have presented four potentially competing problem definitions that currently are driving school reform initiatives in the state, either explicitly or implicitly. Although these problems are not mutually exclusive, in a world of limited resources, policy initiatives that address one problem or another are competing with their counterparts for funding and focus. It would facilitate the policymaking process if political actors could agree on what problems have priority in the state's policy agenda.

WHAT CONUNDRUMS MUST BE CONFRONTED?

In seeking to address certain policy problems, such as improving student and school performance levels, several larger issues are encountered, and decisions must be made about them. In current school reform debates, four large conundrums must be confronted. They include a shift of orientation from input regulation to performance monitoring, a debate about what standards to adopt, the definition of equity, and what is meant by efficiency. The responses to these questions may seem self-evident when first encountered. However, these initial responses frequently give way to knottier issues as competing values come into play.[5]

---

[5] In the following pages, I focus on several specific issues facing Illinois policymakers. I have more fully described the changing assumptions about public education in the United States that undergird much of the national reform effort in Hess, 1995.

Shifting from Input Regulation to Performance Monitoring

Traditionally, states have sought to influence schools by regulating various dimensions of school life: teacher certification, minimum hours of daily instruction, number of days in the school year, and graduation requirements expressed in terms of Carnegie units (i.e., number of specific courses passed in high school). The assumption behind this approach is that if every school in the state uses minimally acceptable inputs, acceptable student learning will result, and differences in student achievement will reflect either the latent talent of the students or the effort they are willing to put forward.

These assumptions were challenged with the publication of *A Nation at Risk* in 1983. The National Commission on Excellence in Education suggested that we should focus more on student performance, leaving the "how" to local districts and schools, but requiring adequate achievement from all students (NCEE, 1983). The 1985 state reform act began to move Illinois toward a focus on student performance by calling for state learning objectives and a state testing program. This shift from *regulating the inputs* while letting student achievement vary widely to *monitoring student performance* and allowing the inputs to vary as needed is a fundamental change in approach that is still only partially being implemented more than 15 years later. There is much attention to student performance now, but the state school code still severely regulates the ways schools and school districts operate.

The state has been pursuing both approaches at once. On the one hand, it added sanctions that could be applied to low-performing schools and school districts (as the General Assembly did in 1995 in amendments to the Chicago School Reform Act and in later creating a state academic warning list). At the same time, the legislature raised graduation course requirements (an input that reinforces subject matter isolation and mitigates against interdisciplinary courses as a way to teach required knowledge and skills). In fall 1997, the General Assembly raised teacher certification standards (another input). The best that can be said is that currently, Illinois is in a transition from the traditional approach of input regulation to a performance-based approach that focuses on monitoring and supervision. The worst case is that state policy is schizophrenic on this issue.

What Standards Do We Want to Achieve?

Many critics of public education in the United States have complained about the "dumbing down" of school textbooks and of the curriculum in general. Sometimes the criticism is oriented to the past ("Kids just aren't learning what we learned in school"); sometimes it is comparative ("American kids aren't doing as well in math as Japanese, German, or Russian kids"). From these criticisms, it is a short step to say that we should have higher expectations of our students and thus higher standards. In response, discipline specialists, such as the pioneering National Council of Teachers of Mathematics (NCTM), have developed higher standards for the teaching of their subject. The federal government has given financial support to similar bodies to develop standards in several other disciplines. The effort to develop higher standards has, however, run into a number of difficulties.

The effort to develop higher standards has shifted the proposed learning objectives beyond basic skills and "procedural" knowledge (e.g., the appropriate steps and their sequencing to solve particular algebraic problems) into a deeper understanding of how mathematics or the process of writing "really works." This conception of higher standards places less emphasis on learning facts and formulas (historical dates and figures, multiplication tables, etc.) and more emphasis on understanding the meaning implicit in combinations of facts and logical operations. However, popular support for such "higher standards" frequently wanes when they are perceived as abandoning basic competencies and forsaking the nation's core cultural knowledge. The debate about desired student outcomes is hotly contested, as "one persisting position emphasizes student absorption of knowledge, and another emphasizes student construction of meaning, or 'teaching for understanding'" (Newmann, King, and Rigdon, 1997, p. 45). Thus, an effort to raise standards becomes perceived by others as lowering standards.

A related problem is that many elementary and secondary school teachers never learned these deeper aspects of their own specialties when they were in college or graduate school, and they have difficulty teaching to these higher standards. James Spillane and his colleagues have been studying efforts of schools and school districts in Michigan to implement the new NCTM math standards. They found that, in a sample of nine school districts with high reputations for implementing the new standards, a majority of teachers and local district policymakers did not understand the dimensions of math that these standards presumed. Of those who did understand the discipline, only a very few could both incorporate an appropriate curriculum and enact a classroom pedagogy capable of leading students toward these higher understandings (Spillane and Zeuli, 1997). This problem is doubly vexing when one remembers that the teachers and administrators in these districts thought they *were* teaching to the new NCTM standards.

The problem is more complex in that there is little external reinforcement for shifting to these new, higher standards. College entrance requirements have not significantly changed to favor students taught to these new standards. School accreditation requirements have not been shifted in comparable ways in most states. The hiring practices of businesses continue to focus on degrees acquired, not competancies achieved. Performance standards for teachers still focus on classroom management skills while ignoring measurements of achievement gains by their students. Public opinion polls indicate parents and other citizens favor more basic instruction (Bradley, 1997).

District and school-level personnel have huge incentives to maintain a traditional skills focus. Beyond the obvious burden of trying to upgrade the inadequately prepared teaching force to teach to higher standards, there are important rewards attached to the current system. As indicated earlier, the vast majority of school districts in Illinois show average student achievement levels above the state average, because the state average is depressed by the large number of low-income Chicago students achieving at low levels. This creates an obvious political advantage for suburban school leaders who can claim that their schools are above average, while schools with mostly low-income students are left to bear the brunt of the blame for low school performance.

In 1997, the Illinois State Board of Education adopted a new set of educational standards for early and middle elementary grades, middle school, and early and late high school. These standards are focused on a narrowed version of the learning standards mandated in the 1985 state reform legislation. Although the standards adopted have been praised by observers as diverse as Diane Ravitch and the American Federation of Teachers, they have been criticized for ignoring politically contentious arenas such as health education.

Even if Illinois citizens could agree on higher achievement standards for students, we probably could not tell whether our students were reaching those standards. Most assessment systems, including the state's IGAP tests, have been inadequate to measure these "high-skills" objectives. The IGAPs were primarily multiple-choice tests, except for the writing section. While multiple-choice questions are easier to score and therefore cheaper to administer, they provide no performance assessments (e.g., the ability of students in science to successfully conduct an experiment), and they are limited to one point in time in a school year (four moments for the same subject in a student's public school career). The same shortcoming is evident in the more recently developed Illinois Standards Achievement Test (ISAT) program, which has replaced IGAP. By contrast, student portfolios span a year's work. Other states, such as Kentucky, have developed testing systems that incorporate both performance and portfolio assessments. Like most, but not all, state testing programs, there are no stakes for the students taking the Illinois assessment, so students who see no sense in taking the tests have no reason to do their best. The General Assembly has recently mandated that test scores be made available to districts on an individual basis and included on student records to try to meet this difficulty, but that effort may have minimal effect on student motivation and creates new reliability problems for the test-makers. The new Prairie State Achievement Examination for eleventh-graders was originally touted as a high school exit exam that students would have to "pass" in order to graduate. However, when the state decided to base this exam on the ACT Assessment, a nationally administered high school test, the exit exam function was ruled out.

The IGAP tests had two other serious problems, with debilitating implications for tracking student achievement in Illinois. The first, to be discussed in more detail later in this chapter, is that the IGAP provided no valid way to measure improvement or deterioration in the achievement levels of either individual students or schools, a critical failure if education reform is about school improvement. Second, several versions of the IGAP were found by researchers at the University of Chicago to contain too few questions at the low end of the achievement scale, leading to large score variations for lower-performing students that reflect only a few more (or less) correct answers (Bryk, 1996). Thus, the test scores were artificially depressed and less stable for those districts already catching blame for low student performance. It is not clear yet that the ISATs have resolved either of these problems.

An examination of test scores in one southwest suburban school district for the six-year period from 1988 to 1993 showed huge variations (as much as 80 points) for the same grade in the same school from one year to the next (see Table 2).[6] Generally speaking, the state mean for these tests was about 250. It is difficult to say anything about school improvement in these schools when scores bounce around as erratically as in Brodnicki's third-grade reading or Wilkins's third-grade math, where the average score fell to 206 in 1991, but then jumped far above the state mean to 290 in 1992. Such huge variations show the unreliability of these tests to accurately report changes in achievement for schools, and the problem is even worse in schools whose students perform at or below the statewide average, as a summary report of tracking reform in 14 Chicago schools showed (Hess, 1996).

TABLE 2: Illinois Goals Assessment Program (IGAP) Test Score Variation in Indian Springs Elementary School District 109

	1988	1989	1990	1991	1992	1993	Low	High
Brodnicki								
3rd-grade reading	259	229	289	289	224	247	224	289
6th-grade reading	281	309	264	289	253	333	253	333
Dosher								
3rd-grade reading	265	284	235	259	254	236	235	284
6th-grade reading	308	267	257	297	223	241	223	308
Wilkins								
3rd-grade reading	256	245	253	223	266	275	223	275
3rd-grade math	----	232	245	206	290	272	206	290

[6] See Hess (1996), for a similar depiction of the variability of IGAP scores from year to year in 14 Chicago schools.

Should Resources to Provide Educational Services Guarantee Equity among All Students or Minimal Adequacy for All?

For more than a decade, school reform advocates in Illinois have been arguing that students should have equal funding.[7] In the late 1980s, a compact of school districts, the Committee for Educational Rights Under the Constitution, was formed to sue the state in an effort to force more equitable funding across school districts. That suit, filed in 1989, was dismissed by the Cook County Circuit Court in 1991. The case was ultimately appealed to the Illinois Supreme Court, which dismissed the case in 1996. Still, school finance reform continues to be an important element in education policy discussions in Illinois.

Proposing a new system of school funding, if more than simply boosting the minimum adequacy level, entails a number of vexing issues beyond simple dollar equivalences. In different regions of the state, there are different educational costs to provide comparable quality (if quality here represents comparable programs available and equal capacity and effectiveness of teachers). The cost of living differs by almost 50 percent among the counties of Illinois, according to a study conducted by Walter McMahon of the University of Illinois at Urbana-Champaign (McMahon and Chang, 1991). Perhaps teacher salaries should vary according to the cost of living.

Teacher labor markets also vary across the state. Districts with harder-to-educate children and in more remote locations have more difficulty in attracting highly competent teachers than do districts serving primarily affluent families. To create comparable teacher capacity among school districts, perhaps districts with recruiting difficulties should be able to pay their teachers higher salaries. Teachers in the Chicago metropolitan area seem to be more mobile, and higher proportions of them are able to move from one district to another to secure more favorable employment. What effect does that mobility have on how funding should be distributed?

Should education be seen as a fundamental right of all students (and thus equally available so as to not advantage one group of children over another)? Or should education be under-

---

[7] An earlier Chicago Assembly book devoted its attention to how government in Illinois should be financed. One chapter focused on school funding (Wong, 1996).

stood as an investment by the state in the development of its human resources? If education is a human capital investment, an argument can be made for higher investment in those persons most likely to provide a higher return on the investment.

Equity is usually focused on the issue of resources available to provide a comparable educational program to students. There is, however, another kind of equity in school funding, the equity of tax burden experienced by property owners. Should some homeowners be forced to bear tax rates that are seven times higher than those of other homeowners, especially if the resources generated are only half of what is available to the children of families with much greater property wealth and much lower tax rates?

How can local "liberty" to provide an education that meets the expectations of local citizens be assured? Should local liberty be equally available to school districts currently too short of resources to have any effective educational choices? Should local liberty be available only to groups of citizens at the school district level, regardless of the size of the district, or should it be available at the school level?

What Is Meant by Efficiency?

The emphasis on "efficiency" in education has not been based on a careful definition of the term. Some scholars, influenced by economic definitions of efficiency, have begun to examine the costs of reaching particular student achievement results. The IGAP tests provided a performance measure, and the cost per pupil of school districts became the input variable. School districts with mid-level costs and low student performance would appear to be inefficient on such measures, but so would high-cost districts with average or slightly above average scores. Such straightforward analyses ignore the differences in student achievement that result from differences in socioeconomic status among enrolled students. These socioeconomic differences both depress student outcomes and increase total student costs as a result of compensatory education programs.

An analysis conducted by Peter Chalos of the University of Illinois at Chicago showed the added benefit in student performance from increasing spending per student, up to a certain point (Chalos, 1998). However, the most inefficient school districts turned out to be the high-cost suburban districts. This finding surprised many policymakers, but not knowledgeable observers, who have wondered for years why it made sense to pay a superintendent of a school district with 4,000 elementary school students a salary comparable to that paid a superintendent in Chicago with more than 430,000 students.

Prior to the availability of comparable outcome measures, efficiency was viewed as running a school system at the lowest possible cost per student. This led, particularly in larger school systems, to the advent of large schools as a way to achieve facility and staffing "efficiencies." However, when outcomes were introduced into the efficiency equation, these large schools were found to be less successful than smaller schools that served similar student populations. For example, a study of eighth-grade graduates of Chicago elementary schools found that larger elementary schools had higher proportions of students who eventually dropped out of high school than did smaller schools serving similar students (Hess and Greer, 1986). Thus, packing more than 1,800 children ages 5-14 into one school, as in Nathan Davis Elementary School and Shields Elementary School in Chicago, might be low in cost per pupil, but it is high in cost per pupils who eventually graduate from high school. The emphasis on performance as a component of efficiency has led to a number of proposals to change the way schools are structured and governed.

One focus involves moving decision-making from large, bureaucratically organized school districts down to the individual school, as was embodied in the Chicago School Reform Act of 1988. Another focus, unforeseen in the 1988 act, is dividing large school buildings into several smaller schools, each using the common facility. These schools-within-schools might resemble different programs within one school under one principal or might be completely separate schools, each with its own principal, acting as co-tenants in the common facility.[8]

A more radical version of school-based management emerged in Minnesota in 1991 with the creation of the first charter schools. Charter schools are public schools directly established by the state or by other entities empowered to do so by the state. These schools provide a free, public education but

---

[8] Equally unforeseen was the emergence of teacher-led schools that contest the assumption that every school should be bureaucratically organized with a principal in charge.

usually are not under the jurisdiction of local school districts. Charter schools are direct extensions of the shift from regulating inputs to monitoring performance; they are generally freed of the many regulations of state school codes in exchange for an agreement about student achievement by the end of the limited charter period (typically five years).

More than half of the 50 states have now enacted charter school legislation. Ted Kolderie, one of the advocates of Minnesota's pioneering law and a supporter of charter schools, has categorized charter laws as either "weak" or "strong" on the basis of the likelihood that innovative schools that do not simply mimic existing public schools will emerge from each state's law. Stronger laws include provisions for allowing sponsors other than the local district, for allowing a variety of groups to organize a charter, for charters to be discrete legal entities, for charters to be schools of choice for teachers and students, and for charters to automatically receive full funding (cited in Bierlein and Mulholland, 1994). On these criteria, the Illinois charter law is considered a weak law, primarily because it vests in local school districts the exclusive decision on whether charters should be granted. Not surprisingly, Illinois school districts, with the exception of Chicago, have refused to grant charters to groups that would compete with local district schools for students. In fact, the Illinois charter school legislation resembles legislation allowing districts to contract with outside agencies to provide schools that will serve a special purpose not easily accomplished in the district's regular schools. The first Illinois charter granted, in Peoria, was to establish a school for special education pupils. At the close of 1997, the Peoria charter was the only one granted by a school district outside Chicago. Subsequently, the General Assembly strengthened the legislation minimally by giving the Illinois State Board of Education the right to override a local district's refusal to approve a charter. However, this remains a much more awkward arrangement than in other states, where the state supports charter schools directly, and local districts have little say in establishing charters.[9]

---

[9] In 2000-2001, Illinois had 19 charter schools—13 in Chicago, three in the metropolitan suburbs (Crete, Grayslake, Des Plaines), and three downstate (Cahokia, Springfield, East St. Louis). Beginning in 1999-2000, Peoria's charter school began operating as a Regional Safe School program for all of Peoria County.

An even more radical attack on the monopoly of the provision of public education is the idea of vouchers or tuition tax credits. Both of these proposals are designed to give parents the right to "vote with their feet" in choosing the kind of education their children will receive at public expense. Tax credits have the obvious limitation of serving primarily parents who earn enough income to pay more taxes than the cost of their children's tuition. Vouchers can be more equitably available to all parents or can be targeted to provide advantages to low-income parents. In Illinois, vouchers have been strongly supported by backers of the state's parochial schools and by large media outlets such as the *Chicago Tribune*.

Currently, there are two major voucher programs, one in Milwaukee, which has been operating since 1991, and the other in Cleveland, which started in 1996. In Milwaukee, 1,500 low-income parents of students in the Milwaukee Public Schools (MPS) or just coming of age to enroll in MPS qualify for tuition vouchers of about $2,500 for use in private, nonsectarian schools. A 1996 effort to expand the program to 15,000 students and allow them to attend religiously sponsored schools was disallowed by the state appellate court in 1997. The Cleveland voucher plan, which allowed students to enroll in parochial as well as private schools, was also challenged in the courts. The plan was found to violate the state constitution and was ordered suspended at the end of the 1999-2000 school year.

Restrictions on who can receive a voucher avoid a major problem faced by many voucher advocates: the cost of extending public support for students currently enrolled in private or parochial schools. Because the advocates of vouchers in Illinois have been closely allied with lobbyists for the parochial schools, it is unlikely that voucher proposals in this state can avoid answering the question of where to find the additional funds to support the nearly 300,000 students now enrolled in private and parochial schools. At even $2,500 per pupil, state costs could increase by about $750 million.

The debate about efficiency in Illinois has turned away from the question of student achievement and has focused instead on reconstituting the balance of labor-management influence on school decision-making. In an effort to seriously weaken the influence of teacher unions, the General Assembly, in 1995, considered legislation restricting the bargaining rights of teachers, but proponents could not muster the votes to adopt the measure on a statewide basis. However, the Chicago School

Reform Amendatory Act did include provisions to severely constrain the rights of the Chicago Teachers Union (CTU), at least temporarily. Those provisions eliminated the CTU's right to strike for the first 18 months after their adoption and removed from the bargaining arena issues of district management and work rules. The amendments also altered the traditional political alliance between the union and the mayor by making the mayor directly responsible for the school district management. Thus, the debate about school efficiency shifted to questions such as how cheaply teachers can be hired or how easily teachers can be fired, as well as how administrators can recover control of prerogatives over class size, programs offered, days worked, and so forth.

WHAT STRATEGIES SHOULD THE STATE PURSUE?

Once state policymakers have decided what problem to focus on, confronted the conundrums outlined above, and chosen the parameters within which they are willing to address the problem, they then must decide which strategies to pursue. Since resources are finite, not all available strategies can be pursued, and among those strategies that can be pursued, not all can have an equal focus. Choices must be made. Following is a discussion of three major strategies that have received significant attention in Illinois: improving teacher quality, improving school performance, and engaging students more successfully.

Improving Teacher Quality

There is a widely held perception that the quality of teachers currently employed in Illinois is not adequate to successfully confront the problems faced by contemporary schools. Different people arrive at this common perception from different situations. In urban schools, there is a perception that too many teachers are incompetent in basic skills or uncaring about the success of their low-income African-American and Hispanic-American students. In suburban schools, the quality issue tends to focus more on teachers' preparedness and disciplinary training for the high-skills reforms being proposed by academics and the discipline specialists. Many researchers are concerned with the capacity of schools to enact an educational program that can

meet the new standards. Newmann, King, and Rigdon concluded that "even if external authorities provided higher quality
standards and inducements, many schools would lack the capacity to meet them" (1997, p. 46). Related questions are, "Do
teachers have the will to change from using outmoded and ineffective practices?" and "Are they willing to admit their teaching
practices have been ineffective?"

There are currently two quite different approaches to improve the quality of teachers in Illinois. One is a continuation
of the traditional "input regulation" strategy to increase certification requirements and participation in national certification
efforts. The other is a "performance focused" approach that
relaxes certification requirements in exchange for a system of
rewards and sanctions.

Generally, the input regulation strategy of increasing certification requirements assumes there is an adequate supply of
potential teachers that can be more carefully screened for entrance into the profession and that existing teachers, given the
opportunity, could and would be willing to improve their capacity and effectiveness. This approach would require higher preparation standards for schools of education (e.g., requiring a
liberal arts bachelor's degree with a subject major and a master's in education) and closing schools of education that do not
produce high-quality teacher candidates.[10]

Historically, states that have raised teacher certification
requirements have later found themselves facing a teacher shortage, as the supply of students choosing to go into teaching and
able to meet the new qualifications decreases. At that point,
states have either rescinded the higher standards or have chosen
to wink at districts with lower resources or more difficult working conditions as they employ "provisionals" or "full-time-basis
substitutes" to fill their classrooms. This pattern is the result of
ignoring the problem of teacher recruitment.

For the past several decades, students entering teaching have
tended to come from the bottom quartile of their entering fresh-
man class and to achieve grade-point averages below those of

---

[10] See the recent report of the National Commission on Teaching
and America's Future (NCTAF, 1996), one of whose signatories was
Illinois Governor Jim Edgar. However, it is not clear that the governor was ready to close any of the state's schools of education, particularly those producing the majority of the state's racial/ethnic
minority teachers.

other students. Raising the standards for entry into teaching without, at the same time, inducing better-prepared undergraduates to switch to a teaching career is unlikely to be a successful strategy. Correspondingly, thinking that large numbers of current teachers would gladly forsake what they consider to be "tried and proven" strategies of instruction for unfamiliar approaches that claim to achieve higher levels of student understanding ignores the evidence of years of research on teacher resistance to change, overlooks teachers' mistaken perceptions that they are already "doing the reforms," and underestimates the importance of the protections offered by tenure and union work rules (McLaughlin, 1978; Hargreaves, 1994; Spillane and Zeuli, 1997).

Since 1995, attention has been focused, not without controversy, on a performance-based set of strategies to improve the quality of teaching in the state's public schools. Other states, such as Kentucky and Maryland, have progressed further down this path than Illinois. However, the mid-decade amendments to the Chicago School Reform Act have put Chicago in the forefront of implementing this strategic approach in Illinois.

Focusing on student achievement changes the basis of judging teacher performance. Competence is no longer judged by the degrees a teacher has acquired or the number of courses passed in a university (or a school district's own offerings). Competence is instead measured by the success of a teacher's students. Such a distinction blurs the traditional line between teaching and learning. No longer is it possible for a teacher to claim, "I taught that, but they didn't learn it!" The performance approach is based on the conviction that teaching does not occur unless learning happens. This is, of course, also affected by the willingness and effort of students to learn, a problem to which I shall return.

If teacher competence is judged on the basis of student achievement, there is ample evidence that many currently certified teachers are not performing at acceptable levels and that certification, at whatever level, does not guarantee competence in teaching (which is quite different from being competent as a university student). Thus, the performance-based strategy de-emphasizes teacher certification requirements, seeks to entice more qualified persons into teaching through alternative certification procedures, and generally focuses more directly on the problems of teacher recruitment by acknowledging the dynamics of the teacher labor market. Alternative certification ap-

proaches seek to capitalize on changes in the wider employment
market, such as higher levels of professional and managerial
unemployment and the negative impact on individuals of downsizing and depersonalization in corporate bureaucracies.

At the same time, performance-based strategies emphasize
using external (rather than intrinsic) rewards and sanctions as
incentives for current teachers to change their practice.   In
Kentucky, rewards of up to $3,500 per teacher have been dis-
tributed in schools in which student achievement exceeds
improvement benchmarks.   These benchmarks were part of a
20-year state program to bring all students to a much higher
level of proficiency than that achieved in most other states.
Implementation of a series of corresponding sanctions on
schools that have failed to meet their improvement goals has
been somewhat curtailed while complaints about the state's
assessment system are being addressed.   The potential sanctions
included installing external monitors (educational experts),
granting students a choice of attending other schools, and
threatening the loss of jobs.   Evidence on the effectiveness of
the rewards in encouraging teachers to change their practice is
inconclusive.[11]   The threat of sanctions rather than the promise
of rewards did motivate some teachers to change their practice
(Appalachia Educational Laboratory, 1996).

Meanwhile, the Chicago Public Schools has implemented a
program of sanctions on low-performing schools, without any
corresponding rewards.   During the 1996-97 school year, 109
of the system's some 550 schools were placed on probation.
Schools on probation are provided "probation managers" to
monitor and oversee the actions of the principal and "external
partners" to provide technical assistance to faculty members
trying to change their practice.[12]   During the summer of 1997,

---

[11] Kentucky invested heavily in professional development as it
began to implement its reforms, thus combining pressure for change
with support in the effort to change.

[12] During the fall of 1997, ISBE announced a similar process,
modeled on the Chicago plan.   At the same time, 125 schools were
placed on an early warning list and promised supervision and technical assistance similar to that provided to schools on probation in
Chicago.   The schools on probation in Chicago continued to be ser-
viced by the Chicago district, while the state limited its focus to the
32 listed schools outside of Chicago.

the School Reform Board of Trustees (board of education) voted to reconstitute the faculties at seven of the lowest-performing high schools. In those schools, about 30 percent of the teachers were replaced, as were five of the seven principals. Replaced teachers were retained in the school system for 10 months and had the option of seeking a permanent position in other schools. Those who did not find another permanent position would be terminated. "Re-engineering," a sanction less sweeping than reconstitution, was introduced in the 1999-2000 school year. "Intervention," a more radical judgment on low-performing schools, was initiated in 2000-2001. For schools subject to this sanction, an external supervisory team will evaluate all teachers over an eight-month period, after which those judged inadequate can be fired outright.

Under these performance-based strategies, teacher tenure is subordinated to student achievement success. Judgments about the competence of teachers are based on student achievement, not on credentials or evaluations of classroom management capability. After four years of performance-based initiatives in Chicago, the number of schools on probation had been halved and student achievement had improved in both elementary and high schools.

Overall, it would appear that strategies to improve teacher quality in Illinois are a strange hybrid of input regulation and performance monitoring. On the one hand, the state has raised teacher certification requirements, which may have more of an effect on currently higher-performing school districts and possibly on schools of education. On the other hand, performance monitoring efforts have focused primarily on lower-performing schools in Chicago, but have been extended to some 30 other schools around the state.

Improving School Performance

While improving teacher quality may be one component of improving school performance, there are a number of other strategies that might also be considered. Strategies to improve school performance require some decisions about previously acknowledged conundrums, which would then lead toward some potential reform strategies.

The state must first decide on standards for school performance. The new Illinois Learning Standards, with their corresponding learning objectives at five points in a student's school career (early and late elementary years, middle school, early and late high school) are claimed to be in line with the high standards promulgated by the various discipline-based standards documents. There has been debate, however, about whether these Illinois standards are indeed high standards or the lowest common denominator of acceptable language, devoid of required knowledge content.[13]

By contrast, Kentucky chose to establish standards of proficiency more in line with those embodied in the National Assessment of Educational Progress (NAEP) tests, under which even the best schools in the state have only 65 percent of their students achieving at proficient levels, according to one prominently placed school superintendent (see Guskey, 1994). Further, if school performance improvement is the goal, then standards of improvement should be set for each school. In Kentucky, the percentage of students achieving the level of proficiency (on a four-position scale of novice, apprentice, proficient, distinguished) was expected to rise to 100 percent in each school in 20 years. Targeted biannual increases for each school were to reflect one-tenth of the difference between the current percentage achieving proficiency and the 20-year goal of 100 percent. Illinois has yet to set specific improvement goals for its schools. Thus, while Kentucky focuses on the improvement of all schools, Illinois largely ignores changes in achievement, either declines or improvement, in its higher-performing and mid-level schools.

Illinois must also come up with a better way to measure "improvement." Its current approach involves a refinement of the input regulation strategy of accreditation. Accreditation reviews, performed at the high school level by an independent association for the North Central states, have proven incapable of guaranteeing an acceptable level of student performance in all of the state's schools (most low-performing high schools in the state are fully accredited).[14] In 1996, the Illinois State Board of Education initiated a quality review process, admini-

---

[13] For contrasting views, see Grossman (1997) and Palmisano (1997).

[14] The North Central Association is also moving toward a performance-based accreditation process.

stered by the state with assistance from local practitioners from schools or districts other than the ones under review. The reviews assess the implementation of an adequate curriculum, appropriate pedagogical approaches, and the existence of a reasonable school improvement plan adopted for or by the school. This approach, while a considerable advance on previous accreditation approaches, continues the regulatory strategy of monitoring the inputs of education and assumes that advising schools on changes in the schooling process will lead to higher student achievement.

Adopting a "performance-based" approach to improving schools is another alternative, but it would require a set of strategies not currently available in Illinois. Improving achievement levels requires a change in orientation that measures schools against their own prior performance, rather than comparing the performance of one school and its students to the performance of other schools and their (not necessarily comparable) students. Prevailing practice in Illinois continues to compare annual school scores with those of other schools, celebrating the above-average performance of two-thirds of the state's districts while loudly bemoaning the performance level of schools in the other third of the districts. No attention is paid to the number of schools improving their levels of achievement or the number in which student achievement is decreasing, which would include many suburban schools with outstanding reputations. Since the students tested in each year by the state are different from those tested in the prior year, little credibility is given to comparisons of scores from one year to the next or even "cohort" comparisons from third grade to sixth grade. Such data are used today in Chicago, and in other districts that test all students every year, to track school-level improvement compared with prior performance.[15]

What is needed is a state assessment system that will show the "value added" by each school to its students' education. This means showing how much growth is achieved by each student from one year to the next and finding a way to aggregate the growth of each student for the school as a whole. Current student assessments, both those administered by ISBE (including ISAT) and those commercially available, are not designed to

---

[15] See Hess (1996) for a more detailed explanation of the problems in this approach.

demonstrate such growth, and such tests would be exceedingly complex to develop, given the range of abilities of students in any one grade. To truly track school improvement, assessments must be developed that explicitly measure growth in student achievement between two grades at certain intervals (e.g., from 3rd to 4th, 6th to 7th, 10th to 11th). Then the aggregate scores of schools could be compared with the growth (not absolute scores) of their own students in succeeding years. This would allow an analysis of whether schools are improving over their previous growth gains or regressing from them.

For anything to matter in encouraging school improvement, changes in student achievement levels at schools must count for something. Consequences for performance must apply to both educators and students. There must be rewards and recognition if schools improve and consequences if they fail to improve. Thus, a system of rewards must be created to meet the state's goals for school improvement, and real sanctions must be applied against the adults, not the students, in schools that do not improve. Such systems are in place in Kentucky, South Carolina, and Maryland.

Frequently, representatives of the business community in Illinois have proposed giving high-performing schools more funds and taking funds away from low-performing schools. These proposals miss the point that such a direct financial system of rewards and sanctions ends up penalizing the students, through program reductions, for the lack of performance of the adults at the school. In addition, such proposals are frequently not very sophisticated about the difficulties encountered by schools seeking to educate greater proportions of low-income students. I will return to the issue of rewards and sanctions for students shortly.

The most difficult part of the strategic question is how to accomplish school improvement, particularly in the lowest performing schools. One obvious strategy is to assure that all schools provide their students an adequate educational program with adequate staff coverage. This is, of course, the intent behind school finance reforms that focus on assuring that all schools receive an adequate amount of funding. However, the assumption that adequate funding will assure an adequate educational program is problematic, at best. Some years ago, under Superintendent Ted Kimbrough, only half of all Chicago high schools employed a faculty member competent to teach physics. If physics is not taught, it is not surprising to find lower test scores in science in those schools than in schools where the full range of sciences is taught. More funding might provide an additional position, even if student enrollment in advanced science classes is low. But securing an additional 30 teachers certified to teach high school physics might still be a problem. Money is part of the answer to ensuring an adequate program offering in every school, but money alone may not be sufficient to solve this part of the problem.

Beyond the issue of adequate staff coverage of subjects to be taught, improving the performance of low-performing schools also entails improving the quality of teaching in those schools. This is a far more difficult problem. Despite state certification requirements, the quality and preparation of teachers varies significantly across the state and within the Chicago metropolitan region. Teachers graduating from the University of Illinois at Urbana-Champaign and Northwestern University generally have far higher scores on college entrance tests such as the ACT than do teachers graduating from Chicago State University or Northeastern Illinois University. Teachers graduating from other regional colleges and universities likely fall somewhere in between. School districts differ significantly in their ability to hire teachers from more competitive universities.

Similarly, districts vary significantly in the proportion of their teachers who have acquired a master's degree. Chicago and districts in the south suburbs have fewer teachers with master's degrees. In 1995, 54 percent of all teachers in suburban Cook County and 57 percent in DuPage County held master's degrees. By contrast, only 43 percent of teachers in Will County and 41 percent in Chicago had those degrees. Within suburban Cook County, the proportion of elementary school teachers with master's degrees was more than 50 percent in the northern suburbs but less than 40 percent in the southern suburbs (Ed.dat, 1996). These differences in teacher preparation correlate inversely with the percentages of low-income and minority students enrolled in those districts and with the revenues per pupil available to the districts.

To spread teacher quality more evenly across the region, not to mention the state, would require significant incentives to attract higher quality teachers to Chicago and the south suburban school districts enrolling the most disadvantaged students and away from the more advantaged northern and western suburbs. Given the unwillingness of state policymakers to entertain funding proposals that would increase equity of resources, it is also highly unlikely that they would enact policies to enable the city and south suburban districts to compete effectively for the best teachers.

An even more problematic strategy is focused on improving the quality of existing teachers in low-performing districts. Given the lower levels of initial preparation for college and attendance at less selective universities by teachers in these districts, improving their quality of teaching is likely to be quite challenging. Add to that the general resistance of teachers to change, and the challenge becomes greater. Thus, it is with both anticipation and skepticism that researchers are closely following the efforts to improve teacher quality as a component of school reform in Chicago.

Engaging Students More Successfully

Appropriately, teachers point out that if the performance levels of students are to improve, these students must be successfully engaged in schools and school-based learning. The problem of student engagement is, however, quite different at different ends of the student achievement scale. In many low-performing schools, students have become disaffected from school institutions that more resemble prisons than vehicles of opportunity. At the higher end of the scale, schools expand their offerings, through advanced placement courses, to overlap with college-level education.

The National Education Commission on Time and Learning pointed out that in the past (under input regulation), schools provided the same amount of time to all students and allowed student performance to vary significantly (NECTL, 1994). The commission recommended that in an era in which we want all students to achieve at high levels, we should allow variation in the time students spend in school. In earlier periods, students who mastered high school subjects could graduate at age 15 or 16 and were allowed to begin their college careers at an earlier age. Currently, school districts serving middle-class parents have devised a system whereby such successful students are provided college-equivalency courses in high school, at taxpayer expense, thereby reducing the number of courses these students must take in college, and the quarters of required tuition their parents must pay.

By contrast, the Commission on Time and Learning recommended that students needing more time to become proficient in the core high school subjects should be provided that extra time. Yet few school districts with high numbers of lower-performing students, who tend also to come from low-income backgrounds, have the resources to provide this extra learning opportunity. Beginning in 1997, the Chicago Public Schools reallocated resources to provide mandatory summer school for more than 28,000 low-performing students in the third, sixth, and eighth grades. The CPS has also announced it will allow students to complete high school in three, four, or five years, beginning with students entering ninth grade in fall 2001. But it has proved more difficult to find ways to extend a low-performing student's day to eight hours while reducing the time required of more successful students to four hours. Our current ways of providing resources to schools would mitigate against fitting the time available for schooling to the differential needs of students.

One strategy for enhancing the engagement of students in low-performing schools is to create higher stakes for the students' own performance levels. Mandatory summer school for low-performing students is one such consequence. Retention of students who then still do not meet required levels of proficiency is another potential consequence. But negative sanctions alone are unlikely to be as successful as might be desired. In addition to making more resources available, such as more time and assistance, schools and society as a whole must find ways to convince disaffected, low-income students of the value of education. Similarly, student incentives and sanctions must be closely aligned with incentives and sanctions for educators regarding school improvement. It will be no easy task to convince low-income students that education matters, given the lack of connection between educational attainment and economic opportunities in many low-income communities.

At the other end of the scale, some high schools have been more innovative in expanding their curriculum to challenge high achievers through advanced placement courses, co-enrollment in higher educational institutions, and international baccalaureate-type programs. Other high schools have made an effort to more closely connect their curriculum offerings to likely career choices of their students. Few schools see the value of reducing taxpayer costs by encouraging early graduation.

WHERE ARE WE IN ILLINOIS?

School reform policy in Illinois has schizophrenically combined elements of the traditional, input-regulation approach with new initiatives that focus on performance, such as more challenging academic standards, statewide testing, and various accountability mechanisms. In 1985, the state began to move toward defining learning goals. In 1997, it adopted new standards to embody those goals, followed by new state assessments in 1999 and 2000 to measure whether the goals are being met. This process can be seen as an effort to shift away from input regulation and toward a performance-based system. State policymakers talk about wanting higher student achievement, although the rhetoric appears to be more directed at low-performing districts and schools than at schools performing in the mid-range or above. Still, both the legislature and the ISBE seem reluctant to abandon the traditional markers of quality, as seen in increasing course requirements for high school graduation (rather than specifying the knowledge and skills students should have to graduate) and in the effort to raise teacher certification requirements. The certification-raising effort proceeded without regard for the economics of the teacher labor market and current student achievement levels. Meanwhile, the legislature has been reluctant to invest significant resources to meet the challenges of the transition toward a performance-based approach (for example, in designing new assessments that could provide needed information about school improvement).

The state appears to be in a period of political uncertainty and lack of consensus about major elements of school reform policy. Although some advocate a commitment to reform based on higher standards, the adopted standards seem to be something of a political compromise. However, the state's new assessments (ISAT) measure adequate achievement at higher thresholds than in the past, at least in math. At the other end of the political spectrum, potent political forces call for a "back to basics" approach that focuses on easily measurable core knowledge and basic computational and reading skills.

On the school finance front, state policymakers have retreated from the pursuit of equity by focusing on adequacy. By pumping more dollars into the poorest districts, the gap between rich and poor districts has been slightly narrowed among elementary districts, and the new funds have provided more adequate resources to nearly 700,000 students. However, the fundamental resource advantages enjoyed by students in the mostly White north and west suburbs—represented by powerful legislators—have been preserved. Meanwhile, there is little discussion about the social and economic burden borne by the state's taxpayers that results from the inequality of educational opportunity maintained under current policies in Illinois.

The low level of support for notions of equality in Illinois is reflected in the stark separation of school districts educating mostly White students and those educating mostly minority students. Further, it would appear that there is little inclination among either Whites or African-Americans to seek to overcome the current separation or to provide resources, both financial and human, to address the unequal outcomes between predominantly White and predominantly minority schools and school districts. There does seem to be some greater interest among Hispanic-Americans to locate in integrated, or at least intermingled, communities in the region's suburbs, and thereby to escape the unequal performance of primarily minority districts. Although there is some willingness among White policymakers to advocate for a minimally adequate education for all children, regardless of race, that willingness clearly does not extend to treating all children equally.

REFERENCES

Appalachia Educational Laboratory (1996).   "Five Years of Education Reform in Rural Kentucky," *Notes from the Field: Education Reform in Rural Kentucky*, vol. 5, no. 1, p. S1.

Bierlein, Louann A., and Lori A. Mulholland (1994). *Comparing Charter School Laws: The Issue of Autonomy.* Policy Brief, Morrison Institute for Public Policy. Flagstaff: Arizona State University.

Bradley, Ann (1997). "Professors' Attitudes Out of Sync, Study Finds," *Education Week*, October 27, 1997, p. 3.

Braskamp, David, G. Alfred Hess, Jr., and Micere Keels (forthcoming). *The State of the States and Provinces, 1999.* San Diego: Special Interest Group on Fiscal Issues, Policy, and Education Finance, American Educational Research Association.

Bryk, Anthony (1996). Personal communication.

Chalos, Peter (1998). Personal communication.

120 *G. Alfred Hess, Jr.*

Ed.dat (1996). *1995 Ed.dat Databook: School Report Card Data*. Riverside, Ill.: Education Data and Consulting Service.

Grossman, Ron (1997). "Blue Book Blather: Why Illinois Ain't Ready for Reform," *Chicago Tribune*, August 3, 1997, sec. 2, p. 5.

Guskey, Thomas R., ed. (1994). *High Stakes Performance Assessment: Perspectives on Kentucky's Education Reform*. Thousand Oaks, Calif.: Corwin Press.

Hargreaves, Andy (1994). *Changing Teachers, Changing Times: Teachers' Work and Culture in the Postmodern Age*. New York: Teachers College Press.

———— (1997). Personal communication.

Hess, G. Alfred, Jr. (1995). *Restructuring Urban Schools: A Chicago Perspective*. New York: Teachers College Press.

————, ed. (1996). *Implementing Reform: Stories of Stability and Change in 14 Schools*. Chicago: Chicago Panel on School Policy.

Hess, G. Alfred, Jr., and David Braskamp (1998). "The 1997 Illinois School Finance Revisions: Less than Meets the Eye." Evanston, Ill.: Center for Urban School Policy, Northwestern University.

Hess, G. Alfred, Jr., and James L. Greer (1986). *Bending the Twig: The Elementary Years and Dropout Rates in the Chicago Public Schools*. Chicago: Chicago Panel on Public School Policy and Finance.

Hill, Paul T., and Mary Beth Celio (1997). "System-Changing Reform Ideas: Can They Save City Schools?" Washington, D.C.: The Brookings Institution.

ISBE (1997). *1996 Annual Report*. Springfield: Illinois State Board of Education.

———— (2000). "1999-2000 Public School Fall Enrollment and Housing Report." Springfield: Illinois State Board of Education.

Kerner Commmission (1968). *Report of the National Advisory Commission on Civil Disorders*. Washington, D.C.: U.S. Government Printing Office.

McLaughlin, Milbrey W. (1978). "Implementation as Mutual Adaptation: Change in Classroom Organization." In Dale Mann, ed., *Making Change Happen*. New York: Teachers College Press.

McMahon, Walter, and Shao-Chung Chang (1991). *Geographical Cost of Living Differences: Interstate and Intrastate,*

Update 1991. Normal: Center for the Study of Educational Finance, Illinois State University.

Mfume, Kweisi, with Rod Stodghill II (1997). *No Free Ride: From the Mean Streets to the Mainstream.* New York: One World.

NCEE (1983). *A Nation at Risk: The Imperative for Educational Reform.* Report of the National Commission on Excellence in Education. Washington, D.C.: U.S. Government Printing Office.

NCTAF (1996). *What Matters Most: Teaching for America's Future.* Report of the National Commission on Teaching and America's Future. New York: Teachers College, Columbia University.

NECTL (1994). *Prisoners of Time: Report of the National Education Commission on Time and Learning.* Washington, D.C.: U.S. Government Printing Office.

Newmann, Fred M., M. Bruce King, and Mark Rigdon (1997). "Accountability and School Performance: Implications from Restructuring Schools," *Harvard Educational Review,* vol. 67, no. 1 (Spring 1997), pp. 41-74.

Palmisano, Michael J. (1997). "Standards Defense," *Chicago Tribune,* August 13, 1997.

Ravitch, Diane (1997). Personal communication.

SCANS (1992). *Learning a Living: A Blueprint for High Performance.* Washington, D.C.: Secretary's Commission on Achieving Necessary Skills, U.S. Department of Labor.

Spillane, James P., and John Zeuli (1997). "The Mathematics Reforms: Mapping the Progress of Reform and Multiple Contexts of Influence." Paper presented to the American Education Research Association in Chicago.

Wong, Kenneth K. (1996). "Toward Fiscal Responsibility in Illinois Public Education." In Lawrence B. Joseph, ed., *Dilemmas of Fiscal Reform: Paying for State and Local Government in Illinois.* A Chicago Assembly Book. Chicago: Center for Urban Research and Policy Studies, University of Chicago; distributed by University of Illinois Press.

COMMENTS: EQUITY IN CHOOSING SCHOOLS AND NEIGHBORHOODS

William Sander and William Testa[*]

Fred Hess provides a thorough and thoughtful overview of the major issues and conundrums that bear on educational reform in Illinois. In our commentary, we focus on one particular area identified by Hess—the improvement of low-performing schools and school districts. We believe this to be the most important issue because low-performing school systems typically serve those families with the fewest resources and fewest choices and opportunities available to them. In our discussion of potential policies, we emphasize program options that have been proposed but largely rejected in Illinois—policies to help low-income families to exercise choice of neighborhoods and schools.

FAMILIES, NEIGHBORHOODS, OR SCHOOLS?

Hess correctly characterizes current policy discussion as emphasizing the improvement of the lowest-performing schools and school districts. In some respects, this emphasis is a sad commentary that good social science does not always drive public policy; that is, a fundamental research finding has not sufficiently penetrated public policy discussion. Statistical findings dating back to at least the Coleman Report are quite consistent in showing that family involvement, family income, and parent education levels are the more important determinants of student achievement (see Coleman et al., 1966). Families and neighborhoods matter to educational outcomes, yet we seem to insist otherwise, as evidenced by our fixation on supporting the monopolistic public school system. Why is it that public policy discussion emphasizes school delivery rather than assisting fami-

[*] The authors thank Margrethe Krontoft of the Federal Reserve Bank of Chicago for assistance.

lies and neighborhoods to produce higher achievement for their children?

There is a common perception that if more money were spent in either poor school districts or districts with a high percentage of poor children, academic achievement could be improved. The effect of educational spending on academic achievement is a matter of some contention (see, e.g., Hanushek, 1986, 1997; Hedges, Laine, and Greenwald, 1994). Teacher education level and teacher experience, two important factors that affect salary, seem only weakly related to student achievement (Grissmer et al., 2000; Rivkin, Hanushek, and Kain, 1999). However, other characteristics of teachers, such as their own standardized test scores, do indicate how successful they will be at improving student learning (Ferguson, 1998). Some research suggests that pupil-teacher ratios within classrooms can matter as well. The benefits of smaller classes tend to be more substantial for early grades and for minority students; for others, the benefits are not very great (Grissmer et al., 2000; Rivkin, Hanushek, and Kain, 1999). Two empirical studies in Illinois show that, in some cases, average teacher salaries and lower pupil-teacher ratios have modest, positive effects on academic achievement and educational attainment (Sander, 1993, 1999).

These various studies suggest that funds are not consistently being well spent, but they have little to say about the practical issue of how to ensure that money and resources *are* well spent. Our current public school systems are structured under the assumption that actual consumers of education—students and their families—cannot be trusted to choose among successful learning environments and cultures for their children. Sadly, the school and neighborhood choices available to many Chicago-area parents are meager, and the outside influences contaminating family love and guidance are most insidious. Low-income families are largely unable to change these circumstances or to move away from them.

VOUCHERS AND OTHER ASSISTANCE TO LOW-INCOME FAMILIES

Ironically, it is in Chicago where we find the strongest evidence that the ability to move to opportunity is effective. The *Gautreaux v. Chicago Housing Authority* judicial decision of 1969, implemented in 1976, required that public housing recipients be given vouchers to obtain private rental housing in either the city or the suburbs. Although housing, and not education, motivated the *Gautreaux* decision, the benefits conferred on families who chose to move to the suburbs are clear. The school dropout rate for suburban movers was 5 percent, compared with 20 percent for city movers. Fifty-four percent of suburban movers attended college, compared with 21 percent of city movers, and 27 percent attended a four-year college, compared with only 4 percent of city movers (Rubinowitz and Rosenbaum, 2000). A ten-year federal demonstration program with similar features, called Moving to Opportunity, has been under way in Baltimore, Boston, Chicago, Los Angeles, and New York (*Economist*, 1995).

However, aside from this small federal program, "voting with one's feet" or "moving to opportunity" for low-income families in Chicago is problematic and, for some, perhaps nearly impossible. Leaving aside the lack of cultural acceptance of minority families in wealthy suburban enclaves, affordable housing is at issue here, perhaps more so than in other metropolitan regions. In Illinois, local community control of land use is quite strong. In particular, the more wealthy suburbs of Chicago frequently enact residential zoning ordinances that prohibit multi-family and other affordable and high-density housing. Such zoning restrictions are encouraged by a school finance system that depends on local property taxation to a greater degree than in other states. For the 1996-97 school year, for example, Illinois state government accounted for only 27 percent of elementary-secondary public school revenue, compared with 48 percent nationwide (NCES, 1999, Table 161). Such local funding means that, other things equal, even if a suburban school system were receptive to having more lower-income families, such actions would be a losing fiscal proposition because the tax stream accompanying such families would put the school system's fiscal health in jeopardy. That is not to say that the answer is a tax system that cedes all education funding responsibility to the state government. As Hoxby (1997) argues, local financing of schools has some important redeeming features. Local financing encourages keen local oversight of school systems because homeowners—whether they have children or not—come to care about school efficiency as their property values hang in the balance. So too, state government's equalization of per-pupil expenditures across school districts, as has occurred in California, has eroded general public support (and financing) for the provision of education (Silva and Sonstelie, 1995). Funding levels in poorer districts can be made relatively lower with state assumption and equalization of school financing. Therefore, it would appear that a policy balance must be struck that leaves an array of choices and responsibilities in the hands of all households, rich and poor alike.

To date, poor families are those without choices. For families that are "zoned out" and left behind to occupy the high-density and depreciating housing of yesteryear, escaping the culture of underachievement is problematic at best. In many poorer communities in both the city and suburbs, the neighborhood school is but a depressing extension of the neighborhood, that is, characterized by low academic achievement, social problems, lack of discipline, little exposure to the successful "world" of commerce, and so forth. Can the urban public school—even if it is on par with typical suburban schools—be sufficient to overcome the shortcomings of family background and neighborhood culture? Some would argue that the Chicago Public Schools (CPS) are making a good try. The CPS Lighthouse Program and other after-school initiatives are notable in delivering learning and social activities throughout the day. Through its aggressive summer programs, the school district is attempting to help students who face possible grade retention. If, however, such efforts fail to shield low-income children from despair and underachievement, should they and their families be held captive by a government monopoly? Should they not have alternatives, as wealthy families do, when public schools fail? Should they not have the opportunity to choose a peer group and school environment that is in accord with the values and structure that they believe will result in success?

Some believe that education vouchers would improve the quality of public education by creating competitive pressures among schools to attract students and, more directly, by offering a safe haven for any families to select a school deemed appropriate for their child (e.g., Friedman, 1962). Other programs would allow publicly funded vouchers to reimburse school districts that accept students who are transported from outside the district, as does Milwaukee's Suburban Transfer Program (see Witte and Thorn, 1995).

Several voucher programs are under way in different parts of the country, including public programs in Milwaukee, Cleveland, and Florida and about 70 privately funded programs. Although education vouchers are controversial, 60 percent of parents who send their children to public schools are in favor of them (*Economist*, 2000). In addition, low-income African-Americans and Hispanics are more likely to support vouchers, while more affluent White parents in suburban areas are less likely to be enthusiastic about vouchers (Viteritti, 1999). To some extent, one's support for vouchers is related to the range of alternatives available. These alternatives are usually perceived as above average for more affluent White parents and below average for poor minority parents.

The voucher program in Milwaukee has probably received the most attention. The program started in the early 1990s and awarded vouchers to a relatively small number of low-income students who could use them at private, non-religious schools. The program now provides vouchers for up to 15,000 low-income children in Milwaukee that can be used at both independent and religious schools. In a rigorous evaluation of the program, Rouse (1998) found that private schools increased test scores of voucher students in mathematics but not in reading. However, it is probably too early to gauge the overall effects of the Milwaukee voucher program since its expansion to include more students and to religious schools. Further, it is also problematic to project what effect a large-scale voucher program might have.

Nonetheless, the effect of existing private schools on academic outcomes might provide some clues to the potential effect of vouchers. Private schools have played an important, albeit modest, role in educating children in the United States. The private share in primary and secondary schooling has held steady at about 10 percent since the 1950s. In the 1950s, Catholic schools accounted for approximately 90 percent of private school enrollment. Catholic schools have become relatively less important over the past 50 years, while independent schools and other religious schools have become more important. Today, the Catholic share in private school enrollment is less than half.

There is controversy over the effects of Catholic and other private schooling on academic achievement and educational attainment. McEwan (2000) provides a review of studies on private school effects. Many studies have focused on the effects of Catholic schools because they account for a large share of private school enrollment. The results of a new study indicate that African-Americans and Hispanics have gained the most from attending Catholic schools (Sander, 2001a). These groups had substantially higher levels of academic achievement and educational attainment when they attended Catholic rather than public schools. Catholic schools had no significant effects, however, on academic outcomes for most non-Hispanic White students. White students in Catholic schools were more likely to graduate from high school and to attain higher test scores, but this was more of a result of Catholic schools selecting better students than providing a superior education.

Although there is controversy in the academic literature on the effects of Catholic schools, data on Chicago Catholic schools illustrate that low-income African-American and Hispanic students may already be gaining from Catholic schooling. More than 100 of the 168 Catholic schools in Chicago are classified as "Big Shoulders" schools—schools that serve mainly low-income minority students. More than 50 percent of the students in Big Shoulders schools are products of poor families, and 80 percent are from minority groups. The dropout rate in Big Shoulders schools is less than one percent, and 97 percent of Big Shoulders students graduate from high school. In 1999, 81 percent of high school graduates in Big Shoulders schools went on to college (Archdiocese of Chicago, 2000). For Chicago's public schools, the high school dropout rate is 15 percent, and the high school graduation rate is only about 62 percent. Further, a much smaller percentage of high school graduates from CPS go on to college (Sander, 2001b). The evidence thus suggests that African-Americans and Hispanics from poor backgrounds do much better in Catholic schools than in public schools.

There is also controversy on the effects of private schools on public school achievement. Although it is possible that a larger private school sector would increase the quality of public education through competitive pressures, it is also possible that there would be no effect (or a negative effect) on quality. It is possible that a larger private school sector could affect resources for public schools by weakening local political support. It is also possible that a larger private sector could result in increasing per-pupil expenditures in the public schools. As students leave the public school system, a smaller tax rate hike would be needed to raise a dollar of additional spending on those students remaining in public schools. If so, local electorates might be swayed to vote for increased public school spending per pupil.

On the down side, if private schools take the best public school students, this could reduce public school achievement both directly, by reducing the number of high-achieving students in public schools, and indirectly, by negative peer-group effects. That is, if the best students leave public schools, the performance of the remaining students could fall if the achievement of students who remain in the public sector is positively related to the achievement of their peers. Some studies (Hoxby, 1994; Dee, 1998) show that private schools raise the quality of public education, but other studies (Jepsen, 2000; Sander, 2001a) do not show such a relationship. Sander's study focuses on the effects of private schools on public school achievement in Illinois. Although the study does not show that private schools increase the quality of public schools, neither does it support the hypothesis that private schools have negative effects. It could be the case that a substantially larger private sector might result in different findings for Illinois, which remains dominated by the public school sector. In fall 1997, about 13 percent of students in Illinois attended private elementary and secondary schools (NCES, 1999, Tables 40, 64).

Another study by Hoxby (1996) focuses on the possible effects of voucher programs. She estimates that a $1,000 voucher would increase private school enrollment from 10 percent to about 14 percent. Enrollment growth would be higher for larger religious groups (such as Catholics) that have tended to support private schools and less for smaller religious groups. Further, enrollment would increase more for groups (such as African-Americans in large cities) with relatively poor public school alternatives. Hoxby also estimates that vouchers would have a negligible effect on total public school spending and a negligible or slightly positive effect on per-pupil spending in the public sector.

FINANCE AND EQUITY

Although Hess does not present an extended critique of vouchers, he does raise a practical issue that voucher proponents must answer. Where will the revenue be found to fund the school operating costs (an estimated $750 million) for those Illinois students who now attend private schools, even before one more dollar is spent to expand attendance at private schools? In principle, of course, the total amount of societal resources devoted to education need not be affected by whether we educate our children in private or public schools. Hess is referring, however, to the political problem of getting from "hither to yon." State and local governments seldom, if ever, make quantum leaps in policy direction. Would it be possible to increase public revenues to pay for private schooling for low-income children without, in the short term, diminishing spending on those public schools serving low-income children?

A possible solution to this dilemma is now blowing in the political winds. The state of Florida has implemented a program, currently under challenge in state courts, that would award voucher opportunities only to those students living within the attendance districts of the worst-performing public schools in the state.[1] A similar initiative was on the statewide ballot in Michigan in November 2000, but it was soundly defeated. Such plans greatly limit the costs and focus of educational vouchers to those who are most in need and to those who have the fewest financial and locational choices at their disposal.

One might argue, however, that targeting vouchers to those who are attending failing public schools creates another inequity—the denial of assistance to financially struggling low-income families that are already attending non-public schools. From meager resources, such families must pay twice for their choice of private school; that is, they must pay both tuition and local property taxes that support the public school system that they have avoided. Some proponents of school choice have argued that tax credits are the remedy for that problem. The recently enacted Illinois Education Tax Credit Program establishes a refundable tax credit of up to $500 per family for those with children in private schools—for 25 percent of tuition, lab, and book fees above $250. In contrast to the tax credit program in Minnesota, the Illinois program is independent of family income. In addition to the absence of vertical equity inherent in this program—that is, both rich and poor are eli-

---

[1] Florida's plan, enacted in 1999, was the first statewide voucher program. The program ranks schools from A to F. Schools that receive high marks or are improving are given additional funding. If a school fails (F) for two years in a row, the students at that school can receive a tuition voucher worth $4,000 to be used at any higher-scoring school. Private schools are barred from requiring students to participate in religious activities. As of 1999, 119 students were using vouchers.

gible—the size is insufficient to give the tax credit much meaning. The small size of the tax credit reduces the likelihood that additional families, especially low-income families, will use the credit to send their children to private schools.

CONCLUSION

Equity in resources spent by governments can sometimes be important, and such equity is thankfully championed by Fred Hess and others. However, the very weak connection between resources spent and educational outcomes suggests that additional reforms are necessary to assist students from low-income families. Such families must often passively accept the education delivered by local government monopolies, and they must do so in a neighborhood environment that is far from conducive to educating and socializing young people into the upwardly mobile mainstream. Therefore, it is also important to think about equity in the alternative choices that are available to parents for their children's schools and neighborhoods. Policy avenues should include broadening family choices in "moving to opportunity," as well as allowing families to apply their tax dollars to their own choice of schools.

REFERENCES

Archdiocese of Chicago (2000). "Shoulder to Shoulder." Chicago: Big Shoulders Foundation, Archdiocese of Chicago.

Coleman, James S., et al. (1966). *Equality of Educational Opportunity*. Washington, D.C.: U.S. Government Printing Office.

Dee, Thomas S. (1998). "Competition and the Quality of Public Schools," *Economics of Education Review*, vol. 17, no. 4, pp. 419-427.

Ferguson, Ronald (1998). "Can Schools Narrow the Black-White Test Score Gap?" In Christopher Jencks and Meredith Phillips, eds., *The Black-White Test Score Gap*. Washington D.C.: Brookings Institution Press.

Friedman, Milton (1962). *Capitalism and Freedom*. Chicago: University of Chicago Press.

Economist (1995). "Housing Policy: From Ghetto to Suburb." U.S. edition, October 7, 1995.

_____ (2000). "Back to School." U.S. edition, September 30, 2000.

Grissmer, David W., Ann Flanagan, Jennifer Kawata, and Stephanie Williamson (2000). *Improving Student Achievement: What NAEP Test Scores Tell Us.* Santa Monica, Calif.: RAND.

Hanushek, Eric A. (1986). "The Economics of Schooling: Production and Efficiency in Public Schools," *Journal of Economic Literature*, vol. 24, no. 3 (September 1986), pp. 1141-1177.

_____ (1997). "Assessing the Effects of School Resources on Student Performance: An Update," *Educational Evaluation and Policy Analysis*, vol. 19, no. 2, (Summer 1997), pp. 141-164.

Hedges, Larry V., Richard D. Laine, and Rob Greenwald (1994). "Does Money Matter? A Meta-Analysis of Studies of the Effects of Differential School Inputs on Student Outcomes," *Educational Researcher*, vol. 23, no. 3 (April 1994), pp. 5-14.

Hoxby, Caroline M. (1994). "Do Private Schools Provide Competition for Public Schools?" Working Paper No. 4978. Cambridge, Mass.: National Bureau of Economic Research.

_____ (1996). "The Effects of Private School Vouchers on Schools and Students." In Helen F. Ladd, ed., *Holding Schools Accountable: Performance-Based Reform in Education.* Washington D.C.: Brookings Institution.

_____ (1997). "Local Property Tax-Based Funding of Public Schools." Chicago: Heartland Institute.

Jepsen, Christopher (2000). "The Private Schooling Market and Its Effects on Student Achievement." Ph.D. dissertation, Northwestern University.

McEwan, Patrick (2000). "The Potential Impact of Large-Scale Voucher Programs." Occasional Paper No. 2. New York: National Center for the Study of Privatization in Education, Teachers College, Columbia University.

NCES (1999). *Digest of Education Statistics, 1999.* Washington, D.C.: National Center for Education Statistics, U.S. Department of Education.

Rivkin, Steven, Eric Hanushek, and John Kain (1999). "Teachers, Schools, and Academic Achievement." Paper presented at a conference on "School Choice and Competition," Federal Reserve Bank of Chicago, April 27-28, 1999.

Rouse, Cecilia Elena (1998). "Private School Vouchers and Student Achievement: An Evaluation of the Milwaukee Parental Choice Program," *Quarterly Journal of Economics*, vol. 113, no. 2 (May 1998), pp. 553-602.

Rubinowitz, Leonard S., and James E. Rosenbaum (2000). *Crossing the Class and Color Lines: From Public Housing to White Suburbia*. Chicago: University of Chicago Press.

Sander, William (1993). "Expenditures and Student Achievement in Illinois: New Evidence," *Journal of Public Economics*, vol. 52, no. 3 (October 1993), pp. 403-416.

_____ (1999). "Endogenous Expenditures and Student Achievement," *Economics Letters*, vol. 64, no. 2 (August 1999), pp. 223-231.

_____ (2001a). *Catholic Schools: Private and Social Effects*. Boston: Kluwer Academic Publishers.

_____ (2001b). "Chicago Public Schools and Student Achievement," *Urban Education*, no. 36, pp. 27-38.

Silva, Fabio, and Jon Sonstelie (1995). "Did *Serrano* Cause a Decline in School Spending?" *National Tax Journal*, vol. 48, no. 2 (June 1995), pp. 199-215.

Viteritti, Joseph (1999). *Choosing Equality: School Choice, the Constitution, and Civil Society*. Washington D.C.: Brookings Institution Press.

Witte, John F., and Christopher A. Thorn (1995). "Who Chooses? Voucher and Interdistrict Choice Programs in Milwaukee." In Thomas A. Downes and William A. Testa, eds., *Midwest Approaches to School Reform*. Proceedings from a conference held at the Federal Reserve Bank of Chicago, October 26-27, 1994.

STANDARDS-BASED REFORM IN THE STATES: PROGRESS AND CHALLENGES

Diane Massell

Standards-based, systemic reform has become the preeminent education policy strategy, used widely by federal, state, and local governments and supported by foundations, national professional associations, and others in the quest to improve teaching and learning. Its ideas are strongly evident in three key pieces of federal legislation: Improving America's Schools Act (1994), which provides federal aid to poor students; Goals 2000 (1994), which provides financial resources to states and local school districts to support standards-based reform; and the reauthorized Individuals with Disabilities in Education Act (1997). By 1999, 49 states had developed, or were in the process of developing, new academic standards for students, and 47 states had adopted or were building student assessments aligned to those standards (AFT, 1999). Local school districts are also embracing standards-based, systemic reform strategies. In addition to Chicago, prominent examples in large urban school districts include Philadelphia, San Diego, and Pittsburgh.

Standards-based, systemic reform generally consists of three key components: a unifying vision and goals that include ambitious curriculum and performance standards for all students; coherent policies that reinforce these ambitious outcomes; and a restructured system of governance that gives local decision-makers more authority and control to reach the student performance goals (Smith and O'Day, 1991). The purpose of this chapter is to explain the background and rationale for the standards-based reform movement and to discuss how it has unfolded in states, school districts, and classrooms. I also lay out issues for educators and public officials to consider as they attempt to move forward with this improvement strategy. This analysis draws primarily on studies of state and district policies, as well as other research on standards-based reform, conducted by the Consortium for Policy Research in Education (CPRE).

EDUCATION REFORM EFFORTS SINCE THE 1980s

The standards-based, systemic reform agenda builds on the foundations of the "educational excellence" movement of the 1980s. In 1983, the National Commission on Excellence in Education published its landmark report, *A Nation at Risk*, which called on state governments to set higher standards by requiring all students to take more credits in core academic subjects as a precondition for high school graduation; raising college entrance requirements; establishing stronger criteria for promotion from one grade to another; imposing longer school days and a longer school year; requiring new teachers to pass basic skills tests and meet other criteria for entry and certification; and expanding states' accountability and oversight functions. In essence, these reforms can be considered "intensification" strategies because they called for more of the kinds of policies that already existed and came largely in the form of mandates about inputs into the educational process.

Beyond Social Relevance and Basic Skills

This focus on core academic subjects and higher standards was intended to remedy the policy emphasis in the 1960s and 1970s, which initially de-emphasized core academic subjects in favor of a more socially relevant curriculum and later focused on guaranteeing that students achieved at least a minimal level of competency in basic skills. In the late 1970s, states and school districts around the country began to require low-level basic skills tests for graduation and grade-level promotion and adopted curricula that reflected this basic skills approach. While these policies were meant to establish a "floor" below which no one would fall, critics charged that they created a "ceiling" beyond which the system infrequently aspired, narrowed the curriculum, and yielded drill-and-practice methods of instruction (e.g., Haertel, 1989; Massell, 1995). These low standards created a vicious cycle of low expectations, which research showed contributed to low performance by students. Indeed, the authors of *A Nation at Risk* concluded that these policies had created "a rising tide of mediocrity" in public education. State and local officials moved at an unprecedented pace to embrace the report's recommendations. For example, 41 states increased high school graduation requirements between

1983 and 1985, and many states imposed more tests in more subject areas and grade levels (Coley and Goertz, 1990).

These intensification strategies yielded a number of positive results. The percentage of high school graduates earning the number of core academic credits recommended by *A Nation at Risk* in English, social studies, science, mathematics, foreign language, and computers rose from just 2 percent in 1982 to 25 percent in 1994. Setting aside the report's recommendations for computer science and foreign language credits, the percentage of graduates taking the recommended number of English, social studies, science, and mathematics credits grew from 31 percent to 75 percent over the same time period. Furthermore, the gains were not just for college-bound or more advantaged students. Course-taking patterns showed that *all* high school students were taking more academic courses (Mirel and Angus, 1994; Legum et al., 1998).

Policymakers began asking, however, whether these courses remained as academically oriented as they had been before a more diverse student body was required to participate. Studies of the curriculum enacted in the classroom showed that courses were not watered down to accommodate students from different academic backgrounds. For example, a study of 18 schools in six states found no significant differences between the algebra courses that were expanded to include the non-college-bound and the courses that were offered to college-bound students (Porter et al., 1993). Instead, schools tended to replace remedial math programs with pre-algebra and algebra, and more students took advanced levels of English (Clune et al., 1991). At the same time, the number of students who entered college in the fall following graduation soared to a new high. More minority students took the Scholastic Aptitude Test (SAT) and did increasingly well, and the number of minorities taking Advanced Placement examinations doubled (CBO, 1993; NCES, 1992; Pitsch, 1991).

Shortcomings of Educational Excellence Reforms

Although significant progress was made in exposing students to core academic content and encouraging them to pursue more education, some studies revealed weaknesses in the coursework that students received. Between 1982 and 1990, trends in student achievement from the National Assessment of Educational

Progress showed that students performed poorly at the most rigorous and challenging levels in mathematics, science, and reading (NCES, 1992; Rothman, 1992; Elley, 1992; Kirst, 1993). Classroom studies showed that teachers, even in upper-level courses, only infrequently asked students to solve problems or use analytical thinking skills (Porter et al., 1993). The textbook materials and tests emphasized broad topic coverage rather than in-depth investigation and understanding, and rote memorization of basic, factual knowledge rather than challenging material and problem-solving.[1]

In fact, the "educational excellence" initiatives simply led to more of the same kinds of minimum-competency-oriented tests, classroom material, and teacher certification policies that had emerged during the basic skills movement. Thus, the first major criticism of the "educational excellence" reforms was that they did not question the quality of the instructional materials and teaching that permeated American public schools. A growing awareness of the increasingly competitive global economy led the business community and policymakers at all levels to call for challenging, "world class" standards. Such standards would promote not only a higher level of content in academic work, but also students' abilities to think critically and apply their knowledge to solving real-world problems (see, e.g., NCEST, 1992).

A second criticism was that policies often sent conflicting signals to local educators, a problem that arose from a fragmented policymaking process that tended to layer new policies on old ones without considering whether they reinforce or contradict one another. For example, to improve the quality of the workforce, policymakers imposed more challenging tests and additional requirements for new teachers. At the same time, they issued emergency credentials or created alternative routes to certification that permitted new teachers to bypass these quality controls.

Finally, the excellence policies were criticized as being mandates from the top that did not actively engage teachers or local educators to use their professional expertise and experience to identify problems or develop solutions. State regula-

---

[1] See Tyson-Bernstein, 1986; CSTEEP, 1992; Resnick and Resnick, 1992; Bowman and Peng, 1972; Frederickson, 1984.

tions and mandates were seen as stifling innovation and fitting poorly with local needs.

As a result of these complaints, state policymakers made efforts to deregulate and shift their central education agencies toward providing technical assistance and away from traditional monitoring and oversight functions. In 1986, the National Governors' Association published a report that called for a "horse-trade" with local educators: less regulation in exchange for better results (NGA, 1986). State and local "restructuring" policies sought to place more authority and control at the local level, especially in individual schools. These included such initiatives as site-based decision-making (SBDM), in which schools were given more control over curriculum, hiring, budgeting, or other decisions, as well as required school-site councils comprised of parents, community members, teachers, and others. Some of these councils were advisory, while others had more direct authority. Overall, the intent was to broaden authority and control beyond administrators. However, research on SBDM and school-site councils has shown that process-oriented reform—without a strong instructional focus and sufficient knowledge, information, and incentives to improve—does not yield significant improvements in student performance (Wohlstetter et al., 1994; David et al., 1989; Malen et al., 1990).

STANDARDS-BASED, SYSTEMIC REFORM

Standards-based, systemic reform attempts to build on these earlier approaches while addressing their weaknesses. To the educational excellence reforms, it says: the emphasis on the core academic curriculum is correct, but the quality of the core academic curriculum needs to be improved. To deregulation and restructuring, it says: yes, but it is important to provide substantive leadership and goals for these initiatives, and to hold local educators accountable for student performance. Overall, advocates claim that by placing standards at the center of all education reform efforts, the educational system will be much more effective in meeting shared improvement goals.

There is general agreement that standards-based, systemic reform involves three key features: challenging academic content and performance standards for all students, coherent policies, and restructured governance. Nevertheless, states have differed in translating these broad goals into specific policy and practice. States have confronted several crucial questions in implementing standards: (1) What is rigorous, challenging academic content? In other words, what should these new state standards look like? (2) What kinds of accountability incentives are necessary to motivate people to make substantial changes in educational practice? (3) What is the appropriate role of policy in helping educators to gain the knowledge and skills they need or in providing sufficient resources and support to yield improvement? State and local officials and educators have addressed these and other questions by adapting the general ideas of standards-based reform to their own political environments and traditions. The result has been wide variation and experimentation across states in the design and implementation of standards and assessments, accountability systems, and approaches to building local capacity to meet the standards.

STATE STANDARDS AND ASSESSMENTS

Standards in academic subject areas and student assessment programs are the primary policy instruments for expressing higher expectations for student learning and performance. While it is not completely new for states to offer curriculum guidance or to mandate student testing, the philosophy and design behind the standards-based reform movement differs in some critical respects from previous reform efforts.

Curriculum Standards

In the late 1970s and 1980s, state-level curriculum guidance consisted of curriculum frameworks or course descriptions with lists of isolated facts and skills organized by specific grade level (Curry and Temple, 1992). All too often, these documents were ignored and sat on shelves gathering dust. Many reformers believe that, to be more relevant, new curriculum standards should focus on the major concepts and ideas of a disciplinary field and convey the underlying goals and principles of reform in a way that is more meaningful to educators and the public (Massell, 1994). In addition, policymakers in states such as California, Florida, Kentucky, and South Carolina have argued against providing grade-by-grade statements of expectation and have focused instead on standards for clusters of grades (e.g., K-3, 4-8, 9-12). Underlying this new approach was the educational argument that students should not be locked into a rigid set of grade-level expectations because students develop at different rates. Further, many believe that overly detailed curriculum standards will lead once again to the kind of lock-step, rote instruction that many reformers have been trying to change. Finally, in many states, there was a powerful political reason for not providing highly detailed standards. At the outset of the standards-based reform movement, many conservative groups and local school districts expressed concern that standards were a way for the state to exert a heavy, controlling hand over local curricula. Aside from these general political pressures, some state constitutions, such as Colorado's, prohibit them from prescribing a school curriculum.

A second change from previous curriculum guidance policies has been in the process that states use to develop standards. Earlier state curriculum guidance documents were usually crafted by isolated committees of teachers that passed on their decisions to higher officials for approval. Many states are now drawing participants from a broader cross-section of interested parties, including teachers, parents, students, administrators, university faculty, and business and community leaders. Content standards in many states, such as Vermont, Kentucky, and Texas, have gone through an extensive period (two years or more) of review and revision in an effort to gain broad consensus and understanding. Minnesota and New Jersey took more than five years to craft standards. Indeed, educators have become more keenly aware of the problems that result when the goals of reform are not widely shared (Carlson, 1992). In emphasizing consensus, standards groups are trying to avoid the mistakes of past curriculum reform projects that too often neglected the political support needed for implementation (McLaughlin, 1991; Elmore, 1993).

Finally, in an effort to counteract the emphasis on low-level skills and rote drill-and-practice routines, many advocates have pressed for the new standards to reflect alternative ideas about learning and teaching arising from psychological studies. This alternative approach to learning is generally known as "constructivism." Proponents of constructivism argue that students can best learn analytic and problem-solving skills when they are actively involved in the material, have an opportunity to apply what they are learning to meaningful situations, and have the opportunity to explicitly lay out and challenge theories about the way things work (Resnick, 1987).

Standards-Based Assessment

New standards have led to new measures of what students learn, which are reflected in recent efforts to improve statewide testing programs. There have been three main improvement strategies. One involves aligning new tests to the more challenging academic content standards. Second, many state policymakers have sought to eliminate the use of commercial, norm-referenced tests, which are seen as disconnected from some of the key goals of standards-based reform. Norm-referenced tests measure student performance compared to other students, rather than to a fixed body of knowledge. In Colorado, state education commissioner Bill Moloney outlined the distinction in the following way:

> Norm-referenced tests compare students to one another, he explained. "Let's say you are a student in a class of 10, and the class is asked, 'How many can spell dog and how many can spell cat?' If nine students can't spell either one, and you can spell cat, you would be above the average. But that doesn't mean you are in good shape." In contrast, tests based on standards "compare what kids do know to what they ought to know," Moloney said. If you picture students climbing a mountain, he explained, norm-referenced tests show where the climbers are in relation to one another, while standards-based tests show where they are in relation to the mountaintop (Bingham, 1997).

Standards-based, criterion-referenced tests measure a student's ability by the actual proportion of correct answers. These tests can be related to a coherent body of knowledge (content standards) that have value and support among educators and the public.

A third major strategy for improving standards-based assessment has been to develop tests that support quality classroom instruction as well as serve their traditional accountability purposes. Abundant research has shown that multiple-choice, fixed-response formats tend to promote rote drill-and-practice teaching techniques that do not engage students in more challenging learning. Thus, one of the most prominent and widespread movements in assessment reform has been to change testing formats away from multiple-choice items and toward more open-ended learning tasks. Called "performance-based assessments," these formats ask students to apply their learning to such tasks as writing a paragraph or essay in response to a question, writing a research paper, conducting scientific experiments, or engaging in computer simulations of scientific activity (Pechman and Hammond, 1991). Collecting and evaluating student work from the classroom over an extended period of time and placing it into portfolios is another new assessment strategy that some advocate as providing a more complete picture of students' knowledge and understanding, and one that reinforces sound classroom teaching and prompts students to reason and solve problems (Wiggins, 1993; CRESST, 1995).

Adapting Standards and Assessments

A major challenge has been to translate these basic designs for curriculum and assessment into specific state-level policies. While constructivist principles have been very influential in the policy world generally, states have varied widely in the extent to which they have adopted these approaches. In the late 1980s and early 1990s, California and Kentucky moved ahead of most states by incorporating the most far-reaching versions of constructivist principles. California implemented a new, statewide assessment program in 1993, known as the California Learning Assessment System, that relied primarily on performance-based tasks. Kentucky adopted an entirely performance-based assessment for accountability, the Kentucky Instructional Results and Information System (KIRIS).[2] KIRIS also used mathematics and writing portfolios and included those results in its accountability index.

Other states took a more modest or incremental approach to testing reform. Connecticut and New Jersey, for example, added performance tasks to their statewide exams but maintained more traditional, multiple-choice items as well. Some states, such as Texas, piloted performance assessments but

---

[2] In 1993, state policymakers in Kentucky completely eliminated multiple-choice items from accountability calculations.

decided to maintain a traditional test format, though keyed to more rigorous content.

The content standards used in California and Kentucky were also among the most constructivist. For example, California's 1992 mathematics framework strongly stressed problem-solving and knowledge application, and its 1987 English-language arts framework focused on whole language instruction.[3] Although basic skills were not completely ignored, they were downplayed in an effort to reorient teachers to new instructional ideas. Kentucky's 1993 standards, the "75 Valued Learner Outcomes," included the kind of "affective" learning goals ("students should work well in groups," "have high self-esteem," or "be tolerant of others") that are associated with "outcomes-based education."

The states that moved ahead in adopting the most far-reaching versions of reform have since moved back to a more middle ground. This modification stemmed from technical and political challenges, as well as from growing concern that the emphasis on problem-solving and critical thinking was eroding students' ability to master basic skills. The challenges confronted by California and Kentucky illustrated the kinds of problems experienced by other states that have pursued the most far-reaching reforms.

California's efforts suffered two major blows. First, the new California Learning Assessment System (CLAS) came under sharp criticism for providing only aggregate, school-level scores rather than scores for individual students; for technical problems that led to questions about accuracy; and—in the eyes of some religious groups—for imposing "liberal" values. As a result, Governor Pete Wilson vetoed funding for CLAS in 1994 after two administrations of the test, and the state renewed its search for a new assessment program. The second blow came when California's performance on the National Assessment of Educational Progress (NAEP) declined. On NAEP reading assessment, California was close to last in 1992 and was dead last in 1994. Similarly, results of student performance on the CLAS test showed serious deficits in basic reading and mathematical skills. Critics blamed the problem on the lack of

---

[3] Generally, whole language emphasizes teaching students to read by decoding words based on the meaning of passages, rather than sounding them out based on phonics. The California framework also emphasized the use of literature rather than basal readers.

emphasis on basic skills and the abandonment of traditional instructional approaches in the English-language arts and mathematics. In fact, one of the chief designers of the new frameworks came to believe that they did underplay the role of phonics, math facts, calculation skills, and other basic skills.[4] Subsequent task forces on these two frameworks have called for "balance" between the new and the old. A 1995 law authorizing a new testing program reestablished a place for traditional testing in addition to measures of applied learning (i.e., performance assessments). This law also provided a monetary incentive to districts to adopt norm-referenced, basic skills tests in grades 2-10 and reintroduced multiple-choice items in a new statewide exam.

Kentucky policymakers have also moved to re-establish some traditional types of standards and assessments while maintaining strong elements of constructivist reform. Critics argued that the state's original goals were difficult, if not impossible, to measure. For example, they questioned how one measures a "student's ability to work well in groups" or "have high self-esteem." Critics also believed that such outcomes intruded into the personal lives and values of students and their families. Kentucky responded by paring down these standards to 57 "Academic Expectations" based on a more tightly construed notion of academic knowledge. The state also made adjustments in its assessment program. As in other states, the public raised questions about how well their students performed relative to other students nationally—a question that the state's own standards-based tests could not answer. In response, the state reintroduced a norm-referenced test, but it did not include the results in its accountability program. In addition, technical

---

[4] Bill Honig, former superintendent of public instruction, wrote that the 1987 English-language arts framework created under his watch "makes important points about the need for literacy-rich classrooms, an integrated language arts program, the necessity of being well-read, the potency of literature, and the ability to understand and discuss ideas. While it does state that phonics and skills are important, it is neither specific enough nor clear enough about the essential beginning-to-read strategies for pre-school, kindergarten, and early primary grades. Consequently, as most people now realize, the framework must be supplemented in these areas." He also warned against allowing the pendulum to swing too far back to focus solely on phonics or basic skills (Honig, 1995).

issues on its mathematics portfolio led the state to remove this component from the accountability index until the problems were resolved.[5] Nevertheless, as of 1997, the major, innovative features of the KIRIS system remained intact.

As state policymakers moved forward with new standards and assessments, it seemed that moving too far on the scale of innovation and doing so too quickly created strong political and educational challenges that pushed policymakers back to a middle ground. States such as Connecticut, Maryland, and New Jersey, which had adopted a more incremental and balanced approach from the outset, experienced less political turbulence and were able to maintain a fairly steady course. Balancing between the new and the more traditional approaches to teaching and learning appears to have become the watchword, although new challenges are still emerging.

STANDARDS AND ACCOUNTABILITY

Accountability programs have been used in the United States for over a century to guarantee sound educational practices and provide incentives for local systems to improve. Accountability programs serve many purposes, including ensuring minimum levels and quality of educational inputs (e.g., staff, libraries), access to programs and services (e.g., course offerings), proper use of resources, and minimum levels of educational outcomes. Other purposes include informing the community about school conditions and performance and stimulating school improvement. Historically, states have focused on input and process standards, relying on school district accreditation processes to monitor compliance (Sebba, Thurlow, and Goertz, 1999).

Under the philosophy of standards-based reform, there have been discernible changes in the design of state accountability programs. The most dramatic change has been a greater emphasis on holding schools responsible for meeting performance standards for all students in exchange for greater flexibility in regulations and oversight. The focus has also shifted away from district-level accountability to school-level accountability,

---

[5] Because of technical problems, few states have adopted portfolios for accountability purposes. Their use is more common in local districts, however.

with great attention paid to low-performing schools. States are employing rewards and sanctions, while de-emphasizing compliance with rules and regulations, to motivate changes in local practice.

State policymakers have also experimented with approaches to accountability that use external market pressures, such as public or private school choice, as an incentive to improve public education. For example, in 1988, Minnesota enacted the first statewide open enrollment program, which allowed parents to select the public school of their choice; by 1995, 16 states had passed similar legislation (CER, 1995). Other mechanisms, such as vouchers, tuition tax credits, and postsecondary enrollment options for high school students, are meant to open up the public K-12 system to market-based incentives for improvement, although these are still rare policies at the state level. In a similar vein, charter schools introduce competition by permitting teachers, parents, university staff, and others to set up alternative public schools, often freed from much state regulation. By 1999, 37 states had enacted charter school laws (CER, 2000). In this chapter, however, I will only explore accountability trends "within the system." The discussion is organized around three key aspects of accountability programs: who is held accountable, for what, and with what consequences.

Who Is Held Accountable?

In the late 1990s, schools became a more prominent target of state accountability programs. They received more policy attention in part because of the prevalent view that schools are the organizational sites that matter in student success or failure. A long line of research on effective schools suggests that school leadership and climate can make a significant difference in student performance. Thus, policymakers are collecting school-level performance data as a way to encourage educators to take greater responsibility for student achievement. Many states have typically produced reports with information aggregated only at the district level, making it impossible to discern how well one school performed in comparison with others. Maryland introduced school-level reporting in the early 1990s so that poorly performing schools could, in the words of one state official, "no longer hide" behind aggregate district results. By

1996, 37 states produced public reports that included school-level data (Clements and Blank, 1997).

While schools are receiving heightened attention, policy-makers also are continuing to hold students, teachers, and districts accountable in a variety of ways. At the student level, the focus is primarily on high school students. Most states require high school students to take certain coursework in order to graduate (CCSSO, 1996a), and, as part of the legacy of *A Nation at Risk,* the number of academic credits required has escalated since 1982. However, few states specify which courses students must take to satisfy these broad academic categories, or require minimum grade-point averages.

Many policymakers have been concerned about legal, ethical, and political challenges to more demanding, high-stakes graduation exams. The precedent set by the *Debra P. v. Turlington* lawsuit in Florida in the late 1970s required the state to demonstrate that students had received a fair opportunity to learn the material covered in exit exams. This legal standard is a major consideration in current discussions, and some policymakers are concerned that more challenging assessments will lead to similar lawsuits. Others are concerned about the potential of such exams to drive students out of high school. As a result of these issues, Minnesota made significant changes in its "graduation rule," which specifies the standards that students must meet in order to graduate. The graduation rule was split into two components: "basic requirements" and more difficult "profile of learning standards." Basic requirements are the "essential" skills and knowledge that all students must meet to earn a diploma. Although the more challenging profile of learning standards is also required for graduation, the rule was modified so that students must only select and pass 24 of the 60 standards. Furthermore, local districts, not the state, evaluate student performance on the profile of learning measures.

Accountability for teachers has often been limited to recertification regulations. These regulations typically require teachers to participate in a certain number of credit hours of professional development. However, few of the 40 states that require these activities specify types of professional development (CCSSO, 1996a). Thus, teachers are often solely responsible for deciding whether these activities actually relate to their current teaching assignments or to reform initiatives. Efforts to exert more control over the recertification process, as well as to institute other quality control measures (such as satisfactory evaluations of teaching performance), are frequently resisted by teachers and their unions as infringements on professional autonomy (Massell, 1998). For example, in an effort to better align the continuing education requirements of relicensure to reform, a 1991 Colorado law mandated that teachers create professional development portfolios in consultation with their supervisors. Complaints from constituents led the legislature to eliminate this provision in 1997 and to prohibit requirements for renewal from exceeding six continuing education units or 90 clock hours of professional development. In addition, the legislature prohibited the state board or state department of education from specifying any particular type of professional development or from requiring teachers to receive approval from anyone for their continuing education activities.

Some states have pursued the strategy of holding teachers accountable for school-level performance measures. Kentucky and Maryland, for example, allow school staff to be transferred if schools are chronically low-performing. Texas plans to include student performance on state tests as one of many factors in a teacher's evaluation package. By and large, however, most states have not imposed direct, high-stakes sanctions or incentives on teachers.

Accountable for What?

Another trend is for state accountability programs to collect data on and build consequences around performance measures such as achievement test scores and drop-out and attendance rates. Again, this is a fairly new phenomenon because states have typically focused on holding local educators responsible for traditional input or process measures. Although states have been administering minimum competency tests since the late 1970s, the tests and performance standards used in accountability systems today tend to be more challenging. (Whereas tests measure the content of what students learn, performance standards are cutoff points at which a student or a school meets an acceptable level of performance.) Schools and districts, not just students, are being held accountable for meeting (or not meeting) the new performance standards.[6]

While some states are retaining input and process accountability alongside new performance requirements (Elmore et al., 1995), other states are taking dramatic steps to remove such regulations. For example, Florida and Texas—traditionally strong, highly mandate-oriented states—have sharply reduced or even eliminated compliance-monitoring, evaluating schools according to inputs, and site inspections, except in cases of chronic low performance. Waivers from state rules and regulations are commonplace.

Some states define performance targets for schools and districts, while others give local districts more latitude in determining these measures. Maryland and Kentucky require schools to demonstrate satisfactory and continuous growth on the state assessments as well as other measures, such as attendance. Schools must also meet predetermined state performance targets. For example, Maryland schools were required to have at least 70 percent of their students meet "satisfactory" or "excellent" levels on the state assessment by the year 2000. This presented a difficult challenge, given that in 1996 only one elementary school, one middle school, and 18 high schools achieved the state's satisfactory performance levels on all variables.

---

[6] Expected levels of performance vary across states and even within states. A study comparing performance standards in 11 states with those used by NAEP revealed substantial differences in how challenging these various state standards were. In Wisconsin, for example, 88 percent of 4th-grade students were proficient in reading on state tests, but only 35 percent were proficient on NAEP. Similarly, 88 percent of Louisiana's students were proficient on state exams, while only 15 percent were proficient on NAEP. Only New Hampshire and Delaware had more rigorous proficiency criteria than NAEP (Musick, 1997). Indeed, this sort of variability was one of the major arguments the Clinton administration used in trying to develop national testing. Even within states, rigor can vary across different measures. In Maryland, for example, it has been easier for high schools than for elementary and middle schools to meet satisfactory standards of performance. In 1993, the state introduced a new, more rigorous assessment for grades 3, 5, and 8, but it continued to rely on a basic skills exit exam at the high school level. A new high school assessment is scheduled for implementation beginning with students entering grade 9 in fall 2001.

In strongly decentralized states, accountability policies give school districts considerable flexibility to determine how performance will be evaluated. For example, Colorado planned to require districts to submit an "Enterprise Accreditation Contract" in which districts themselves established the criteria by which they would evaluate their schools' performance. Similarly, Florida's 1991 reform law permitted schools to determine their own criteria for improvement in their school improvement plans. These plans must show how schools define levels of adequate yearly progress toward their own goals, as well as the mechanisms they would use to evaluate their performance. However, the Florida Department of Education, after finding that schools did not impose rigorous measures, established its own criteria for school performance.

Another challenge involves designing accountability systems to ensure that schools and districts are accountable for the performance of *all* students. An issue that plagues most testing programs is the problem of educators "working the numbers" to raise scores and accountability ratings. A common technique for raising scores is to keep poorly performing students from taking the tests in the first place. In Michigan, for example, some principals advised parents of low-performing students to exercise their right to exempt their children from taking the 1996-97 state test, with warnings about possible ill effects on their children's self-esteem or educational career. Other educators have inappropriately labeled children as special education students because, under most guidelines, these students do not have to take tests that are deemed inappropriate for them.

Kentucky, Colorado, and Maryland tried to address this issue by adding disincentives for excluding students from testing. Maryland, for example, conducted more rigorous monitoring to ensure that students were not being inappropriately exempted from state tests. Each of these states also included the total number of students in a school to calculate the aggregate accountability score, regardless of whether all students took the test. Texas requires that each subgroup of the student population within a school achieve state performance targets for a school to receive an acceptable rating. In other words, all racial and ethnic groups, as well as economically disadvantaged students, must meet the state standards.

Efforts to include all students under the same accountability tent have been bolstered by federal legislation. The Improving America's Schools Act of 1994 required that economically disadvantaged students be tested using the same assessments as all other students. The 1997 amendments to the Individuals with Disabilities in Education Act required states to report the number of students with disabilities who participate in state and district assessments. The law also specifies that scores of these students be publicly reported.

With What Consequences?

States have established a range of consequences for districts and schools regarding student performance. Perhaps the most common is public reporting of performance data, a strategy used to raise public awareness and place pressure on the districts and schools to improve. For some states with strong local control, the idea of publicizing student achievement data is still highly controversial; in Minnesota, for instance, the publication of these data contributed to the resignation of the state superintendent.

Most of the attention, however, has been focused on low-performing schools and districts. These schools are subject to a range of interventions, such as being placed on a state "watch list," being required to produce school improvement plans, receiving special technical assistance and support, and becoming subject to a form of "reconstitution," which involves transferring some or all staff out of the school. Some states, such as Kentucky and Texas, also give students the right to transfer if their school is found to be failing. New Jersey, among other states, has taken over chronically failing school districts.

The impact of these various interventions is disputed and complex. Reporting test results can be powerful, even in affluent communities, where real estate values are strongly linked to perceived school quality. Many policymakers argue, however, that reporting results alone provides insufficient motivation for improvement and have instituted more attention-getting sanctions as well as rewards. One study of Kentucky's school-based performance award program found that many teachers were motivated by a desire to avoid the negative publicity associated with sanctions, by professional pride and a desire for positive public recognition, and by the satisfaction of seeing students achieve. Some teachers and principals also feared the loss of professional autonomy and job security that could attend to chronically poor performance. But for most teachers, the fiscal rewards were viewed as a pleasant bonus but not a strong in-centive. In fact, the money led to such problems among teach-ers and so negatively affected the professional climate that the Kentucky Education Association opposed funding bonuses and suggested that the money be channeled into professional devel-opment (Kelley, 1998).

Kentucky also trained a network of "distinguished educa-tors" to assist poorly performing schools with school improve-ment planning and change processes. Many of these low-performing schools received training and support in curriculum alignment using both state standards and national content stand-ards. After receiving assistance, many of these schools made significant gains on test scores. Thus, a critical aspect of any reform strategy is the extent to which the capacities of schools and individuals in the system are considered.

STRATEGIES FOR BUILDING CAPACITY

Over the past ten years or so, policymakers' energies have been focused on establishing the architecture of reform: standards, tests, incentives, and accountability systems. More recently, they have paid greater attention to building the capacity needed to achieve the higher standards. Analysts have introduced the notion of capacity to emphasize that simply having clear ideas about learning goals or high motivation does not automatically yield improvements in student learning.[7] Wanting to achieve a certain goal or standard is a necessary but not a sufficient condition for doing so. Teachers and administrators need the knowledge, skills, resources, and organizational capacity to achieve the desired ends. Standards-based reform requires teachers to know more about their subject, to teach in a more dynamic style, to respond to the knowledge and dispositions that their students bring to the classroom, to engage in continuous learning, and to take on new professional roles with site-based management and other activities. Research has shown that teacher knowledge of subject matter, the way different students learn, and teaching methods are critical elements of teacher effectiveness (Darling-Hammond, 1996). However, less than

---

[7] See, e.g., Berman and McLaughlin, 1978; McLaughlin, 1987, 1991.

75 percent of teachers nationwide have a degree in the subject they teach, have studied child development or teaching methods, or have passed tests of teaching knowledge and skill (McMillen et al., 1994, cited in NCTAF, 1996).

Policymakers generally think first of building the capacity of the teaching force. While this is clearly a critical piece of the reform puzzle, studies have shown that capacity for reform should be conceived more broadly. Ball and Cohen (1996) argue that in addition to teachers' knowledge and skills, capacity at the classroom level requires sufficient and appropriate instructional materials and students who are ready and motivated to learn. Others have argued that successful reform—in particular, positive effects of standards-based reform policies on instruction—also depends on capacity at the organizational level (schools, districts, states). Goertz, Floden, and O'Day (1995) argue that effective instruction depends on factors such as school leadership, a school's willingness and ability to support teachers' professional learning and collaboration, and whether the district and state policy infrastructure is sending coherent and strong signals about instructional goals.

In this section, I describe recent trends in state efforts to build both individual and organizational capacity to undertake reform. These findings are drawn primarily from a study of eight states: California, Colorado, Florida, Kentucky, Maryland, Michigan, Minnesota, and Texas (Massell, 1998).

Decentralized Support Infrastructure

To provide teacher training and professional development as well as technical assistance to schools, states have established, supported, or relied on a set of infrastructures external to state education agencies. This strategy often supplemented or supplanted the support offered by state agency staff. In the early 1990s, for instance, the Texas Education Agency eliminated the direct provision of technical assistance to schools or districts. Instead, it handed those responsibilities over to its 20 regional Education Service Centers (ESCs), which are responsible for technical assistance, staff development, technology support, and federal program assistance. Texas also established Centers for Educator Development to provide subject-specific professional development in math, social studies, science, and English-language arts at the University of Texas at Austin and Texas A&M University.

This decentralization trend emerged, in part, from the view that those in closer proximity to the schools could best access and support local needs, a notion compatible with support for greater local control and autonomy from the state. The strategy also resulted from more pragmatic considerations; state education agencies simply do not have the personnel or resources to provide direct support. In the late 1980s and early 1990s, education agency staff in many states were cut sharply because of fiscal distress, as well as longstanding legislative mistrust and complaints about the burden of central agency control and monitoring (Fuhrman and Rosenthal, 1981; Massell and Fuhrman, 1994).

Thus, central education agency staff were moving further away from providing direct assistance and services to districts and schools. The infrastructure they used included regional service providers, such as intermediate education units, as well as the expertise and support of universities and professional organizations. States were also encouraging or supporting teachers, schools, and administrators to network around reform issues.

California, for example, has networks (e.g., Math Renaissance) that focus on specific academic content areas; a middle-school initiative funded by the National Science Foundation; a network for restructuring schools; and a pilot network of schools focusing on early literacy. Perhaps the best-known example is its content-focused, teacher-based networks: the Subject Matter Projects (SMP). Through summer institutes and follow-up training during the school year, participating teachers have the opportunity to reflect on and develop instructional and curricular strategies and projects. Building on this model, new SMPs were created in different subjects to expand the number of teachers who are knowledgeable about curriculum related to the state frameworks. In 1987, the legislature provided the SMPs with funding in three-year cycles, which both offered stability and enabled interested teachers to make a long-term commitment and evolve into a cadre of teacher leaders.

Some states, such as Minnesota, Florida, and Kentucky, have trained individuals to provide support to schools and teachers for reform efforts. For example, the Kentucky Department of Education created a network of experienced Distinguished

Educators to provide direct assistance to poorly performing schools.

Studies suggest that the kind of support provided through networks can help improve student performance if the networks are strongly focused on the content of reform rather than vague prescriptions about reform processes. For example, in a survey of California elementary school teachers' responses to state mathematics reforms, researchers found important classroom practice effects from teacher participation in workshops centered on the new student curriculum. Compared with involvement in more generic types of professional development, these experiences prompted more reform-related activities and instruction. The study also found that these changes translated into student success on the statewide mathematics test (Cohen, Wilson, and Hill, 1997). Similarly, with the focused support of the Distinguished Educators, 63 percent of the Kentucky schools listed as in decline made enough gains to be placed in the reward category in the next accountability cycle, although further studies are needed to better understand the role of these experts in building school capacity to change (Davis et al., 1997).

It is important to note that some states simply do not have regional institutions to provide the support needed by schools and districts. Furthermore, staffing in these regional entities can be limited and constrained. For example, Kentucky's Regional Service Centers have one staff person to provide curriculum support to about 25 school districts and at least four or five times that many schools. They also have a high rate of staff turnover. Some of Colorado's service centers had only two staff members. Some states also do not have strong universities in all regions.

Even in states with a relatively strong regional capacity, these institutions have a mandate to serve the lowest-performing schools and districts first. Indeed, Maryland established a new regional infrastructure to serve low-performing, low-capacity districts. This strategy of targeting resources to the neediest schools is common in many states, but it begs the question of how schools in the middle of the performance distribution can gain the knowledge and skills they need to make progress. Many of these mid-range schools are far from fully meeting state performance standards.

Professional Development Standards

Another major strategy to improve teacher knowledge and skills has been to create voluntary standards for professional development, which are generally aligned with the principles of standards-based reform. Officials have used these standards to guide professional development activities, to review state and federally funded professional development grants, or to help local districts plan staff development. For example, Colorado used professional development standards during itsr review of local applications for Goals 2000 grants. In Texas, each school district had to develop its own plan and criteria for the use of professional development dollars, although the state was also creating a framework for professional development to be aligned with the new state curriculum.

These efforts signal state policymakers' growing concerns about improving the quality of professional development. Politicians are typically skeptical about the worth of professional development, often seeing it as payoff to the teachers' unions rather than a critical component of reform. For example, Michigan's governor eliminated a $10 million fund that provided state resources for staff development. In Colorado and Minnesota, local districts resisted state efforts to set aside dollars for professional development out of concern that it would cut into badly needed general education revenues.

States typically provide professional development resources in the form of grants or as part of special programs such as California's Reading Initiative. Much of what many states could offer districts for professional development has come from federal sources, such as Goals 2000 and Title II of the Improving America's Schools Act. Including professional development dollars in special programs and grants may have the political value of making these funds less vulnerable to budget-cutting maneuvers, but it also may prevent state agencies, local districts, and schools from making strategic use of these resources.

Curriculum Clarification

One of the chief dilemmas confronting standards-based reform is the balance between state-mandated academic content and performance standards, on the one hand, and maximum local flexibility in determining strategies for meeting the standards, on the other hand. For political, legal, and philosophical reasons, state policymakers have hesitated to create standards with high degrees of specificity. However, most educators wanted more—not less—external guidance and support for instruction than they had been receiving from the state or other groups (Massell et al., 1997). The most frequent complaints about state standards were that they were too general and that district and school staff did not have the capacity, resources, time, or expertise to convert broad standards into practice. In fact, local administrators and teachers have historically lacked the kind of expert knowledge and skills necessary to develop curriculum programs and materials, leading them to depend heavily on textbook and testing publishers for structure and guidance (Walker, 1990).

Local educators in Kentucky demanded that the state provide them with more specific guidance and support for meeting state standards. The Kentucky State Department of Education consequently created a state framework, "Transformations," and another more detailed document called "Core Content for Assessment." Education groups in California, Texas, and other states have argued for a return to the more conventional kinds of grade-by-grade standards that list very precisely the expected skills and content. However, policymakers in Colorado, Maryland, and other states remain wary of the political or legal repercussions of being too proactive and specific about curriculum, even to the point that state agency staff are hesitant to offer advice about curriculum programs that are aligned with standards.

One strategy states have developed for walking this tightrope has been to provide plenty of curriculum resources for local educators to learn about different materials. Policymakers have infused their standards documents with more concrete examples of what standards-based instruction would look like, provided curriculum frameworks or other supporting documents, set up resource banks of materials and instructional tools—often through the use of new technologies, or encouraging relationships with national curriculum projects or programs. For example, Texas has developed standards-based curriculum and teaching vignettes on compact disks, putting materials on the Internet, and using video teleconferencing to allow teachers to view demonstration lessons, to discuss them with a master teacher or expert, and even to try to model the lessons. Even in Texas, however, a major textbook adoption state, policy leaders and education professionals were cautious about identifying reading programs that school districts might use. Because of these competing forces, it is likely that states will continue to pursue a range of curriculum policies, depending on their own political traditions and mix of interests. Districts and schools will still have the lion's share of the burden of determining effective curriculum to meet state standards.

School Improvement Planning

For many of the eight states in the CPRE study, school improvement planning was a pivotal strategy for building local capacity, specifically, the capacity to survey their own resources and needs and determine how to reallocate them to meet new goals. Indeed, school improvement planning was a key way for states to marry top-driven state standards with bottom-up decision-making about instructional practice. For example, the Maryland accountability program required every school not meeting state performance standards to develop a school improvement plan. Because the state viewed this planning as critical, it targeted a wide range of resources to facilitating the process, both in the department and in state-supported regional centers. However, as with its regional support system, these resources were targeted on the lowest-performing schools, though the vast majority of schools did not meet state standards in all areas. Kentucky and Texas embedded school improvement planning in regulations governing site-based decision-making (SBDM). For instance, Kentucky required SBDM teams to develop school transformation plans every two years, while Texas called for annual plans by SBDM teams.

One of the key assumptions of school improvement planning—and indeed, of the overall trends in accountability under standards-based reforms—is that information on performance will drive change in schools and districts. This theory presumes that the kinds of performance data provided by states are readily understandable by teachers and administrators. But the performance data are often very complex, especially on state accountability indices, which aggregate information across different measures (achievement in different subjects, attendance, drop-out data, and the like). A study of accountability programs in Kentucky and Mississippi found that the programs were so complex that few policymakers or educators could begin to explain how they worked (Elmore et al., 1995).

Just translating performance data into action in schools and classrooms can be difficult, for a variety of reasons. For example, a number of states assess only a small range of subjects or a few grade levels, whereas schools offer a much broader curriculum and teach students in multiple grades. These assessments, then, do not provide feedback on non-tested subjects or grades. Even when teachers do receive individual student data, interpreting the data can be a difficult task; teacher education programs often offer little training in interpreting or using assessments (Massell, 1995). A major challenge for policymakers is ensuring that teachers and administrators have the requisite knowledge and skills to bridge the gap between accountability and testing data and the kinds of organizational and instructional changes needed to address the new performance goals.

CONCLUSION

Standards-based, systemic reform represents a synthesis of earlier strategies for improving instruction in America's public schools. It attempts to wed the top-down, state-mandated educational excellence reforms that flowed from *A Nation at Risk* with a second wave of bottom-up reforms that called for empowering schools and restructuring governance. Policymakers and analysts have diagnosed both the benefits and the problems that flow from these reform strategies and have come up with a model of change that calls for coherent state-mandated academic standards and policies, leaving local districts and schools with the discretion to determine the best instructional strategies to meet those goals.

State academic standards have often embraced some portion of new constructivist ideas about teaching and learning. As implementation proceeded, policymakers faced numerous challenges over these approaches. Indeed, discussions about what students should know and be able to do have frequently opened a Pandora's box of competing social and political values, which most policymakers have historically preferred not to discuss publicly. Rather, decisions about the academic content of education were often left in the hands of commercial testing and textbook publishers and teachers. Standards-based reform defied that silence and argued that such discussions must be held openly to build a common framework for public education. However, forging change and bringing forth new ideas about teaching and learning is difficult, both because educational institutions are resistant to change and because parents and educators have long-established images of what educational practice should look like. Moreover, reform ideas were not always well-researched and tested in classrooms, and teachers were not always adequately trained to teach in the new styles.

By the late 1990s, a mixed model of the new and the old emerged. Indeed, the persistence of standards-based reform and its wide adoption across the states can be attributed to the fact that policymakers adjusted their ideas in response to public and professional concerns and developed reform models that balanced between newer and more traditional approaches to content, assessment, and instruction. To be sure, the debate about standards and teaching practice is not settled in some states, and the pendulum may swing even further back toward older methods. At this point, however, balance is still the theme of the day in state education policy. One challenge will be to ensure that this balance is carefully constructed so that administrators and teachers receive coherent signals about instruction. If, for example, academic content standards are rigorous and challenging, while assessments measure low-level skills and competencies, the goals of the reform movement will be undermined.

Accountability is an integral component of standards-based reform, and state accountability systems demand higher performance from schools in exchange for granting greater flexibility and local control. States have established challenging performance targets for schools. Recognizing that there can be many good and many poor schools within districts, policymakers have required that school results be reported so that problem schools are not masked, and they have established consequences for schools based on performance.

Policymakers in some states have also attempted to use the accountability system as an equity lever. They have created incentives for schools to include all students in assessments so that results will not be artificially inflated by the absence of the weakest performers. Schools have been known to inappropriately exempt or exclude some students in order to raise test scores. More study is needed to determine the overall impact of the effort to include all students in accountability measures. Evidence suggests, however, that even under these more rigorous requirements, some schools find it easier to ignore the weakest students and concentrate on those closest to meeting satisfactory performance levels defined by the accountability system. More study is also needed on the effects of rewards and sanctions on teacher motivation and student performance. Some research suggests that the prospect of sanctions on low-performing schools, accompanied by strong and targeted support to help them meet their goals, may have a substantial impact on teacher motivation and student achievement.

A critical aspect of any reform strategy is the extent to which policymakers address the capacity of individuals and schools to meet the challenges of reform. Policymakers are beginning to attend to the issue of capacity, although the comprehensiveness of their actions varies substantially from state to state. Some states have turned to regional infrastructures to provide technical assistance and professional development to teachers and administrators in local schools. Not all states, however, have a strong group of regional institutions or associations—service centers, universities, professional associations, or more formal networks of teachers and schools—that can provide such support. In addition, regional service centers often have a mandate to focus on low-performing schools, leaving schools in the middle of the performance distribution without much targeted assistance. Similarly, policymakers are using school improvement planning to encourage schools to use state performance data in assessing their own needs and developing strategies to meet state goals. At the same time, the implications of performance data for school change are not always obvious, and policymakers must help schools acquire the skills to undertake sound analysis.

Another lesson that is emerging from reform is the need to provide more sustained professional development and support to teachers' daily practice. Standards-based reforms challenge teachers to move beyond the status quo of "teacher talk" and drill-and-practice activities, to know their subjects in greater depth, and to help all students master more challenging material. Teachers need access to richer opportunities that specifically relate to the content of reform, not vague professional development about the principles of reform. Research is beginning to show that this more substantive kind of professional development can translate into meaningful changes in classroom practice and student learning. State professional development standards are a major way policymakers are trying to address the quality of these activities, but without direct and substantial state financial assistance for professional development, it is uncertain how much impact these standards will have.

Teachers also need access to curriculum material that is linked to standards-based reform and is strongly grounded in evidence of effectiveness. Teachers and school districts often do not have the time or expertise to create an entire curriculum from the bottom up. Consequently, states have begun to provide more specific curriculum direction, but political and legal constraints bar them from taking more aggressive action or, in many cases, from even recommending high-quality curriculum programs to their constituents. Policymakers may want to consider supporting more independent external agencies to broker information and advice about sound curriculum practices.

We still have a long way to go to fulfill the hopes and dreams of standards-based reform. However, the power of its ideas and the notion that it is a logical and useful strategy to improve the system have been broadly accepted by teachers, parents, and policymakers. And thus the work continues.

REFERENCES

AFT (1999). *Making Standards Matter 1999: An Annual Fifty-State Report on Efforts to Raise Academic Standards.* Washington, D.C.: American Federation of Teachers.

Ball, Deborah Loewenberg, and David K. Cohen (1996). "Reform by the Book: What Is—Or Might Be—the Role of Curriculum Materials in Teacher Learning and Instructional Reform?" *Educational Researcher*, vol. 25, no. 9 (December 1996), pp. 6-8, 14.

Berman, Paul, and Milbrey W. McLaughlin (1978). *Federal Programs Supporting Educational Change, Volume VIII: Implementing and Sustaining Innovations.* Santa Monica, Calif.: The Rand Corporation.

Bingham, Janet (1997). "New Tests Will Bring Bad News, Good News," *Denver Post*, October 29, 1997.

Bowman, Clair M., and Samuel S. Peng (1972). "A Preliminary Investigation of Recent Advanced Psychology Tests in the GRE Program: An Application of a Cognitive Classification System." Unpublished report. Princeton, N.J.: Educational Testing Service.

Carlson, Carol Gordon (1992). *The Metamorphosis of Mathematics Instruction.* Princeton, N.J.: Educational Testing Service.

CBO (1993). *The Federal Role in Improving Elementary and Secondary Education.* Washington, D.C.: Congressional Budget Office.

CCSSO (1996a). *Key State Education Policies on K-12 Education: Content Standards, Graduation, Teacher Licensure, Time, and Attendance.* Washington, D.C.: Council of Chief State School Officers.

_____ (1996b). *State Education Accountability Reports and Indicator Reports: Status of Reports Across the States.* Washington, D.C.: Council of Chief State School Officers.

CER (1995). *School Reform in the United States: State by State Summary.* Washington, D.C.: Center for Education Reform.

_____ (2000). *Charter Schools Today: Changing the Face of American Education.* Washington, D.C.: Center for Education Reform.

Clements, Barbara S., and Rolf K. Blank (1997). "What Do We Know About Education in the States? Education Indicators in State Reports." Paper presented at the Annual Meeting of the American Educational Research Association.

Clune, William H., et al. (1991). *Changes in High School Course-Taking, 1982-88: A Study of Transcript Data from Selected Schools and States.* New Brunswick, N.J.: Consortium for Policy Research in Education, Rutgers University.

Cohen, David K., Suzanne Wilson, and Heather Hill (1997). "Teaching and Learning Mathematics in California." Paper presented at the annual meeting of the American Education Research Association.

Coley, Richard J., and Margaret E. Goertz (1990). *Educational Standards in the 50 States: 1990.* Princeton, N.J.: Educational Testing Service.

CRESST (1995). *How "Messing About" with Performance Assessment in Mathematics Affects What Happens in Classrooms.* Los Angeles: National Center for Research on Evaluation, Standards, and Testing, Graduate School of Education and Information Studies, University of California, Los Angeles.

CSTEEP (1992). *The Influence of Testing on Teaching Math and Science in Grades 4-12: Executive Summary.* Chestnut

Hill, Mass.: Center for the Study of Testing, Evaluation, and Educational Policy, Boston College.

Curry, Brian, and Tierney Temple (1992). *Using Curriculum Frameworks for Systemic Reform.* Alexandria, Va.: Association for Supervision and Curriculum Development.

Darling-Hammond, Linda (1996). "Teaching and Knowledge." In John Sikula, ed., *Handbook of Research on Teacher Education: A Project of the Association of Teacher Educators.* 2nd edition. New York: Macmillan Library Reference.

David, Jane L., Stewart C. Purkey, and Paula White (1989). *Restructuring in Progress: Lessons from Pioneering Districts.* Washington, D.C.: National Governors' Association.

Davis, Mimi Mitchell, Deborah H. McDonald, and Bert Lyons (1997). *A Preliminary Analysis of the Kentucky Distinguished Educator Initiative: A New Approach to Educational Change.* Frankfort: Kentucky Department of Education.

Elley, Warwick B. (1992). *How in the World Do Students Read? IEA Study of Reading Literacy.* Netherlands: International Association for the Evaluation of Educational Achievement.

Elmore, Richard F. (1993). *The Development and Implementation of Large-Scale Curriculum Reforms.* New Brunswick, N.J.: Consortium for Policy Research in Education, Rutgers University.

Elmore, Richard F., Susan H. Fuhrman, and Charles Abelmann (1995). "The New Accountability in State Education Reform: From Process to Performance." In Helen F. Ladd, ed., *Holding Schools Accountable: Performance Based Reform in Education.* Washington, D.C.: The Brookings Institution.

Frederiksen, Norman (1984). "The Real Test Bias: Influences of Testing on Teaching and Learning," *American Psychologist*, vol. 39, no. 3 (March 1984), pp. 193-202.

Fuhrman, Susan, and Alan Rosenthal, eds. (1981). *Shaping Education Policy in the States.* Washington, D.C.: Institute for Educational Leadership.

Goertz, Margaret E., Robert E. Floden, and Jennifer O'Day (1995). *Studies of Education Reform: Systemic Reform.* New Brunswick, N.J.: Consortium for Policy Research in Education, Rutgers University.

Haertel, Edward H. (1989). "Student Achievement Tests as Tools of Education Policy: Practices and Consequences." In Bernard R. Gifford, ed., *Test Policy and Test Perfor-*

mance: Education, Language, and Culture. Boston: Kluwar Academic Publishers.

Honig, Bill (1995). "How Should We Teach Our Children to Read?" *Minutes of the Superintendent's Reading Task Force*, May 19, 1995.

Kelley, Carolyn (1998). "The Kentucky School-Based Performance Award Program: School-Level Effects," *Educational Policy*, vol. 12, no. 3 (May 1998), pp. 305-324.

Kirst, Michael W. (1993). "Strengths and Weaknesses of American Education," *Phi Delta Kappan*, vol. 74, no. 8 (April 1993), pp. 613-618.

Legum, Stanley, et al. (1998). *The 1994 High School Transcript Study.* Washington, D.C.: National Center for Education Statistics, U.S. Department of Education.

Malen, Betty, Rodney T. Ogawa, and Jennifer Kranz (1990). "What Do We Know About School-Based Management? A Case Study of the Literature—A Call for Research." In William H. Clune and John F. Witte, eds., *Choice and Control in American Education, vol. 2: The Practice of Choice, Decentralization, and School Restructuring.* New York: Falmer Press.

Massell, Diane (1994). "Achieving Consensus: Setting the Agenda for State Curriculum Reform." In Susan H. Fuhrman and Richard F. Elmore, eds., *Governing Curriculum.* Arlington, Va.: Association for Supervision and Curriculum Development.

_____ (1995). *What We Know about Assessing What Students Know: A Literature Review on Assessment.* Prepared for the Annie E. Casey Foundation. Co-sponsored by the Consortium for Policy Research in Education, Rutgers University.

_____ (1998). *State Strategies for Building Capacity in Education: Progress and Continuing Challenges.* Philadelphia: Consortium for Policy Research in Education, University of Pennsylvania.

Massell, Diane, and Susan H. Fuhrman (1994). *Ten Years of State Education Reform, 1983-1993: Overview with Four Case Studies.* New Brunswick, N.J.: Consortium for Policy Research in Education, Rutgers University.

Massell, Diane, Michael Kirst, and Margaret Hoppe (1997). *Persistence and Change: Standards-Based Systemic Reform in Nine States.* Philadelphia: Consortium for Policy Research in Education, University of Pennsylvania.

McLaughlin, Milbrey W. (1987). "Learning from Experience: Lessons from Policy Implementation," *Educational Evaluation and Policy Analysis*, vol. 9, no. 2 (Summer 1987), pp. 171-178.

_____ (1991). "The RAND Change Agent Study: Ten Years Later." In Allan R. Odden, ed., *Education Policy Implementation*. Albany: State University of New York Press.

McMillen, Marilyn M., Sharon A. Bobbitt, and Hilda F. Lynch (1994). "Teacher Training, Certification, and Assignment in Public Schools: 1990-91." Paper presented at the annual meeting of the American Educational Research Association, New Orleans, La., April 1994.

Mirel, Jeffrey, and David Angus (1994). "High Standards for All? The Struggle for Equality in the American High School Curriculum, 1890-1990," *American Educator*, vol. 18, no. 2 (Summer 1994), pp. 4-9, 40-42.

Musick, Mark (1997). "Setting Education Standards High Enough." Paper presented at the Annual Assessment Conference of the Council of Chief State School Officers, June 1997.

National Commission on Excellence in Education (1983). *A Nation at Risk: The Imperative for Educational Reform.* Washington, D.C.: U.S. Government Printing Office.

NCES (1992). *The Condition of Education, 1992.* Washington, D.C.: National Center for Education Statistics.

NCEST (1992). *Raising Standards for American Education.* Washington, D.C.: National Council on Educational Standards and Testing.

NCTAF (1996). *What Matters Most: Teaching for America's Future.* Report of the National Commission on Teaching and America's Future. New York: Teachers College, Columbia University.

NGA (1986). *Time for Results.* Washington, D.C.: National Governors' Association.

Pechman, Ellen M., and P. A. Hammond (1991). "A Background Report on Educational Assessment." Washington, D.C.: National Research Council of the National Academy of Science.

Pitsch, Mark (1991). "350,000 Took AP Exams this Year, Board Reports," *Education Week*, November 13, 1991, p. 9.

Porter, Andrew, Michael W. Kirst, Eric J. Osthoff, John L. Smithson, and Stephen A. Schneider (1993). *Reform Up*

Close: A Classroom Analysis. Madison: Wisconsin Center for Research in Education.

Resnick, Lauren B. (1987). *Education and Learning to Think.* Washington, D. C.: National Academy Press.

Resnick, Daniel P., and Lauren B. Resnick (1992). "Assessing the Thinking Curriculum: New Tools for Educational Reform." In Bernard R. Gifford and Mary Catherine O'Connor, eds., *Changing Assessments: Alternative Views of Aptitude, Achievement and Instruction.* Boston: Kluwer Academic Publishers.

Rothman, Robert (1992). "Science Reform Goals Elusive, NAEP Data Find," *Education Week*, April 1, 1992, p. 1.

Sebba, Judy, Martha L. Thurlow, and Margaret Goertz (1999). "Educational Accountability and Students with Disabilities in the United States and in England and Wales." In Margaret McLaughlin and Martyn Rouse, eds., *Special Education and School Reform in the United States and Britain.* New York: Routledge.

Smith, Marshall S., and Jennifer O'Day (1991). "Systemic School Reform." In Susan H. Fuhrman and Betty Malen, eds., *The Politics of Curriculum and Testing.* Bristol, Pa.: Falmer Press.

Tyson-Bernstein, Harriet (1986). "The Great Textbook Machine and Prospects for Reform," *Social Education*, vol. 50, no. 1 (January 1986), pp. 41-45.

Walker, Decker (1990). *Fundamentals of Curriculum.* Saddlebrook, N.J.: Harcourt, Brace, Jovanovich.

Wiggins, Grant (1993). "Assessment: Authenticity, Context, and Validity," *Phi Delta Kappan*, vol. 75, no. 3 (November 1993), pp. 200-214.

Wohlstetter, Priscilla, Roxane Smyer, and Susan Albers Mohrman (1994). "New Boundaries for School-Based Management: The High Involvement Model," *Educational Evaluation and Policy Analysis*, vol. 16, no. 3 (Fall 1994), pp. 268-286.

COMMENTS: THE CONCEPT OF SYSTEMIC REFORM

Maris A. Vinovskis

Reform of education in America has a long and frustrating history. Starting with the attempts by the Puritans to legislate improved schooling, policymakers and the public have repeatedly been dissatisfied with the state of our society and our schools and called for reforms in American education. An educational reform effort that captured the attention of many policymakers and educators in the 1990s is standards-based, systemic reform.

School reform efforts in the past have followed a typical pattern—one that overemphasizes the then-current crisis in education, denounces earlier educational reforms, and issues a simple but highly plausible set of proposals to solve the problem. Proponents usually exaggerate the extent to which the reforms by themselves can quickly improve education; therefore, they soon face a disillusioned public that once again is disappointed with the slow pace of educational improvement. Are the systemic reform initiatives pursued by the Clinton administration destined to be yet another example of the ebb and flow of educational reform efforts? Or have we finally arrived at a more sophisticated and complex appreciation of the nature of educational changes in order to avoid the disillusionment that has so often accompanied school reform efforts in the past?

Diane Massell's thoughtful and balanced discussion of the implementation and adjustment of standards-based, systemic reform in the states provides some encouragement for those who hope that this latest reform effort will succeed and survive. She points out how systemic reform is built on the perceived failures of the work of the "educational excellence" movement in the early 1980s; how it was written into federal legislation in 1994 and has been accepted and implemented (in varying degrees) by almost every state; that despite the difficulties with systemic reform in several states, most seem to have coped with the numerous problems and challenges; and that by 1997, state and local educators and policymakers had merged old and new approaches to teaching and learning—an important prerequisite for almost any educational innovation to survive and thrive.

Although I find much to admire in many aspects of standards-based, systemic reform, I am somewhat more skeptical than Massell about the overall logic and clarity of the concept of systemic reform. I also have some doubts about the ways in which systemic reform has been interpreted and implemented in practice, the likelihood that systemic reform will significantly improve the educational well-being of the most disadvantaged students, and the actual extent of its understanding and acceptance by educators, policymakers, and the general public.

The concept of standards-based, systemic reform has much to offer. It emphasizes ambitious national and state curriculum standards and appropriate assessment and performance measures; it also calls for the alignment of curriculum standards, performance standards, and assessments, as well as restructured systems of governance. Yet my own review of the development and use of the concept of systemic reform raises questions about its analytic clarity and utility. All of the key elements of systemic reform are not exactly clear. Are "opportunity to learn" standards an integral part of systemic reform? If so, what is meant by "opportunity to learn"? Is the provision of comprehensive services to K-12 students an important part of systemic reform? Have the proposed voluntary national tests become a vital component of systemic reform? Given that systemic reform is such a broad, general approach, what are the specific aspects that are particularly important or essential to improving elementary and secondary education? Despite the importance and widespread use of the concept, there has been surprisingly little effort to analyze and debate systemic reform. For example, as a member of the U.S. Department of Education's congressionally mandated Independent Review Panel for the National Assessment of Title I (which oversaw and commented on most of the new initiatives), I know that the panel did not have a thorough, in-depth discussion of the strengths and weaknesses of the concept of systemic reform (see U.S. Department of Education, 1999).

Massell's chapter provides a thoughtful analysis of the problems of implementing systemic reform. One could expand on her useful discussion even further. Initially, proponents of systemic reform stressed the need to develop national curriculum standards, but the Clinton administration downplayed the need to support those efforts in several subjects. The current national assessments of these standards also are heavily focused on reading, writing, math, and science, with very little attention devoted to social studies. At the state level, many of the curriculum standards in areas such as social studies are so vague as to be almost useless; some of the state assessments are so conceptually and statistically limited that they will not be of much help to parents and educators in telling them what children actually know. Perhaps one of the reasons that so many people believe in the value of systemic reform is that they have been allowed broad latitude in interpreting the concept in theory and in practice. Although federal legislation and administrative guidelines presumably clarified the interpretation of systemic reform, almost anything has been accepted in practice. The U.S. Department of Education, for example, certified that Iowa met the minimum criteria for a systemic reform approach, even though the state had explicitly rejected the notion of statewide curriculum standards.

Some proponents of systemic reform have argued that this approach would be particularly helpful to at-risk children and would promote improvements in schools that serve large numbers of these children. While we still lack adequate outcome data, many analysts fear that the reforms may not be as useful for at-risk children as had been hoped. If there are some gains, they probably will be too small to close the large achievement gap between at-risk students and their more fortunate counterparts. My own analysis of the long history of federal compensatory education programs provides little evidence of the type of dramatic improvements that many policymakers and the public have been led to expect from systemic reform.

Finally, Massell may have exaggerated the current support for systemic reform and underestimated the intellectual and political opposition to it. Many analysts have expressed doubts about the concept of systemic reform; some have rejected it altogether. Many members of Congress have expressed serious doubts about the Goals 2000 legislation. Rather than funding the existing Title I systemic reform initiatives, Congress provided $120 million for promoting comprehensive school reforms on the local level. Moreover, the bitter controversy over voluntary national tests has not helped to prepare the way for a broad, bipartisan consensus that is necessary for educational reform at the national and state levels. Elements of the standards-based, systemic reform effort will undoubtedly survive. I would not be surprised, however, if the next Title I reauthorization moves in yet another direction, especially if the initial student achievement gains are more modest than promised by some advocates of standard-based education reform.[1]

REFERENCES

CQ (2000). "2000 Legislative Summary: ESEA," *CQ Weekly*, December 16, 2000, p. 2899.
U.S. Department of Education (1999). *Promising Results, Continuing Challenges: The Final Report of the National Assessment of Title I.* Washington, D.C.: Planning and Evaluation Service, Office of the Under Secretary, U.S. Department of Education.

---

[1] The 106th Congress was unable to reach agreement on reauthorization of the Elementary and Secondary Education Act (ESEA). Instead, they funded ESEA programs for an additional year in an omnibus spending bill (CQ, 2000).

COMMENTS: STANDARDS-BASED REFORM IN ILLINOIS

Richard D. Laine

The challenge for those concerned with education reform in Illinois is to look widely, in terms of both time and geography, but talk locally. Without an understanding of the progression and context of Illinois education reform, it will be impossible to influence the direction and quality of the next steps in Illinois's path to better public education. Several chapters in this book lay out the key education reforms—and the state context—that have occurred in Illinois. A broader view of the standards-based reform movement, however, is necessary to put the whole of Illinois's reform agenda in context. Diane Massell's chapter does this both conceptually and by using examples from several states. My commentary focuses on some of the major issues of standards-based reform that were not developed in Massell's chapter.

Massell describes the major components of standards-based, systemic reform as:

- challenging standards that define what students should know and be able to do, as well as how well students must perform to meet the standards;
- assessments that measure students' attainment of the standards and their higher-order thinking skills;
- accountability mechanisms that focus on improved results while providing greater flexibility in the inputs and processes to educate students;
- consequences for failure or success;
- building capacity in people, tools, and the system's infrastructure.

While these are the major components of a standards-based reform agenda, there are several other fundamental issues that must be raised, and ultimately answered, to truly engage in standards-based reform. These issues fall under two categories: alignment of the system and overcoming barriers.

ALIGNMENT OF THE SYSTEM

The first category focuses on a central concept of a standards-based system—"alignment." Unlike the traditional state-level policy focus of prescribing inputs and processes, a standards-based system necessitates a focus on clear standards and then strong alignment of all parts of the system in order to achieve the standards. Thus, the major issues yet to be addressed for a standards-based system are the following:

(1) How does the system that adopts a standards-based reform agenda ensure that there is alignment between what occurs at the state level and what occurs at the district and school levels? In other words, how does a state balance the traditional notion of local control, in which the link between state and local activities could be minimal, with the notion of local responsibility, in which the link between the state and local efforts would be leveraged?

(2) Must the education of students be effective only within each school they attend or over their entire public education career? In other words, how can we expect students to acquire the highest quality education over their 12 years in public school when coordination or alignment between elementary, middle, and high schools is often limited? Although this problem is present in larger districts, it is probably a greater problem for dual districts in which more than one elementary district sends students to a central high school. When this occurs, alignment of curriculum, standards, and other activities is limited or becomes convoluted, and attainment of high standards for all students becomes difficult.

(3) How can the public education system enhance its alignment with what comes before it and what comes after it? Research shows us that what happens with children before they enter their first classroom will have a significant effect on their future learning. We also know that what students learn in public schools must give them some knowledge and ability to move into the job market or to continue their education before entering the job market. A standards-based education system requires that students have certain learning opportunities prior to entering the traditional K-12 system and that attainment of standards be tied to tangible preparations for students' next steps. Therefore, how should the public education system enhance its connection or integration with the systems surrounding it?

OVERCOMING BARRIERS

The second category, overcoming barriers, builds on the alignment theme. Within a standards-based system, it is imperative to assess the processes of the system in terms of alignment to the standards and whether the processes are catalysts or barriers to achieving the standards. The major issues to be addressed in regard to barriers in a standards-based system are the following:

(1) We know that a large percentage of teachers are teaching in fields in which they do not have a college major or minor. We also know that nearly 80,000 teachers across Illinois will need to be hired over the next decade. Who will provide existing teachers and new teachers with the professional development that is necessary to support a standards-based system? More important, if we are expecting teachers to teach differently, who will teach the teachers of teachers?

(2) If we are expecting greater learning from our students, can it be done in the traditional means within traditional time constraints? In other words, how can students be expected to meet higher standards using the traditional time structure of 180-day school years, with 2-3 months off in the summer, and typically only 5-6 hour days using traditional methods? If all students are expected to meet and exceed the challenging standards, and we know that students learn differently and at different speeds, then how can time be maintained as a constant and in such a rigid structure?

(3) If standards are set at challenging levels to prepare students for later success, does it not further elevate the issues of equity and adequacy, in terms of both quantity and quality of resources? In other words, does raising the bar—but not providing greater or sufficient opportunities for success through better methods, better trained staff, better technology, and better educational and economic incentives—just provide a clearer picture of how far from the standards many students will fall?

CONCLUSION

Massell's chapter provides an excellent starting point from which to better understand a standards-based education system. As she correctly points out, a large majority of the states across the nation have embarked on some form of the standards-based journey. In most cases, however, the states have focused on building key state-level components that Massell correctly identifies as necessary aspects of a standards-based system. Beyond these components, though, states and school districts are very quickly being forced to address many of the issues identified here. These are not easy issues to address; if they were, they would surely have made some politician's agenda. The next wave in standards-based reform—the wave that will distinguish this effort from past efforts and prove the worth of this reform agenda—will continue to revolve around the components identified by Massell, as well as the issues raised in this commentary.

STANDARDS AND ASSESSMENT IN SCHOOL ACCOUNTABILITY SYSTEMS IN ILLINOIS

John Q. Easton and Sandra L. Storey

In the past decade or so, many states have shifted their education accountability focus away from process and "input" measures and toward performance outcomes. This shift in emphasis moves away from monitoring compliance with regulations and statutes and toward looking more closely at student outcomes, most often student achievement levels. States have indicated less interest in how schools or local districts achieve results than on the outcomes themselves. This change has created a strong focus on student achievement measures, through standardized tests and various other assessments. This new emphasis on accountability is often accompanied by incentives and sanctions, most notably intervention in weak or failing schools (Elmore, Abelmann, and Fuhrman, 1996).

A system to hold schools accountable for student performance should have the following components:

- academic content standards that explicate what students should know and be able to do;
- assessments (tests) to measure student performance in relation to content standards;
- a set of statistical indicators that show how students perform on these assessments;
- standards for school performance as measured by the indicators, with rewards, sanctions, intervention, and support tied to how schools do in relation to these performance standards.

This chapter discusses these four accountability components, with specific reference to their implementation in Illinois and in Chicago, and makes recommendations on how to improve accountability systems in the years ahead.

ACADEMIC CONTENT STANDARDS

Underlying the issue of educational accountability is the question of what schools, teachers, and students are accountable for. Although there is often a great deal of debate about the specific domains and content of learning, there is little doubt that student learning is the primary goal of schooling. Academic content standards make this goal concrete and provide a framework for determining what students are expected to know and be able to do.

National Developments

The national movement toward adopting academic content standards (or learning standards) gained momentum with the 1989 Education Summit, where the nation's governors agreed on six national education goals. In the same year, the National Council of Teachers of Mathematics created a set of content standards that became widely used (Commission on Standards for School Mathematics, 1989). Since then, federal legislation, especially the Improving America's Schools Act of 1994 (which reauthorized the Elementary and Secondary Education Act), has stimulated standards-based reform initiatives across the country. Title I (compensatory education for disadvantaged students) now requires assessments to measure student progress in reaching academic content standards, including assessments that measure higher-order skills and understanding and that use multiple measures of the content standards. The changes in Title I also promote standards-based reform in that they expect to identify schools and districts in need of improvement. The Title I requirements also push for more demanding standards that are applied to more students, with more challenging and difficult assessments.

Learning standards have been created by professional education organizations (e.g., math teachers, science teachers), by state boards of education, and by local school districts. By July 1996, 49 states had developed academic standards or were in the process of developing them (CCSSO, 1996). Many large districts, such as Chicago, also have developed their own learning standards or have adopted standards developed elsewhere. In a survey of its members in 1996, the Council of Great City Schools reported that virtually all responding districts either already had completed content standards in at least four core content areas or were in the process of developing or adopting such standards (CGCS, 1996).

The New Standards Project, a collaboration of education researchers and state and urban school districts, has attempted to bring together the best of content standards in three subject areas (math, English language arts, and science) and in a fourth area, applied learning (New Standards Project, 1997). New Standards has also developed assessments around these internationally benchmarked standards, which have been adopted by the New York City Board of Education. The standards and associated "reference exams" are in use in several states and districts across the country.

Developments in Illinois

In July 1997, the Illinois State Board of Education (ISBE) adopted a new set of learning standards for public schools in the state. The new "Illinois Learning Standards" cover seven subject areas: English language arts, mathematics, science, social science, physical development and health, fine arts, and foreign languages. In addition to the seven subject areas, the ISBE framework stresses the application of learning, crossing disciplines, and reinforcing learning in other areas. The "applications of learning" include solving problems, communicating, using technology, working on teams, and making connections within and across learning areas. The standards specify outcomes for five critical points in students' schooling: early elementary school, late elementary school, middle/junior high school, early high school, and late high school (see sidebar on next page). The 1997 Illinois state learning standards evolved from a set of 34 broader goals created in 1985. The newer standards are much more specific and detailed than the original learning goals. In ISBE's words, these more specific standards can "communicate to students, teachers, and parents exactly what is expected for students to learn" (ISBE, 1997, p. iv).

ILLINOIS LEARNING STANDARDS: AN EXAMPLE

The Illinois Learning Standards framework states what children should know and be able to do in both general and specific terms. The framework begins with broad statements, called state "goals." The goals are then broken down into more specific guidelines, called "standards," which specify the knowledge and/or skills needed to reach the goals. Finally, "learning benchmarks" are progress indicators for gauging student achievement at each grade-level cluster. Here is an example of how goals, standards, and learning benchmarks fit together.

Goals: The framework contains five mathematics goals that cover the range of mathematical learning from counting, performing basic operations, measuring, estimating, using algebra and analytic methods to describe and to predict, using statistics, probability, geometry, and other mathematical fields. The first math goal is: "Demonstrate and apply a knowledge and sense of numbers, including numeration and operations (addition, subtraction, multiplication, division), patterns, ratios, and proportions."

Learning standards: This goal is broken into four standards that define learning needed to reach the goal. For example, the fourth standard in this goal is: "Solve problems using comparison of quantities, ratios, proportions, and percents."

Learning benchmarks: Each standard is explicated at the five grade clusters. The learning benchmarks are generally oriented toward basic skills in the early grades and become more complex in the later grades. Here are examples of learning benchmarks at different grade groupings.

Early elementary school: Compare the numbers of objects in groups.

Middle/junior high school: Apply ratios and proportions to solve practical problems.

Late high school: Solve problems involving loans, mortgages, and other practical applications involving geometric patterns or growth.

ASSESSMENT SYSTEMS

The learning standards tell schools what students are expected to learn, but they do not tell administrators what students actually are learning. Therefore, the key to a meaningful academic accountability process is the assessment of student learning based on these standards. As the ISBE says, "Specific standards make clear the types of tests and measures that accurately gauge student progress" (ISBE, 1997, p. iv). Creating assessments and performance indicators based on these standards is not a simple task. It requires decisions about which standards will be measured, how they will be measured, and at what cost.

Good assessments are critical to an accountability system because they may have a much more forceful influence on what is taught and how it is taught than the standards themselves do. In fact, many educational reforms have been called "measurement-driven" because assessment is thought to influence teaching methods and content more powerfully than any other single factor (Noble and Smith, 1994; Haertel, 1994). Most accountability systems rely heavily on standardized, multiple-choice assessments. Critics believe that overreliance on these tests has the effect of narrowing the curriculum (Haertel, 1994). That is, teachers concentrate their efforts on the type of learning that can be easily measured by multiple-choice questions, while devoting less time and energy to more complex and demanding instruction that leads to problem-solving, evaluation, and integration of learning. Multiple-choice tests are typically appropriate for only a small fraction of current academic standards.

Some school systems are moving toward assessments that use fewer multiple-choice items and instead focus more on "performance assessment," which generally involves asking open-ended questions and requiring students to perform tasks. Performance assessment includes "on-demand" testing methods that have long been a part of many of the large-scale testing systems in European nations, such as timed tests in which students write essays or solve math problems where they must show their work. More recent developments in large-scale assessment systems involve external assessments of student work done over a longer period of time, including science projects, term papers, or portfolios of student work.

There are several reasons why performance assessments have not been used more widely. Clearly, an important issue with these types of assessment devices is whether they are reliable and objective. When performance assessments are used for large-scale, high-stakes accountability systems, attention must be paid to scoring student work in an objective, rigorous way. In addition, these types of assessment systems are much more costly to implement and take longer to score than multiple-choice tests that are scored by a machine.

Despite these difficulties, some states have decided that the benefits outweigh the costs and have moved far in creating standards-based performance assessments. For instance, Kentucky's accountability system is based primarily on performance assessments and performance demonstrations. The reference examinations of the New Standards Project are another example of standards-based assessments requiring students to show their work solving problems, rather than answering multiple-choice questions.

New assessments have been under development by both the Illinois State Board of Education and the Chicago Public Schools. The ISBE has replaced the Illinois Goals Assessment Program (IGAP) with the Illinois Standards Achievement Test (ISAT), which is aligned more closely with the new learning standards. This new test includes more items that are not multiple choice, such as short-answer questions. The CPS has created its own set of academic standards and is developing a set of asessments—the Chicago Academic Standards Exams (CASE)— to be aligned with its new Chicago Academic Standards. Chicago plans to design assessments that "use fewer multiple-choice tests and more of the open-ended performance tests that mirror what students will have to do in the 'real world'" (CPS, n.d., p. 5).

Assessments Used in Illinois and Chicago

Although both Illinois and Chicago are moving to standards-based systems with new assessments, they have relied on available tests to drive the accountability process. Chicago still relies primarily on the Iowa Tests of Basic Skills (ITBS) in elementary grades, and its counterpart, the Tests of Achievement and Proficiency (TAP) in high school. All public schools in the city are required to test reading and math at nearly every grade. Science, social studies, and maps and diagrams tests are required at selected grades. Like many commercially published tests, the ITBS and TAP are entirely composed of multiple-choice questions.

ITBS and TAP are "norm-referenced" tests, which are designed to measure student performance in comparison with national average performance. (By contrast, "criterion-referenced" tests measure performance in relation to specific curriculum standards.) The content of norm-referenced tests is deliberately designed to sample broadly from a wide range of curricula in order to provide a basis for comparing students in a particular school with those in a national sample. These tests are not aligned with any specific curricular strategy or specific content and thus may be used across a range of schools.[1]

Illinois has relied primarily on the IGAP test, which was developed for and used exclusively by public schools in the state. The IGAP measured student and school achievement in five areas: reading, mathematics, writing, science, and social science. Each of these subjects was assessed at selected grades. The IGAP was primarily a multiple-choice test, although it did include a writing test that required students to write one or two essays, depending on their grade. In addition, the IGAP reading test, while multiple-choice, did not follow the format of most standardized reading tests. It included two lengthy reading passages instead of several shorter passages. For each question on the IGAP reading test, students were asked to evaluate the correctness of each response separately, rather than simply choosing the "best" answer. That is, a given question could have more than one correct answer.

Comparison of Trends on IGAP and ITBS

Table 1 compares ITBS and IGAP reading and math scores in the Chicago Public Schools. The table compares only the grades in which students took both tests (3rd, 6th, and 8th) and uses the only method of reporting scores that the two tests have in common—the percentage of students in the top two quartiles. (More on statistics for reporting scores in a later section.)

---

[1] The Chicago Academic Standards Exams will be used to supplement ITBS and TAP.

TABLE 1:　Trends in Mathematics and Reading in the Chicago Public Schools

Percentage of students above national norms in Grades 3, 6, and 8:

	Mathematics		Reading	
	IGAP	ITBS	IGAP	ITBS
1993	29	30	29	23
1994	30	28	27	23
1995	31	30	25	23
1996	37	31	23	26
1997	40	35	19	26
1998	42	38	21	29

IGAP = Illinois Goals Assesssment Program
ITBS = Iowa Tests of Basic Skills

Note: IGAP scores for 1998 were reported against a different set of norms from previous years.

The math results on the two tests were roughly parallel from 1993 to 1997, although after 1994 IGAP scores were higher, and, in fact, the IGAP scores increased more rapidly than the ITBS scores. The reading results were quite different and are an example of why the IGAP reading test was often criticized. While ITBS scores increased in 1996 and 1997 compared with the previous three years, IGAP reading scores steadily declined. Other school districts have claimed similar discrepancies between IGAP reading and other standardized tests used in those districts, although we do not have data from those districts to validate the claims. This comparison is not free of problems; as we discussed earlier, differences in ways that the tests measure reading could account for some discrepancies. Nonetheless, we still would not expect such markedly different patterns in the reading results.

External reviewers have carefully studied the IGAP over several years to determine both its technical and substantive adequacy. In 1995, one panel of distinguished reviewers concluded that IGAP was a "carefully thought out program" that "may well serve as a model for other states" (Roeber et al., 1995). A technical review of the equating procedures used to score tests on the same scale each year found no errors or other problems in the scoring and equating (Wright, Linacre, and Thum, 1996). Despite these expert assurances, the discrepancies in reading scores in Chicago (and apparently other districts) continued to raise questions about IGAP results.

STATISTICAL INDICATORS

In order for assessments to be used in school accountability, school-level test results must be reported in some statistical fashion. There are several different types of statistics available for examining achievement results. We have grouped the various aggregate indicators that are available into the following broad categories: average scores (performance of the average student), distribution of scores (proportion of students scoring at different performance levels), and measures of student growth (changes in student test scores over a specified time period).[2]

Average Scores

Most assessment systems report some sort of average score or "measure of central tendency." These averages are reported as means (the most commonly used) or medians (the score of the middle-scoring student).[3] Mean ISAT "scale scores" for each school are available, although they do not appear on the Illinois School Report Card. The CPS reports ITBS and TAP median "grade equivalents" and median "national percentile ranks" for each school (see sidebar on next page).

---

[2] Table 2 shows sample statistical indicators for a Chicago elementary school.

[3] Both means and medians can be used in different situations; the median is more stable with smaller numbers of test scores.

TYPES OF TEST SCORES

Norm-referenced statistics: Norm-referenced tests are designed to measure student performance in comparison with a sample group, often a national sample.   Nationally normed tests are primarily designed to compare the performance of particular students and schools against a national sample of students and therefore provide an external yardstick by which to measure a school's achievement.

Scale score: On the IGAP, the basic level of reporting for student scores in reading, mathematics, science, and social science was the "scale score" ranging from 0 to 500.   ISAT scale scores for the same subjects range from 120 to 200.   A scale score is a type of standard score based on the raw score (the overall number of items that the student answered correctly).   Scale scores are aggregated to produce average (mean) scores at the school level.

Grade equivalent: A grade equivalent is a decimal number that describes student performance in terms of the typical performance of students tested in a given grade and month.   A grade equivalent of 8.5 indicates that the student performed at the level of a "typical" student in the fifth month of eighth grade.   Typical performance is determined by the performance of students in the national sample of students used to norm the test.

National percentile rank: A student's national percentile rank shows a student's performance relative to the national norming sample. Specifically, it indicates the percentage of students in the national norming sample whose scores were lower than the student taking the test.   For example, a national percentile rank of 89 means that the student scored higher than 89 percent of students in the national sample.

National quartile: Students are grouped into national quartiles based on their national percentile ranks.   National percentile ranks of 1 to 25 are in the first (bottom) quartile.   The second quartile includes percentile ranks of 26 to 50.   The third quartile includes 51 to 75. Finally, the fourth (top) quartile includes percentile ranks of 76 to 99.

TABLE 2: Sample Statistical Indicators for an Elementary School's Sixth-Grade Reading, 1996

	IGAP	ITBS
Average scores:		
Average scale score	227	NA
Median national percentile	NA	44
Median grade equivalent	NA	6.5
Score distributions:		
Pct. of students at or above national norm	NA	40.5
Pct. of students in each national quartile		
First (bottom) quartile	30	26.2
Second quartile	31	38.1
Third quartile	27	26.2
Fourth (top) quartile	12	9.5
Pct. of students meeting state goals		
Not meeting state goals	32	NA
Meeting state goals	57	NA
Exceeding state goals	11	NA
Measures of growth:		
Mean gain from 5th to 6th grade (in grade equivalents) of current sixth-graders	NA	1.1

IGAP = Illinois Goals Assesssment Program
ITBS = Iowa Tests of Basic Skills
NA = Not available

Distributions of Scores

In addition to statistics of the average student, test scores are also reported in terms of the distribution among students. These statistics show how many children are scoring at different levels of performance.

Percentage of students at or above the national norm: The CPS reports the percentage of students scoring at or above the 50th percentile as the "percentage of students scoring at or above the national norm." National percentile ranks are norm-referenced, that is, they compare performance relative to the performance of students in the national sample (see sidebar). The median student in the national sample is always assigned a national percentile rank of 50; by definition, the median student has scored higher than 50 percent of the other students. The state did not report IGAP in this way, although it is possible to compute the percentage of students scoring *above* the national norm by adding together those in the third and fourth national quartiles.[4] Although the IGAP was not itself nationally normed, it was statistically equated to a nationally normed test in order to report the percentage of students scoring in each of the four national quartiles.

Percentage of students in each national quartile: The percentage of students in each of the four national quartiles is reported for ITBS and TAP. This is a norm-referenced measure in that the categories are based on how student performance compares with the performance of students in the norming sample.

Looking at the percentage of students in each national quartile over time provides more information than the percentage of students at or above national norms. It is especially useful in schools where students typically score well above or well below the 50th percentile; year-to-year changes that might not be evident in the percentage at or above national norms might be discerned by looking at the quartiles.

---

[4] "At or above" the national norm includes those in the 50th percentile or higher; "above" the national norm excludes those in the 50th percentile.

Percentage of students meeting state goals: The state has set specific scale scores that students must achieve for each subject and grade in order to meet state goals or standards. IGAP scores were categorized as not meeting, meeting, or exceeding state goals.   At the school level, IGAP reported the percentage of students in each of these three categories for each subject and grade.   The new ISAT uses four categories of scale scores: exceeds standards, meets standards, below standards, and "academic warning."   For both IGAP and ISAT, the top two categories have often been combined, with the emphasis placed on the percentage of students who meet or exceed state goals or standards.

In addition to reporting these results for each subject and grade level, the Illinois State Board of Education reports aggregate results combining all subjects and grades tested.   This aggregate result calculates the number of individual scores (rather than students) in each category.   It is this aggregate result that is typically used for accountability purposes.

Statistics that Measure Student Growth

Most of the other statistics we have discussed are "status outcomes."   That is, they measure the status of student performance in a school at a particular point in time.   For accountability purposes, however, it is more important to measure average annual student growth because a school should be accountable for what students learn while they are enrolled. A measure of student growth shows how much students gained, on average, from one year to the next on skills measured by the test.   It gives schools credit for students who may have entered school with low test scores, but who gained a great deal during the school year.   Such a measure also shows schools where students may have entered with high scores but gained little in terms of achievement on the test.

The CPS reports average annual gains on the ITBS for all students tested and for only those students who were in a school for the entire school year.[5]   Gains are reported in terms of the

---

[5] The CPS does not calculate gains on the TAP test, primarily because the TAP is not mandatory for every grade.   Similarly, the IGAP test was given only at selected grades.

average annual growth of students as measured in grade equivalents. For example, a school's current eighth-graders have a mean grade equivalent of 8.7. The previous year, when these same students were in seventh grade, they had a mean grade equivalent of 7.5. From this, we calculate that the mean annual growth was 1.2 (8.7 minus 7.5). The 1.2 can be interpreted as one year and two months' growth (assuming a ten-month school year). This can be compared with the national norm, which is 1.0 by definition.[6]

USE OF SCHOOL PERFORMANCE INDICATORS FOR ACCOUNTABILITY: PERFORMANCE STANDARDS

In the prior sections, we discussed academic content standards (which tell schools what students are expected to know), assessments (which measure what students actually do know), and performance statistics (which provide a way of reporting the results of assessments). One more piece is needed to hold schools accountable: a performance standard for schools that indicates how well schools should perform in terms of the various statistics.

The performance indicator at the heart of Illinois's accountability efforts is the aggregate percentage of student test scores (all subjects and grades combined) that do not meet state goals. A school is categorized as not meeting state standards if more than 50 percent of its test scores do not meet state goals in a given year. The Chicago Public Schools has relied mainly on results from the ITBS and TAP for its accountability system. The CPS has set a performance standard that schools must have at least 15 percent of their students at or above national norms on ITBS or TAP reading in order to avoid academic probation. Schools with slightly higher levels of performance can be placed on remediation. Schools with even lower reading results (in conjunction with other considerations, as discussed later) may be reconstituted.

---

[6] Bryk et al. (1998) and others have demonstrated weaknesses in the grade equivalent metric as a measure of change. The changing of test forms each year exacerbates these problems, and there are real questions about how "equivalent" the grade equivalents really are.

Another informal performance standard is often used for ITBS and TAP. These tests are designed to have 50 percent of students in the national sample at or above national norms. Chicago schools tend to perform at a much lower level. In 1988, the Illinois legislature enacted school reform legislation that used this 50 percent figure as a performance standard that Chicago schools were expected to attain. Although this criterion does not currently have formal status as a performance standard, it is generally used among CPS officials and others as a mark of good achievement that deserves recognition.

Schools not meeting the Illinois or Chicago academic performance standards become candidates for intervention. The next sections provide more detail on how these performance standards are used by the accountability systems in Illinois and Chicago.

The State Accountability System in Illinois

In January 1997, the Illinois General Assembly amended earlier accountability legislation to create a new system of identifying and intervening in troubled schools. The new system is based solely on test results and has two tiers. First, a school can be placed on an "Academic Early Warning List." Second, schools that do not improve within a specified time period can then be placed on the "Academic Watch List."

Under the new system, a school can end up on the Academic Early Warning List for one of two reasons:

- If more than 50 percent of its test scores do not meet state assessment standards for two consecutive years.
- If the proportion of test scores meeting state standards declines by 20 percent over a four-year period.

Schools in the first group (not meeting assessment standards) can be removed from the list whenever 50 percent of student scores meet or exceed state expectations. If, within two years, these schools are still on the list and have not shown adequate yearly progress (as defined by the state), they can be moved to the more serious Academic Watch List.

Schools in the second group (declining test scores) can be removed from the list when the percentage of scores not meeting state goals is reduced so that it is equal to or less than an average from prior years. These schools will not be put on the Academic Watch List unless they fail to meet state assessment standards for two consecutive years.

In September 1997, 125 schools in the state were placed on the Academic Early Warning List. Of these, 93 were in Chicago, and most were already on academic probation as designated by the Chicago Public Schools (see section below).[7] Once a school is on the Early Warning List, it is supposed to receive additional assistance from the state, including a staff member assigned to help the school, more frequent school quality reviews, targeted school improvement funds, and assistance in obtaining services. The school must also revise its school improvement plan. The Academic Watch List carries consequences including the appointment of an external improvement panel and the possibility that an independent authority may be appointed to oversee the school, and pupils and administrative staff may be reassigned.[8]

The Chicago Public Schools Accountability System

Prior to the development of the Illinois system described above, the Chicago Public Schools developed its own accountability system as a result of the 1995 state legislation that created the Chicago School Reform Board of Trustees. That legislation made it much easier for the school board to intervene in troubled schools. The CPS subsequently established a system of intervention with three-levels of increasing external control: remediation (introduced in the 1995-96 school year), probation

---

[7] In the 1998-99 school year, there were 87 schools on the Early Warning List, including 58 in Chicago. Because of the replacement of IGAP by ISAT, the state board decided that no new schools would be placed on the Early Warning List for 1999-2000 and that no school would be placed on the Academic Watch List based on a single year of ISAT data.

[8] In April 2000, the State Superintendent of Education appointed a School Designation Task Force to make recommendations regarding the alignment of school accountability measures with the Illinois Learning Standards. The task force report, issued in September 2000, proposed an accountability system that would include a continuum of incentives, interventions, and sanctions (ISBE, 2000).

(introduced in 1996-97), and reconstitution (introduced in 1997-98).[9] In 1997-98, 25 schools were placed on academic remediation, which introduced some additional resources into the schools. In the same school year, 115 schools were placed on academic probation as a result of having fewer than 15 percent of students at or above national norms on ITBS/TAP reading.[10]

All schools on probation are paired with an external partner that provides both educational and organizational guidance. Most external partners are affiliated with local universities, and many have had extensive experience working with Chicago Public Schools. The external partners vary widely in their strategies for improving student achievement, and the schools are given some choice in selecting their external partners. In addition to an external partner, each probation school is assigned a probation manager to oversee the process. These probation managers are typically experienced principals, either still serving schools or retired, and come from both the public and private school sectors.

Reconstituted schools remained on probation and continued to receive the support given to other probation schools. However, reconstitution also involved a serious restructuring of the school, including possible removal of the principal and staff. In June 1997, the Chicago Academic Accountability Council (a legislatively mandated body broadly charged with evaluating school progress in the CPS) recommended ten schools (eight high schools and two elementary schools) for intervention or reconstitution. The ten schools were selected because of their extremely low test scores (7% of students or fewer scoring at or above national norms in four of the last five years), poor student attendance rates, and, in the high schools, very low graduation rates. The CPS leadership decided to reconstitute seven high schools from this list of ten. During the summer of 1997, five of the seven principals were replaced. In the schools where principals were not replaced, one school had just appointed a new principal, and one principal was assigned a "co-principal." All staff (teachers and support staff) were re-

---

[9] Although the previous superintendent attempted to initiate a remediation program, it was introduced on a large scale by the new administration in the 1995-96 school year.

[10] In the 2000-2001 school year, there were 24 schools on remediation and 76 on probation.

quired to reapply for their jobs. Interview teams rehired about two-thirds of the teachers.

In the 1999-2000 school year, after negotiating a new contract with the Chicago Teachers Union, the CPS introduced "re-engineering" as a step between probation and reconstitution. Re-engineering includes peer evaluation of teacher performance as well as teacher involvement in reviewing school improvement plans. The following year, the CPS replaced reconstitution with "intervention," which allows teachers and other staff a year to demonstrate their ability before facing expedited removal.[11]

RECOMMENDATIONS

We have discussed developments in standards-based testing and the current use of test scores for accountability purposes. The Illinois State Board of Education and Chicago Public Schools have developed new accountability systems around new standards and assessments. We offer six recommendations on how these new systems should use standards-based assessment results for school accountability:

- Designing assessments to encourage good teaching;
- Accurately measuring the achievement of all students;
- Holding schools accountable for gains in student learning;
- Developing assessments for special education, limited-English-proficient, and younger students;
- Tracking a variety of other statistical indicators in order to ensure the integrity of high-stakes assessments;
- Creating an overall, long-term assessment plan.[12]

Designing Assessments to Encourage Good Teaching

Both Illinois and Chicago have adopted new academic standards, and both are developing assessments based on these

---

[11] See Siple, 1998; Kelleher, 2000; Ortiz, 2000.

[12] Several of these recommendations draw from the work of Bryk et al. (1998), who write specifically about the use of achievement test results for accountability purposes in the Chicago Public Schools.

standards. The development of assessments and statistics that explicitly measure school performance in relation to the standards is probably the most critical part of the accountability system because schools will inevitably target instruction in order to improve performance on the test (sometimes called "teaching to the test"). This is not necessarily a bad thing, so long as the assessments are designed such that "teaching to the test" means good teaching. Assessment design should include: (1) tests that are actually based on academic content standards; (2) a variety of testing techniques; (3) measurement of both basic and higher-order skills; and (4) reporting results in ways directly related to the academic standards.

(1) Assessment development should proceed from the standards and not the other way around: Clearly, when a state or school system adopts standards, it is making decisions about what students should know and what teachers should teach. Schools, however, are not as likely to focus instruction on these standards as on what is tested (or more specifically, what is reported and what they are held accountable for). Therefore, if we want schools to teach the material embodied in the standards, assessments should be specifically tailored to the standards. The development of an assessment system should begin with questions concerning how a standard can best be measured, as well as the kinds of test questions that will give reliable information about whether students have achieved a standard. In this way, assessment development proceeds directly from the standards. A less desirable alternative is to select from a range of previously developed tests the one that most closely matches the standards and try to extrapolate measurement of standards from the items on the test.

(2) The assessment system should contain a variety of testing techniques and not solely multiple-choice questions: Some schools may place inappropriate emphasis on teaching students test-taking skills and may construct classroom work that mirrors the multiple-choice test format. Therefore, it is important to use a variety of assessment techniques that measure student performance on the kind of work (e.g., writing essays, solving math problems) that teachers should be assigning. Moreover, multiple-choice items will likely be inadequate to measure performance for all academic standards.

(3) The assessment system should measure not only basic skills, but also higher-order thinking: The system should administer more in-depth and demanding tests of students' higher-order skills as described in the learning standards.   Such tests could exist at selected grade levels or benchmarks, could play a role in entrance and exit decisions about individual students, and could be reported at the school and district levels in the accountability system.

(4) Assessment results should be reported in concrete ways directly related to the standards: The tests used in Illinois and Chicago are reported in ways that are abstract and separate from the actual content of the tests.   For instance, if we are told that 60 percent of third-graders meet or exceed state goals for math, we do not know exactly what these students can do. Have the students mastered multiplication?   Similarly, if the median ITBS grade equivalent for third-grade math is 3.8, we know that, on average, the students are at or above the national norm, but we do not know what that means in terms of skill mastery.   In short, standards-based assessments should be constructed to produce results that provide direct information about what materials and information students have mastered and what they have not.   Standardized tests can be constructed and scaled such that scores give an indication of what students can and cannot do.

Accurately Measuring the Achievement of All Students

Illinois focuses on the percentage of student test scores that do not meet state goals, and Chicago focuses on the percentage of students at or above national norms.   Although these statistics are useful and meaningful measures of the current status of a school, they are limited in their ability to track changes in performance over time, particularly in schools where most students are well above or well below the specified criterion.

The percentage of students meeting a particular criterion puts the focus on those students very near the criterion.   Students with very low scores may improve considerably but not reach the cutoff.   Students with very high scores may also improve, yet these improvements would not be detected because they started above the criterion.   The mean (average) score is a better indicator for detecting change across the distribution of scores because it reflects changes of all students.

Choosing the correct indicator becomes very important in a high-stakes environment because of the incentives that may be created by the particular indicator. If schools face sanctions based on the percentage of students scoring at or above a particular cutoff, they may focus their attention on the particular students who can most easily be moved up to the threshold. The statistical indicators should also create incentives for broader-based improvements—including lower and higher scoring students. Because the mean is affected by all scores, it is more informative than the percentage of students reaching a particular cutoff score.

Holding Schools Accountable for Gains in Student Learning

Both the Illinois and Chicago assessment programs hold schools accountable based on student achievement status at a given point in time. Status scores do not, however, tell enough about where the students started and how much gain (growth) they made in achievement while enrolled in a school. These factors should be considered when holding schools accountable for student performance.

Schools should be held accountable for overall (average) student gains: Reliance on the measurement of current status can be misleading because schools whose students start out with high skills are likelier to do better on achievement tests than schools whose students come to the school with few skills, regardless of the quality of the instructional program. Although using mean test scores over time is better than using a percentage of students who reach a specified criterion, it is still not the best way to measure school improvement. A change over time in the student body that the school is serving can either lower or improve the status scores, regardless of changes in school quality. For instance, annual average test scores can actually decrease at the same time that the degree of student learning within the school is increasing because new students with lower skills are entering the school (Meyer, 1996).

Student mobility is a major problem in many school systems, including the Chicago Public Schools. In the typical elementary school, about 80 percent of students tested in one year were also tested the previous year at the same schools (Bryk et al., 1998). In order to assess how well a school is educating the students who have been there long enough to learn from that school, we need an indicator that focuses on growth rather than just current status. Therefore, we should focus on gains in achievement for students who have been taught in that school for at least a minimum length of time (probably close to a full year). An indicator of student learning should have good measures of where students begin as well as where they end up.

A gains-based accountability system can also be pushed further in a "value added" direction. How much does the school contribute to the child's learning above and beyond contributions of the home and community? What is the value that the school adds to the student's learning?[13] This value-added approach requires additional information about the schools and the students themselves. These variables would be included in a statistical model to estimate a school's value-added contribution to student learning.

Regardless of the specific model used, gains in achievement are key to using assessment results in an accountability system. The gains form the basis for asking whether the degree of learning in a school is increasing or decreasing over time. Any gains-based system necessitates that the assessment results themselves be comparable from year to year. Such comparability requires careful equating procedures that will provide a stable indicator over time.

Ideally, schools should also be held accountable for the gains of students who start at different levels, although adequate methods for measuring this are not yet available: The accountability system should ensure that all students are included and that special attention is focused on the lowest-achieving students. Under the current system, schools may have incentives to exclude low-scoring students. Holding schools accountable for students' growth may provide incentives for better serving these students.

With the use of status (point in time) scores, a school may appear to be serving students well, even if it provides weak instruction to students with low skills. This can happen if a

---

[13] See Meyer, 1996; Bryk et al., 1998; Bryk et al., 1994.

school has high-scoring students who raise the overall status scores. For example, one school in Chicago gave up its gifted program to another school in order to make space available for more students from the local neighborhood. The first school had been among the better-performing schools in the city, but its performance had been inflated by a program that operated separately from the rest of the school. The school became a below-average performer after the gifted program was transferred. In 1996, about 50 percent of its students in grades 3-8 were reading at or above national norms; the following year, this performance indicator dropped to just under 25 percent.

Schools with mixed populations are often let off the hook because they have high-scoring students who keep the schools from being subject to intervention. Schools should be accountable for the instruction that they offer to *all* students. Using gain scores would mitigate these problems, but this solution is not sufficient because students with weak backgrounds and little outside support may still post lower annual gains (in the long run) than high-achieving students. Therefore, we recommend that the accountability system focus not only on overall student gains, but also on the gains of students with different achievement levels. Unfortunately, adequate methods for this type of analysis are not yet available, but we believe they are worth pursuing.

Developing Assessments for Special Education, Limited-English-Proficient, and Primary Grade Students

Some special education students can be tested using the assessments developed for the general school population, but this is not always appropriate. These students are often excluded from testing or at least from score reporting. It is critical to find a way to hold schools accountable for special education students. We note, however, that simply including these students in the regular testing system may be inappropriate in many cases. Illinois and Chicago should actively pursue development of assessments for special education students that are based on academic standards for the general student population.

Similarly, students with limited English proficiency must be included in the assessment system. These students should be tracked both in their progress on the academic standards and in their progress in learning English. The state has developed the

Illinois Measure of Annual Growth in English (IMAGE), which assesses student progress in reading and writing in grades 3-11.

Finally, the assessment system should address how younger students are to be assessed. Most standardized tests are of questionable reliability with the youngest students, yet there is little doubt that the early school years are crucial for learning literacy and math skills. Other means of checking progress with younger students are needed, such as teacher observation instruments and portfolios of student work that can be reliably scored.

Tracking Other Statistical Indicators

An accountability system needs safeguards to prevent key high-stakes performance indicators from being corrupted. Building in a variety of other indicators can help to preserve the integrity of performance-based statistics.

First, it is important to calculate the percentage of students tested as well as the percentage of students exempt from testing. Schools may attempt to improve school test performance by not testing students who they believe will not do well on the assessments. Therefore, it is critical to calculate the percentage of students actually tested. It is also important to track the percentage of students who are exempt from testing (such as new students with limited English proficiency or certain categories of special education students), although they should not be counted against the school in its percentage tested. Chicago plans to calculate percentage tested, and Illinois has already done so, although the Illinois percentage does not exclude students who are exempt from testing.

In addition to tracking test scores, careful attention should be given to a school's graduation, dropout, and out-mobility rates. These indicators are important in their own right as critical measures of student success in school. While these measures may reflect changes in school demographics over time, they can also be important reflections of whether students remain in school and are not pushed out to raise school test scores.

Creating a Long-Term Assessment Plan

An assessment plan requires a long-term vision. Because of test security needs, the majority of questions on tests must be changed each year. However, one danger of changing tests annually is that scores may not be sufficiently comparable from one year to the next because of the frequent variation in items and content. Therefore, tests used in different years and tests used at different grade levels must be statistically equated. The equating procedures can be planned ahead, using an embedded core of items that will be repeated in order to provide the necessary comparability.

A long-term assessment plan should also allow for making some of the test content public on an annual basis. In releasing test results, a small sample of items can be used to illustrate the meaning of specific scores and refer back to the academic standards. This will help to focus discussions about student achievement and educational accountability on subject material and content rather than on abstract numerical scores.

CONCLUSION

The Illinois State Board of Education and the Chicago Public Schools have both moved to develop standards-based assessment and accountability systems. Accountability systems can be an integral component in an overall school improvement program if carefully conceived and implemented. We have made recommendations for accountability systems that we hope will further this work. First, an accountability system should start with solid, clearly defined, and well thought-out academic content standards that specify what students should know and be able to do.

Second, these standards should be translated into a system of high-quality assessments. A good assessment system is critical because assessments may drive teaching methods and curriculum more powerfully than any other factor. These assessments should be explicitly designed to test attainment of the content standards. General tests meant to be "curriculum neutral" are not appropriate in a standards-based system. These assessments should measure the full range of academic standards and not be limited exclusively to multiple-choice tests or basic-skills testing, which might result in narrowing or "dumbing down" the curriculum. Better assessments are also needed for special education students, students with limited English proficiency, and very young students to show how these students are progressing on the academic content standards. Finally, the assessment system should be well equated from year to year, and parts of its content should be made public each year to help educators, parents, and policymakers understand the meaning of test results in a concrete way.

Third, for standards and assessments to be useful for accountability purposes, the assessments must be reported through a set of performance indicators. These indicators should accurately reflect what schools are doing and should not create perverse incentives for schools to manipulate test scores. Therefore, performance indicators should be designed to have concrete meaning in terms of the content standards. The indicators should take into account how much students have gained in knowledge, in addition to the current status of students at a given point. Emphasis should be placed on measures of average (mean) performance, rather than on percentages of students meeting certain cutoff points, which can be insensitive to changes in very low-performing schools or very high-performing schools, and thus have more potential for manipulation. Finally, indicators of other factors in addition to achievement results should be reported. Such measures, including percentage of students tested, percentage of students graduating or dropping out, and attendance, can be safeguards to ensure that schools are not manipulating achievement results.

REFERENCES

Bryk, Anthony S., Paul E. Deabster, John Q. Easton, Stuart Luppescu, and Yeow Meng Thum (1994). "Measuring Achievement Gains in the Chicago Public Schools," *Education and Urban Society*, vol. 26, no. 3 (May 1994), pp. 306-319.

Bryk, Anthony S., Yeow Meng Thum, John Q. Easton, and Stuart Luppescu (1998). *Academic Productivity of Chicago Public Elementary Schools*. Chicago: Consortium on Chicago School Research.

CCSSO (1996). *States' Status on Standards: 1996 Update*. Washington, D.C.: Council of Chief State School Officers.

CGCS (1996). *Becoming the Best: Standards and Assessment Development in the Great City Schools.* Washington, D.C.: Council of the Great City Schools.

CPS (n.d.). *Expecting More: Higher Standards for Chicago's Students.* Chicago: Chicago Public Schools, Office of Accountability.

Commission on Standards for School Mathematics (1989). *Curriculum and Evaluation: Standards for School Mathematics.* Reston, Va.: National Council of Teachers of Mathematics.

Elmore, Richard F., Charles H. Abelmann, and Susan H. Fuhrman (1996). "The New Accountability in State Education Reform: From Process to Performance." In Helen F. Ladd, ed., *Holding Schools Accountable: Performance-Based Reform in Education.* Washington, D.C.: Brookings Institution.

Haertel, Edward H. (1994). "Theoretical and Practical Implications." In Thomas R. Guskey, ed., *High Stakes Performance Assessment: Perspectives on Kentucky's Educational Reform.* Thousand Oaks, Calif.: Corwin Press.

ISBE (1997). *Illinois Learning Standards.* Springfield: Illinois State Board of Education.

_____ (2000). *School Designation Task Force: A Report and Recommendations to the State Superintendent.* Springfield: Illinois State Board of Education, September 30, 2000.

Kelleher, Maureen (2000). "Great Principals Needed to Rescue Intervention," *Catalyst: Voices of Chicago School Reform,* August 2000.

Meyer, Robert (1996). "Value-Added Indicators of School Performance," In Eric Hanushek and Dale W. Jorgenson, eds., *Improving the Performance of America's Schools.* Washington, D.C.: National Academy Press.

New Standards Project (1997). *Performance Standards.* Three volumes. Washington, D.C.: National Center for Education and the Economy, and the University of Pittsburgh.

Noble, Audrey J., and Mary Lee Smith (1994). *Measurement-Driven Reform: Research on Policy, Practice, Repercussion.* Los Angeles: National Center for Research in Evaluation, Standards, and Student Testing.

Ortiz, Mario G. (2000). "Board Scrambles to Launch New Effort," *Catalyst: Voices of Chicago School Reform,* September 2000.

Roeber, Edward, et al. (1995). "Preliminary Draft of the Illinois Goals Assessment Program Initial Report." Unpublished manuscript. Springfield: Illinois State Board of Education.

Siple, Julie (1998). "Board, Union Split on Reconstitution, Advisory," *Catalyst: Voices of Chicago School Reform*, December 1998.

Wright, Benjamin D., John Michael Linacre, and Yeow Meng Thum (1996). "IGAP Reading Tests, 1993-95: Re-equating and Disaggregating Analyses." Technical Report for the Illinois State Board of Education. Chicago: MESA Psychometrics Laboratory, University of Chicago.

IMPROVING STUDENT LEARNING: HOW DOES MONEY MATTER?

Lawrence O. Picus

Ask most teachers or school administrators if they could do a better job educating children if they had more money, and virtually every one of them would offer a resounding "yes." Ask them what they would do with that money, and their answer would be less clear. Often they do not have a strategic sense of how the money could be used, and more often than not, the answer will conflict with what other teachers or administrators say is needed. Worse, despite the fact that there is substantial evidence our schools could be doing better, most will suggest spending the new money exactly as existing funds are spent.

Despite the general belief that "money matters," the statistical evidence of a relationship between spending and student outcomes has been mixed. For the last 15 years or more, Eric Hanushek has conducted in-depth analyses of "education production function" studies (studies that attempt to link changes in student outcomes with certain school characteristics such as per-pupil expenditures) and has concluded that there is little evidence to support the existence of a relationship between the level of school funding and student achievement (see, e.g., Hanushek, 1997). Others have questioned Hanushek's conclusion, arguing that money can, in fact, matter.[1] A study by Wenglinsky (1997), relying on national databases, suggests that money does matter but that the relationship between school spending and student achievement not direct. He found that in the fourth grade, increased expenditures for instruction and district administration yielded lower pupil-teacher ratios that increased student achievement. In the eighth grade, expenditures for instruction and administration also yielded lower pupil-teacher ratios. Behavior problems were reduced, and the

---

[1] See, e.g., Murnane, 1991; Ferguson, 1991; Hedges, Laine, and Greenwald, 1994a, 1994b.

school's social environment was improved, which, in turn, led to better performance in math.

To date, the debate over whether money matters has focused on complex statistical analyses and detailed discussions about whether the production function approach is appropriate for estimating relationships between spending and student achievement. Much of the debate on the effect of resources on student achievement has been based on the production function approach. Yet as Monk (1992) points out, most efforts to define an educational production function have failed. Despite the inability to relate educational inputs to outcomes, the strong belief that money is important to improving school performance still has a strong following.

A number of researchers, notably Picus and Fazal (1996) and Cooper (1993), have looked closely at how school districts and school sites use the dollars they receive. The most stunning conclusion from this work is the consistency in the pattern with which schools spend their resources. Across the United States, schools spend approximately 60 percent of their resources on direct student instruction. This figure holds true regardless of how much is spent per pupil and seems to be consistent across grade levels. These findings suggest that the effectiveness of new money on student achievement may be limited by the fact that these new resources are used in the same way as existing resources, limiting the potential effectiveness of those new dollars.

Given that the United States spent over \$340 billion on K-12 public education in 1998-99, understanding the impact that money has on student outcomes is important. The purpose of this chapter is twofold: (1) to review existing studies that attempt to answer the question of whether money matters and to provide an objective analysis of the debate in terms of policy outcomes; and (2) to consider alternative approaches to answering the question of whether additional resources lead to gains in student outcomes.

Wenglinsky (1997) offers two perspectives on the relationship between money and student outcomes. The traditional focus, based on the school finance community's long-standing interest in equity, assumes that all spending has an impact on student performance and that it is important to ensure that all children have access to equitable and adequate levels of resources. The second perspective focuses on productivity, arguing that low-performing school districts need to change spending patterns and focus their resources on factors that have been shown to improve student performance, such as reduced class size. A corollary of this view is that central bureaucracy should be reduced and school sites be given more autonomy to make budgetary and resource allocation decisions.

The next section of this chapter focuses on the traditional view, offering data on how educational spending and resource allocation has changed over time and describing some of the major shifts that have taken place in the litigation that is so much a part of school finance reform. The third section attempts to describe what we know about the productivity perspective, offering more details on the debate over whether money matters and trying to find a common thread to help make sense of the complex statistical analyses on which this work is based. In the fourth section, the focus shifts to what we know about how educational resources are used at the district, school, and even classroom levels. If how money is spent does make a difference, then it is important to understand how current patterns are similar to, or different from, the patterns that our research indicates might lead to improved student learning. The fifth section of this chapter offers some policy strategies for more effective use of resources to improve student performance.

EQUITY IN SCHOOL FUNDING: CURRENT STATUS

Spending for Education

Hanushek (1994a) observes that real expenditures (in inflation-adjusted 1990 dollars) for public K-12 education in the United States increased from $2 billion in 1890 to nearly $190 billion in 1990. He further points out that growth in expenditures for education was more than three times the rate of growth in the Gross National Product (GNP); K-12 education represented some 3.6 percent of GNP in 1990, compared with less than 1 percent a century before. Picus and Fazal (1996) show that real per-pupil expenditures in the United States increased by nearly 70 percent during the 1960s, almost 22 percent in the 1970s, and over 48 percent in the 1980s. The increases in the 1960s appear to reflect additional expenditures by the federal government under the Elementary and Secondary Education Act of 1965, as well as the resulting additional efforts on the part of states. In the 1970s, the increases in per-pupil spending resulted from new special education programs and, in many school districts, from declining enrollments that were proportionately greater than real declines in total available resources. In the 1980s, much of the increase in expenditures seems to be the result of reform efforts sparked by the publication of the report of the National Commission on Excellence in Education (NCEE, 1983) and by various education interest groups.

As Table 1 shows, spending on public elementary and secondary schools represented 3.1 percent of Gross Domestic Product (GDP) in 1959-60. This figure rose to 4.4 percent of GDP in 1970-71, declined to 3.5 percent in 1985, and has stood at about 4 percent since 1990. Table 2 shows that real per-pupil expenditures increased by 215 percent between 1959-60 and 1996-97. There was also dramatic variation in spending increases across the 50 states and the District of Columbia during that 37-year period. At the extremes, expenditures in New Jersey increased by nearly 400 percent, more than three times the growth rate in Arizona, where the increase was about 125 percent. In 1959-60, real per-pupil expenditures in New Jersey were actually lower than they were in Arizona. However, by 1996-97, New Jersey was spending more than twice as much per pupil as Arizona. The increase in real per-pupil expenditures in Illinois was less than the national average, measuring approximately 175 percent between 1959-60 and 1996-97 (see Table 2).

What has this additional money bought? The most obvious answer is more teachers. Barro (1992) estimated that teacher salaries account for 53 percent of all current spending by school districts. Moreover, he estimated that as districts receive additional funds, they spend approximately half on teachers, with 40 percent going to reductions in class size and 10 percent devoted to increased teacher salaries. To demonstrate the effect of this emphasis on reducing class size, the *Digest of Education Statistics* shows that nationally, the pupil-teacher ratio in public K-12 schools declined from 26.9 in 1955 to 16.8 in 1998. Moreover, the pupil-teacher ratio declined every year but one between 1955 and 1990 (NCES, 1999, Table 65). Although the pupil-teacher ratio is not a perfect measure of class size, reductions of this magnitude reflect smaller classes in virtually all states.

TABLE 1:   Total Expenditures for Public Elementary and Secondary
Schools, 1959-60 to 1998-99

	$ millions	As pct. of GDP
1959-60	15,613	3.1
1961-62	18,373	3.4
1963-64	21,325	3.5
1965-66	26,248	3.7
1967-68	32,977	4.0
1969-70	40,683	4.1
1970-71	45,500	4.4
1971-72	48,050	4.3
1972-73	51,852	4.2
1973-74	56,970	4.1
1974-75	64,846	4.3
1975-76	70,601	4.3
1976-77	74,194	4.1
1977-78	80,844	4.0
1978-79	86,712	3.8
1979-80	95,962	3.8
1980-81	104,125	3.7
1981-82	111,186	3.6
1982-83	118,425	3.7
1983-84	127,500	3.6
1984-85	137,000	3.5
1985-86	148,600	3.6
1986-87	160,900	3.6
1987-88	172,699	3.7
1988-89	192,977	3.8
1989-90	212,770	3.9
1990-91	229,430	4.0
1991-92	241,055	4.1
1992-93	252,935	4.1
1993-94	265,307	4.0
1994-95	279,000	4.0
1995-96	293,646	4.0
1996-97	313,131	4.1
1997-98	329,800	4.1
1998-99	344,200	4.1

Source: NCES, 1999, Tables 31 and 32.

TABLE 2:   Current Expenditures Per Pupil in Public Elementary and
Secondary Schools, in Constant 1996-97 Dollars, 1959-60 to 1996-97

	1959-60	1969-70	1979-80	1989-90	1996-97	Pct. change 1960-97
United States	$2,029	$3,433	$4,650	$6,232	$6,392	215.0
Alabama	1,304	2,288	3,299	4,164	4,903	276.0
Alaska	2,955	4,722	9,677	10,552	9,097	207.9
Arizona	2,183	3,029	4,034	5,073	4,940	126.3
Arkansas	1,218	2,388	3,223	4,361	4,840	297.4
California	2,293	3,648	4,642	5,495	5,414	136.1
Colorado	2,142	3,104	4,955	5,907	5,728	167.4
Connecticut	2,358	4,002	4,954	9,808	8,901	277.5
Delaware	2,465	3,786	5,856	7,257	7,804	216.6
Dist. of Columbia	2,332	4,284	6,671	11,207	9,019	286.7
Florida	1,718	3,081	3,867	6,254	5,986	248.4
Georgia	1,371	2,473	3,327	5,350	5,708	316.3
Hawaii	1,755	3,536	4,752	5,567	6,144	250.1
Idaho	1,567	2,538	3,396	3,852	4,732	202.0
Illinois	2,371	3,826	5,294	6,405	6,557	176.5
Indiana	1,994	3,062	3,853	5,765	6,605	231.2
Iowa	1,989	3,551	4,762	5,573	6,047	204.0
Kansas	1,881	3,243	4,448	5,947	6,158	227.4
Kentucky	1,260	2,293	3,482	4,687	5,929	370.6
Louisiana	2,012	2,726	3,668	4,885	5,201	158.5
Maine	1,529	2,913	3,733	6,724	6,774	343.0
Maryland	2,124	3,863	5,318	7,854	7,543	255.1
Massachusetts	2,211	3,614	5,771	7,806	7,818	253.6
Michigan	2,245	3,803	5,405	6,941	7,568	237.1
Minnesota	2,300	3,801	4,886	6,221	6,371	177.0
Mississippi	1,114	2,107	3,406	3,872	4,312	287.1
Missouri	1,860	2,981	3,963	5,640	5,823	213.1
Montana	2,222	3,289	5,069	5,928	6,112	175.1
Nebraska	1,822	3,098	4,401	6,059	6,472	255.2
Nevada	2,328	3,237	4,274	5,153	5,541	138.0
New Hampshire	1,878	3,042	3,922	6,638	6,236	232.1
New Jersey	2,096	4,275	6,532	10,186	10,211	387.2
New Mexico	1,961	2,974	4,163	4,399	4,674	138.3
New York	3,037	5,581	7,087	10,089	9,658	218.0
North Carolina	1,283	2,576	3,591	5,369	5,315	314.3
North Dakota	1,983	2,901	3,931	5,243	5,198	162.1

TABLE 2 (continued)

	1959-60	1969-70	1979-80	1989-90	1996-97	Pct. change 1960-97
Ohio	1,974	3,071	4,247	6,313	6,517	230.1
Oklahoma	1,684	2,543	3,943	4,390	5,150	205.8
Oregon	2,425	3,890	5,510	6,851	6,792	180.1
Pennsylvania	2,214	3,709	5,188	7,794	7,686	247.2
Rhode Island	2,236	3,749	5,324	7,969	8,307	271.5
South Carolina	1,190	2,577	3,586	5,108	5,371	351.3
South Dakota	1,876	2,902	3,905	4,669	4,924	162.5
Tennessee	1,288	2,381	3,348	4,585	5,011	289.1
Texas	1,797	2,626	3,921	5,194	5,736	219.2
Utah	1,744	2,634	3,391	3,459	4,045	131.9
Vermont	1,860	3,396	4,088	7,793	7,171	285.5
Virginia	1,483	2,978	4,032	5,846	5,677	282.8
Washington	2,274	3,851	5,257	5,885	6,182	171.9
West Virginia	1,398	2,818	3,931	5,457	6,519	366.3
Wisconsin	2,234	3,713	5,070	6,913	7,398	231.2
Wyoming	2,436	3,601	5,172	6,980	6,448	164.7

Note: Expenditures per pupil calculated on basis of average daily attendance.

Source: NCES, 1999, Table 171.

One reason for this decline in the pupil-teacher ratio is often thought to be the increase in the number of children with disabilities.   Because these children are more difficult to educate, they often are enrolled in much smaller classes.   Yet Hanushek and Rivkin (1994) show that special education programs account for less than one-third of the recent decline in the pupil-teacher ratio.   This means that efforts to reduce regular class sizes have succeeded as well in most states.

Of course, if Barro's estimates are correct, then half of the average increase in spending goes to factors other than teachers. One factor that is responsible for considerable growth in spending in recent years has been benefits paid to school personnel. Hanushek (1994a) estimates that these so-called "fixed charges"

grew from 7 percent to 14 percent of total spending between
1960 and 1980.   Table 3 shows that employee benefits
accounted for 15 percent of spending in 1996-97.   These
increases are tied both to the growing number of teachers and
other personnel and to the growing costs of providing benefits
such as health care and retirement.   There are a number of
other important functions that must be considered in the opera-
tion of a school system.   Central administration, for example,
represents only about 2 percent of total expenditures, while
operations and maintenance account for less than 9 percent.
Table 3 provides a breakdown on how the more than 15,000
school districts in the United States allocated their funds in
1996-97.
     Table 3 shows that school districts spent an average of
approximately 60 percent of their current funds on instruction.
Earlier research by Picus (1993a, 1993b) and Picus and Fazal
(1996) not only confirmed this proportion, but also found that
there is very little variation in that 60 percent figure, despite
substantial variation among school districts in total expenditures
per pupil and in expenditures per pupil for direct instruction.
This pattern has been confirmed by other researchers, most
notably Cooper (1993, 1994).   The lack of variation in the pattern of resource allocation may be part of the reason links
between spending and student outcomes have been hard to find
and may well offer possibilities for making the allocation of
resources more productive in the future.

The Role of the Courts

One cannot consider the implications of changes in spending on
education without looking at the history of school finance litigation in the past 30 years.   The primary trend one sees in court
rulings has been an effort to improve the equity or equality of
spending per pupil across school districts within individual
states.   The first state supreme court decision in this set of
cases was *Serrano v. Priest* (1971).   In that case, the California
Supreme Court held that the state's school finance system
allowed some districts to spend substantially more than other
districts, often with considerably lower property tax rates.
Holding that this violated the equal protection clauses of both
the state and federal constitutions, the court called for substantial equalization of spending across districts.

TABLE 3: Total Public School K-12 Expenditures, 1996-97

	Expenditures ($ mill.)	Pct. distr.	Pct. distr.
Total expenditures[1]	$313,131	100.0	----
Current expenditures	270,152	86.3	100.0
Expenditures by object			
Salaries	175,019	55.9	64.8
Employee benefits	47,119	15.0	17.4
Purchased services	23,042	7.4	8.5
Tuition	1,648	0.5	0.6
Supplies	20,375	6.5	7.5
Other	2,949	0.9	1.1
Expenditures by function			
Instruction	167,148	53.4	61.9
Students support[2]	13,156	4.2	4.9
Instructional services[3]	10,902	3.5	4.0
General administration	6,045	1.9	2.2
School administration	15,558	5.0	5.8
Operation and maintenance	26,837	8.6	9.9
Transportation	10,990	3.5	4.1
Other support services	7,554	2.4	2.8
Food services	11,248	3.6	4.2
Other	714	0.2	0.3
Other current expenditures	4,647	1.5	1.7
Capital outlay	31,434	10.0	----
Interest on school debt	6,899	2.2	----

[1] Excludes expenditures for state education agencies.

[2] Includes health, attendance, and speech pathology services.

[3] Includes curriculum development, staff training, libraries, and media and computer centers.

Source: NCES, 1999, Table 168.

Since that time, many other state courts have made similar rulings, and many states have acted to equalize spending across districts to avoid unfavorable court actions. Federal action was precluded in 1973, when the U.S. Supreme Court, in a 5-4 ruling in *San Antonio Independent School District v. Rodriguez* held that, important as education was for American citizens and for discharging citizen responsibilities, it was not mentioned in the Constitution. Further, all public school students in Texas (where the case was filed) were provided some type of education program. Thus, the Court was unwilling, on its own, to recognize education as a fundamental right. This ruling effectively foreclosed further school finance litigation at the federal level.

There was, however, a great deal of action in the states in the late 1970s and early 1980s, with court rulings in New Jersey and Minnesota, among others, forcing states to make substantial changes to their school finance formulas. In all, some 23 states were involved in school finance litigation during the 1970s and early 1980s, with approximately half of the state courts ruling for the plaintiffs.

Although school finance litigation declined in the early 1980s, there was a resurgence in the late 1980s. This increased judicial activity continued in the 1990s, with some new twists to the old issues. The primary addition to many recent lawsuits has been the idea of "adequacy." Plaintiffs argue that spending is so low in some districts in their state that children living in those districts do not have access to adequate educational opportunity. While this argument met with some success, notably in Kentucky, judges have generally been reluctant to tell the state what an adequate level of funding for education might be.

Two recent rulings in Vermont and Ohio, both in favor of the plaintiffs, may be signals of the future (*Brigham v. Vermont*, 1997; *DeRolph et al. v. Ohio*, 1997). In both states, the high court ruled that the existing state funding formula was unconstitutional, and the court indicated that conditions in the lowest-spending districts were unacceptable and that improvements were needed. Both courts also indicated that low-wealth districts were entitled to greater access to the total wealth of the state. However, neither court specified a minimum level of adequate funding, and both went to lengths to say that nothing in their rulings should be construed to mean that the wealthiest districts should be restricted in what they could spend on their children's education. In the Vermont and Ohio cases, the courts were willing to let some districts spend more, provided the poorest districts also had access to more resources. On the other hand, the Illinois Supreme Court, after 20 or more years of litigation, has allowed that state's school finance structure to stand (*Committee for Educational Rights v. Edgar*, 1996).

One of the results of this litigation over time has been dramatically increased state appropriations for education, largely to provide for greater equalization. Illinois has been an exception to this trend. The state share of total public school costs in Illinois declined from 48 percent in 1976 to 32 percent in 1996. Although many claim that states have been forced to equalize everyone down, the reality is that, over time, substantial amounts of new money have flowed to school districts as a result of school finance reforms (see, e.g., Picus, 1994a). A few of the wealthiest districts in each state have suffered, but many poor districts have reaped revenue windfalls in the early years of school finance reform. In fact, in recent years, a new phenomenon has developed. Even with access to substantially higher revenue through equalization formulas, many low-wealth, low-spending districts elect to remain low spenders and choose to reduce taxes as well. The implications of these decisions in terms of the debate over how money matters are critical; it appears that many school districts may already believe that they have enough money to do the job they want to do, a far cry from the usual expectation that schools want as much as possible.

Up to this point, this chapter has focused on expenditures and how much is available to schools and school districts. It is clear that over time, our schools have benefited from real increases in resources. Whether they have been able to use those resources to improve student performance is less clear. The next section focuses on that debate more closely.

LINKING SPENDING TO STUDENT OUTCOMES

The education community typically focuses on student outcomes that are measured through assessment systems, usually standardized tests. Education production function research attempts to link changes in school spending, or changes in spending patterns, to changes in test scores. Other measures of student performance that are sometimes used include school attendance, dropout rates, college enrollment, and job longevity following high school.[2]

A production function is a model that identifies the possible outcomes that can be achieved with a given combination of inputs. With knowledge of the quantities of inputs available, it is possible to calculate the maximum output that can be achieved. What is important to this process is how the inputs are translated into those outcomes, as well as finding the most efficient way of doing so. The difficulty with identifying production functions in education results from the complexity of the educational process and the number of inputs that can affect outcomes. In addition, it is often difficult to reach agreement on the desired outcomes of the educational system. Even if there is agreement on outcomes, many of the factors that appear to have an impact on the educational process may well be outside the control of educators.

Production functions are estimated using statistical techniques that measure the relationship between a mix of inputs and some identified output. Among the most common outcomes used in educational production functions are the results of standardized tests, graduation rates, dropout rates, and labor market outcomes. The inputs most often considered include per-pupil expenditures, pupil-teacher ratios, teacher education, teacher experience and salaries, school facilities, and administrative inputs. Unfortunately, the results of studies that have attempted to measure the effects of these inputs often conflict or show inconclusive results. Others, beginning with the well-known Coleman Report (Coleman et al., 1966) have shown that factors such as students' socioeconomic status may be more important in determining how well they do in school than many, if not all, of the inputs listed above.

---

[2] Another approach to measuring the impact of educational resources looks at future lifetime earnings. Some economists suggest that education is an investment and that high investment in education will yield higher returns in the form of higher lifetime earnings. Many studies using this "human capital" approach find that money makes a difference (see, e.g., Card and Krueger, 1996).

Does Money Matter? The Recent Debate

Although there has long been interest in the question of whether money matters, renewed debated was sparked by the publication of an article by Hedges, Laine, and Greenwald (1994a). Prior to their article, the most often cited research in this field was the work of Eric Hanushek (1981, 1986, 1989). In that work, as well as his more recent research, Hanushek argued that there did not appear to be a systematic relationship between the level of funding and student outcomes:

> These results have a simple interpretation: There is no strong or consistent relationship between school resources and student performance. In other words, there is little reason to be confident that simply adding more resources to schools as currently constituted will yield performance gains among students (Hanushek, 1997, p. 148).

Hanushek analyzed over 90 different studies. In looking across those studies, at different outcome measures and different types of inputs, Hanushek argues that the variation in findings is such that systematic relationships between money and outcomes have not yet been identified. He states:

> The concern from a policy viewpoint is that nobody can describe when resources will be used effectively and when they will not. In the absence of such a description, providing these general resources to a school implies that sometimes resources might be used effectively, other times they may be applied in ways that are actually damaging, and most of the time no measurable student outcome gains should be expected (Hanushek, 1997, pp. 148-149).

He then suggests that what is needed is to change the incentive structures facing schools so that they have incentives to act in ways that use resources efficiently and that lead to improved student performance.

Hedges, Laine, and Greenwald (1994a, 1994b) conclude that money can, in fact, make a difference. They argue that although Hanushek found a positive, statistically significant relationship in only a minority of the studies he reviewed, the number with such a relationship exceeds what one would expect to find if the relationship were random. They also point out that one would expect the statistically insignificant studies to be evenly divided between positive and negative effects, but that as many as 70 percent of the relationships between per-pupil expenditures and student performance are positive. Relying on this and other evidence, Hedges, Laine, and Greenwald conclude that school resources are systematically related to student achievement.[3]

A number of other studies have looked at this issue. Ferguson (1991) looked at spending and the use of educational resources in Texas. He concluded that "hiring teachers with stronger literacy skills, hiring more teachers (when students-per-teacher exceeds eighteen), retaining experienced teachers, and attracting more teachers with advanced training are all measures that produce higher test scores in exchange for more money" (Ferguson, 1991, p. 485). His findings also suggest that teachers' selection of districts in which to work is affected by the education level of adults in the community, the racial composition of the community, and the salaries in other districts and alternative occupations. This implies, according to Ferguson, that better teachers will tend to move to districts with higher socioeconomic characteristics if salaries are equal. If teacher skills and knowledge have an impact on student achievement (as Ferguson and others suggest), then low socioeconomic areas may have to offer substantially higher salaries to attract and retain high-quality teachers. This would help confirm a link between expenditures and student achievement.

A more recent study by Wenglinsky (1997) looked at three large national databases to determine whether expenditures had an impact on the achievement of fourth- and eighth-graders. He found that the impact of spending occurred in steps or stages. For fourth-graders, increased expenditures on instruction and on school district administration were related to higher teacher-student ratios. Increased teacher-student ratios (smaller class sizes), in turn, led to higher achievement in mathematics. In the eighth grade, the process was more complex. Increased expenditures on instruction and central administration were also related to higher teacher-student ratios, which led to an improved school environment or climate, and the improved climate and its lack of behavior problems resulted in higher achievement in math.

---

[3] See also Laine, Greenwald, and Hedges, 1996; Greenwald, Hedges, and Laine, 1996a, 1996b.

On the surface, it is hard to see why higher expenditures for administration would lead to smaller class size. However, school district expenditure patterns are remarkably similar, regardless of spending level. Thus, higher spending districts (which could afford smaller classes) would also have more money available for additional administrative support. Wenglinsky's findings suggest that the combination of smaller classes and more administrative support leads to improved student performance. This makes sense in that teachers are able to focus more time on teaching and have more supportive resources both to help improve their teaching and to deal with students who may be disruptive in class.

Equally interesting was Wenglinsky's finding that capital outlay (spending on facility construction and maintenance), school-level administration, and teacher education levels could not be linked to improved student achievement. This is particularly intriguing in light of the finding that increased spending for central or district administration was associated with improved student outcomes. These findings are certain to be controversial and, to some extent, conflict with the conventional wisdom about school administration. What makes his findings important is the point that additional spending on district administration leads to improved teacher-student ratios, whereas that is not so with increased school site administration. The reason for this is not clear, but it is something that should be considered as schools move to more site-based management.

One of the problems with class size research has been the lack of a true experimental design. In fact, only one study with such a design has been undertaken. In the Tennessee Student-Teacher Achievement Ratio (STAR) experiment, children were randomly assigned to classes with low pupil-teacher ratios and high pupil-teacher ratios. Students were placed in one of three groups: an experimental group with an average class size of 15.1 students, a control group with an average class size of 22.4 students, and another control group with an average class size of 22.8 students and a teacher's aide. Under the study design, each student was to stay in the original class-size assignment until the third grade. Following third grade, the experiment was concluded and all students were assigned to regular-size classrooms. Standardized tests were given each school year to measure student achievement. Although there are some methodological and data problems in any study of this magnitude, some respected researchers have argued that the

Tennessee STAR project is the best designed experimental study on this topic to date (e.g., Mosteller, 1995; Krueger, 1998). Krueger summarized the major findings of the Tennessee STAR project as follows:

- At the end of the first year of the study, the performance of students in the experimental classes exceeded that of students in the two control groups by five to eight percentage points.
- For students who started the program in kindergarten, the relative advantage of those assigned to small classes grew between kindergarten and first grade, but the differences were relatively small beyond that.
- For students who entered in the first or second grade, the advantage of being in a small class tended to grow in subsequent grades.
- There was little difference in performance between students in regular-sized classrooms and students in regular-sized classrooms with teacher aides.
- Minority students and students who qualified for free and reduced-price lunches tended to receive a larger benefit from being assigned to small classes.
- Students who were in small classes have shown lasting achievement gains through the seventh grade.

A number of important policy issues arise from the Tennessee STAR findings. First, the results of the evaluation suggest that smaller classes can lead to improved student performance and that those performance gains are maintained at least through the seventh grade. Moreover, the results suggest that alternative models that rely on the use of teacher aides to reduce "effective class size" may have little impact. The research also suggests that simply reducing class size without changing how teachers deliver instruction is unlikely to improve student performance. It is important that teachers take advantage of the smaller classes to offer material in new and challenging ways identified through research. Absent that effort and the training needed to accompany such a change, expenditures for class-size reduction may be relatively ineffective.

In summary, there remains considerable disagreement over the impact of additional resources on educational outcomes of students. The complexity of the educational process, combined with the wide range of outcomes we have established for our schools and the many alternative approaches we use to fund our schools, makes it difficult to come to any unqualified conclusions about how money matters in improving student performance.

Studies of Resource Allocation and Use

One of the problems with the studies described above is they do not consider the tremendous similarity in spending patterns among school districts. Several studies have shown resource allocation across school districts to be remarkably similar, despite differences in total per-pupil spending, student characteristics, and district attributes. Picus's early studies showed that approximately 60 percent of school district funds were spent on direct instruction, which was defined as teacher compensation (salary and benefits) and instructional materials (Picus, 1993a, 1993b). Picus and Fazal (1996) argue that the non-instructional 40 percent does not represent a so-called "administrative blob," but rather spending for important functions such as maintenance and operations, student transportation, site administration, and instructional support in the form of staff to help teachers and students. They also found considerable evidence that central office administration as a percentage of total district expenditures is lower in large urban districts. Those districts have high expenditures for administration, but the spending is spread over even larger student and employee bases.

These findings on the similarities in school spending patterns do not mean that all children receive the same level of educational services. Picus and Fazal (1996) point out that a district spending $10,000 per pupil and $6,000 per pupil for direct instruction is able to offer smaller classes, better paid and presumably higher-quality teachers, and higher-quality instructional materials than a district spending $5,000 per pupil and only $3,000 per pupil for direct instruction.

What we do not know is what the impact on student performance would be if schools or school districts were to dramatically change the way they spend the resources available to them. Odden and Picus have suggested that the important message from the research summarized above was that "if additional education revenues were spent in the same way as current education revenues, student performance increases were unlikely to emerge" (1992, p. 281). Therefore, knowing whether high-performing schools utilize resources differently from other schools would be very helpful in resolving the debate over how money matters.

Nakib (1996) looked at the allocation of educational resources by high-performing high schools in Florida and compared those allocation patterns with the way resources were used in other high schools. Seven different measures were used to compare student performance. Per-pupil spending and per-pupil spending for instruction were not significantly higher in high-performing high schools, largely because of the highly equalized school funding formula used in Florida. On the other hand, Nakib found that the percentage of expenditures devoted to instruction was lower in the high-performing high schools, implying that such schools may actually spend more money on resources not directly linked to instruction than do other high schools. Nakib did not offer an explanation for this finding. However, it is possible that providing a variety of support functions to teachers, which enable them to focus more of their time and attention on the task of teaching, might foster improved student performance.

Unfortunately, the results of this Florida analysis do little to clarify the debate on how money matters. Comparisons of high-performing high schools with all other high schools in Florida showed no clear distinction in either the amount of money available or in the way resources were used. As with many other studies, it was student demographic characteristics that had the greatest impact on student performance.

More recently, Odden (1997) found that the school reform models developed as part of the New American Schools project have generally led to increased student performance.[4] In each of the seven models he studied, schools were required to substantially reallocate resources away from instructional aides and teachers with special assignments. Instead, the schools focused on increasing the number of teachers in regular classrooms, thus lowering average class size. In addition, each of the designs has required substantial investments, in both time and

---

[4] The New American Schools were initially established through corporate grants growing out of President Bush's America 2000 initiative. The New American Schools Development Corporation (predecessor to the New American Schools) funded eleven "break the mold" school reform models.

money, for professional development. Odden suggests that the costs of such professional development can often be funded by eliminating a position vacant through attrition. His optimistic assessment is that for relatively little additional money, schools can identify existing programs and organizational structures that will help them improve student learning.

STRATEGIES TO IMPROVE STUDENT PERFORMANCE

The evidence presented above makes it difficult to reach a strong conclusion on how money matters in improving student performance. Even though virtually all educators believe that additional resources will lead to higher student performance, few can tell how best to spend the funds to achieve that goal. As a result, their demands for more money, absent a well-reasoned description of how the money will be used, do not build confidence that money, by itself, will make a difference. We need to focus on and understand those factors—such as teacher quality and class size—that are most likely to affect student performance. The problem is that research shows that there are few differences in the way school districts spend the money they have or in what they choose to do with new re-sources. The remainder of this section proposes four strategies for focusing resources to improve student performance, with or without new funds: reallocation of existing resources, incentives for improved performance, a more market-based budgeting environment, and developing the concept of "venture capital" for schools and school systems.

Reallocation of Existing Resources

Regardless of what impact additional funds might have, it is important that existing resources be used as efficiently as possible. In a case study of the Boston public schools, Miles (1995) found that if all individuals classified as teachers were to teach equal-sized classes, the average class in the district could be reduced from 22 to 13 students. Although this would place all children with disabilities in regular programs, Miles also provides estimates of what the average class size would be if some of the most severely disabled children continued to receive services under current programs. Dramatic class size reductions were still possible. Miles's work highlights the fact that in many school districts, it may be possible to reduce class size through different teacher assignments throughout the district. To the extent that smaller class size improves student performance, these changes would offer an improvement in student performance at little or no cost.

Odden (1997), in his analysis of the costs of the New American Schools, argues that schools can find the additional funds (which range from $50,000 to $250,000 per school per year) to finance the various school designs through a combination of creatively using categorical funds, eliminating classroom aides, and reallocating resources (e.g., eliminating one or two teaching positions). Some of these options may result in larger classes or fewer teachers, but the more intensive use of staff and greater professional development activities available seem to result in improved student performance in many of the schools that have adopted these designs.

In sum, aside from seeking additional funds, there may be ways to restructure what is done with current funds. Henry Levin's Accelerated Schools, the New American Schools program designs, and careful analyses of current staffing patterns could all yield improved student performance.[5]

Incentives

The use of incentives to improve school performance is not a new idea (see, e.g., Picus, 1992). Unfortunately, the incentives that seem to have the most success are negative sanctions. Schools faced with threats of intervention often act quickly to improve performance rather than risk the stigma of a sanction. By contrast, many positive incentives have been less successful. For example, high-performing schools are often granted waivers from state regulation. But why reward districts that have succeeded within the regulatory system with relief they do not seem to need? Perhaps the more appropriate incentive would be to provide waivers to underperforming schools with the hope that increased flexibility would lead to improvements.

---

[5] Accelerated Schools are designed to provide a fast-paced educational program to all students, who, it is assumed, are able to learn the material. See, e.g., Levin, 1987.

Hanushek (1997) argues that the incentives currently in place do not encourage teachers to work to improve student performance, and that those incentives need to be changed. He suggests that we do not really know enough about what kinds of performance incentives work and that more experimentation and research is needed. Incentives can be directed at schools or at teachers. Although many incentive programs offer modest amounts of money (often to be used for things other than payments to teachers or other school staff), the funding for these programs is generally limited. If the program offers an incentive for attaining a certain level of performance, the value of the incentive declines as more schools qualify. Alternatively, if the top-performing schools receive a fixed reward until the funds are exhausted, schools that perform well may miss the cutoff point despite substantial growth or improvement. Similarly, incentives focused on teachers run the risk of creating competition among teachers, reducing teamwork, and potentially harming student performance. Creating incentives that reward groups of teachers or schools seem to be more effective (Odden and Picus, 2000).

Sanctions are often the most effective way to motivate low-performing schools. This may be because these schools do not believe they have a chance to earn a high-performance reward and thus are not motivated. Facing the threat of take-over, or even just poor publicity through a state or district accountability program, often provides the incentive for schools to focus on strategies that will improve student performance. It may be that different forms of incentives and sanctions will work better, depending on the current level of student performance at a school. This means that incentive programs must be carefully crafted so that rewards and sanctions are focused on those schools needing improvement. The focus must be on the change or improvement in student outcomes, not simply overall achievement levels. If schools are simply compared based on average or median test scores, low-performing schools will see no benefit from attempting to make changes. On the other hand, if the program rewards improvement in student performance, low-performing schools will have more incentive to change.

Market Approaches

Many of today's reformers call for market-based changes in the organization of our schools. They propose choice programs, vouchers, and other models that ostensibly force out low-performing schools and allow high-performing schools to grow and multiply. It seems unlikely, particularly in large, over-crowded urban districts, that poor-performing schools would actually close as a result of such programs. More likely, students whose families have the resources, time, or acumen to work the system will get into the better schools, while others will continue to suffer.

Market mechanisms can be a powerful tool for improving the performance of an organization. Current proposals for market structures in public education have met with tremendous resistance. An alternative approach suggests that what is needed is market-type mechanisms within public school systems (see Picus, 1994b). For markets to succeed, failure is an essential ingredient. Since it is unlikely that schools will close (or fail), a proxy for failure is needed. Schools would be given more authority over the use of their resources, particularly professional development funds, and they would be held accountable for student outcomes. Schools implementing successful programs would meet their goals, while those selecting inappropriate programs most likely would fall short of those goals. Schools purchasing services that did not lead to improved student performance would change to new programs and providers. Providers of educational programs or stratgegies that did not seem to work in improving student performance would sell their strategies to fewer and fewer schools, eventually going out of business—creating the failure that is part of a market. On the other hand, providers of programs that were successful in improving student performance would thrive. These providers might be school districts, consortia of school personnel, or private companies. The market for teachers within a district could also be made less restrictive, with principals seeking teachers who share their management style and programmatic vision.

Venture Capital

In a study of the costs of implementing California's "Caught in the Middle" reforms for middle schools, Marsh and Sevilla (1992) found that the annual costs of restructuring schools under the program were 3-6 percent higher than average current expenditures per pupil in California schools. However, they also concluded that the first year "start-up" costs amounted to approximately 25 percent of annual costs. These costs included new instructional materials and substantial funding for professional development, both for teacher release time during the school year and to compensate teachers for additional training programs during the summer or other periods when they were not in the classroom. The problem schools face is finding those start-up funds. For example, in a large district with ten middle schools, each with a budget of $10 million, the initial start-up costs would be $25 million, a figure that would be hard to find in a district budget. However, if the program were started in two schools a year, the annual cost would be $5 million. Since the money would be for start-up purposes only, the $5 million could be used for two different schools each year until all ten schools had implemented the program. Then, the district would have $5 million to put to some other good use.

The problem today is that once funds are appropriated to a school or program, they generally become the possession of that entity. Finding a way to use the money in a revolving fashion would facilitate continued improvements in educational programs. The major problem is determining who gets the venture capital funds first and who must wait. In many large school districts, superintendents are publishing lists of the best- and worst-performing schools; clearly such lists could be used to prioritize the allocation of start-up funds. Another issue is the equity of the distribution. Although some schools will get more in a given year than others, over the established time period, all schools will receive the funds. One has to accept the idea that equity is measured over some longer time frame, not simply on an annual basis.

CONCLUSION

Those who argue that it is not how much money you have, but how it is used that matters must provide more than a vague statement about the use of resources in schools. It is hard to argue that providing more money to schools will not help. However, discerning the relationship between the amount of money spent and how well students perform has, to date, been elusive. Clearly, it is crucial that schools focus the resources they have on strategies that research shows will lead to improvements in student learning. The four proposals outlined above are grounded in the belief that authority over fiscal matters should be established as much as possible at the school site, but that district and state structures must be in place to create incentives for performance and to ensure that schools have access to adequate levels of resources.

REFERENCES

Barro, Stephen M. (1992). "What Does the Education Dollar Buy? Relationships of Staffing, Staff Characteristics, and Staff Salaries to State Per-Pupil Spending." Working paper prepared for the Finance Center of the Consortium for Policy Research in Education.

Brigham v. Vermont (1997). 692 A.2d 384.

Card, David, and Alan B. Krueger (1996). "The Economic Return to School Quality." In William J. Baumol and William E. Becker, eds., *Assessing Educational Practices: The Contribution of Economics*. Cambridge, Mass.: MIT Press.

Coleman, James S., et al. (1966). *Equality of Educational Opportunity*. Washington, D.C.: U.S. Department of Health, Education, and Welfare.

Committee for Educational Rights v. Edgar (1996). 672 N.E.2d 1178.

Cooper, Bruce S. (1993). "School-Site Cost Allocations: Testing a Micro-Financial Model in 23 Districts in Ten States." Paper prepared for the Annual Meeting of the American Education Finance Association, Albuquerque, N.M., March 1993.

_____ (1994). "Making Money Matter in Education: A Micro-Financial Model for Determining School-Level Allocations, Efficiency, and Productivity," *Journal of Education Finance*, vol. 20, no. 1 (Summer 1994), pp. 66-87.

DeRolph et al. v. Ohio (1997). 677 N.E.2d 733.

Ferguson, Ronald F. (1991). "Paying for Public Education: New Evidence on How and Why Money Matters," *Harvard*

Journal on Legislation, vol. 28, no. 2 (Summer 1991), pp. 465-498.

Greenwald, Rob, Larry V. Hedges, and Richard D. Laine (1996a). "The Effect of School Resources on Student Achievement," *Review of Educational Research*, vol. 66, no. 3 (Fall 1996), pp. 361-396.

_____ (1996b). "Interpreting Research on School Resources and Student Achievement: A Rejoinder to Hanushek," *Review of Educational Research*, vol. 66, no. 3 (Fall 1996), pp. 411-416.

Hanushek, Eric A., with Bruce D. Spencer and David E. Wiley (1981). "Throwing Money at Schools," *Journal of Policy Analysis and Management*, vol. 1, no. 1 (Fall 1981), pp. 19-41.

Hanushek, Eric A. (1986). "The Economics of Schooling: Production and Efficiency in Public Schools," *Journal of Economic Literature*, vol. 24, no. 3 (September 1986), pp. 1141-1177.

_____ (1989). "The Impact of Differential Expenditures on School Performance," *Educational Researcher*, vol. 18, no. 4 (May 1989), pp. 45-51.

_____ (1994a). *Making Schools Work: Improving Performance and Controlling Costs*. Washington, D.C.: Brookings Institution.

_____ (1994b). "Money Might Matter Somewhere: A Response to Hedges, Laine, and Greenwald," *Educational Researcher*, vol. 23, no. 4 (May 1994), pp. 5-8.

_____ (1997). "Assessing the Effects of School Resources on Student Performance: An Update," *Educational Evaluation and Policy Analysis*, vol. 19, no. 2, (Summer 1997), pp. 141-164.

Hanushek, Eric A., and Steve G. Rivkin (1994). "Understanding the 20th Century Explosion in U.S. School Costs." Working paper no. 388. Rochester, N.Y.: Rochester Center for Economic Research.

Hedges, Larry V., Richard D. Laine, and Rob Greenwald (1994a). "Does Money Matter? A Meta-Analysis of Studies of the Effects of Differential School Inputs on Student Outcomes," *Educational Researcher*, vol. 23, no. 3 (April 1994), pp. 5-14.

_____ (1994b). "Money Does Matter Somewhere: A Reply to Hanushek," *Educational Researcher*, vol. 23, no. 4 (May 1994), pp. 9-10.

Krueger, Alan B. (1998). "Reassessing the View that American Schools Are Broken," *Federal Reserve Bank of New York / Economic Policy Review*, vol. 4, no. 1 (March 1998), pp. 29-43.

Laine, Richard D., Rob Greenwald, and Larry V. Hedges (1996). "Money Does Matter: A Research Synthesis of a New Universe of Education Production Function Studies." In Lawrence O. Picus and James L. Wattenbarger, eds., *Where Does the Money Go? Resource Allocation in Elementary and Secondary Schools*. Thousand Oaks, Calif.: Corwin Press.

Levin, Henry A. (1987). "Accelerated Schools for Disadvantaged Students," *Educational Leadership*, March 1987, pp. 19-21.

Marsh, David, and Jennifer Sevilla (1992). "Understanding the Cost Implications of California's Caught in the Middle Program." In Allan Odden, ed., *Restructuring School Finance for the 1990s*. New York: Jossey-Bass.

Miles, Karen Hawley (1995). "Freeing Resources for Improving Schools: A Case Study of Teacher Allocation in Boston Public Schools," *Educational Evaluation and Policy Analysis*, vol. 17, no. 4 (Winter 1995), pp. 476-493.

Monk, David H. (1992). "Educational Productivity Research: An Update and Assessment of Its Role in Education Finance Reform," *Educational Evaluation and Policy Analysis*, vol. 14, no. 4, pp. 307-332.

Mosteller, Frederick (1995). "The Tennessee Study of Class Size in the Early School Grades," *The Future of Children: Critical Issues for Children and Youths*, vol. 5, no. 2 (Summer/Fall 1995), pp. 457-464.

Murnane, Richard J. (1991). "Interpreting the Evidence on 'Does Money Matter'?" *Harvard Journal on Legislation*, vol. 28, no. 2 (Summer 1991), pp. 458-464.

Nakib, Yasser A. (1996). "Beyond District-Level Expenditures: Schooling Resource Allocation and Use in Florida." In Lawrence O. Picus and James L. Wattenbarger, eds., *Where Does the Money Go? Resource Allocation in Elementary and Secondary Schools*. Newbury Park, Calif.: Corwin Press.

NCEE (1983). *A Nation at Risk: The Imperative for Educational Reform*. Report of the National Commission on Excellence in Education. Washington, D.C.: U.S. Government Printing Office.

NCES (1999). *Digest of Education Statistics, 1999.* Washington D.C.: National Center for Education Statistics, U.S. Department of Education.

Odden, Allan (1997). "The Finance Side of Implementing New American Schools." Alexandria, Va.: New American Schools.

Odden, Allan R., and Lawrence O. Picus (1992). *School Finance: A Policy Perspective.* New York: McGraw-Hill.

_____ (2000). *School Finance: A Policy Perspective.* 2nd ed. New York: McGraw-Hill.

Picus, Lawrence O. (1992). "Using Incentives to Stimulate Improved School Performance: An Assessment of Alternative Approaches." In Allan R. Odden, ed., *Rethinking School Finance: An Agenda for the 1990s.* San Francisco: Jossey-Bass.

_____ (1993a). "The Allocation and Use of Educational Resources: School Level Evidence from the Schools and Staffing Survey." Working paper no. 37. Los Angeles: University of Southern California, Center for Research in Education Finance.

_____ (1993b). "The Allocation and Use of Educational Resources: District Level Evidence from the Schools and Staffing Survey." Working paper no. 34. Los Angeles: University of Southern California, Center for Research in Education Finance.

_____ (1994a). "The Local Impact of School Finance Reform in Four Texas School Districts," *Educational Evaluation and Policy Analysis*, vol. 16, no. 4 (Winter 1994), pp. 391-404.

_____ (1994b). "Achieving Program Equity: Are Markets the Answer?" *Educational Policy*, vol. 8, no. 4 (December 1994), pp. 568-581.

Picus, Lawrence O., and Minaz B. Fazal (1996). "Why Do We Need to Know What Money Buys? Research on Resource Allocation Patterns in Elementary and Secondary Schools." In Lawrence O. Picus and James L. Wattenbarger, eds., *Where Does the Money Go? Resource Allocation in Elementary and Secondary Schools.* Newbury Park, Calif.: Corwin Press.

San Antonio Independent School District v. Rodriguez (1973). 411 U.S. 1, 93 S.Ct. 1278.

Serrano v. Priest (1971). 5 Cal 3d 584, 96 Cal. Rptr. 601, 487 p.2nd 1241.

Wenglinsky, Harold (1997). *When Money Matters*. Princeton, N.J.: Educational Testing Service.

COMMENTS: EDUCATION FUNDING IN ILLINOIS

Dea Meyer

Lawrence Picus's chapter reviews much of the research on school resources and educational outcomes. Picus concludes that, given the complexity of the educational process, the wide range of educational outcomes, and the variations in the way that schools are funded, it is difficult to reach a strong conclusion about how money matters in improving student performance. However, given that the spending patterns of the vast majority of school districts are quite similar, there could be improvements in results with changes in the way resources are used. Picus suggests four strategies that could improve student performance with or without more money: reallocation of existing resources; incentives for improved performance; a more market-based budgeting environment; and developing the concept of "venture capital" for schools and school systems. Picus's discussion of the impact of money and potential changes in resource allocation raises important issues for debates over public school funding in Illinois.

SCHOOL FINANCE REFORM IN ILLINOIS

On December 4, 1997, Governor Jim Edgar signed House Bill 452 into law. This education reform and funding legislation provided tools that could help to improve educational outcomes in elementary and secondary schools in Illinois. The law unfortunately did not provide for systemic change in the way schools are funded. It did, however, represent the first time that the legislature had formally recognized the state's role in ensuring that each child has access to sufficient resources for a quality, basic education. In addition, the law included provisions to improve educational quality and accountability, as well as a state capital program for buildings and technology infrastructure.

The impact of both the additional resources and changes in school administration will depend heavily on strong management strategies and execution at both the state and local levels. To be effective, this law must build on previous efforts by the General Assembly, the State Board of Education, and others to develop a system of challenging and well-articulated academic standards, an effective assessment system, innovative instructional programs, and a well-organized and constructive accountability and technical assistance system to ensure that all children meet society's increasing educational demands.

Given the large disparities in the amount of resources provided to elementary and secondary education in Illinois, the manner in which schools are funded has been debated over much of the past 20 years. There have been various efforts to change the ways schools are funded legislatively, constitutionally, and through the courts. These efforts have been largely unsuccessful due to varied perceptions among different constituencies regarding the state's role in funding public education. The impetus for HB 452 came from the 1994 gubernatorial election and the 1996 report of Governor's Commission on Education Funding. The recommendations of the Governor's Commission, which included a proposed constitutional amendment to strengthen the state's commitment to public education, were endorsed by Governor Edgar but never brought up for a vote in the General Assembly. Nonetheless, the commission's work and the Governor's attention to it drew the focus of voters and legislators to the issue of education funding and reform. Many of the principles of the commission's report were encompassed in HB 452.

The Foundation Level

The Governor's Commission recommended that the state ensure that each child have access to a "quality basic education" (Governor's Commission, 1996, p. 9). The state should guarantee a foundation level from combined state and local resources, based on the spending of efficiently operated, high-performing schools.[1] The foundation level was estimated to be $4,225 per

---

[1] These schools were defined in terms of (1) high academic performance (as measured by state achievement tests) relative to other schools serving students of similar socioeconomic backgrounds, and (2) below-average per pupil expenditures relative to the state as a whole (Governor's Commission, 1996, Appendix B).

student for the 1995-96 school year. The new foundation level would be phased in over a three-year period. The state was to fund 50 percent of the aggregate statewide amount of the foundation level, and this amount would be reviewed every two to three years.

The Governor's Commission also noted the funding advantages of high school districts in Illinois—despite educational research indicating the importance of the early years of a child's education. The state's per-pupil funding formula included a system of grade-weights: 1.0 for elementary schools, 1.05 for middle schools, and 1.25 for high schools. The commission recommended elimination of grade-level weighting.

The 1997 legislation represented the first time that a specific foundation level of school funding was enacted into law. The General Assembly established a foundation level of funding of $4,225 for FY 1999, which would increase by $100 per pupil over the following two years. The legislature committed to a continuing appropriation for three fiscal years (1999-2001). In addition, grade-level weighting was eliminated, although the legislation included a "hold harmless" provision. School districts would receive no less state aid in 1998-99 and any subsequent year than they received in 1997-98.

Poverty Grants

The previous state funding formula included additional weighting for low-income pupils, ranging from zero to a maximum of .625. The Governor's Commission recommended replacing per-pupil weighting with separate graduated grants for districts with low-income student populations of 20 percent of more.

The 1997 legislation established supplemental general state aid based on the concentration of students from low-income households within the school district. The per-pupil grant levels for the 1998-99 school year were $800 for 20-35 percent low-income, $1,100 for 35-50 percent, $1,500 for 50-60 percent, and $1,900 for 60 percent or more. In each of the subsequent two years, grant levels would be increased for school districts with low-income enrollment of 35 percent or more. Under the new law, state aid was more targeted to those districts with the highest concentrations of low-income students (20% or more), but the total amount of state aid distributed on the basis of low-income enrollment was actually much smaller (see Dye, Gold-stein, and McGuire, 1998).

The question that must be evaluated is whether these are the appropriate dollar amounts and allocations to effectively help schools with concentrations of children from low-income families. Although some have argued that this manner of poverty funding will bring additional resources to poorer districts, others contend that by separating these grants from the per-pupil formula, funds will be cut when tough resource allocation decisions are made in the future. In addition, as under the previous formula, these allocations are based on the most recent U.S. Census counts, which gradually become outdated.

Sources of Funding

The commission's recommendations for increased state funding for education were coupled with a proposal to reduce reliance on local property taxes. Property taxes for school districts were to be reduced by 25 percent statewide. The commission emphasized the importance of using "growing and predictable funding sources" to finance public schools. Revenue sources should provide sufficient funding for the long term and preserve a better balance between state and local sources. The primary source of new funding would be an increase in the state income tax; other sources would include efficiencies in state government, growth in state revenues, an expansion of the sales tax base, and taxes on gaming, including river boats.

The education funding increases under HB 452 were to be financed through general revenue growth, an increase in the cigarette tax, an increase in the telephone message tax, a graduated tax on gaming, and an increase in fees paid by late taxpayers. Given that only the message tax is a growing source of revenue and the current fiscal situation is "as good as it gets," a change in the state's economic circumstances will most likely necessitate a review of these revenue sources to continue to support the state's new commitment to providing a quality education to all of the state's children.

Promoting Efficiency and Innovation

The report of the Governor's Commission maintained that the overriding goal should be "improved educational performance" and that additional state funding must be linked to clearly defined academic standards, a strong assessment and account-ability process, and incentives for improved performance. The commission made several recommendations to promote greater efficiency, innovation, and flexibility at the local level. These included reviewing and eliminating unnecessary or overly pre-scriptive sections of the state's school code in favor of greater focus on educational results; undertaking innovative program-ming such as charter schools and greater site-based manage-ment; and revising the teacher certification and personnel sys-tem in order to attract and retain high-quality professionals, as well as enhancing accountability.

Under the 1997 legislation, a three-tiered, standards-based teacher certification process was established, tenure was ex-tended, and the dismissal process for underperforming teachers was streamlined. In addition, performance contracts for super-intendents and principals based on educational results were to be implemented, powers of school districts to enter into con-tracts with third parties for non-instructional services were clarified, and the State Board of Education's authority to over-rule local school boards on charter school disapprovals was expanded.

CONCLUSION

The 1997 legislation was a step forward in the funding of edu-cation and in improving educational quality across the state. The achievement of the foundation level is the result of an injection of over half a billion dollars, as well as a reallocation of dollars within the current funding system with the elimination of student weighting. Although it did not restructure school funding, it did commit the state to providing resources for an adequate education for all children in Illinois. In addition, changes were made in the teacher certification processes to en-sure that candidates possess the necessary skills and perform on the job, as well as making it easier for career-changers to join the profession. Establishing charter schools to create educa-tional competition was made easier, performance contracts were introduced for administrators, and some operations were stream-lined.

Despite these changes, there is still much work to be done. The continuing appropriation for the new school funding formula ends in June 2001. The 1997 legislation mandated the creation of an Education Funding Advisory Board to recommend revisions in the foundation level, as well as changes in supplemental state aid to districts with concentrations of students from low-income households. In June 2000, Governor George Ryan appointed five voting members and 13 ex-officio members to the Education Funding Advisory Board, with Robert Leininger, former state superintendent of education, as chairman.

Beyond the school funding issue, education policy in Illinois remains a mix of state mandates and efforts to establish a performance-based system. The framework for a performance-based system exists, but strong leadership is needed for effective implementation. We must continue to focus on the recruitment and continued training of high-quality professionals at all levels of the educational system, as well as the construction of a strong performance-based accountability system and the long-term goal of changing the way schools are funded. Whether the new resources improve educational results will depend as much on state and local leadership as on any of the changes enacted into law. With the substantial amount of new resources some districts are receiving, strong professional development programs and remediation for underperforming students can be implemented. In addition, we need studies of how districts with significant funding increases spent their new resources and whether there has been any improvement in educational performance.

REFERENCES

Dye, Richard F., Scott Goldstein, and Therese J. McGuire (1998). *An Evaluation of Illinois' 1997 School Reforms.* Chicago: Institute of Government and Public Affairs, University of Illinois, and Metropolitan Planning Council.

Governor's Commission (1996). *Report of the Governor's Commission on Education Funding for the State of Illinois.* Chicago: Office of the Governor, March 1996.

SO MUCH REFORM, SO LITTLE CHANGE: BUILDING-LEVEL OBSTACLES TO URBAN SCHOOL REFORM

Charles M. Payne

Since the Chicago School Reform Act of 1988, the city's public schools have, on the whole, aggressively adopted innovations in virtually every area of school life. After several years of such massive experimentation, there seems to be fairly broad agreement that the system is improved (Lenz 1997; Bryk et al., 1998). The pace of change, however, has been a good deal slower than school reformers anticipated. The original legislation envisioned transforming schools within five years. Yet, during the 2000-2001 school year—after ten years of implementation—one out of six schools in the system were on remediation or probation because of poor academic performance.

What slows down the rate of progress? What obstacles prevent innovations from living up to their advertising? This chapter suggests some ways of thinking about these issues, at least in terms of obstacles that are visible from the level of the individual school building. Such a perspective omits a great deal that is important, including state and local politics and questions about resource inequities. Nevertheless, what we can "see" from the school-building level is a significant part of the problem.[1]

Since 1990, I have had a number of perspectives from which to observe school reform in Chicago: as the director of a six-year ethnographic study of the Chicago implementation of James Comer's School Development Process, as a member of the Citywide Coalition for School Reform, as a member of the group that brought the Algebra Project to Chicago, and as a consultant to local foundations involved with school reform and to the Chicago Board of Education. Most of my contact has been with bottom-quartile schools as measured by pre-reform

---

[1] On the disadvantages of stressing the individual school, see Sarason, 1996.

test scores. This chapter is a reflection on all those experiences. The first section presents a typology of impediments to change, a map of possible stumbling blocks. The second focuses in greater detail on one kind of obstacle, the "social demoralization" of schools. The concluding section discusses implications for school reform and educational policy.

TOWARD A TYPOLOGY OF IMPEDIMENTS TO CHANGE

This discussion will draw on illustrations from several school reform programs, including Comer's School Development Process and Theodore Sizer's Coalition of Essential Schools, two of the most visible and influential models. Comer's program, which began at Yale in 1968, tries to improve schools by improving the working relationships among adults. The program creates several teams in a school, one for overall performance, one to increase parent participation in the life of the school, and a third to improve the delivery of support services to individuals and to the school as a whole. Aside from their specific functions, the teams are expected to lead cultural change in their buildings, inculcating a collaborative, consensus-seeking ethos that specifically eschews fault-finding (Comer, 1980; Comer et al., 1996; Comer, 1997). According to the Comer model, such a climate increases the likelihood that adults will be able to work together on behalf of children.

The Coalition of Essential Schools, started in 1984 at Brown University, takes an explicit intellectual stance against the mindlessness of the American high school. Members of the Coalition subscribe to a set of common principles, chief among them the radical notion that the purpose of schooling is to enable students to learn to use their minds well, which means that it is more important to achieve genuine mastery over a limited number of essential skills and areas of knowledge than to be exposed to a "comprehensive" curriculum. In addition, member schools agree that:

- their goals should apply to all students;
- teaching and learning should be personalized;
- the governing metaphor of the school should be that of the "student-as-worker";
- student competence should be demonstrated through projects, not just test scores;

- schools should stress high expectations and decency in personal relationships;
- teaching loads should be no more than 80 students;
- teachers have substantial time for collective planning.

By 1997, some 700 schools nationwide had subscribed to these principles, roughly comparable to the number implementing the Comer program.[2] Whereas the Comer program was developed specifically in response to the problems of urban schools, the Coalition includes schools of all types, although a significant number serve low-income, urban populations.

Think of yourself as a principal considering implementation of an innovative program such as Sizer's or Comer's, or perhaps something more limited, such as a new reading program. Whatever the innovation, what might you anticipate as possible problems? I have had numerous conversations with building-level leaders about the progress of various reform initiatives. The typology in Table 1 summarizes some of the issues that arose repeatedly in those discussions; it also takes into account some of my own observations about what was happening in the schools that I visited regularly.[3]

Table 1 is more illustrative than comprehensive; it omits an entire set of issues on the characteristics of students and communities.[4] For example, the table says nothing directly about the violence that surrounds and permeates many schools and nothing about how deeply disengaged from school many adolescents are. It also fails to reflect some of the sources of disorganization peculiar to high schools. Limited as it is, however, the table offers a sense of what building leaders must confront.

---

[2] See Gibboney, 1994; Miller, 1996a, 1996b; Muncey and McQuillan, 1996; Sarason, 1996; Viadero, 1994; Wasley, 1991.

[3] The table borrows some language from Berman and McLaughlin, 1978. It is also similar to a list developed by the Consortium on Chicago School Research.

[4] I could add more about the ways in which students present problems, but principals, in particular, said very little about that. The omission may reflect a post-reform leadership culture in which it was becoming increasingly unacceptable to blame students.

TABLE 1: Impediments to Changing Urban Schools

Social Infrastructure

- Distrust, lack of social comfort among adults; low mutual expectations.
- Predisposition to suspicion of "outsiders"; generalized anger.
- Tensions pertaining to race, ethnicity, age cohort; predisposition
    to factions; resulting communications problems.
- Various patterns of withdrawal as major coping strategy.
- "Happy talk" culture; unwillingness to discuss problems in public settings.
- Poor internal communications.
- Institutional inability to learn from experience.

Building-Level Politics

- Patronage, favoritism; tendency to give new programs to "safe" people.
- Tendency to protect existing power arrangements, formal or informal.
- Pattern of contestation among principal, teachers, local school council,
    union, others; pattern of stalemated power.
- Pattern of autocratic power or vacillation between autocratic and more
    collaborative leadership styles.
- Principals not open to new ideas, criticism; principals unable to
    understand how they are perceived by staff.
- Unwillingness to talk aboout certain issues for fear of offending
    the principal or other powerful people.

Instructional Capacity

- Teacher skepticism about students' learning capacity.
- Weak sense of teacher agency.
- Inadequate instructional supervision skills of principals; absence of
    accountability for instructional program.
- Rigidity of teacher attitudes about how students learn.
- Reluctance of teachers to assume leadership.
- Tradition of teacher autonomy: "What goes on in my classroom is my
    business."
- Content knowledge of staff; classroom management skills.
- Poor fit between curriculum and assessment procedure; being made to
    teach one thing while students are being tested on another.
- Ineffective discipline practice; atmosphere unconducive to teaching.
- General belief in program failure: "We've seen programs come, we've
    seen them go."
- Inadequate informal staff knowledge of student backgrounds and interests.
- Resource needs, including personnel, material, and space needs.
- Instability of good instructional staff.

TABLE 1 (continued)

Environmental Turbulence

- Perception of patronage, favoritism, cronyism in central office practices.
- Instability of leadership at central office.
- Hierarchical culture at central office; perception that "the only way to get something done is to kiss somebody's behind."
- Absence of accountability for central office personnel.
- Political, organizational, resource issues at school district or state level.
- Inadequate support services from central office, including its inability to function as information resource.
- Poor communication with central office; seemingly contradictory, arbitrary directives from central office; building leaders taken away from substantive work.

Structure of Support for Implementation

- Lack of time, including time for retraining, shared planning, reflection; competing time demands made by different programs.
- Narrow base of support; lack of ownership; inability to offer appropriate blend of top-down and bottom-up incentives/sanctions.
- Inappropriate pace and scale of change; trying to do too much too quickly.
- Narrow base of leadership; tendency for everything to fall back on the principal and/or a few others: "The same few people do everything."
- Leadership's lack of deep understanding of particular innovations; lack of comparative knowledge regarding innovations.
- Absence of quality substitute support.
- Instability of key administrative personnel.
- Absence of mechanism for ongoing, accurate assessment of innovations.
- Absence of follow-through, inability to make mid-course corrections.

Social Infrastructure

In the worst schools, the basic web of social relations is likely to be severely damaged. These schools are angry, discouraged places where people trust only those in their personal clique—which is ordinarily defined, at least in part, in terms of race or ethnicity—and where people can be quick to interpret the behavior of everyone outside that clique in the most negative way.[5]   One important reason school reformers underestimated how long it would take to change the system was widespread underappreciation of the salience of social relations.   For many programs, the first two years of implementation were almost wholly given over to clearing away the social and political underbrush; rather than implementing the programs, they were trying to get into a position where they could begin to do so.[6]

The Comer program tries to anticipate relationship problems, but even the staff involved in the Chicago implementation initially underestimated the depth and tenacity of these problems.   They were aware, for example, of the tensions between teachers and parents and of the very strong sense among Chicago teachers that inner-city parents are insufficiently interested in the education of their children.   Thus, in their first schools, the staff put a great deal of energy into increasing the visible participation of parents in schools, thinking that would reduce some of the tensions.   In fact, in almost every case, increased parental involvement led to increased parent-teacher tension, at least initially.   Mere interaction did not change the deeply ingrained tendency of one group to interpret the behavior of the other group in the most negative way possible.[7]

Pervasive distrust means that schools cannot make use of financial and technical resources even when they become available.   Inner-city schools typically have severe resource prob-

---

[5] For recent descriptions of dysfunctional school climates, see Anyon, 1997; Devine, 1996; Fine, 1991.   The portrait they create, however, hardly differs from that in older literature, including Comer, 1980; Fuchs, 1969; Gouldner, 1978; Kohl, 1967; Payne, 1984; Rogers, 1968; Rosenfeld 1971.

[6] While schools were struggling through this period, some researchers were pronouncing various programs as ineffectual (Walberg and Niemiec, 1994).

[7] This example, like many in this section, can be misleading in that it separates the social climate from the resource base.   If we could take away from a North Shore school 40 percent of its funding, 40 percent of its teachers, and the top-performing 50 percent of its students, what would that do to school climate?   I suspect the tone of interaction might change substantially.   We could also think of physical safety as a kind of resource.

lems. In demoralized schools, however, making resources available does not mean that the resources will ever be brought to bear on the problems. Expensive teaching materials sit on a shelf because teachers believe that the materials will make no difference, or the materials end up in the room of a teacher who has political pull. Outsiders with potentially useful expertise are rejected simply because they are outsiders.

Social demoralization also means that communicating the simplest information accurately is difficult even when no one is deliberately sabotaging the flow of information. In such environments, programs that are inherently complex may operate at an extra disadvantage. The sheer complexity of the program may militate against the development and communication of an accurate, shared understanding of what the program is about. This is all the more so in high schools where size and departmentalization further frustrate communication. This has been a problem for both Essential Schools and Comer schools. Essential Schools have found that staff members in a given school may have significantly different understandings of what the program does. Comer facilitators in Chicago have commented frequently on the number of people who say that they still do not understand the program at all.

A climate of distrust also contributes to one of the most frustrating characteristics of these institutions: their inability to learn from experience. Over a period of just a few years, some schools have implemented 10 or 15 different programs, none of which have gone particularly well. These same schools continue to implement more programs in ways that reflect little or no learning from previous attempts.[8] In part, the inability to learn from experience has to do with the lack of time for shared reflection and pooling of information, but even if there were

---

[8] Another hypothesis about the inability to learn from experience is that building-level leaders do not perceive implementation in the way that they perceive and understand program structure. Beyond a few very broad generalizations about the "change process," they may not have clear paradigms for thinking about how innovations develop. They are interested in having programs rather than developing them. Alternatively, it may be that one of the paradigms they do have, the "inadequate personnel" paradigm ("It didn't go well because the people I put in charge blew it"), pushes out more instructive explanations.

time, distrustful people have a hard time learning from one another.

The inadequate social infrastructure may also mean that inner-city schools are distinctively personality-driven institutions. In a socially chaotic environment, strong personalities may find a kind of leverage not available in more structured environments. Suburban schools have plenty of staff personality problems of their own, but the lack of structure in urban schools, especially the absence of effective sanctions for poor performance, leaves them particularly vulnerable to strong, aggressive personalities. That is, given inadequate evaluation of personnel, a protectionist union, dauntingly complex procedures for disciplining uncooperative teachers, and a weak professional culture, there are fewer institutional constraints on individual behavior than one might find elsewhere (see Chicago Tribune Staff, 1988, pp. 61-85; Vander Weele, 1994, pp. 61-74). Thus, the constellation of personalities associated with a particular reform effort may be a critical predictor of how implementation will fare.

Building-Level Politics

The category of "building-level politics" will be intuitively familiar to suburban as well as urban school teachers. Seymour Sarason quotes one teacher as saying that in schools, "no good idea ever goes anywhere; it gets buried in endless discussion and power plays that make you sorry you ever got involved in the first place" (1996, p. 336). The tendency for decisions to reflect the desire of those in power to maintain and augment their power may be nearly universal but, again, especially salient in inner-city schools. In wealthier schools, political considerations are more likely to be offset to some degree by higher levels of social skill, greater availability of resources (and thus less need to fight over who gets what), a more even distribution of social capital, and a more stable set of power arrangements. These restraints are less evident in urban schools. As a result, outside agencies trying to lead reform efforts are frequently embedded in the extant political conflicts before they are astute enough even to recognize it.

Instructional Capacity

We have ample evidence that in inner-city schools, the modal teacher belief is that by the time students start school, the great majority of them have already been so damaged that only a handful can be saved; thus, it does not matter what teachers do (see, e.g., Chicago Tribune staff, 1988; Gouldner, 1978). This is an ideology in the sense that teachers are clearly invested in the idea of the ineducability of most children and the apathy of their parents, so much so that when teachers encounter evidence to the contrary, there is a predisposition to reject it (Kohl, 1967; Rosenfeld, 1971). Within the context of school reform, teachers may try new methods, but they do so with the same old attitudes.

Chicago school principals have never been known for their skills at instructional supervision, and reform has not changed that, at least not in the bottom-tier schools. Principals who have not been comfortable supervising traditional instruction are being asked to lead the implementation of new, often more complicated, instructional initiatives. Principals claim, with much justification, that the other things they are required to do leave little time for classroom supervision, but other factors play a role—fear of confrontation with individual teachers or with the union, a sense that classroom observations are not very useful, and a lack of confidence among some principals in their own instructional skills.

The universal answer to problems of instruction is staff development, despite the fact that it usually fails—another testimony to the inability of schools to learn from experience. It may well be that there is a new consensus emerging about the nature of effective professional development (Miller, 1995). Among other things, it should be responsive to teacher-identified needs, be school-based and built into basic school operations, be ongoing, and help teachers develop a theoretical understanding of their work. In fact, "drive-by" staff development seems to be the modal type of development in troubled schools. One study of four urban districts found that "the traditional model—short-term passive activities with limited follow-up—was still common, even though teachers generally found such training boring and irrelevant" (Miller, 1995, p. 2). As much as 90 percent of what teachers "learn" in such activities is quickly forgotten.

Good professional development can change teachers. Both the National Writing Project and the Illinois Writing Project have been successful in changing teacher behavior. Part of the reason seems to be that these projects create long-term relationships with the teachers and generate long-term professional dialogue among teachers (Smith, 1996). Other programs (e.g., Children's Math Worlds and the Algebra Project) seem to achieve similar results by having a more experienced teacher maintain regular contact with new teachers for a significant time after their training (Davis and Harris, 1994).

Environmental Turbulence

One of the things that make it difficult for schools to concentrate on core issues of teaching and learning is the class of problems that Table 1 labels "environmental turbulence," that is, the ways in which the characteristics of the school district can affect individual schools. Even when the Chicago system was supposedly decentralized, principals thought that too much time was spent responding to central-office directives that were dubiously connected to the schools' educational mission. That problem persists. Although the central office seems to be getting more points for both competence and good intentions than it did several years ago, principals still expect central office staff to undercut them on a regular basis (see Lenz, 1997). Principals expect that the central office will lose track of funds in the computer that make it possible to hire new staff, will issue conflicting and ever-changing policy directives, or will just give out thoroughly erroneous information. Principals still cultivate friends downtown to look out for them; no one wants to be dependent on the official channels of explanation and assistance.

Structure of Support

Much of what I have listed under "structure of support" is at least implied by some of the problems above, but the factors in this category are important enough to discuss separately. Determining how much "ownership" a project has turns out to be more complicated than it may sound. Some programs (e.g., the Algebra Project and Accelerated Schools) require that teachers vote before the programs come into a school. Even so, a few strong personalities may unduly influence the voting, or the principal may have twisted arms to influence votes. In some instances, teachers may agree to a program only to learn that they had no idea what they were getting themselves into. A traditional math teacher may get very excited by a training session on inquiry-based math but be unable to really understand what the transition entails until it has been tried for a substantial period of time. Robert Moses of the Algebra Project believes that it takes a year of exposure before a teacher can make a truly informed decision about whether to buy in.[9] As a part of that process, it is very useful for teachers who are about to implement a new program to have substantial contact—preferably including classroom visits—with other teachers who have implemented the same program recently. In practice, principals rarely have the resources, including substitute teacher support, to make this possible. As a result, teachers continue trying to implement programs about which they may have a superficial understanding. Only after an earnest effort to change their teaching can teachers understand the costs in terms of preparation time, disruption of classroom routines, and so forth.[10]

There is a parallel process at the school level. Many schools are trying to push change at a pace that makes little sense for their level of organizational development, which is just one of many reasons for the widespread difficulty schools have in following through. It is not unusual for a school to set clear priorities at the beginning of the year and then never talk about them again after December. The priorities get lost in the shuffle, pushed aside by new concerns and new initiatives.

---

[9] On the Algebra Project, see Moses et al., 1989; Silva and Moses, 1990; Davis and Harris, 1994.

[10] Students may play a larger role in impeding teacher change than we realize. One of the ways teachers keep the lid on classrooms, especially in the older grades, is by giving healthy doses of seat-work (i.e., simple in-class writing assignments). It becomes a safe and comfortable routine for both sides; teachers who try to make the shift to more interactive classrooms are likely to face a period during which students, removed from their calming routines, are bouncing off the walls. Eventually, students are likely to appreciate and enjoy the interactive classrooms, if teachers have the strength to endure that initial period.

Implementation as a Learning Process

The partial list of obstacles in Table 1 should be enough to remind us that the problems of urban schools are multidimensional, intertwined, and "overdetermined." The worst schools suffer from deeply rooted cultures of failure and distrust, are politically conflicted and personality-driven, have difficulty learning from their own experiences, have internal communication problems, have unstable staffs and narrow pools of relevant professional skill, and exist in a larger environment that is politically unstable. In such an organizational context, we should assume that most program implementation will be superficial. There are just too many problems and too few resources. Harried principals will work on one problem or another for a little while, unable to give most problems meaningful or sustained attention. Thus, across the school system, one sees a remarkable outpouring of reform activity, but many schools cannot get past the outward structures of reform—committees, meetings, materials, specialized vocabularies. New educational programming is being constantly erected over weak social, political, and professional scaffolding. When deeply troubled schools do manage to put something worthwhile in place, we should be skeptical about how long they will be able to hang on to it.

As Chicago schools begin to experience some success, they are learning how fragile it is. In the Chicago Comer program, schools that develop high-functioning teams may be unable to sustain the effort, often because of personnel changes. Other schools are finding that teachers who experience success with a given instructional program do not necessarily want to use the program again the next year. A number of probation schools that have made progress have had difficulty getting their faculties to continue the effort. Similarly, the Coalition of Essential Schools has found that even when teachers have invested great effort in transforming their teaching styles, many slowly begin reverting to traditional practices by the third, fourth, or fifth year. Schools also find progress undermined by high turnover among administrators (Viadero, 1994). Comer believes that about a third of the schools in his program make gains but then have difficulty sustaining them (Comer, 1997, p. 72).[11] We

---

[11] See also Muncey and McQuillan, 1996; Payne, 1984, pp. 59-67.

should expect that our toughest schools will have as much trouble sustaining successful initiatives as they do establishing them. Reformers typically assume that once teachers have some success using new methods, they will buy into those methods. That may be naive. If schools continue to improve, positive synergies will develop at some point, but they take longer than most of us supposed. These schools have been failing for so long that little bits and pieces of success do not take root.

Table 1 may also suggest ways for contrasting the strengths and limitations of various models of reform. All the major reform models address some of the important issues raised by the table. Comer is right to stress the salience of social climate; Total Quality Management (TQM) is right to stress the managerial and administrative deficits of schools; the Coalition of Essential Schools is right in its critique of schools as lacking intellectual coherence. On the other hand, none of these models fully anticipates the realities of low-capacity schools. Comer has never had a clear curricular component or method for supporting teachers in the classroom; TQM and the Coalition both seem to consistently underestimate the social and political implications of their work. Most models have what Paul Hill calls "zones of wishful thinking"—areas of predictable problems that go unaddressed (Hill and Celio, 1998).[12] Blind spots do not mean that programs cannot be effective. There are thousands of "medium-bad" schools where there is enough infrastructure in place that the direction provided by a model and the energy provided by its proponents may be enough to help. In the most troubled schools, however, failure to anticipate weak capacity will consistently prevent anything real from being implemented.

There is little evidence on the success rates of different models, but the available evidence is suggestive. Sizer says that his greatest disappointment has been the small number of schools that have broken through (Miller, 1996a). Richard Gibboney, a very sympathetic observer, is not sure whether any of the Coalition's schools had achieved thorough school reform by 1993, despite many cases of excellent work in some of the schools (Gibboney, 1994). Sarason (1996) comes to essentially

---

[12] This might be taken as an argument for more cooperation among programs. Although there are discussions of this sort at the national level, they are running into the bedrock problems of ego and competitiveness.

the same conclusion, partly on the basis of the detailed ethnographic work of Donna Muncey and Patrick McQuillan, who note that all the change efforts they studied contributed to "increased political contentiousness, within faculties and between teachers and administrators" (Muncey and McQuillan, 1996, p. 278). Given the available evidence, it is not clear that even 10 percent of the implementation efforts in urban areas have produced sustained change in schools by any of the usual measures.

As originally conceived, the Essential Schools model may have been an especially difficult model for dysfunctional schools. On the one hand, urban schools in the Coalition have adopted some good policies—lower teacher-student ratios, more reading and writing requirements, more active learning activities, and generally higher standards. On the other hand, the Coalition has traditionally lacked a clear model of implementation. Gibboney believes that the major weakness in the Coalition's approach is that "it severely underestimates the quality and depth of supportive education that teachers, administrators, school board members, and key community leaders require to mount and sustain their fundamental reform initiative." The support offered is "too thin and too superficial" (Gibboney, 1994, pp. 68, 70). The lack of a support structure was deliberate to some degree. According to Muncey and McQuillan, the Coalition's central staff "does not offer member schools a model or even a suggested starting point for change but rather emphasizes local control and autonomy" (1996, p. 8). One can easily appreciate the philosophical basis for that position, but it can be an invitation to disaster in the inner city. Some schools have enough leadership talent and other infrastructure to make something out of the vision, but inner-city schools generally need a great deal more support in the early stages. Without it, even if they start moving in positive directions, they are likely to founder. The Coalition has been in the process of re-examining its implementation style and putting more emphasis on making "coaches" available to schools.[13]

---

[13] When philanthropist Walter H. Annenberg decided to donate $500 million for improving urban education, he essentially put the Coalition in charge of the effort. Recent reports suggest that the gift became entangled in local politics, one of the dimensions of change that always seems to catch the Coalition off guard (Sanchez, 1997).

Comer has expressed some frustration with the fact that after three years, only about one-third of the schools with which he works demonstrate significant improvement (Comer, 1997, p. 72). If that is accurate, it is probably quite good, considering. Compared with the Coalition, the Comer program has a fairly clear implementation process. The facilitator represents the program on site and assists in problem-solving. In some districts, facilitators clearly speak with the authority of the district superintendent, which gives them substantial leverage. In the early phases of implementation, much of their problem-solving focuses on social and political issues. There is also a team structure, with detailed guidelines for how teams should operate, as well as a series of training sessions for school and district leaders. The Comer program has been developing a series of partnerships with universities in order to offer more follow-up support. The curriculum component is still evolving.

Other programs move beyond a general framework for implementation. Early childhood reading programs—Reading Recovery, Reading One on One, Success for All—seem to be among the most replicable programs, and some have very precisely articulated implementation procedures. Success for All, for example, was operating in 300 schools by 1995 (see Madden et al., 1993; Slavin et al., 1995). It has its own reading curriculum featuring both phonics and literature-based instruction, along with cooperative learning. Student progress is assessed frequently. Weaker readers have tutors, who are certified teachers with additional training from the program. There is an ongoing staff development program that puts less emphasis on initial training and more on subsequent follow-up in the classroom. A family support team offers parenting education programs, encourages more parental involvement in school, and helps solve problems concerning individual students. All of this is overseen by a half-time or full-time facilitator who supports teachers, coordinates the various program components, and helps with problem-solving. This approach represents the opposite end of the spectrum from early versions of Essential Schools. The program comes with curriculum, pedagogy, new staff roles, professional development, social supports, and significant trouble-shooting capacity. It imports so much infrastructure of its own that the organizational and cultural weaknesses of schools matter less.

Most of the well-known urban school reform models, even those led by experienced and dedicated individuals, assume more social and organizational infrastructure than actually exists in bottom-tier schools. Comer and Sizer have both indicated that they initially underestimated the difficulty of instituting real change. Noting that it took eleven years longer than expected to reach certain program goals, Comer explains he did not anticipate the "multiple and complex problems we encountered in and beyond the schools" (Comer, 1997, p. 72). Similarly, Sizer, reflecting on twelve years of reform work, says, "I was aware that it would be hard, but I was not aware of how hard it would be, how weak the incentives would be, how fierce the opposition would be." He now has a finer appreciation of the salience of school culture and governance (Miller, 1996a, p. 4).

The record of institutional intransigence—for schools in general and urban schools in particular—is ample: "The history of education during the 1960s and 1970s is replete with examples of superior curricula and instructional programs, developed in and for urban schools, that were rejected one by one by urban school cultures in favor of more traditional schooling." Even when schools were changed, the changes did not have long lifespans: "They appear on the scene, bloom, and rather quickly revert to the old school culture" (Parish and Aquila, 1996, p. 303).

Three decades ago, Sarason cautioned that we should expect little or nothing from school reform efforts because reformers consistently failed to understand schools as organizations with their own cultures and power arrangements (Sarason, 1971). In a recent retrospective piece, he noted that for 15 years, he kept a file of letters from people who had mounted failed reform efforts. One of the strongest themes in those letters was that reformers "had vastly underestimated the force of existing power relationships and had vastly overestimated the willingness of school personnel to confront the implications of those relationships on the level of action" (Sarason, 1996, p. 340). Paul Berman and Milbrey McLaughlin studied nearly 300 federally funded educational innovations, concluding that successful implementation was rare, that it was difficult to sustain success over a number of years, and that replication of programs in new sites usually fell short of the performance at original sites (Berman and McLaughlin, 1978). Again, most of the innovations were in less troubled environments than the inner city. Much federal spending on educational innovation, the study concluded, was being wasted. A few years later, Larry Cuban examined high school pedagogy and concluded that it had hardly changed over the last century, surviving wave after wave of school reform (Cuban, 1984; see also Gibboney, 1994).

There is a substantial body of very visible research pointing to the intractability of schools. This point seems not to have been adequately appreciated by contemporary reformers, despite the fact that virtually all reformers claim their work is "research-based." It is unclear what they mean by that, but they apparently do not mean research on the history of past reforms and their implementation.

Richard Elmore has recently revived the discussion, point-ing out that school reforms tend to be either short-lived or shallowly implemented, in part because "curriculum developers proved to be inept and naive in their grasp of the individual and institutional issues of change associated with their reforms. They assumed that a 'good' product would travel into U.S. classrooms on the basis of its merit, without regard to the complex institutional and individual factors that might constrain its ability to do so" (Elmore, 1996, p. 14). As Muncey and McQuillan conclude, "research on educational reform often rediscovers the wheel, finding out what has already been learned in previous studies" (1996, p. 288). Much like the schools that they are trying to change, the reform community seems to have an institutionalized inability to learn from experi-ence. We should have learned far more than we have from the thousands of schools that have been restructured over the years. Sarason rightly points out that many reformers act as if they have nothing to learn:

> [The] educational reform movement has been almost totally unaware that its initial models *never* should have been regarded as other than just that: first approximations that would be found wanting in very important respects. On the contrary, each discrete effort at change seemed to assume that its rationale was *the* model, not an initial one that would lead to better ones (Sarason, 1996, p. 355).

The factors preventing the reform community from adopting a systematic learning mode are too complicated to be explored here.[14] However, there are three issues that should be part of

---

[14] The findings of Berman and McLaughlin (1978) on factors affecting successful educational change still stand up extremely well. They concluded that one-shot, pre-implementation training is ineffec-

any exploration. First, we need to consider the possibility that reformers simply take their own models too seriously and get too invested in their own ideas to think critically about implementation. They come to be communities of true believers, forever reassuring themselves of the rightness of their models and the wrongness of everyone else's (Gibboney, 1994, p. 71). Second, we need to understand the role of foundations in encouraging nonreflective implementation. The Coalition of Essential Schools made a decision to expand rapidly because foundations would take them seriously only if they were growing (Muncey and McQuillan, 1996). This pattern has been replicated by foundations in Chicago. Finally, recalling the tone of public debate about Chicago school reform, we should consider the possibility that reformers tended to hold educators in contempt, which led to simplistic ways of thinking about change. In this respect, there was little difference between the views of business leaders such as those who created Chicago's "Corporate/Community School" and community-based activists coming from a leftist perspective.[15] Both tended to construct problems in reductionist terms—teachers and principals who did not care, who were not trying, or who failed to appreciate "good" models of practice. The implication always seemed to be that once "we" come to power, things will quickly be set right.

Why reformers have been so slow to appreciate the complex causes of failure in inner-city schools is open for debate. The consequence is a cycle we have seen often. Reformers develop visions that are morally compelling, well-supported with intellectual rationale, but underconceptualized with respect to the day-to-day realities of inner-city schools. The reformers have

---

tive, that teachers should receive classroom assistance and should observe similar projects in other schools, and that principals should participate in training and teachers in project decision-making. High schools are harder to change than elementary schools. Veteran teachers are less likely to implement changes successfully. Quality of relations among teachers, active support of principals, and effectiveness of project directors all strongly affect implementation. I would also argue, however, that Berman and McLaughlin undervalue administrative pressure and overvalue local development of program materials.

[15] The Chicago Corporate/Community School opened in the North Lawndale neighborhood in 1988. Because of funding problems, it was absorbed into the public school system in 1994.

some early successes, perhaps in smaller schools or in schools with particularly good leadership or in situations where the program founder is actively involved in implementation. They sell their vision on the basis of those early successes and expand their program, probably with foundation encouragement. As they move into more schools and more difficult situations, they find that their earlier experiences did not fully prepare them for dealing with the array of problems that urban schools present. With dozens (or hundreds) of schools, they cannot adjust to the problems of the environment in the same way they could with two or three schools. Program results become more mixed. Some of the original success stories begin to deteriorate. The same people who encouraged rapid expansion—the policymaking community, the foundations, the media—become disappointed. The intellectual and humanistic premises of reform are called into question. Traditionally, at this juncture, another cycle of collective despair about inner-city schools begins. Indeed, we are already hearing arguments that "reform doesn't work" (e.g., Steinberg, 1996; Miller, 1996b).

Another fork in the road is possible. Reformers may learn the hard way, but the reform community has clearly learned a great deal and is translating that into more comprehensive and intensive methods for implementation. Nationally, the question is whether reformers will be given enough time to put what they have learned into practice before the relevant publics give up on urban schools again. The situation is quite different in Chicago, where despair is no longer an option, a point discussed in the next section.

"I DON'T WANT YOUR NASTY POT OF GOLD": THE SOCIAL DEMORALIZATION OF SCHOOLS[16]

The problems created by the social demoralization of urban schools may be the least understood obstacle to reform, at least by policymakers. Again, the issue is not lack of research. Three decades of ethnographic work attest to the power of dys-

---

[16] This section is an abbreviated version of Payne (1997). I am grateful to Michelle Adler, Chicago Comer facilitator, for the "nasty pot of gold" story.

functional relationships in urban schools.[17]   Nonetheless, programs and mandates continue to be thrown at schools with little discernible concern for their social infrastructure.

This section examines in more detail the disjunction between public policy and the daily reality of urban schools. We can begin with a story:

> One day a stranger strolled into an urban school and asked if he could address the teachers. When they were gathered, he held up a big, shiny pot of gold and announced that it belonged to the school—he had brought it as a gift. The teachers, especially the veteran teachers, immediately started firing hostile questions at him. Why was he being so nice to them? Who was going to divide up the gold? Did the union approve of bringing gold into schools? Besides, some of them had heard that he had already given a pot of gold to the school down the street. Was this pot of gold as large as the pot of gold he gave the school down the street? Because if not, they didn't want it. They didn't need any second-rate pot of gold, thank you very much. One stern matron rose to her feet, shaking a finger at the befuddled stranger, to testify that she had been teaching for 35 years, and if you needed gold to teach, she sure would have figured it out before now. She knew the students and parents in this neighborhood, which was more than she could say for the stranger, and they just weren't the kind of parents and kids who could appreciate gold. Maybe gold made a difference in other neighborhoods, but it wasn't going to do a bit of good here.

People who have been involved in efforts to change schools recognize the pot of gold scenario. Distrust and suspicion, which are at the heart of what I mean by demoralization, can wreak havoc with the most benign programs. One of Chicago's Comer schools will be used to illustrate this point.

---

[17]   See Kohl, 1967; Kozol, 1967; Fuchs, 1969; Leacock, 1969; Rogers, 1968; Rosenfeld, 1971; Gouldner, 1978; Simon, 1982; Rogers and Chung, 1983; Payne, 1984; Fine, 1991; Anyon, 1997.

Woodbine School is one of the 16 Chicago schools that have tried to implement the Comer process.[18]   Among Comer schools, Woodbine is very much in the middle of the pack in most aspects.   A K-8 school, its reading scores place it in the third quartile among all city schools, well ahead of most Comer schools.   Serving an overwhelmingly low-income, Black and Hispanic population on the city's West Side, it has an engaged, energetic principal and a hardworking staff.   Although many Chicago schools are virtually empty of staff soon after the afternoon bell, several Woodbine teachers regularly come early and stay late, suggesting a staff that has higher-than-normal expectations.   At least two well-known street gangs operate in the area, but this is not a school serving one of Chicago's housing projects, with all the additional social problems that entails.

Even with its relative advantages, Woodbine's staff has significant problems trusting one another.   Some of this lack of trust originates with the leadership team, but it emanates to relationships throughout the building.   Mrs. Clinton, the principal, is very concerned with test scores but, like most Chicago principals, would be considered more of a manager than an instructional leader.   Her classroom observations—which are infrequent—seem geared toward identifying the weaker teachers so that she can weed them out rather than working with them to improve.   She has, however, hired some assistant principals who are respected by staff for their knowledge of instruction, something not all principals are secure enough to do.

The principal's operating style, though, makes it difficult for her to get the best out of her staff.   She is described as impetuous and much quicker to reprimand—often in public—than to praise.   The principal is not very patient with the frequent criticisms of her insensitivity to staff; she hires people because she hopes they are professional enough to do their jobs without being stroked every few minutes.   Despite the fact that the school is committed to shared decision-making, Mrs. Clinton has difficulty making her staff, even the senior staff, feel that they have a real voice.   She vacillates between asking for collaboration and consensus one day and expecting staff to respect her decision-making prerogatives as principal the next.

---

[18] To protect its anonymity, I have changed some details about "Woodbine" school and its staff.

Her vacillation keeps senior staff constantly off balance. Is this a day when it is okay to disagree with the boss or not?

A staff member who guesses wrong can wind up in big trouble. At one point, the principal decided that she wanted to reshuffle job assignments of members of the leadership team (the assistant principals, the counselor, the social worker, the curriculum resource specialist) in ways that, from her viewpoint, would allow for more effective curriculum supervision and more support for teachers on disciplinary matters. From the viewpoint of almost everybody else, it looked as if the reassignments failed to take advantage of the particular strengths and weaknesses of team members. Mrs. Clinton originally presented the decision as a done deal, but when she saw how clearly shocked the leadership team was at not being consulted sooner, she claimed that she was only making suggestions. She had presented the realignment so forcefully that no one really believed that it was open for discussion. Few objections were voiced until she stepped out of the room, and the Comer facilitator pressed people for their reactions, which turned out to be almost entirely negative. Mrs. Clinton was clearly annoyed to walk back in the room and find the issue still under discussion. According to the field notes, she sighed and, in a combative tone, asked the group, "What is the problem? Is there someone here who is unable to do what I have asked them to do?" When Mrs. Johnson, one of the assistant principals, expressed her doubts about the new plan, Mrs. Clinton repeatedly asked her if she was saying that she could not accomplish what she had been asked to do, and Mrs. Johnson repeatedly responded that she was "perfectly willing" to do her "very best" but she still had concerns. After going back and forth for awhile, Clinton pushed her chair back from the table and said angrily, "This is an administrative decision, and I am the administrator. This is no longer up for discussion. As far as I am concerned, this meeting is adjourned." With that, she stormed out.

The observable fallout from this little brouhaha continued for months. In the short term, Mrs. Johnson was frightened—almost to tears at one point—that for voicing an honest opinion, she was going to get written up. Mrs. Clinton was certainly in a mood to do that for awhile. She felt betrayed by her assistant. This was not the first time that Clinton thought that Johnson had betrayed her by speaking out of turn, but it marked a turning point in their relationship. Mrs. Clinton several times expressed skepticism about Mrs. Johnson's intentions, and Mrs. Johnson, who prided herself on being a hard worker, seemed to withdraw for awhile. She did her job, but she was not always invested in it the way she had been. Perhaps it should not be surprising that the assistant principal's relationship with teachers sometimes replicated the principal's relationship with her. Johnson made several decisions that directly affected teachers without consulting them and then seemed surprised when teachers were upset or felt devalued.

It may seem that Mrs. Clinton overreacted to a minor disagreement, but one must appreciate the context within which she works. Like all Chicago school principals, she was on a four-year contract, renewable at the pleasure of her local school council (LSC). For much of the period under discussion, relations between the principal and the LSC were markedly tense. The principal seemed to be right in her judgment that some LSC members were out to get her. At least two members seemed to automatically take the opposite side from her on any issue. There were periods, negotiated by the Comer facilitator, when the hostile LSC members tried to be less oppositional, but even during those truce periods the principal had a hard time believing they were sincere. She continued to interpret their behavior in the light of their previous behavior, perceiving attacks when none were intended. The principal was thus always on the defensive, confronted with a central administration that was becoming increasingly aggressive about insisting on test score improvement and an LSC that seemed to be waiting for her to slip up. The last thing she needed was senior staff openly disagreeing with policy. From the principal's point of view, that kind of betrayal was not merely personal, it jeopardized her ability to continue to run and improve her school. A principal may firmly believe in collaborative, egalitarian ideals—Mrs. Clinton brought the Comer program to Woodbine, after all—and yet bracket them off as not being applicable to particular situations. You cannot have everybody expressing their feelings on every single point when you are in the middle of a battle. The principal believed, with some justification, that there had been plenty of issues on which she had gone out of her way to solicit and respond to staff input. She could not do it on every issue.

Her leadership staff would have almost certainly agreed with her. Still, they wanted to know, more clearly than the principal had communicated in the past, which issues were the principal's prerogative and which were open for input. Realistically, though, principals were themselves going through the reform process for the first time, and the political context in which they work is shifting constantly. They could not always know in advance which issues could comfortably be thrown open for discussion.

However understandable, what is perceived as inconsistent behavior from principals can wreak havoc with their staff. Soon after the blowup, Mr. Ford, another assistant principal and perhaps the member of the leadership team least likely to disagree with the principal, seemed to become the favorite. He seemed to have gained Clinton's confidence in a way the others did not and seemed to have access to information sooner than anybody else. Other members of the team resented what they saw as favoritism, and in subsequent meetings when people disagreed with Mr. Ford, it was not always clear whether they were disagreeing substantively or because he was the principal's new favorite. At least one other member seemed to be always trying to protect Ford from any criticism. For several months, the atmosphere on the team was defensive and mutually suspicious, enough so that there were open discussions about distrust on the team. The simplest administrative tasks—supervising the lunchroom, devising a detention policy—became Byzantine exercises in intrigue, with each faction trying to discredit the other and always questioning the motives of the other.

This squabbling, backbiting group was supposed to be leading Woodbine School through a comprehensive revision of its K-8 curriculum. The school had embarked on this project a year and a half earlier; the project was intended to spur more professional collaboration among teachers and to align the material taught in one grade with that taught in contiguous grades, while encouraging the use of more innovative teaching methods. It seemed to be largely an idea that the school administration was pushing, but there was some degree of enthusiasm among staff at the beginning, which was rather quickly frittered away. The external consultant got off to a rocky start; teachers initially thought he was talking down to them. Many teachers were visibly uncomfortable with the idea of sharing what they were doing in the classroom. Re-examination of the curriculum required dozens of meetings, after school and on weekends, and even the initially hopeful became resentful. Some teachers made earnest efforts to coordinate with teachers in other grades, but many others did not, and some of the latter involved cases of pre-existing friction among teachers. Other disagreements started off as curricular—including one between a proponent of whole language in the early grades and a proponent of phonics—but came to take on a personal cast as well, preventing any rational search for compromise. When the administration failed to react forcefully to these problems, they sent a message to teachers about just how serious they were. In any case, most teachers seemed to find the whole process rather abusive. Even so, it was clear that they learned a great deal about what their colleagues were doing; despite all the problems, there was a new level of professional dialogue. The fruit of their labor was a sizable new curriculum handbook, completed just as long-festering leadership tensions were coming to a boil. The administrators acted as if the handbook was a great victory, while teachers generally shrugged.

With or without a handbook, school leadership was much too fractured to implement anything in the classroom. Mrs. Johnson was probably the staff member with the most pertinent expertise, but the project was assigned to one of the assistants with whom Johnson was frequently at odds. Johnson clearly knew about some of the problems as they were developing, but given her tenuous relationship with the principal and some of her colleagues, she did not feel comfortable about raising issues too forcefully. Nevertheless, raise them she did, and, as she expected, her questions were interpreted as personal attacks, and the other assistant countered with a series of optimistic reports that glossed over reality. Eventually, Mrs. Johnson was given more direct responsibility for the project, but teachers' attitudes were well hardened by that time. They did not want to hear the phrase "curriculum revision." The very idea of visiting someone else's classrooms was still commonly referred to as "spying."

Eight or nine months after the handbook was produced, few teachers could have found a copy of it, much less teach from it. With reasonable leadership, the process might have had a chance; other schools gained a good deal more from the process. At Woodbine, the fragile social situation made it impossible for the school to use the expertise of its staff. It is almost certain that the entire episode deepened teacher cynicism about large-scale change. Pity the next person who tries to sell this group on a new academic program, no matter how valuable.

Even when Woodbine School attempted more modest initiatives, they too frequently floundered on the social infrastructure. Consider a teacher-initiated attempt to address discipline problems. Teachers had long complained that the central office did little to help them with misbehaving students. Largely at the urging of Mr. Steele, a White fifth-grade teacher, the middle-grade teachers initiated their own discipline policy. Each transgression earned students a certain number of points, and as points added up, so did sanctions—calls to parents, detention, loss of in-class privileges, and so on. It may not have been the most creative response, but it worked. There was apparently unanimous agreement that so long as all teachers were enforcing it, and students faced the same rules and punishments in every classroom, it made a real difference. Classrooms and corridors were noticeably more quiet, referrals to the office were reduced. Most of the changes occurred fairly rapidly, and even the most chronic offenders seemed to improve after several marking periods.

Teachers had collectively identified a problem of vital importance to them, collaborated, and come up with a way to substantially alleviate the discipline problem. Naturally, it did not last. It is hard to say exactly when things started falling apart, but it was clear that by the end of the first year, there was less consistency of effort. Mr. Steele, the person most visibly associated with the discipline project, lost some leverage after becoming involved in a conflict with the administration that took on a personal tone—with Steele referring to the main office as the "lunatics." At least one teacher decided to stop using the point system. By the beginning of the next school year, there were two nonconformants, one of whom went so far as to bad-mouth to students the teachers who were enforcing the rules. Her colleagues thought she was trying to win a popularity contest with the students. There was some thought given to asking the administration to intercede and get everybody back on the same page, but the teachers decided that there was no purpose in that. Their thinking may have been affected by the fact that one of the nonconformants was widely perceived to be among the principal's pets. The program just withered away, as teachers gradually tired of beating their heads against the wall. Midway through the second year, only a few classrooms were even trying.

One cannot be certain what was happening at the level of individual motivation, but outwardly, there seems to have been an inability to sustain minimally cooperative relationships, even when everyone involved was profiting, as well as an apparent absence of professional respect and confidence in the ability of the administration to act impartially. Teachers could craft a small victory, but holding on to it took more social capital than they had.

It would be mistaken to think of these problems as incidental. If only a particular teacher had avoided getting into a spitting match with the principal, maybe things would have worked out. But even if that situation had not developed, another incident would have occurred. In the inner city, hostility must be understood not merely as interpersonal, but as structural. If underprepared people are put in a highly stressful, resource-deficient, stigmatized environment where no one typically has authority to invoke effective sanctions and where class and racial tensions are always present, then hostile, dysfunctional relationships become as much a part of the social landscape as outmoded textbooks.

Woodbine School is emphatically not among the worst schools in Chicago; I think of it as "medium bad." The worst schools would not have a principal giving conflicting messages; they might have an out-and-out autocrat running the school with an "in" group, whose members are distinguished only by their skill at political intrigue or ardor at butt-kissing or who happen to be of the same racial group as the principal. In some schools, teachers can be so intimidated that it is difficult to get them to talk inside the building; we called them "parking lot schools" because that is where we had to do our interviews. For all the problems Mrs. Clinton had, her staff almost universally acknowledged her desire to see children learn and her willingness to select staff on the basis of professional competence. She flew off the handle but would listen after calming down. For all their problems, the hardworking staff saw test scores on the rise. The tragedy of Woodbine is that with a staff that decidedly had not given up, they still could not sustain a level of internal cooperation that would allow them to predictably maintain simple positive innovations, even with staff ownership of the innovations.

SOCIAL INFRASTRUCTURE AND SCHOOL REFORM

With a variation here or there, what occurred at Woodbine—reform efforts undermined by distrust and a lack of confidence among staff—is being acted out across the Chicago public schools. The Consortium on Chicago School Research used a

survey of teachers at 210 schools to identify those characteristics shared by schools that were improving.[19]   When the 30
highest-rated schools were compared with the 30 worst schools
on a composite indicator of "cooperative adult effort toward
school improvement," social trust was a key factor.   Teachers
almost unanimously agreed that relationships with their colleagues were cordial, but that did not mean there was much
respect or trust among them.   More than 40 percent of teachers
disagreed with the statement, "Teachers in this school trust each
other" (Sebring, Bryk, and Easton, 1995, p. 60).[20]   How teachers in a given school felt about that issue correlated highly with
whether the school was perceived as improving or stagnating:

> Teachers in the top 30 schools . . . generally sense a great
> deal of respect from other teachers, indicating that they
> respect other teachers who take the lead in school improve-
> ment efforts and feel comfortable expressing their worries
> and concerns with colleagues.   In contrast, in the bottom 30
> schools, teachers explicitly state that they do not trust each
> other.   They believe that only half of the teachers in the
> school really care about each other, and they perceive limited
> respect from their colleagues (Sebring, Bryk, and Easton,
> 1995, p. 61).

There were similar patterns in terms of teacher-parent trust in
the bottom 30 schools: "Teachers perceive much less respect
from parents and report that only about half of their colleagues

---

[19] School "improvement" was based on teachers' assessments of
changes in factors such as their own effectiveness, professional
growth opportunities, and learning from other teachers; relationships
with students, parents, and the community; and student behavior and
academic performance.   The study did not include any direct measure
of student achievement (Sebring, Bryk, and Easton, 1995, p. 4).

[20] While "social climate" is a multidimensional concept (Anderson, 1982), the issue of "trust" cuts right to the heart of what is
problematic about the social climate in many urban schools.   Broadly
conceived, "trust" takes into account how people assess each other's
intentions *and* each other's capacities.   Do principals trust that their
teachers have enough content knowledge to be effective?   Do teachers
believe that their children really are capable of learning?   It might be
clearer to say that the central issues are both trust and confidence.

really care about the local community and feel supported by parents" (Sebring, Bryk, and Easton, 1995, p. 61).

For Chicago, this description probably applies to one-quarter to one-third of the city's schools, and these are the schools that public policy has the least chance of affecting.[21] What difference would it make if policymakers, whether of the ideological left or the ideological right, better appreciated the social demoralization of schools? For one thing, they might be less confident that structural change in and of itself means real change. As a report from the Wisconsin Center for Educational Research puts it:

> Our research suggests that human resources—such as openness to improvement, trust and respect, teachers having knowledge and skills, supportive leadership and socialization—are more critical to the development of professional community than structural conditions.
>
> Structural conditions—including time to meet and talk, physical proximity, interdependent teaching roles, communication structures and teacher empowerment—are important, to be sure. But if a school lacks the social and human resources to make use of those structural conditions, it's unlikely that a strong professional community can develop.
>
> This finding adds weight to the argument that the structural elements of restructuring have received too much emphasis in many reform proposals, while the need to improve the culture, climate, and interpersonal relationships in schools have received too little attention (Kruse, Louis, and Bryk, 1995, p. 7).

As noted earlier, we have repeatedly seen apparently meaningful structural reforms dissipate like dew in sunshine. In the late 1980s, for example, there was widespread confidence among researchers and educational activists that changing governance structures—decentralizing, democratizing, empowering everybody—would lead to real change. At least one-third of school districts in the country tried some form of site-based management between 1986 and 1990 (David, 1995). After more than 15 years of experimentation, it is clear that the rela-

---

[21] See Payne (1997) for a fuller discussion of the numbers of demoralized schools.

tionship between changing structures of building-level power and improving education is not necessarily a direct or reliable one.[22]

Take Chicago as a case in point. Part of the rationale for school reform in Chicago was that empowering parents could create more accountable schools. Thus, the reform law gave parents six out of the eleven seats on each local school council, including the chair. Does changing the formal structure of power change the reality? Not necessarily. According to the best estimate we have (now somewhat dated), in at least 40 percent of the city's schools, principals consolidated power in their own hands (Bryk et al., 1993). Principals who learned to adjust to the new situation probably became more powerful than they were before parents were formally empowered.[23] Parents have a numerical majority on the councils, but parent members are least likely to come to meetings. If they do come, they are the least likely to participate (Easton and Storey, 1994). If they do participate, there is a substantial likelihood that the professionals on the council will pointedly ignore them. In several respects, parents do not have the social capital, including the self-confidence, to take full advantage of the formal change in the arrangement of power.

Another contemporary example is the "best practices" movement, which is based on the straightforward idea that there are certain educational practices that are demonstrably superior to others (Zemelman, Daniels, and Hyde, 1993). If research can identify those practices and make them available to schools, there can be dramatic changes in educational outcomes. Perhaps this is a little too straightforward for the inner city. Most discussion of best practices, including Chicago's attempt to systematize their use, pays little attention to social context (CPS, 1994). At the extremes, that means taking a teaching methodology from, say, New York's Central Park East—that is, a situation with faculty who are highly skilled, share a common edu-

---

[22] See Conley, 1991; Malen, Ogawa, and Kranz, 1990; Weiss, Cambone, and Wyeth, 1992; Weiss, 1993; Wohlstetter and Mohrman, 1994; Ross and Webb, 1995; Weiss, 1995.

[23] At least this was true until a 1995 revision of the reform legislation gave the Mayor of Chicago significantly enhanced powers vis-à-vis the school system. Chicago now has a system that is simultaneously decentralized and recentralized.

cational vision, and have a personal and political commitment to its success—and trying to export it to the normal ghetto school where staff are of questionable competence, alienated, distrustful of one another, and skeptical of the idea that what they do can matter for children. That is to say, the Best Practices movement lends itself to decontextualized thinking, reducing the problem to a cognitive one—if only our teachers knew how they do it in Podunk.

Consider the various "systemic initiatives" that the National Science Foundation (NSF) has been advocating since 1991 (West, 1994; CPRE, 1995). The NSF's Statewide Systemic Initiative and their associated Urban Systemic Initiative aim at nothing less than a complete overhaul of math and science teaching in this country, an overhaul that will not leave poor and minority children behind. To do that, they want to invoke higher standards for learning and assessment, align state and local policies concerning finance, curriculum, teacher preparation and development in support of these higher standards, and develop and provide teachers with materials that will support their use of innovative, inquiry-based curriculum. The statewide initiative in Georgia, for example, intends to produce "creative problem-solvers, critical thinkers, questioners, experimenters, innovators, effective communicators, and reflective learners" (CPRE, 1995, p. 4).

These are entirely laudable aims, but how are all the sensible-sounding plans likely to play when they reach, say, inner-city Atlanta? In a certain number of schools, the principal, well aware that any new program can be disruptive, will put a "safe" person in charge, which, in itself, can cause the program to lose legitimacy with the faculty. Almost inevitably, in some schools, teachers who are firmly convinced that their children will never learn multiplication tables are going to reject the new teaching procedures out of hand. If someone makes them go through the motions, they will do so, but no more than that. The main mechanism for bringing the program into a building is a design team, the members of which are supposed to represent all the teachers in a building concerned with math or science education. These teams will have all the problems other supposedly democratic committees have in demoralized environments. If staff members are sufficiently factionalized and the level of individualism sufficiently high, it may not be possible for any teacher to "represent" other teachers or to meaningfully communicate new ideas to them. If nothing else, some of the teachers are going to be Black, some of the curriculum experts are going to be White, and some of those Black teachers have heard enough White experts on Black children to last them this lifetime and the next. The moment the "experts" start to pontificate, the teachers will shut down.

How can reform programs be made more rugged so that whatever they offer of value can survive the actual conditions of inner-city schools? Part of the answer is to be wary about allowing programs to grow too fast. We are all anxious for change, but given the record of large-scale failures in the past, the NSF might have been better off trying to have a real impact in bottom-tier schools in one city before going nationwide. Being "systemic" at the local level is challenge enough right now. In the early years of school reform in Chicago, foundations said they wanted some bang for their buck. The more schools in a program, the happier the foundations were. Comer wanted to start off in Chicago with just two schools, but local foundations wanted him to start with 16. As a compromise, the program began with four schools the first year and added four more the second year, which, in retrospect, was self-defeating. The program was moving into new schools before getting a handle on what was happening in the first group.

Ironically, as suggested earlier, there are reasons to wonder whether even the national Comer project has grown too rapidly. Begun in the 1960s, the program grew rapidly in the 1980s. In 1990, at least 100 schools around the country were trying to implement Comer programs; by 1994, the number had risen to 300, and by the fall of 1995, it was 563 (Haynes and Comer 1993; Comer et al., 1996). It is now estimated to be more than 700. The very pace of growth suggests questions about whether the small national staff can adequately monitor the degree to which individual projects continue to focus on relationships. In the absence of some such monitoring, one would expect the program to become a caricature of itself, with much energy spent on maintaining the visible structures and many a rhetorical bow in the direction of the program's official philosophy.

The small schools movement is another reform driven by concern with social relationship issues. Inspired, in large measure, by the success of some New York City sub-districts in creating smaller, more personal schools with staff that shared a vision, it seems to offer one relatively reliable policy tool for addressing social demoralization. Here, again, though, much depends on how the program is implemented. In practice, at least in Chicago, some principals have simply ordered their staffs to develop small schools, like it or not, a kind of "be personable or you're going to get hurt" policy. This is likely to lead to schools that are administratively broken down into smaller units but with little of the ethos and commitment that should accompany reform—structural reform without social change, which, as it were, is where we came in.

When one considers how difficult it is to get American schools to change and how the urban context intensifies those difficulties, the progress of Chicago schools is quite impressive. Test scores have been rising, and schools are safer (Bryk et al., 1998; Lenz, 1997; Williams, 1994). Reform can be thought of as going through several phases. Perhaps what was most important about the bottom-up emphasis of the earlier phase is that it opened schools to new ideas and new ways of thinking about teaching, and gave them the financial flexibility to institute new programs without waiting for approval (see Mirel, 1993). The more entrepreneurial schools, usually estimated to be about a third of the system, were able to make progress in this environment (Bryk et al., 1993). Another third of the schools were moribund, many of them too wrapped up in internal conflict to generate collective direction. The progress they have made seems largely attributable to the aggressive, top-down management style introduced when Paul Vallas became CEO of the Chicago Public Schools in 1995. In retrospect, there is no reason to believe that those schools were ever going to change from the bottom up, except in a handful of cases with unusual leadership on site. Indeed, perhaps one of the larger lessons of the Chicago experience is that singular reliance on bottom-up measures is least appropriate in the most demoralized schools. Large-scale change in urban systems may require at least a period of top-down pressure.

The Vallas administration has been roundly criticized for implementing programs with insufficient planning, for being authoritarian, and for lacking regard for due process (Lenz, 1997; Lenz and Forte, 1996). Nonetheless, judging from test scores and other measures, the administration has managed to get the attention of bottom-tier schools. Ironically, the various reform models may have a better chance of making a dent in "tough schools" in Chicago than elsewhere. There is more leverage for change in an environment where the administration is constantly sending the signal that failure is not acceptable for any reason and that poorly performing schools will be sanctioned. The irony is that much of the Chicago reform community is animated by models of democratic, collegial change processes, and it is uncomfortable with anything that seems to be top-down reform. Most reform groups disagree either with the way probation sanctions have been carried out or with the idea of probation itself (or both). Nevertheless, they nearly all seem to agree that they have more leverage in those schools that have been put on probation. School staff are more willing to listen and cooperate under the threat of more serious sanction, and they are less likely to indulge in the old pattern of rejecting offers of help just because it comes from "outsiders."

I know one principal whose summary judgment of the Vallas administration is that they are "hard-headed people," but they do learn. That, of course, is very much the picture of the reform community that emerged in the first part of the chapter—they learn slowly, but they learn. If all parties can maintain a posture of learning, we will have a much better chance of seeing the city's schools move to a new plateau. Some of the critical issues are clear enough. We must begin thinking about preserving the improvements made to date. Otherwise, as much historical experience tells us, the successes will be lost. Schools must be given much more time—not just a few in-service days a year—to devote to reform activities. Building leaders need help thinking in more complex ways about what they are doing. Too often, they do not know enough about either the particular reforms they are implementing or the general history of urban school reform. Too often, they do not have the skills to usefully assess the programs they are implementing. This also applies to the central office, which must develop multidimensional ways of measuring school change, not just test scores and certainly not just scores from tests measuring narrow skills. The task, as Sarason reminds us, is changing organizational culture, not raising test scores. Doing so means that the central office must maintain high expectations of schools while becoming more supportive of them. Even if one grants that the punitive tone of the administration has achieved some good in the second phase of school reform, it is not clear that the same stance makes as much sense in the next phase. People cannot be forced into developing professional subcultures. These issues are predictable, and others will arise. If school staff, reformers, and the administration are all willing to do what we admonish our students to do—to approach new experiences as learners—they should have a better chance to work through whatever new problems they encounter. If that can be accomplished, Chicago may be uniquely poised to blend the creativity and commitment that bottom-up reform can generate with the bottom-line mentality of business in ways that will help the neediest children in the toughest schools. Given the historical record, of course, that is an enormous "if."

REFERENCES

Anderson, Carolyn (1982). "The Search for School Climate: A Review of the Research," *Review of Educational Research*, vol. 52, no. 3 (Fall 1982), pp. 368-420.

Anyon, Jean (1997). *Ghetto Schooling: A Political Economy of Urban Education Reform.* New York: Teachers College Press.

Berman, Paul, and Milbrey McLaughlin (1978). *Federal Programs Supporting Educational Change, Vol. 8: Implementing and Sustaining Innovations.* Santa Monica, Calif.: RAND Corporation.

Bryk, Anthony S., John Q. Easton, David Kerbow, Sharon Rollow, and Penny Sebring (1993). *A View from the Elementary Schools: The State of Reform in Chicago.* Chicago: Consortium on Chicago School Research.

Bryk, Anthony S., Yeow Meng Thum, John Q. Easton, and Stuart Luppesco (1998). *Academic Productivity of Chicago Public Elementary Schools.* Chicago: Consortium on Chicago School Research.

Chicago Tribune Staff (1988). *Chicago Schools, "Worst in America": An Examination of the Public Schools that Fail Chicago.* Chicago: Chicago Tribune.

Comer, James (1980). *School Power.* New York: Free Press.

_____ (1997). *Waiting for a Miracle: Why Schools Can't Solve Our Problems, and How We Can.* New York: Dutton.

Comer, James, Norris Haynes, Edward Joyner, and Michael Ben-Avie, eds. (1996). *Rallying the Whole Village: The Comer Process for Reforming Education.* New York: Teachers College Press.

Conley, Sharon (1991). "Review of Research on Teacher Participation in School Decision-Making. In Gerald Grant, ed., *Review of Research in Education.* Washington, D.C.: American Educational Research Association.

CPRE (1995). *Reforming Science, Mathematics and Technology Education: NSF's State Systemic Initiatives.* New Brunswick, N.J.: Consortium for Policy Research in Education.

CPS (1994). "Pathways to Achievement: Self-Analysis Guide." Chicago: Department of Research, Evaluation, and Planning, Chicago Public Schools.

Cuban, Larry (1984). *How Teachers Taught: Constancy and Change in American Classrooms, 1890-1980.* New York: Longman.

David, Jane (1995). "The Who, What and Why of Site-Based Management," *Educational Leadership,* vol. 53, no. 4 (December-January 1995-1996), pp. 4-9.

Davis, Frank, and Linda Harris (1994). "Evaluation Report: The Algebra Project, 1992-1993." Cambridge, Mass.: Program Evaluation and Research Group, Lesley College.

Devine, John (1996). *Maximum Security: The Culture of Violence in Inner-City Schools.* Chicago: University of Chicago Press.

Easton, John, and Sandra Storey (1994). "The Development of Local School Councils," *Education and Urban Society,* vol. 26, no. 3 (May 1994), pp. 220-237.

Elmore, Richard (1996). "Getting to Scale with Good Educational Practice," *Harvard Educational Review,* vol. 66, no. 1 (Spring 1996), pp. 1-26.

Fine, Michelle (1991). *Framing Dropouts.* Albany: State University of New York Press.

Fuchs, Estelle (1969). *Teachers Talk.* New York: Anchor.

Gibboney, Richard A. (1994). *The Stone Trumpet: A Story of Practical School Reform, 1960-1990.* Albany: State University of New York Press.

Gouldner, Helen (1978). *Teachers' Pets, Troublemakers, and Nobodies.* Westport, Conn.: Greenwood.

Haynes, Norris, and James Comer (1993). "The Yale School Development Program," *Urban Education,* vol. 28, no. 2 (July 1993), pp. 166-199.

Hill, Paul T., and Mary Beth Celio (1998). *Fixing Urban Schools.* Washington, D.C.: Brookings Institution Press.

Kohl, Herbert (1967). *36 Children.* New York: New American Library.

Kozol, Jonathan (1967). *Death at an Early Age.* Boston: Houghton-Mifflin.

Kruse, Sharon, Karen Seashore Louis, and Anthony Bryk (1995). "Teachers Build Professional Communities," *WCER*

Highlights (Wisconsin Center for Education Research), vol. 7, no. 1 (Spring 1995), pp. 6-8.

Leacock, Eleanor (1969). *Teaching and Learning in City Schools*. New York: Basic.

Lee, Valerie, and Julia Smith (1996). "Collective Responsibility for Learning and Its Effects on Gains in Achievement for Early Secondary School Students," *American Journal of Education*, vol. 104, no. 2 (February 1996), pp. 103-47.

Lenz, Linda (1997). "Winning Ugly," *Chicago Tribune*, October 26, 1997.

Lenz, Linda, and Lorraine Forte (1996). "Blind Spot in Glowing Record?" *Catalyst: Voices of Chicago School Reform*, February 1996.

Madden, Nancy, Robert Slavin, Nancy Karweit, Lawrence Dolan, and Barbara Wasik (1993). "Success for All: Longitudinal Effects of a Restructuring Program for Inner-City Elementary Schools," *American Educational Research Journal*, vol. 30, no. 1 (Spring 1993), pp. 123-148.

Malen, Betty, Rodney T. Ogawa, and Jennifer Kranz (1990). "What Do We Know about School-Based Management? A Case Study of the Literature—A Call for Research." In William H. Clune and John F. Witte, eds., *Choice and Control in American Education, vol. 2: The Practice of Choice, Decentralization, and School Restructuring*. New York: Falmer Press.

Miller, Edward (1995). "The Old Model of Staff Development Survives in a World Where Everything Else Has Changed," *Harvard Education Letter*, vol. 11, no. 1 (January-February 1995), pp. 1-3.

_____ (1996a). "Hard-Won Lessons from the School Reform Battle: A Conversation with Ted Sizer," *Harvard Education Letter*, vol. 12, no. 4 (July/August 1996), pp. 3-6.

_____ (1996b). "Idealists and Cynics: the Micropolitics of Systemic School Reform," *Harvard Education Letter*, vol. 12, no. 4 (July/August 1996), pp. 1-4.

Mirel, Jeffrey (1993). "School Reform, Chicago Style: Educational Innovation in a Changing Urban Context, 1976-1991," *Urban Education*, vol. 28, no. 2 (July 1993), pp. 116-149.

Moses, Robert P., Mieko Kamii, Susan McAllister Swap, and Jeffrey Howard (1989). "The Algebra Project: Organizing in the Spirit of Ella," *Harvard Educational Review*, vol. 59, no. 4 (November 1989), pp. 422-443.

Muncey, Donna E., and Patrick J. McQuillan (1996). *Reform and Resistance in Schools and Classrooms: An Ethnographic View of the Coalition of Essential Schools.* New Haven: Yale University Press.

Parish, Ralph, and Frank Aquila (1996). "Cultural Ways of Working and Believing in School: Preserving the Way Things Are," *Phi Delta Kappan*, vol. 78, no. 4 (December 1996), pp. 298-308.

Payne, Charles (1984). *Getting What We Ask For: The Ambiguity of Success and Failure in Urban Education.* Westport, Conn.: Greenwood.

———— (1997). "I Don't Want Your Pot of Gold: Urban School Climate and Public Policy." Evanston, Ill.: Institute for Policy Research, Northwestern University.

Rogers, David (1968). *110 Livingston Street: Politics and Bureaucracy in the New York City Schools.* New York: Random House.

Rogers, David, and Norman H. Chung (1983). *110 Livingston Street Revisited: Decentralization in Action.* New York: New York University Press.

Rosenfeld, Gerry (1971). *Shut Those Thick Lips: A Study of Slum School Failure.* New York: Holt, Rinehart, and Winston.

Ross, Dorene D., and Rodman B. Webb (1995). "Implementing Shared Decision-Making at Brooksville Elementary School." In Ann Lieberman, ed., *The Work of Restructuring Schools: Building from the Ground Up.* New York: Teachers College Press.

Sanchez, Rene (1997). "Can $500 Million Make a Dent? Expectations Diminishing for Gift to Public Education," *Washington Post*, October 13, 1997, p. A1.

Sarason, Seymour B. (1971). *The Culture of the School and the Problem of Change.* Boston: Allyn and Bacon.

———— (1996). *Revisiting "The Culture of the School and the Problem of Change."* New York: Teachers College Press.

Sebring, Penny Bender, Anthony S. Byrk, and John Q. Easton (1995). *Charting Reform: Chicago Teachers Take Stock.* Chicago: Consortium on Chicago School Research.

Silva, Cynthia M., and Robert P. Moses (1990). "The Algebra Project: Making Middle School Mathematics Count," *Journal of Negro Education*, vol. 59, no. 3 (1990), pp. 375-391.

Simon, John (1982). *To Become Somebody: Growing Up against the Grain of Society.* New York: Houghton-Mifflin.

Slavin, Robert, Nancy Madden, Lawrence Dolan, and Barbara
    Wasik (1995). "Success for All: A Summary of Research."
    Paper presented at the American Educational Research
    Association, 1995.
Smith, Mary Ann (1996). "The National Writing Project after
    22 Years," *Phi Delta Kappan*, vol. 77, no. 10 (June 1996),
    pp. 688-692
Steinberg, Laurence (1996). *Beyond the Classroom: Why
    School Reform Has Failed and What Parents Need to Do*.
    New York: Touchstone.
Vander Weele, Maribeth (1994). *Reclaiming Our Schools: The
    Struggle for Chicago School Reform*. Chicago: Loyola Uni-
    versity Press.
Viadero, Debra (1994). "Success with Coalition Reforms Seen
    Limited in Some Schools," *Education Week*, April 14,
    1994, p. 12.
Walberg, Herbert, and Richard Niemiec (1994). "Is Chicago
    School Reform Working?" *Phi Delta Kappan*, vol. 75,
    no. 9 (May 1994), pp. 713-715.
Wasley, Patricia (1991). "Stirring the Chalkdust: Three
    Teachers in the Midst of Change," *Teachers College Rec-
    ord*, vol. 93, no. 1 (Fall 1991), pp. 28-58.
Weiss, Carol (1993). "Shared Decision-Making about What?
    A Comparison of Schools with and without Teacher Partici-
    pation," *Teachers College Record*, vol. 95, no. 1 (Fall
    1993), pp. 69-92.
_____ (1995). "The Four 'I's' of School Reform: How
    Interests, Ideology, Information, and Institution Affect
    Teachers and Principals," *Harvard Educational Review*,
    vol. 65, no. 4 (Winter 1995), pp. 571-592.
Weiss, Carol, Joseph Cambone, and Alexander Wyeth (1992).
    "Trouble in Paradise: Teacher Conflicts in Shared Decision-
    Making," *Educational Administration,* vol. 28, no. 3
    (August 1992), pp. 350-367.
West, Peter (1994). "A Man with a 'Systemic' Science-Reform
    Plan," *Education Week*, November 30, 1994, p. 20.
Williams, Debra (1994). "Violence in Schools Drops as Secu-
    rity Staff Grows," *Catalyst*, vol. 6, no. 3 (November 1994),
    pp. 1, 4-5, 15.
Wohlstetter, Priscilla, and Susan Mohrman (1994). *School-
    Based Management: Promise and Process*. New Bruns-
    wick, N.J.: Consortium for Policy Research in Education,
    Rutgers University.

Zemelman, Steven, Harvey Daniels, and Arthur Hyde (1993). *Best Practice: New Teaching and Learning Standards for America's Schools*. Portsmouth, N.H.: Heinemann.

COMMENTS: SOME LESSONS FROM CATHOLIC SCHOOLS

Valerie E. Lee

Charles Payne's chapter describes several types of impediments to reform in urban public schools, one of which is weak social infrastructure. The climate in such schools is marked by weak social relations, pervasive distrust, social demoralization, and a pervasive belief that many students are ineducable. The purpose of my commentary is to describe several characteristics of Catholic secondary schools that stand in stark contrast to Payne's description of the damaged social infrastructures of urban public schools. Because most Catholic schools are located in cities and because they serve increasingly large numbers of disadvantaged students (many of whom are not Catholic), their successes with such students offer examples that may be illuminating in light of discussions of the problems of (and solutions for) contemporary urban public schools.[1]

SOME BACKGROUND

There are several reasons why anyone interested in urban school reform might draw some valuable lessons from examining Catholic schools in the United States: a rich intellectual and social history; their numerical predominance among the nation's private schools; the spare structure that guides their internal operations; and the favorable outcomes for students and families that choose the schools. Although Catholic schools have repre-

---

[1] The ideas in this commentary are drawn from a long collaborative relationship with Anthony Bryk (see Bryk, Lee, and Holland, 1993). Because we have worked together so closely, it is impossible to separate which ideas, writing, and conclusions have sprung from which person. Some of these ideas are also discussed in Lee, 1997, 2001.

sented one vehicle for social mobility for successive waves of immigrants, they also provide an educational alternative for students beyond those from Catholic families.

Most Catholic schools were, and still are, located in cities where Catholic immigrants settled. Catholic schools began to experience serious pressures during the late 1960s and 1970s, as masses of White families, many Catholics among them, fled the cities for the suburbs. Between 1965 and 1990, enrollment dropped by half.[2] The response of the church to this crisis, and the intellectual milieu in which this response was crafted, has shaped the nature of today's Catholic schools. In the mid-1960s, Vatican II wrought enormous changes in the Catholic church and its schools. A major thrust was an explicit commitment to social justice: The church decided to aggressively and firmly resist a tide of "White flight" enrollments; to redress racial injustice directly; and to hire lay faculty to replace religious order members who left. As a consequence of remaining in the inner city, serving many students from low-income families, and paying faculty salaries instead of relying on contributed services, the Catholic educational sector faced substantial financial difficulties. These pressures still plague Catholic schools in every American city.

Today, about 5 percent of the nation's secondary school population attends Catholic schools. This represents about 75 percent of all students in private high schools.[3] Between 1965 and 1990, when enrollments fell by half, many Catholic schools closed; others opened their doors to students who were

---

[2] From a high of 5.5 million students in 1965, Catholic school enrollment dropped to 2.5 million in 1990. Although they enrolled 12 percent of the school-age population in 1965, in 1990 the schools enrolled only 5.4 percent. The numbers of schools declined accordingly, from 13,000 in 1965 to around 9,000 in 1990 (NCEA, 1990).

[3] Catholic high schools enrolled about 618,000 students in 1997-98, which was 6 percent higher than five years earlier but 41 percent lower than it was in 1969-70. All private secondary schools enrolled about 1.3 million students in fall 1997, compared with 13.1 million students in public secondary schools. Catholic elementary schools enrolled about 6 percent of the total elementary school population in fall 1997. Catholic schools are still closing, but at much less precipitous rates than in the late 1960s and 1970s (NCES, 1999, Tables 3, 63).

not part of the schools' historical mission. These developments coincided with the philosophical thrust toward social justice from Vatican II. Between 1970 and 1990, the proportion of minority students in Catholic schools increased from less than 10 percent to over 20 percent; at the same time, non-Catholic enrollment quadrupled. In Catholic schools in many of the nation's largest cities, these trends have been even more pronounced. Compared with other private schools, Catholic schools enroll a non-elite clientele. Over the past 20 years, tuitions have skyrocketed. Catholic high schools, somewhat more selective than Catholic elementary schools, charge higher tuition (averaging around $3,000, with a wide range). School-financed scholarships are uncommon.

Although Catholic schools enroll somewhat more advantaged children than do public schools, the social differences are modest. They are often called the "poor man's private school." Many Catholic school parents still have working-class backgrounds, and many have never attended college. The major difference between students in the two sectors is self-selection: families that send their children to Catholic schools choose and pay to do so. Many parents make considerable financial sacrifices to pay the tuition. Although most students in Catholic schools are Catholic, increasing proportions of inner-city families that choose this type of education for their children do so despite the religious orientation, not because of it.

The rationale for a discussion of Catholic schools in this commentary relates to the realities of where the schools are (in the cities) and whom they serve (substantial proportions of disadvantaged students). The vast majority of U.S. children attend public schools, and our nation views those schools as troubled. As a non-Catholic, my own motivation for studying these schools has been what their story has to say about urban public schools. This commentary explores some explanations for why contemporary Catholic high schools seem to produce favorable outcomes for their students. Much of the discussion is based on findings from *Catholic Schools and the Common Good* (Bryk, Lee, and Holland, 1993).

ELEMENTS OF CATHOLIC SCHOOLS' EFFECTIVENESS

Delimited Academic Core

The academic program of Catholic high schools is organized as a core curriculum. Almost the same program of study is followed by virtually all students, regardless of family background, academic preparation, or future educational plans. The structure of this curriculum is predicated on distinctive views among faculty and administrators about what all students can and should learn. These views connect to long-standing church traditions about the capacities and proper aims of human beings and about what constitutes a proper education. Required courses predominate, with elective courses limited in content and number.

Compared with public schools, the amount of tracking in a Catholic high school is modest. Whatever program differentiation exists does not produce the invidious consequences found in public schools, in part because explicit school policies allocate more resources to the students who need them most—that is, those at the lower end of the academic spectrum.[4] This reflects a fundamental institutional purpose: a common education of mind and spirit for all. The consequences for students are profound. When all students have common and high-level academic experiences, they all learn more. The academic organization of Catholic high schools also makes efficient use of the limited fiscal and human resources that typify these schools. Furthermore, their small size acts as an organizational correlate of their academic structure. Although there is no reason why large schools should necessarily offer more differentiated academic and social experiences to students, it is both logical and easier when there are more students to accommodate.

---

[4] The nature of remediation is also quite different in public and Catholic high schools. Typically, a Catholic ninth-grader without adequate skills to succeed in Algebra 1, for example, would be placed in an Algebra 1 class but would also be required to take another math class each day until his or her computational skills reached the class level. In a public high school, on the other hand, such a student would likely be enrolled in a general math class instead of Algebra 1. That student would be unlikely to ever learn algebra.

Communal School Organization

The academic structure of Catholic high schools is embedded in a communal organization with three key features. First is an extensive array of school activities whose purpose is to provide frequent opportunities for face-to-face interactions and shared experiences among school members, both adults and students. This occurs through both the common curriculum and the numerous school events that promote high levels of participation and more informal interactions (e.g., athletics, drama, musical events, religious activities). Established traditions allow current students to share experiences with former members.

A second component focuses on the role of teachers, which is more diffuse than that of their public school counterparts. Rather than defining themselves as subject-matter specialists, teachers in Catholic high schools see their responsibilities as extending to any encounters with students: in hallways, on school grounds, in the surrounding neighborhood, and sometimes in their homes. Many teachers define their profession in moral terms—forming character as well as developing skills. Collegiality among teachers is common. School decision-making is less conflictual and more often characterized by high levels of mutual trust and respect. Again, small school size facilitates a more personalized role for teachers, as well as community-building as a whole.

A third component is a set of shared beliefs about what students should learn, about proper norms for instruction, and about how people should relate to one another. Expressing these beliefs is facilitated in an environment defined by a general set of moral understandings about the dignity of each person, a commitment to genuine dialogue, and a commitment to work toward an ethos of caring. The idea of community was spelled out in Vatican II documents about Catholic education. Both the language and living of a community defined in this way is very evident in Catholic schools.

Decentralized Governance

The administrative layer in Catholic schools is thin. Management responsibilities are held mainly by staff members who also teach. The principal has considerable control over daily operations, a tradition that very likely flows from the strong governance by religious orders that formerly characterized almost all Catholic high schools. Even with the expansion of a lay principalship, deference to the principal's authority is common. Principals are often selected from the faculty, rather than from a professional cadre of administrators. The decision to seek or accept an administrative role is often motivated by the opportunity it provides to help the school, rather than for professional advancement or a "plum job downtown." Catholic schools are linked to one another only very loosely, with virtually all important decisions made at the school site. Current reform efforts in public schools toward decentralization are very modest in comparison with the level of school-site autonomy among Catholic schools.

An Inspirational Ideology

Within the ideological thrust from Vatican II that energized Catholic education are two inspirational ideas that shape life in the schools: "personalism" and "subsidiarity." Personalism motivates Catholic schools to pay attention to numerous small social encounters in shaping school life. It motivates the extended teacher role that encourages teachers to care about the kind of people that students become, as well as the knowledge and skills that they acquire. Social behavior is seen in moral terms, as practices within a just community. Personalism makes claims on individuals to act beyond their own particular interests and toward the common good.

The principle of subsidiarity gives human meaning to voluntary associations that act as buffers between the individual and an impersonal society. Subsidiarity motivates the schools to provide a public place for acting on moral norms. Instrumental considerations about such issues as work efficiency and subject-matter specialization, so common in public comprehensive high schools, are mediated in Catholic schools by a dominant concern for human dignity. The social solidarity that flourishes in small group associations gives meaning to the lives of teachers and students.

The inspirational ideology underlying the organization of Catholic schools binds together their members into a functioning whole. This ideology, connected to the basic religious philosophy that links these schools together, was energized by Vatican II. However, it could also be argued that the "religiousness" of this ideology is not crucial to the effects that it generates. After all, the schools enroll large numbers of non-Catholics. The ideas underlying these understandings are quite consistent with basic democratic ideals.

THREE "LESSONS" FOR PUBLIC SCHOOLS

A Core Curriculum

The findings from our book that received the most attention are "common school" factors. Catholic schools seem able to induce high achievement in their students—all their students. What makes the most difference to student learning is the courses they take. With few exceptions, all Catholic high school students follow a narrow academic curriculum, one that normally defines the college-preparatory track. Students have few choices in their courses of study. Regardless of students' academic or social background, irrespective of their plans or aspirations for their post-high-school futures, Catholic schools direct their students to academic undertakings that are defined as appropriate intellectual preparation for all students.

These findings have relevance for public schools. Social stratification in the public education system is reinforced by policies of responding to individual differences in ability or background, offering a smorgasbord of courses from which students must choose, and then asking students who make poor choices to suffer a lifetime of responsibility for them. Poor and minority students often "choose" (or are pushed toward) undemanding, low-track courses. The direction that curricular change should take seems clear from these findings. Catholic schools, particularly those in the inner city that enroll large proportions of disadvantaged students, serve as models that might guide the direction for curriculum change.

The School as a Community

There are profound organizational differences between Catholic and public high schools. The differentiated environment of the average public high school acts against the formation of high levels of personal interaction. Recent school reform initiatives have focused on trying to engage students with their education

by offering extrinsic rewards and punishments.[5] Our research
on Catholic schools challenges the premise of such reforms and
argues against their efficacy. Such initiatives, which draw on
basic tenets of individualism, represent appeals to personal
interest or to the utilitarian calculus of the "carrot and stick" to
encourage good behavior and discourage bad behavior.

Catholic schools direct their attention to the social (or
common) rather than the individual basis of human engagement.
We have considerable evidence that daily life in these schools
represents a source of considerable meaning for members of the
community. Our work on school communal organization provides evidence that schools (Catholic or non-Catholic) organized
around the social principles described earlier have much power
to engage their participants.

Education as a Cultural and Moral Enterprise

Enculturation occurs in all schools. Although contemporary
public schools do not have religious classes or direct and
deliberate efforts toward forming a coherent social life, they do
convey a distinct vision of society—one in which individuals
strive for personal success while pursuing their own self-
interest. Accounts of contemporary public high schools describe institutional norms that are competitive, individualistic,
and materialistic.[6] These norms are embedded in the differentiated curriculum, the tracking structure, and teacher assignments

---

[5] A common claim is that greater student engagement can be
developed by offering students more choices within a diverse curriculum taught in a more stimulating fashion. A related argument holds
that teachers will expend more effort when they teach classes and subjects in which they have a high degree of personal interest. Still
other reforms aimed at accountability offer extrinsic rewards to students for simply staying in school—promised jobs or college tuition
upon graduation. Related ideas threaten students with sanctions for
dropping out—cancelled drivers licences, cuts in parents' welfare payments. Merit pay proposals represent a complementary reward initiative for teachers, who would be rewarded for special performance in
comparison with their colleagues.

[6] See Cusick and Wheeler, 1988; Grant, 1988; Metz, 1986;
Lightfoot, 1983.

that often find good teachers rewarded with classes filled with the most able students. They are also embedded in the routine social encounters that are regulated by explicit codes of conduct specifying prohibited behaviors and elaborate individual rights. Over the last 50 years, self-interest has displaced the common good as the social milieu in which students are directed. In fact, the common good is distinct from what is best for most individuals.

The Catholic school vision stands in direct contrast to the culture of the individual. It is grounded, at its best, in a belief system that focuses on the dignity of each human being and in every person's responsibility to advance the goals of peace, justice, and human welfare. Catholic schools define education in terms of forming the conscience of all students toward an awareness of what they share in common. According to this definition, a proper education cannot be affectively neutral.

CONCLUSION

Some philosophy of education drives every school. Embracing democracy depends on developing a dialogue about the nature of individual and group interests and on fostering a civic conscience that makes moral claims on citizens to act in accord with this balance. Education for democratic citizenship requires sustained encounters that pose questions for students about the nature of individuals and society and about appropriate and worthy personal and social aims. Such encounters are surely simpler to foster in school settings that are small and explicitly formed around a moral core. I argue, however, that a democratic education—not training, but true education—requires more. Besides imparting technical knowledge and skills to negotiate a complex world, students must be helped to develop a moral vision toward which those skills should be pointed, as well as a conscience that encourages them to pursue that vision. In this sense, education is fundamentally a moral enterprise.

As argued at the outset, some "lessons" from Catholic schools are quite relevant for the reform of urban public schools. The purposes served by public education are now under intense scrutiny and criticism. Many have argued that the existing system of public education has lost its position as an agent of the common good. Arguments about common schools ring hollow when measured against the reality of

schools that afford unparalleled opportunities for some, while
simultaneously undereducating large segments of our society
and denying basic human dignity to the most disadvantaged.

It seems clear that although the public schools alone have
not created the extreme social inequities in our society, they are
organized in ways that more frequently magnify than diminish
inequities by family income, race, and ethnicity as students pass
through American public schools. I hope that my comments
will not be interpreted as demeaning the efforts and motivations
of individual public school teachers, principals, and administrators. One purpose of using a comparative framework—public vs. Catholic schools—is to highlight the difficult organizational conditions under which most public educators work. The
work of these educators and their students could be more effective and more personally rewarding if it were performed in
environments similar to those we have documented in Catholic
high schools.

REFERENCES

Bryk, Anthony S., Valerie E. Lee, and Peter B. Holland
    (1993). *Catholic Schools and the Common Good.* Cam-
    bridge, Mass.: Harvard University Press.
Cusick, Philip A., and Christopher W. Wheeler (1988). "Edu-
    cational Morality and Organizational Reforms," *American
    Journal of Education*, vol. 96, no. 2 (February 1988),
    pp. 231-255.
Grant, Gerald (1988). *The World We Created at Hamilton
    High.* Cambridge, Mass.: Harvard Univerity Press.
Lee, Valerie E. (1997). "Catholic Lessons for Public Schools."
    In Diane Ravitch and Joseph P. Viteritti, eds., *New Schools
    for a New Century: The Redesign of Urban Education.*
    New Haven: Yale University Press.
_____, with Julia B. Smith (2001). *Restructuring High
    Schools for Equity and Excellence: What Works.* New
    York: Teachers College Press.
Lightfoot, Sarah Lawrence (1983). *The Good High School:
    Portraits of Character and Culture.* New York: Basic
    Books.
Metz, Mary H. (1986). *Different by Design: The Context and
    Character of Three Magnet Schools.* London: Routledge
    and Kegan Paul.

NCEA (1990). *United States Catholic Elementary and Secondary Schools, 1989-1990: Annual Statistical Report on Schools, Enrollment, and Staffing.* Washington, D.C.: National Catholic Educational Association.

NCES (1999). *Digest of Education Statistics, 1999.* Washington, D.C.: National Center for Education Statistics, U.S. Department of Education.

LESSONS OF CHICAGO SCHOOL REFORM: FROM RADICAL DECENTRALIZATION TO ADMINISTRATIVE PRAGMATISM

Dan A. Lewis

More than a decade has passed since Chicago embarked on its experiment with radical school reform. Beginning with legislation passed by the Illinois General Assembly in 1988 and continuing with legislation enacted in 1995, Chicago entered an era of reorganization for its public school system. The purpose of this chapter is to assess the experience of Chicago school reform and make some judgments about the lessons we have learned.[1]

Chicago school reform has shifted power to a "public-regarding" middle class of professionals and bureaucratic managers. Over the decade of reform, participatory decentralization produced recentralized power in the hands of the mayor. Decentralization begat more power for the very institutional forms it was meant to replace. Surely the lesson here is to be careful what you wish for—it may turn into its opposite. The political alliances that have produced this outcome were built around a middle-class ideology of the public interest that drew together suburban legislators, the mayor, and reformers. The emphasis on "school reform," rather than teacher or student improvement, provided the rationale for centralization of power in the hands of individuals from outside the school district hierarchy. As political power shifted to the suburbs, reformers teamed with business interests and the mayor to centralize authority in the hands of a chief executive officer. Educators have been replaced by managers who have the confidence of this more middle-class electorate as they focus on "fixing the schools."

---

[1] See Appendix for descriptions of the Chicago School Reform Act of 1988 and the Chicago School Reform Amendatory Act of 1995.

THE FIRST LESSON: SCHOOL REFORM
IN ITS HISTORICAL CONTEXT

Supporters of the 1988 reforms have argued that changes in the law transformed the school system and that law shapes practice. Many advocates of school reform tell the story of a citizen movement that swept away an old bureaucratic system and replaced it with one that, while not perfect, gave parents and community members a strong voice in the governance of local schools. Their story begins in 1987 with a teacher strike, as if that strike started a process that had no precedents and was not shaped by previous history. Reform resulted from community outrage and the development of a strong popular movement that won the day in a legislature that saw the wisdom of the new directions. This interpretation is misleading. Reforms have a history, as does the context into which reform is introduced. One must understand that history to make sense of the recent reform process. I believe that an understanding of the reform process must begin much earlier, as Chicago coped with the migration of some 500,000 African-Americans from the South. The decentralization approach of 1988 was born in the struggles of the mid-1960s to desegregate the Chicago public schools.[2]

The Chicago public school system was centralized in the decades following World War II. Centralization was the approach favored by "administrative progressives," a group of superintendents, school administrators, and university professors who believed that scientific management of the school system would improve student learning and district efficiency (Tyack, 1974). The way to do this was to centralize under a strong superintendent. Benjamin Willis, superintendent of the Chicago Public Schools from the late 1950s to the mid-1960s, was the epitome of that trend. Willis was recognized as an administrative progressive, someone who was trying to improve public schooling by using scientific management techniques to overcome the influences of patronage and corruption. He was president of the National Association of School Superintendents and was considered a model of the successful manager.

---

[2] For other accounts of the story of Chicago school reform, see, e.g., Hess, 1990, 1995; Katz, Fine, and Simon, 1997; Mirel, 1993; Moore, 1990; Vander Weele, 1994; Vasquez, 1994.

In the mid-1960s, Chicago's public school system was composed of 525,000 students taught by 25,000 teachers (who had recently been unionized) and supervised by 1,000 administrators. The city was 25 percent African-American, compared with about 14 percent in 1950. African-Americans represented about a third of public school enrollment and more than half of the student population in elementary schools. Willis was forced out in 1965 by pressure from civil rights activists who were dissatisfied with his responses to segregation in the schools. His forced retirement signaled the beginning of the end of the era of administrative progressivism, as the civil rights struggle and racial conflict challenged the legitimacy of centralized administration. Ironically, it was Willis who clung steadfastly to the concept of the neighborhood school in the face of demands for radical transfer policies to achieve some form of racial balance. Chicago's civil rights movement in the 1960s demanded an end to segregated schools and an end to Willis's leadership. They achieved the latter, but not the former.

The Willis story demonstrates the necessity of managing outside pressures if the system is to maintain its legitimacy. The dilemma for the managers of the school system is to cope with those pressures without losing the support of other key constituencies. The first Mayor Daley would have lost the political support of Whites in Chicago if he had allowed serious racial mixing in the schools. His son (the current mayor of Chicago) faced a very different situation a generation later, when the key problem was the legitimacy of the entire public school enterprise in the eyes of external stakeholders throughout the state, as well as in the city itself. The business community, state legislators, community activists, and downtown reformers (the external pressure groups) have continued to pressure the system for changes that were not forthcoming.

The 1960s were also the period in which the teachers were formally unionized, and Martin Luther King, Jr., came to Chicago to lead a movement for civil rights. This period began the transformation of a system that had been controlled by professional school administrators, with the backing of the Democratic machine, into one in which sharing power with the community became the way to achieve legitimacy. In the 20 years following Willis's resignation, it became apparent that changes in the superintendency were no longer meaningful responses to these demands for improvement. There are several reasons why contemporary school reform began in this period. First and foremost, the pressure from outside the school system, as well as the school district leadership's inability to respond to that pressure, created the changes in how the schools were run. Morever, the question of control over the schools and the demand for more control by African-Americans over their education has remained at the core of school reform in Chicago.

The two decades following Willis's departure would see the system grope toward accommodation with the bitter White resistance to desegregation and the growing difficulty superintendents had directing the massive system of some 400,000 students. As White enrollment continued to decline, dropping from some 65 percent of the students in the mid-1960s to about 10 percent in the 1990s, the issues of managing the system shifted from maintaining neighborhood schools to lifting student achievement levels. The school system lost 100,000 students from the mid-1960s to the early 1980s. Between 1985-86 and 1995-96, White enrollment continued to decline (by more than 16,000). African-American enrollment also dropped (by more than 34,000), while Hispanic enrollment grew by more than 31,000. Over the same period, high school graduation rates declined from 61 percent to 51 percent, and dropout rates rose from 11 percent to 16 percent. As we look at this history, the true measure of school reform may not be how much test scores have improved, but rather, how little they have eroded, given the staggering impact of changes in the composition of the student body.

The Chicago School Reform Act of 1988 was the culmination of the decentralization process; it completed the transition from a strong superintendent model of administration that had started to weaken with the removal of Benjamin Willis in 1966 to a decentralized leadership model in 1988. If the 1988 reforms were about decentralization, and the 1995 reforms were about recentralization, then together these reforms pushed the administrative progressives to the sidelines and suggested that the public schools were now being run by local elected officials in coalition with powerful external constituencies. More than ten years into school reform, the real losers in the process have been the administrative progressives, while "administrative pragmatists" have gained control.

In both the 1960s and 1980s, school reform began with the loss of elite confidence in and support for administrative leadership. Willis failed to maintain that support, as did the leaders of the school district just prior to the 1988 reforms. The loss of power by central administration in 1988 did not automatically mean that reform goals would be achieved. Indeed, the rising expectations for what reform could accomplish created pressures that made radical decentralization very difficult to maintain. The more pressure the political environment put on the district, the more likely the district would recentralize in order to both control what was going on in the schools and respond to pressure from the broader political environment.

The irony should be obvious: decentralization produces its opposite. Decentralization puts pressure on the school district, including the pressure produced by local school councils and their advocates, which in turn impels the system's leadership to centralize in order to control what is going on in the district. The more pressure there is on the district for higher student achievement, the more need for centralization to respond in a systematic way. Demands for change lead to demands for accountability, which makes decentralization unrealistic. A political environment that wants more from its public schools will not be satisfied with a system that cannot manage itself. The skills of senior management in meeting those expectations will, to a large extent, determine the well-being of the school district. It is only when external political pressure abates that central administration can loosen the reins and allow decentralization to flourish. Because decentralization nurtures racial isolation, the wider (read White) political environment will find decentralization useful in supporting the status quo.

External pressures make centralization a likely strategy for organizing an urban school district.[3] Political pressures demand assertive action to avoid the loss of policy control over the system. Thus, the pressure to decentralize the system in 1988 sowed the seeds of recentralization in 1995. The system had a growing need to speak for itself after the first round of reform, but it had less capacity to do so with the weakening of the central administration. Given that policy control is usually defined by the authority of the chief executive, both local officials and state officials saw the need to strengthen the central administration as a way improve the decentralized schools.[4]

---

[3] On the centralizing tendencies that external political pressure generates in school districts, see Hannaway, 1993.

[4] See, e.g., Wong and Sunderman, 1996; Wong et al., 1997.

The current hybrid design combines aspects of decentralization and centralization in an effort to respond to the dual pressures faced by Chicago's public schools. This structure of governance balances the need for legitimacy with the need for control. At the same time, administrative pragmatism replaces administrative progressivism. The forces that shape educational expectations reside outside the school system in the form of reformers, business leaders, and politicians who decide when change should come about. The form of that change depends on how the issues are defined by those same groups.

Nearly half of all the low-income students in Illinois go to school in Chicago, while voters from Chicago make up an ever decreasing percentage of Illinois voters, roughly 20 percent of the statewide electorate. It is no wonder that the debate over how to improve the Chicago system has shifted toward a more suburban set of priorities. The genius of the 1988 reforms was the continued demand for neighborhood schools, but this time in the name of all parents rather than just White parents. Another important difference between the 1988 reforms and those of a generation earlier was that the educational professionals now under attack were mostly middle-class African-Americans.

THE SECOND LESSON: SCHOOL IMPROVEMENT

Much of the research on the first phase of Chicago school reform centered on school improvement. The 1988 reforms were founded on the belief that the key to improving the schools lies within the governance structure of each school: "At base was the belief that the expanded engagement of local participants in the work of the schools would sustain attention and provide substantial support for improvements in classroom instruction and in student learning" (Bryk, Easton, et al., 1994, p. 75). The reform philosophy thus assumed that changes in governance that transferred formal authority to the local school councils would improve student achievement. The early research assumed that this logic of school reform was correct and asked how it could be achieved. Case studies describing how individual schools went about implementing the reforms were the conventional research design. The research that followed from this approach compared schools either to themselves over time or to other schools in Chicago, looking for factors that would predict improvement.[5] The emphasis was on changes in governance, participation by parents, and performance of principals. The researchers were looking for exemplars that could be used to guide other schools. Local school councils (LSCs) were seen as the key to success.

The emphasis on the individual school mirrored the emphasis in the 1988 reform on the LSCs. This research approach was very important in the first few years of school reform, but there was often no baseline against which to compare the post-reform schools, and little effort was made to look at how individual students fared over the reform period.[6] High mobility rates among students were often ignored. Variations in student achievement within schools were seldom analyzed. Instead, average scores of students on national tests (or the percentage above the national norm) became the criteria for success.

On the positive side, these case studies gave the public a view (perhaps a bit too rosy, but a view nevertheless) of what was going on in the Chicago Public Schools. The implicit goal of many of these researchers was to create the impression that while there may be bumps in the road, the successful implementation of the 1988 reforms was an imperative that all Chicago should support. The underlying assumptions of the reform were taken as a given, and that what was needed were more models of how to make that design work.

Typologies of LSCs were developed. Researchers offered recommendations for improving LSCs, suggesting the need to strengthen their leadership. Administration of LSCs needed improvements such as minute-taking, knowledge of rules about quorums and votes, and translators. There was a consensus that LSC members needed to be trained if they were to succeed. LSCs met, on average, twelve times a year, with eight of eleven members present, with three to four members commenting on each issue (Easton and Storey, 1994).[7] A survey of teachers found that two-thirds felt represented fairly by colleagues on the LSCs. A majority (57%) felt that LSCs re-

---

[5] See, e.g., Hess, 1994a.

[6] See, e.g., Bryk, Deabster, et al., 1994.

[7] See also Easton, Storey, et al., 1990; Designs for Change, 1991; Ford et al., 1991; Easton, Flinspach, et al., 1991, 1993.

spected the views of teachers, but 20 percent of teachers had very negative views about LSCs in terms of lack of cooperation and lack of respect for teachers' views. Although there were some teachers who found the situation wanting, they were, on the whole, positive about LSCs (Easton, Bryk, et al., 1991).

Most of the research on LSCs was not connected to student achievement. Many researchers believed that in the years following the first reform, it was simply too early to expect to find such improvements. Thus, the research said little about the connection between school operations and student achievement. Parent involvement was key to the 1988 reforms, and many studies described how that involvement was progressing, with suggestions made on how to improve participation.

Many schools also developed relationships with businesses, universities, and reform organizations to help school improvement efforts. These partnerships were seen by many as one of the best outcomes of reform. Although most of the research involved case studies, they did show that the walls between the school and other institutions had been broken down, with good results. New programs were introduced, tutors became involved, and new resources were brought to bear on the learning enterprise. Very little of this was possible before reforms were initiated. Much innovation and experimentation was introduced where little was evident before.

The role of principals was also viewed as an important part of school improvement. The 1988 reforms eliminated tenure for principals, with LSCs making the determination about who would be principal. Principals were to be held accountable for school improvement, and if they failed to meet the expectations of the LSC, they could be terminated. Some researchers were not so sure that the loss of principal tenure was a good thing. The insecurity that followed made management more difficult, and the principals were being held accountable for decisions made by the LSCs. The principals' jobs were more complicated after the 1988 reforms because they had to answer to both the LSCs and the central administration. The 1988 reforms certainly put principals on the hot seat. Many principals, however, reported not having enough time to attend to all their new responsibilities and roles, with professional development and teacher evaluation feeling the brunt of the time crunch. Researchers generally believed that although principals had a more difficult job after school reform, many were rising admirably to the task. The conclusion was that the principals had to learn how to lead in new ways, and when they learned how to do this, schools would improve (Ford and Bennett, 1994).[8]

One of the consequences of decentralization was that systemwide school improvement became more difficult. LSCs had the power to reform their schools, but if one school achieved great success, there were few mechanisms for expanding that success to other schools. How could one school be made to try a successful approach that was pioneered by another? How would one school know what another was doing? The central administration could play a role in addressing these questions, but its authority was weak until the 1995 reforms.

The lessons of Chicago school reform regarding school improvement cannot be summarized easily. The fear that poor parents would not be able to govern their schools proved to be unwarranted, although there was wide variation among LSCs. New and energetic principals were hired in many schools with apparently good results. After more than ten years of reform, the key factors for school improvement have become clear: good leadership by the local school council, an energetic and committed principal, and parents and teachers that can work together with a common vision. How to produce these pieces is a bit more complicated, but the research on school improvement shows it can be done. Whether those successes can be routinized is more problematic.

THE THIRD LESSON: TEACHER IMPROVEMENT

The research on teaching under Chicago school reform did not demonstrate any sustained improvement in the quality of instruction. Most of this work was not very sanguine about instructional improvement. The authors offered various reasons for this failure to improve. Some suggested that teachers were preoccupied with preparing students for standardized tests, while others emphasized the lack of a professionally supportive culture in the schools. The fact remains that the research literature does not show a systematic improvement in the quality of instruction. It can also be said that instructional improve-

---

[8] On the role of principals, see also Designs for Change, 1990; Peterson, 1990; Ford, 1991; Bennett et al., 1992; Smylie et al., 1994; Flinspach and Ryan, 1994.

ment has not been the focus of most researchers. This lack of focus on what teachers were doing in the classroom also reflects another of the assumptions of the 1988 legislation: that the teachers were not an essential part of the reform process. In particular, many reformers and legislators thought that the Chicago Teachers Union was a major impediment to improving the schools. Instructional improvement was seen as something that would emerge from governance reform.

Teacher satisfaction, however, was studied. There was considerable attention paid to how teachers felt about what was going on around them. Teachers have reported a mixture of opinions, from feeling left out of the reform process, to seeing some of their schools improving after the 1988 reforms. A survey of elementary school teachers found that 60 percent thought that their school was getting better. A large majority (75%) of teachers reported that they were "pro-reform," and half thought that there was more cooperation within schools after the 1988 reforms. This general picture of satisfaction suggested a positive attitude toward reform, although more than half reported that reform had not changed their teaching practice, with almost all the teachers (95%) reporting that they felt competent in their teaching (Easton, Bryk, et al., 1991). A later survey of teachers showed highly varied perspectives on the progress of reform in elementary schools and generally pessimistic views from high school teachers (Sebring et al., 1995). Teachers seemed to have accepted reform and found that it had brought some benefits, but there was little evidence that instruction had improved.[9] In some ways, this lack of attention to instruction is odd, given the interest of so many in school improvement. One would have thought that researchers would have been interested in tracking the impact of the reforms in the classroom, assessing how local school councils and their principals affected—failed to affect—what was going on in the classroom. There was, however, little serious attention to this issue. The reforms of 1988 and 1995 were both aimed primarily at changes in governance, not instructional improvement, and many researchers seemed to have adopted the logic of the reform in the design of their studies.

---

[9] See also Hess, 1994b.

THE FOURTH LESSON: STUDENT IMPROVEMENT

Prior to the 1988 school reforms, there was a pervasive feeling of pessimism about the Chicago public school system. Chicago students were consistently scoring among the lowest in the nation on standardized achievement tests. There was a consensus among educators, parents, and business people alike that improvement was an urgent necessity—a consensus that still exists. In the second phase of Chicago school reform, there has been greater emphasis on improving student achievement, as expressed by the Chicago Academic Accountability Council, which was established under the 1995 reform legislation:

> The impact of school reform policy on classrooms has been mixed and uneven. School-based management and restructuring only work when the focus is on student achievement. Reform efforts must reach into every classroom to improve what transpires between students and teachers on a daily basis. Teachers must become engaged as learners, too. They must improve their knowledge of content, increase their repertoire of strategies to meet the diverse learning needs of their students, and stay focused on quality instruction (1997, p. iv).

Much of the more recent research on Chicago school reform also reflects the policy agenda of student improvement.[10] Chicago public school students must do better, but the research over the past decade has not shown consistent results that would let us conclude with confidence that school reform has brought about student improvement.[11] Scores on national tests show improvements in some areas but not in others. Dropout rates have been erratic, with some positive results recently. What is, of course, difficult to discern is whether school reform has been responsible for the improvements that have occurred.

To determine the impact of school reform on achievement, we must look at whether the experiences of individual students over time in schools have an impact on how they do on the

---

[10] See, e.g., Bryk, Thum, et al., 1998.

[11] See, e.g., Bryk, Deabster, et al., 1994; Walberg and Niemiec, 1994; Downes and Horowitz, 1995; Bryk, Kerbow, and Rollow, 1997.

tests, especially after controlling for other factors that influence the results. Parental background, student capacity, and socio-economic status are but a few of the factors that shape achievement. To date, there have been only a few carefully conducted studies of individual achievement among a randomly selected sample of Chicago public school students. There have been no studies, as far as I am aware, that look at the classroom experiences of students and relate those experiences to student achievement. Some studies have looked at changes in the scores of students in schools, using school averages for comparison, but these gross measures tell us little about individual students. Schools can improve, but that tells us little about the individual students in them and how they are doing. Some of these studies of gross measures give reason for optimism, while others are quite pessimistic. There is a need for careful research on samples of students that track their achievement over time and control for factors that affect that achievement. Individual-level as well as school-level and classroom-level variables must be measured. With such research in hand, managers could make grounded decisions about what kinds of interventions have an impact. This work is essential if Chicago is to build on more than a decade of effort.

CONCLUSION

An urban school system can be viewed as a "time machine," displaying patterns of values and behavior—rooted in choices made in the past—over basic questions of how children should be educated (Wirt, 1974, p. 3). A school system responds to pressures in the present, weighted down by those earlier decisions and their residues in the bureaucracy. The system reacts to pressures from outside organizations and tries to meet the expectations of those organizations if it is to remain viable politically, economically, and culturally. The time machine must react to demands for change, but in doing so, it does not have a free hand. Chicago school reform was the result of the system's history and the pressure to change.

When we observe how a school system operates in the present, those past decisions can be seen just below the surface of current procedures and plans. Many discussions of Chicago school reform seem to argue that the reforms of 1988 were somehow freed from the past, that new ideas won the day in

Springfield, moving the system to a radically new way of doing business. This assumption overlooks a complex political history. Illinois is dominated by a political culture that is pragmatic, often cynical, and usually quite conservative. The reforms of 1988 signaled a shift in power, a shift that had more to do with racial politics and the district's loss of legitimacy than it did a commitment to a community-centered approach to decision-making in the school district. Important external organizations (the Chicago business community, middle-class reformers, and state legislators) had enough power to overcome the strength of the school board, the teachers' union, and the superintendent in shifting power to a new coalition of interests that developed an ideology to rationalize the shift. The change in the ideology of reform from 1988 to 1995 reflected the political strength of Mayor Daley and his willingness to form a coalition with Republican legislators. The two phases of reform show what can happen when the district fails to respond adequately to external pressure.

Advocates of the first reform argued that new ideas had won the day, when in fact what had won the day back in 1988 was the power of the urban reform pressure group composed of middle-class reformers, local business elites, and state legislators to overcome the power of a declining urban machine (composed of Democratic politicians, unions, and minority voters). The reform groups had been critical of big-city machine politics for decades, arguing that corruption and the focus on political gain had eroded the ability of Chicago's public agencies (including the school district) to meet the needs of the working and poor people who lived in its jurisdiction. The fact that the city government was reflecting the growing political strength of African-Americans only compounded the desire of state politicians to weaken the control of these big-city interests over the school system. Neighborhood control over the schools was a powerful rhetoric in 1988, as it was a generation earlier.[12]

The biggest lesson of this reform period is that the decentralization of 1988 gave birth to the recentralization of 1995. Pressure to change impels managers to exert control. There is no doubt that change has occurred. Now we have a school system with local school councils, principals who no longer have lifetime tenure in their jobs, and considerable amounts of state

---

[12] See Lewis and Nakagawa, 1995.

funding going directly to the schools to be used at the discretion of LSCs. There has been considerable turnover in principals. Successful administrators have learned a new rhetoric to respond to new demands from a variety of groups. The talk is now of inclusion and openness to change rather than of hierarchy and responsiveness to bureaucratic demands. It is a rhetoric that plays well in a cynical state political culture where government action and bureaucracy are discredited. The present system presents a tension between a strong centralizing manager and an infrastructure that is very decentralized and "loosely coupled." The legitimacy of the Chicago system depends on integrating these tendencies.

Although support for decentralization has had some short-term benefits, over the longer term we need to focus on issues of teacher effectiveness and student learning. We must move from governance to instruction. We must seek ways to increase the competitive advantage of Chicago students in labor markets and in higher education. Do Chicago public school graduates fare better today than they did a decade ago in competing for jobs? Are they doing better in admission to postsecondary educational institutions? What learning strategies are paying off in better skill acquisition? The lesson of Chicago school reform is that we had better start asking those questions now, before another decade slips by, and we have lost the advantage produced by past reforms. Chicago is a "world-class" city competing in a global economy. The city's public schools must contribute an educated workforce to the metropolitan region if we are to be successful in that competition. The reforms of the next decade must be about student learning, and the pressure to change must be about how to improve that learning. The basic questions we address are about how children should be educated. If we learn from the past, we can answer those questions intelligently.

APPENDIX: CHICAGO SCHOOL REFORM
LEGISLATION HIGHLIGHTS[13]

Provisions of the Chicago School Reform Act of 1988 became
effective on July 1, 1989. Major revisions under the Chicago
School Amendatory Act of 1995 became effective on July 1,
1995. Additional revisions regarding school principals were
enacted in 1996.

LOCAL SCHOOL COUNCILS

Composition, Selection

Each school was to establish a local school council (LSC) consisting of the principal, six parents, two community residents,
two teachers, and, in high schools, one student. Parents and
community residents on the LSC could not be Chicago Public
Schools employees. Members were to be elected by their peers
at each school.

> *1991 amendment in response to a court ruling on LSC elec-*
> *tion provisions*: Parents and community members were
> given five votes each to divide among parent and commu-
> nity candidates; teachers and students were to be appointed
> by the School Board following advisory elections among
> their peers.

Powers, Duties

(1) LSCs were given authority to appoint the principal under a
four-year contract. The only requirement for new principals
would be a state administrative certificate; the Board of Education could not impose additional eligibility requirements.

---

[13] This material is drawn from *Catalyst: Voices of Chicago School
Reform* < http://www.catalyst-chicago.org. >. Reprinted with per-
mission.

1996 Amendment: The school board was given the authority to impose its own requirements for becoming and remaining a principal. The board used its authority to require Chicago residency, six years' experience as a teacher and administrator with consistently good performance, and internship and training beyond the standard administrative certificate.

(2) LSCs were given authority to write and approve a performance contract with the principal. LSCs could make additions to the basic systemwide performance contract, provided these were neither discriminatory nor in opposition to the board's basic contract provisions.

(3) LSCs were to evaluate the performance of principals and decide whether to renew contracts at the end of four years.

1996 Amendment: The system's chief executive officer was given veto power over the retention of principals; the School Board became a court of appeal.

(4) LSCs were to help create and to approve a school improvement plan, which would detail how the school would boost test scores, cut truancy and dropout rates, and ensure that children are prepared for the future. An LSC could request policy waivers from the board, and/or waivers of union agreements, to help implement its school improvement plan.

(5) LSCs were to help create and to approve a school budget, using a lump-sum allocation from the board.

1995 Amendment: LSCs were authorized to approve receipts and expenditures for schools' internal accounts.

Training

An eight-hour training session for new LSC members was "strongly encouraged" but not required.

1995 Amendment: The state mandated three full days of training for new LSC members. The legislation also changed some of the content of the training, emphasizing legal issues and ways to improve student achievement, and shifted LSC elections so that members could be trained in the summer. LSC members who did not complete the training would be removed by the board.

CENTRAL AUTHORITY

School Board Membership

The existing 11-member Board of Education was abolished. A School Board Nominating Commission was created; it included 23 parent and community representatives from LSCs across the city and five members appointed by the mayor. It screened candidates and gave the mayor a slate of three candidates for each vacant position on an expanded 15-member board. The mayor had 30 days to act; his choices needed approval by the City Council. If the mayor rejected all three slated candidates for a particular slot, the commission would select three more.

> *1995 Amendment*: The 15-member Board of Education and the Nominating Commission were abolished. The mayor was given unfettered authority to appoint a five-member School Reform Board of Trustees to serve through 1999. Thereafter, the mayor would name a seven-member board, with staggered, four-year terms.

Board Responsibilities

The board was given responsibility for setting curriculum goals and standards; supervising special and bilingual education; providing meals and transportation; developing a discipline code; and building, renovating, and closing school facilities.

The board was requried to write specific educational reform objectives and goals, which were to be approved by the Chicago School Finance Authority. The board would choose a General Superintendent, who served under a three-year contract.

1995 Amendment: The mayor chose a chief executive officer to serve for four years; thereafter, the School Board would choose a general superintendent.

The new School Reform Board of Trustees was directed to trim costs of non-educational services; to provide a long-term, balanced budget; to streamline the administration; to create an Academic Accountability Council to ensure schools' progress; and to establish any structures deemed necessary to help the system work better.

The new board was given authority to hire outside contractors to do work currently done by board employees; staff could be laid off with 14 days' written notice.

The board would determine, subject to judicial review, whether a teacher or principal should be fired. Previously, those decisions had been made by state hearing officers, who now could only provide findings of fact and recommendations.

The teachers' union was stripped of authority to bargain over a wide range of operational and educational issues, including class size, school schedules, and staff assignments.

The board was no longer required to submit educational and financial plans to the Chicago School Finance Authority for approval.

The board was given greatly increased flexibility in the use of state and local funds, which paved the way for four-year union contracts and dozens of new programs.

PRINCIPALS' AUTHORITY

(1) Principals could fill vacant educational positions without regard to seniority. Tenured teachers who lose their positions at a school because of falling enrollment or curriculum changes (so-called reserve teachers) were guaranteed some form of employment by the system for 20 months.

1995 Amendment: Protections for reserve teachers were eliminated.   Principals could use non-teachers for library duties and school-sponsored extracurricular activities.

(2) The in-class remediation time principals must grant to unsatisfactory teachers was cut from one year to 45 days.   However, principals could extend remediation up to a total of one year, part of which could take place outside the classroom.

(3) The principal, along with the school engineer, could keep a set of keys to the building.   The principal, along with subdistrict supervising engineers and lunchroom managers, would conduct regular evaluations of the school engineer and school lunchroom manager.   The subdistrict superintendent would handle conflicts between principals and their engineers and lunchroom managers.

1995 Amendment: Principals were given sole authority to evaluate engineers and lunchroom managers.   In the case of a negative evaluation, they could reprimand, suspend, or recommend the dismissal of the employee.

(4) Each principal, with his or her LSC, was given responsibility for developing a school improvement plan and a curriculum. A Professional Personnel Advisory Committee (PPAC) was created to help.   Each PPAC was to consist of certified teachers; its size and manner of selection was left up to each school.

(5) Principals were required to give LSCs copies of audits of internal accounts and any pertinent information generated by reviews of programs or operations.

ACCOUNTABILITY

Each of the 23 existing elementary and high school subdistricts were to establish subdistrict councils, composed of one elected parent or community member from each LSC in the subdistrict.

The subdistrict superintendent was to suggest actions to remedy low-performing schools, including drafting remediation plans and, if problems continue, placing schools on probation.   The subdistrict council was to approve or disapprove the subdistrict superintendent's recommendations.

In cases in which a school had failed to make progress after being on probation for a year, the Board of Education could order new LSC elections, replace the principal, replace teachers, or close the school.

> *1995 Amendment*: Subdistricts were abolished. Authority for moving against low-performing schools was transferred to the CEO and a reconstituted board. The board and CEO were given new options for intervention and did not have to wait for a year of probation to act. The CEO also assumed authority to evaluate principals, who continued to be evaluated by LSCs as well.

STATE CHAPTER 1 FUNDS

State Chapter 1 funds must be distributed to schools based on their enrollment of poor children. Those funds must be used only on programs that supplement the basic curriculum (e.g., reduced class size, early childhood enrichment). These changed were to be phased in gradually, with full compliance by 1994. Principals were given the lead in developing spending plans, which must be approved by LSCs.

The law suggested that the board use revenue from "administrative reductions" to plug budget holes caused by the transfer of these funds to individual school budgets.

> *1995 Amendment*: The amount of state Chapter 1 funds distributed to schools for use at their discretion was capped at $261 million, with the Reform Board gaining control over annual increases above that amount.

REFERENCES

Bennett, Albert, Anthony Bryk, John Easton, David Kerbow, Stuart Luppescu, and Penny Sebring (1992). *Charting Reform: The Principals' Perspective.* Chicago: Consortium on Chicago School Research.

Bryk, Anthony, Paul E. Deabster, John Q. Easton, Stuart Luppescu, and Yeow Meng Thum (1994). "Measuring Achievement Gains in the Chicago Public Schools," *Education and Urban Society*, vol. 26, no. 3 (May 1994), pp. 306-320.

Bryk, Anthony S., John Q. Easton, David Kerbow, Sharon G. Rollow, and Penny A. Sebring (1994). "The State of Chicago School Reform," *Phi Delta Kappan*, vol. 76, no. 1 (September 1994), pp. 74-78.

Bryk, Anthony S., David Kerbow, and Sharon Rollow (1997). "Chicago School Reform." In Diane Ravitch and Joseph P. Viteritti, eds., *New Schools for a New Century: The Redesign of Urban Education.* New Haven: Yale University Press.

Bryk, Anthony S., Yeow Men Thum, John Q. Easton, and Stuart Luppescu (1998). *Academic Productivity of Chicago Public Schools: A Technical Report Sponsored by the Consortium on Chicago School Research.* Chicago: Consortium on Chicago School Research, University of Chicago.

Chicago Academic Accountability Council (1997). "High School Academic Trends Report." Chicago: Chicago Academic Accountability Council, June 1997.

Designs for Change (1990). *Chicago Principals: Changing of the Guard.* Chicago: Designs for Change.

_____ (1991). *The Untold Story: Candidate Participation in the 1991 LSC Elections.* Chicago: Designs for Change.

Downes, Thomas A., and Jacquelyn L. Horowitz (1995). "An Analysis of the Effect of Chicago School Reform on Student Performance." In Thomas A. Downes and William A. Testa, eds., *Midwest Approaches to School Reform.* Proceedings of a Conference Held at the Federal Reserve Bank of Chicago, October 26-27, 1994. Chicago: Federal Reserve Bank of Chicago.

Easton, John Q., Anthony S. Bryk, Mary E. Driscoll, John G. Kotsakis, Penny A. Sebring, and Arie J. van der Ploeg (1991). *Charting Reform: The Teachers' Turn.* Chicago: Consortium on Chicago School Research.

Easton, John Q., Susan Leigh Flinspach, Darryl Ford, Jesse Qualls, Susan Ryan, Sandra Storey, Paula Gill, and Todd Ricard (1991). *Decision Making and School Improvement: LSCs in the First Two Years of Reform.* Chicago: Chicago Panel on School Policy and Finance.

Easton, John Q., Susan Leigh Flinspach, et al. (1993). *Local School Governance: The Third Year of Chicago School Reform.* Chicago: Chicago Panel on School Policy and Finance.

Easton, John Q., Sandra Storey, Cheryl Johnson, Jesse Qualls, and Darryl Ford (1990). *Local School Council Meetings During the First Year of Chicago School Reform.* Chicago: Chicago Panel on School Policy and Finance.

Easton, John Q., and Sandra L. Storey (1994). "The Development of Local School Councils," *Education and Urban Society*, vol. 26, no. 3 (May 1994), pp. 220-237.

Flinspach, Susan Leigh, and Susan P. Ryan (1994). "Diversity of Outcomes: Local Schools Under School Reform," *Education and Urban Society*, vol. 26, no. 3 (May 1994), pp. 292-305.

Ford, Darryl (1991). "The School Principal and Chicago School Reform: Principals' Early Perceptions of Reform Initiatives." Chicago: Chicago Panel on School Policy and Finance.

Ford, Darryl, and Albert Bennett (1994). "The Changing Principalship in Chicago," *Education and Urban Society*, vol. 6, no. 3 (May 1994), pp. 238-247.

Ford, Darryl, Susan Ryan, Jesse Qualls, Sandra Storey, and John Easton (1991). *Making the Most of School Reform: Suggestions for More Effective Local School Councils.* Chicago: Chicago Panel on School Policy and Finance.

Hannaway, Jane (1993). "Political Pressure and Decentralization in Institutional Organizations: The Case of School Districts," *Sociology of Education*, vol. 66, no. 3 (July 1993), pp. 147-163.

Hess, G. Alfred, Jr. (1990). *Chicago School Reform: What It Is and How It Came to Be.* Chicago: Chicago Panel on Public School Policy and Finance.

_____ (1994a). "School-Based Management as a Vehicle for School Reform," *Education and Urban Society*, vol. 26, no. 3 (May 1994), pp. 203-219.

_____ (1994b). "The Changing Role of Teachers: Moving from Interested Spectators to Engaged Planners," *Education and Urban Society*, vol. 26, no. 3 (May 1994), pp. 248-263.

_____ (1995). *Restructuring Urban Schools: A Chicago Perspective*. New York: Teachers College Press.

Katz, Michael B., Michelle Fine, and Elaine Simon (1997). "Poking Around: Outsiders View Chicago School Reform," *Teachers College Record*, vol. 99, no. 1 (Fall 1997), pp. 117-157.

Lewis, Dan A., and Kathryn Nakagawa (1995). *Race and Educational Reform in the American Metropolis*. Albany: State University of New York Press.

Mirel, Jeffrey (1993). "School Reform, Chicago Style: Educational Innovation in a Changing Urban Context, 1976-1991," *Urban Education*, vol. 28, no. 2 (July 1993), pp. 116-149.

Moore, Donald R. (1990). "Voice and Choice in Chicago." In William H. Clune and John F. Witte, eds., *Choice and Control in American Education, Volume 2: The Practice of Choice, Decentralization, and School Restructuring*. New York: Falmer Press.

Peterson, Kent (1990). "The New Politics of the Principalship: School Reform and Change in Chicago." In Stephen Clements and Andrew Forsaith, eds., *Chicago School Reform: National Perspectives and Local Responses*. Proceedings of a conference sponsored by the Educational Excellence Network and the Joyce Foundation, November 19, 1990.

Sebring, Penny Bender, Anthony S. Bryk, John Q. Easton, Stuart Luppescu, Yeow Meng Thum, Winifred A. Lopez, and BetsAnn Smith (1995). *Charting Reform: Chicago Teachers Take Stock*. Chicago: Consortium on Chicago School Research.

Smylie, Mark, Robert L. Crowson, Victoria Chou, and Rebekah A. Levin (1994). "The Principal and Community-School Connections in Chicago's Radical Reform," *Educational Administration Quarterly*, vol. 30, no. 3 (August 1994), pp. 342-364.

Tyack, David B. (1974). *The One Best System: A History of American Urban Education*. Cambridge, Mass.: Harvard University Press.

Vander Weele, Maribeth (1994). *Reclaiming Our Schools: The Struggle for Chicago School Reform*. Chicago: Loyola University Press.

Vasquez, Rosetta (1994). *Reforming Chicago Public Schools: The Intended and Unitended Consequences.* DeKalb, Ill.: LEPS Press.

Walberg, Herbert, and Richard Niemiec (1994). "Is Chicago School Reform Working?" *Phi Delta Kappan*, vol. 75, no. 9 (May 1994), pp. 713-715.

Wirt, Frederick M. (1974). *Power in the City: Decision Making in San Francisco.* Berkeley: University of California Press.

Wong, Kenneth K., Robert Dreeben, Laurence Lynn, and Gail Sunderman (1997). *Integrated Governance as a Reform Strategy in the Chicago Public Schools.* Chicago: Department of Education and Harris Graduate School of Public Policy Studies, University of Chicago.

Wong, Kenneth K., and Gail Sunderman (1996). "Redesigning Accountability at the System-Wide Level: The Politics of School Reform in Chicago." In Kenneth K. Wong, ed., *Advances in Educational Policy*, Volume 2. Greenwich, Conn.: JAI Press.

COMMENTS: INTEGRATED GOVERNANCE

Kenneth K. Wong

Dan Lewis's essay is a thoughtful account of school reform in Chicago. His analysis pays particular attention to Chicago's experience in implementing the "parent empowerment" model enacted in 1988, which established local school councils (LSCs) in every school. He also refers to the 1995 "integrated governance" reform that enabled the mayor to exercise control over the public schools.

Lewis's essay offers several valuable lessons on the status of Chicago reform for the policy and academic community. First, Chicago school reform must be understood in historical perspective, which includes the demise of "progressive administrators" as a result of the two strands of reform. Second, an understanding of school reform is incomplete without full consideration of the interplay of political institutions and social and racial stratification. Third, given the seemingly opposing sets of values that guide the two reforms, it is not surprising to see a great deal of tension between decentralized forces (LSCs and their supporters) and "recentralized" practices (i.e., systemwide guidelines issued by the Vallas administration). Finally, the politics of evaluating school reform has been dominated by those who accept the positive side of decentralization reform. In reviewing the research conducted on the parent empowerment phase, Lewis questions the usefulness of many of the studies.

The many contributions of the chapter notwithstanding, one key issue that is not systematically addressed is the nature of the 1995 reform. The 1995 restructuring was not simply "recentralization." Instead, it redefined the authority structure and enhanced accountability. The national significance of the 1995 reform cannot be underestimated. After all, despite intense media and academic publicity, the 1988 parent empowerment model has not been adopted by any major urban school system. In contrast, within three years of implementation, the "integrated governance" reform was adopted by Cleveland and Baltimore and was being considered by several other cities. Major initiatives of the Vallas administration, such as an end to "social promotion" and the creation of "summer bridge" programs, have been endorsed by national, state, and local leaders from both major political parties. In my view, the 1995 reform created the conditions that are necessary to improve teaching and learning for the Chicago public school system as a whole.[1]

WHAT IS INTEGRATED GOVERNANCE?

Decentralization is no longer the dominant reform strategy in the Chicago Public Schools (CPS). The Chicago School Reform Amendatory Act, which took effect in July 1995, reversed a seven-year trend toward decentralization of authority over school operations and redesigned governance so that power and authority are integrated. This new structure of integrated governance would reduce competing authorities and coordinate activities in support of systemwide policy goals. The legislation provided for:

- mayoral appointment of board members and top administrators;
- elimination of competing sources of authority, such as the School Board Nominating Commission and the School Finance Authority;
- a reconstituted Chicago School Reform Board of Trustees to hold LSCs accountable to systemwide standards;
- a new position of a chief executive officer (CEO) to oversee the top administrative team.

With integrated governance, fewer policy actors compete for decision-making authority. The 1995 law suspended the power of the School Finance Authority, eliminated the School Board Nominating Commission, and diminished the ability of the LSCs to operate independently. Further, integrated governance is designed to facilitate policy coherence and improve organizational collaboration among major actors. As a result of the 1995 reforms, the board, top administration, and the mayor's office are closely linked by appointment decisions emanating from the mayor's office. Finally, integrated governance relies

---

[1] For more detailed discussion of integrated governance, see Wong et al., 1997; Wong, 1998; Wong et al., 1999.

on an administration that enjoys strong managerial authority. The 1995 law expanded the financial powers of the board and enhanced the powers of the CEO to manage the system.

REDUCING INSTITUTIONAL AND POLICY FRAGMENTATION

Although the 1995 legislation left intact some features of the previous arrangements, it reduced competing sources of authority and strengthened central administration. The law reduced the size of the board from 15 members to five and put the mayor in charge of appointing board members, the board president, and the CEO. Because the board appoints the top administrative officers, these changes facilitate an effective link between the mayor's office and the central office. Under this arrangement, education becomes a part of the mayor's policy agenda; the mayor can decide how much political capital he is willing to invest in improving the schools. The board and CEO undertook a series of actions to improve public confidence in the ability of the central administration to govern the schools.

The new administration acted swiftly to demonstrate a commitment to efficiency by adopting a business management model. The management and maintenance of school buildings, for example, were reorganized to stress customer service and contracting out to private firms. The board eliminated the Bureau of Facilities Planning in the central office, reduced the number of positions in the Department of Facilities Central Service Center by half, and reduced the citywide administration of facilities. Services for the management and maintenance of school property were contracted out to private firms.

By strengthening the centralized authority of the school system, the 1995 legislation shifted the balance of power between the central office and the LSCs. Prior to 1995, the central office competed with the LSCs for authority over the educational agenda. The LSCs had broad authority, but there was little direct accountability or oversight. For example, state Chapter 1 funds (state aid distributed on basis on low-income student enrollment) went directly to the schools, but the board remained accountable if the money was misused. Selection of principals by the LSCs was often influenced by the constituencies of the particular neighborhood.

The new administration signaled the LSCs that they could no longer operate with complete independence and incorporated the LSCs into the overall system by defining standards and responsibilities to which they must adhere. This policy established 15 criteria covering the actions of the principal, staff, LSC, and LSC members. Under the new policy, the board declared that an "educational crisis" existed at Prosser Preparatory Center and Nathan Hale School. The LSC was disbanded at each school. The LSC at Prosser was declared non-functional in part because of its failure to approve a school improvement plan or evaluate the principal. At Hale, the LSC was suspended after members were found to have intruded in the day-to-day operations of the school, entered classrooms unannounced and uninvited, and failed "to follow the law regarding their powers and responsibilities."

IMPROVING FINANCIAL MANAGEMENT

The 1995 governance redesign enhanced the ability of the central administration to perform financial and management functions efficiently. The 1995 law suspended the budget oversight authority of the School Finance Authority, removed the balanced budget requirement, and placed the inspector general under the authority of the board. A number of state-funded categorical programs (e.g., K-6 reading improvement, substance abuse prevention, Hispanic programs, and gifted education) were collapsed into a general education block grant and an educational services block grant. Although total revenues available to the board declined by 8 percent in FY 1996 from the previous year, revenues going into its general funds increased by about 2 percent. In addition, the board acquired greater flexibility over the use of pension funds and Chapter 1 funds not allocated to the schools. Finally, there were no longer separate tax levies earmarked for specific purposes.

These changes increased board discretion over school revenue, allowing the board to prepare a four-year balanced budget and negotiate a four-year contract, including a raise, with the Chicago Teachers Union. These actions brought both financial and labor stability to the system. Both Standard and Poor's and Moody's raised the CPS bond rating, allowing the board to issue bonds for the construction of new buildings under lower interest rates than before. The four-year teachers' contract meant the board could focus on developing and implementing its education agenda.

INTERVENING IN LOW-PERFORMING SCHOOLS

The 1995 law incorporated a focus on accountability and academic achievement that compelled the administration to target the lowest-performing schools for intervention. Declaring that an "educational crisis" existed in Chicago, the 1995 legislation directed the Board of Trustees and the CEO to increase the quality of educational services within the system. It enhanced the powers of the CEO to identify poorly performing schools and place these schools on remediation, probation, intervention, or reconstitution. Prior to 1995, subdistrict superintendents had the primary responsibility to monitor the performance of the schools and identify non-performing schools. In the past, to place a school on remediation or probation required the approval of the subdistrict council, which was made up of parent or community members from each LSC within the subdistrict.

In January 1996, the CEO placed 21 schools on remediation for failing to meet state standards on Illinois Goals Assessment Program (IGAP) tests for three consecutive years. Only six schools had been placed on remediation by the previous administration. At the same time, the board removed two elementary school principals because the schools failed to improve after a year on remediation.

In September 1996, the CEO placed 109 schools (20% of all schools in the system) on probation because 15 percent or less of their students scored at grade level on nationally normed tests. These schools were held accountable to their school improvement plans as well as to improvements in student test scores. Since this initiative began, nine schools have been removed from the list, and 15 have been added.

Seven schools were targeted for reconstitution based on continued low performance of standardized tests. (None of the reconstituted schools had more than 7% of its students reading at or above grade level.) Five of the seven schools had their principals replaced, and 188 of 675 teachers (29%) were not rehired.

Another new initiative has been the end of "social promotion." In an expanded program from the previous summer, third-, sixth-, eighth-, and ninth-grade students who did not meet set levels on one of two nationally normed tests—the Iowa Tests of Basic Skills (ITBS) or the Tests of Achievement and Proficiency (TAP)—were required to participate in a Summer Bridge program. For example, 61 percent of eighth-graders who participated in the program met the cutoff scores after the seven weeks. By the end of the summer, 92 percent of all eighth-graders had met the school system's new promotion standards. Teachers in this program were provided with day-by-day lesson plans. Students were promoted to the next grade if they brought their scores to the cutoff point set for their grade. If they did not, they were required to repeat the grade. Repeating students returned to their original schools, unless they were older eighth-graders. Half of the repeating eighth-graders attended one of 13 transition centers that featured a curriculum emphasizing basic skills.

The board and top administration reorganized the central office to reflect the focus on accountability and established the improvement of IGAP scores as the primary objective of the system. While other departments within the central office were eliminated or significantly downsized, the administration created the Office of Accountability to monitor school performance, identify low-performing schools, and intervene in poorly performing schools. The Office of Accountability has several departments that launched various programs to improve schools with low test scores. The Department of School Quality Review works with the Illinois State Board of Education to develop a review process to evaluate all schools once every four years. The Department of School Intervention works with schools on the state's Academic Watch List or in remediation.

BROADENING THE POLITICAL BASE OF SUPPORT

The link between the mayor's office and the board can facilitate political support for the school system. With the redesign of the governance system, Mayor Richard Daley has been more willing to invest his political capital in the Chicago schools. To restore public confidence, the Vallas administration projected an image of efficient, responsive, and "clean" government. The administration also took a number of steps to strengthen the support of the business community for the public schools. This support can be crucial in strengthening the board's credibility with the state legislature.

The mayor's appointments to the Board of Trustees reflected a concern with consolidating business support for the schools. Three of the five board members had extensive experience in the private sector. Moreover, the distribution of appointments within the central office reflected the mayor's commitment to improving the fiscal conditions and management of the system. The top appointments in the central office made between July 1995 and December 1996 reflected a diversity of expertise from the private sector, nonprofit organizations, city agencies, and the ranks of the CPS.

To further enhance business support for the schools and the perception of efficient management, the new administration reorganized the central office according to business principles that stressed downsizing and privatization. The strategy of focusing on management and budget issues early on paid off with improved public confidence in the ability of the administration to manage the schools and with stabilized relations with the teachers' union.

Believing that raising test scores is the basis for long-term political support, the mayor, board, and CEO have adopted this as their primary strategy. Better test scores, it was hoped, would form the basis for increased state funding and the continuation of the current centralized governance with the mayor in control of the schools. This arrangement is likely to shift additional power back to the central office, including the establishment of qualifications for the appointment of principals, and to further diminish the role of LSCs. Indeed, in August 1996, the General Assembly adopted legislation that allows the Board of Trustees to develop additional standards and requirements to become a principal.

AN AMBITIOUS AGENDA AND CHALLENGES AHEAD

Under integrated governance, the CEO and the board have initiated a broad reform agenda that includes the following components:

- The system has designed and disseminated its own standards (Chicago Academic Standards) in the areas of English-language arts, mathematics, biological and physical sciences, and social sciences. Achievement tests aligned with those standards are being developed.

- High schools are dividing students into junior academies (grades 9-10) and senior academies (grades 11-12).
- Teachers are expected to participate in professional development that is supportive of and consistent with their school's action plan.

In the longer run, the success of the integrated governance model in Chicago depends on the extent to which the district is able to address several of the key policy challenges:

- How will the system provide support for repeating students? How will high schools address failure rates in the ninth grade?
- How will the system implement curriculum standards in 550 schools? How will teachers make use of assessments to improve curriculum and instruction?
- What incentives will the system provide to expand the supply of well-qualified teachers?
- How will the system monitor progress in the reconstituted schools? What kinds of interim benchmarks are helpful to schools under probation and reconstitution?

These concerns notwithstanding, integrated governance is a promising strategy. Chicago was the first major urban school district to adopt an approach involving highly visible mayoral commitment and political capital to improve the system. Further research is needed to better understand how this can work in other cities and to identify the crucial components of the redesigned system that are transferable.

REFERENCES

Wong, Kenneth K. (1998). *Transforming Urban School Systems: Integrated Governance in Chicago and Birmingham (UK)*. Chicago: Department of Education, and Harris Graduate School of Public Policy Studies, University of Chicago.

Wong, Kenneth K., Dorothea Anagnostopoulos, Stacey Rutledge, Laurence Lynn, and Robert Dreeben (1999). *Implementation of an Educational Accountability Agenda: Integrated Governance in the Chicago Public Schools Enters Its Fourth Year*. Chicago: Department of Education, University of Chicago.

Wong, Kenneth K., Robert Dreeben, Laurence Lynn, and Gail
Sunderman (1997). *Integrated Governance as a Reform
Strategy in the Chicago Public Schools*. Chicago: Depart-
ment of Education, and Harris Graduate School of Public
Policy Studies, University of Chicago.

EDUCATION REFORM FOR THE 21st CENTURY

Report of the Chicago Assembly*

Public school reform efforts across the nation have increasingly focused on standards, performance, and accountability. These themes arise from widespread concern that America's schools are not adequately preparing students for workforce participation, for higher education, and for the economic and technological challenges of the 21st century. A particularly critical task involves improving educational outcomes for children in poverty and other "at-risk" students who represent an increasing proportion of public school enrollment. There has been a growing consensus—at the national, state, and local levels—on an overall agenda and direction for education policy. This agenda centers on the general principles of "standards-based" education reform:

- setting more rigorous standards for what students should know and be able to do;
- measuring the performance of students and schools against those standards;
- providing schools and educators with the tools, skills, and other resources needed to prepare students to achieve higher standards;
- holding schools accountable for the results—i.e., for educational outcomes (U.S. Department of Education, 1996, p. 3).

The seventh Chicago Assembly, "Education Reform for the 21st Century," was held on January 26-27, 1998. Participants included leadership from state government, local school dis-

---

* This is a revised version of a report that was originally released in August 1998. The background section and other descriptive material have been updated. The substance of the findings and recommendations is unchanged.

tricts, community and civic organizations, business, labor, professional associations, advocacy groups, foundations, and universities. Chicago Assembly participants engaged in two days of intensive discussion and deliberation on policy strategies for enhancing learning opportunities and improving educational outcomes for student populations in metropolitan Chicago. The findings and recommendations of the Chicago Assembly Report reflect broad agreement on some of the major issues in standards-based education reform:

Achieving higher standards

- A central goal of education reform should be to assure that all students acquire the basic skills and higher-order skills to prepare for the 21st century.
- The state has the responsibility to supply equitable and adequate resources to establish and implement minimum standards; local school districts have the responsibility of enabling students to meet and exceed those standards.
- A variety of assessment methods should be used to measure student performance in relation to state learning standards.
- A major obstacle to achieving higher standards for all students in the Chicago metropolitan region is a "two-tiered" education system that produces widely disparate outcomes for advantaged and disadvantaged students.

Enhancing accountability

- Education reform for the 21st century requires a strong system of accountability involving multiple stakeholders.
- A primary focus of accountability should be principals and teachers at the school level.
- Effective accountability systems involve both positive and negative incentives; greater emphasis should be put on rewards and recognition for improvement, as well as appropriate intervention in low-performing schools.

Building capacity for reform

- Education reform for the 21st century must involve building the capacity needed to achieve higher standards.

- Building capacity for reform should focus on strategies to improve the quality of teaching. Such efforts should include attracting and retaining talented teachers, strengthening incentives to improve teacher performance, and investing in effective professional development.
- Effective educational partnerships can be important tools for expanding resources and building long-term support for school reform. Capacity-building should involve collaboration with a wide variety of stakeholders at the community, regional, and state levels.

BACKGROUND

NATIONAL POLICY TRENDS

In 1983, *A Nation at Risk*, the landmark report of the National Commission on Excellence in Education, galvanized public attention on the issue of educational quality. The report warned that "the educational foundations of our society are presently being eroded by a rising tide of mediocrity." The commission's recommendations included stronger high school graduation requirements with core curriculum content focusing on the "new basics" (English, mathematics, science, social studies, and computer science); more rigorous standards and expectations for academic performance; more classroom time devoted to learning the new basics; and efforts to improve the preparation of teachers and to make teaching a more rewarding and respected profession (NCEE, 1983).

A *Nation at Risk* generated several different waves of education reform at state and local levels across the country. The "educational excellence" movement of the 1980s saw increased state activism in education policy and focused largely on the "inputs" of the educational process, including exposing more students to core academic curriculum, mandating more standardized tests for more subject areas and grade levels, strengthening high school graduation requirements, and instituting higher teacher certification standards.[1]

A second wave of reform, emerging in the middle-to-late 1980s, emphasized strategies for "restructuring" the process of

---

[1] See Massell, 2001.

learning, the practice of teaching, and the organization and governance of public schools. Genuine education reform was seen as requiring decentralization of decision-making to the school and community level. These "bottom-up" approaches to reform included school-based or site-based management, which gave teachers and principals, as well as parents and other community members, more control over curriculum, hiring, budgeting, and other decisions. The empowerment theme in school restructuring was often accompanied by the idea of schools as "learning communities" in which teachers, students, and administrators actively participate in and take responsibility for the educational process.[2] The movement for school-based reform also involved growing interest in comprehensive reform models—such as James Comer's "School Development Process," Henry Levin's "Accelerated Schools," Robert Slavin's "Success for All," and Theodore Sizer's "Coalition of Essential Schools"—that are designed to raise expectations and achievement for all students, especially disadvantaged students.[3]

By the mid-1990s, a third wave of education reform drew on elements of both "top-down" and "bottom-up" approaches and focused on improving *educational outcomes* by setting higher standards for what students should know and be able to do. "Standards-based reform" involves establishing more rigorous academic standards for all students, measuring the performance of students and schools against those standards, and holding schools accountable for educational outcomes.[4] According to some formulations, standards-based reform means "systemic" reform, which involves the following key features:

- curriculum frameworks (or academic content standards), typically developed at the state level, to provide direction and vision for improving educational outcomes;
- a coherent, coordinated set of policies regarding academic content and performance standards, assessment tools,

---

[2] See Elmore, 1990; Newmann, 1993; Wohlstetter, Mohrman, and Robertson, 1997.

[3] See Murnane and Levy, 1992, pp. 195-196; Barnett, 1996; CPRE, 1998; Payne, 2001.

[4] See Murnane and Levy, 1992, pp. 196-207; McLaughlin and Shepard, 1995; Ladd, 1996.

teacher preparation and professional development, and accountability for results;
* changes in governance to reduce state regulations and mandates and to give local school districts and individual schools the flexibility, control, and resources to design and implement strategies for preparing students to achieve higher standards.[5]

Elements of standards-based reform were reflected in the 1989 Education Summit convened in Charlottesville, Virginia, by President Bush and the nation's governors, which led to the adoption of National Education Goals for the year 2000. A more detailed formulation appeared in the 1992 report of the National Council on Education Standards and Testing, which was charged by Congress with making recommendations regarding the desirability and feasibility of national standards and tests (NCEST, 1992). In 1994, the "Goals 2000: Educate America Act" authorized a National Education Standards and Improvement Council (NESIC) to develop voluntary national standards and established federal grants for systemic education improvement plans at the state and local levels. The emerging consensus on national education standards was stalled, however, in the aftermath of Republican victories in the 1994 congressional elections. President Clinton never appointed members to the NESIC, and Congress abolished it in 1996.[6]

Despite political difficulties at the federal level, the movement toward standards-based reform continued at the state level. By the late 1990s, nearly all states had implemented or were developing academic content standards, performance standards, and student assessment tools. The idea of standards-based reform was embraced by organizations such as the National Governors' Association, the National Conference of State Legislatures, the Education Commission of the States, the Council of Chief State School Officers, the National Association of State

---

[5] See Smith and O'Day, 1991; O'Day and Smith, 1993; Massell, 2001.

[6] See McLaughlin and Shepard, 1995, pp. 1-4; Ravitch, 1995, pp. xvi-xvii.

Boards of Education, and the American Federation of Teachers.[7]

Although standards-based reform has generated broad support, the actual design and implementation of academic content standards, assessment tools, performance indicators, and accountability measures have been more complex matters. Some reformers maintain that setting high standards should move beyond minimum competencies and basic skills and should emphasize higher-order thinking, conceptual understanding, and complex problem-solving. The new standards should "reflect changing conceptions of the types of knowledge and skills required for productive employment, responsible citizenship, and personal fulfillment in the 21st century" (McLaughlin and Shepard, 1995, p. 10). Some critics of this approach believe that emphasis on higher-order thinking can divert attention from teaching basic skills and transmitting a common body of substantive knowledge to all students. Other observers reject such a dichotomy and insist that standards-based reform should emphasize both basic skills and higher skills.[8]

A related set of issues surrounds designing assessment tools that are aligned with academic content standards and that provide accurate and reliable measures of student achievement. Some critics warn that "high-stakes" testing, especially traditional multiple-choice formats, can have adverse effects on classroom instruction such as "narrowing the curriculum" and "teaching to the test." Several states have introduced alternative assessment tools (e.g., portfolios of classroom work) that enable students to demonstrate that they understand and can apply what they have learned. Questions have been been raised, however, about the reliability and objectivity of these alternative assessments, which have sometimes met with implementation problems and political controversy.[9]

---

[7] See, e.g., CCSSO, 1997; AFT, 1997.

[8] See Massell, 2001; Hess, 2001.

[9] See Ravitch, 1995, pp. 106, 167-168; Massell, 2001. The logic of standards-based reform also implies shifting from widely used "norm-referenced" tests, which are designed to measure a student's performance in comparison with national norms or averages, to "criterion-referenced" tests, which measure student performance in relation to specific academic content standards.

Aside from the selection of assessment tools, designing appropriate performance indicators is a technically complex task. Holding schools accountable for student performance (i.e., gains in student learning) requires measuring the "value added" in the educational process, that is, how much a school contributes to student learning above and beyond prior student achievement and the effects of home and community.[10]

Another contested issue concerns the link between higher standards and educational equity. For some proponents of systemic reform, the principle of higher standards and higher expectations *for all students* should be a tool for achieving greater equity in the educational system. Content standards and performance standards must be accompanied by "opportunity-to-learn" (OTL) standards regarding the resources, programs, and qualified teachers needed to enable all students to meet the expectations reflected in new performance standards.[11] The idea of OTL standards became one of the most contentious issues in education policy debates at the federal level; in most states, OTL standards have not been prominent items on the education policy agenda.[12]

STATEWIDE POLICY TRENDS IN ILLINOIS

State education policy in Illinois in the 1980s and 1990s focused on both "inputs" and "outcomes." In 1985, in response to both the *Nation at Risk* report and the recommendations of the Illinois Commission on the Improvement of Elementary and Secondary Education, the General Assembly enacted a comprehen-

---

[10] See Easton and Storey, 2001; Bryk, et al., 1998; R. Meyer, 1996.

[11] See NCEST, 1992; O'Day and Smith, 1993; McLaughlin and Shepard, 1995, pp. 10-12, 42-48.

[12] Elmore and Fuhrman, 1995; Porter, 1995; Massell, Kirst, and Hoppe, 1997. The federal Goals 2000 legislation enacted in 1994 provided for voluntary national OTL standards and required state systemic education improvement plans to include OTL standards or strategies. In 1996, however, Congress abolished the NESIC, which had been charged with developing national OTL standards, and eliminated requirements for OTL standards at the state level.

sive package of statewide reforms. The centerpiece of the legislation required the Illinois State Board of Education (ISBE) to identify state goals for learning in six subject areas and to institute a statewide testing program for public school students. As a result, ISBE created the Illinois Goals Assessment Program (IGAP) to measure student achievement every year in the third, sixth, eighth, and tenth grades. In addition, local school districts were required to develop learning objectives consistent with the state learning goals and, as a means to "better schools accountability," to issue annual "school report cards" that assess the performance of schools and students.[13]

Although Illinois began to shift attention to educational outcomes in the 1980s, it did not abandon the traditional concern with regulating school inputs and processes. In 1983, the legislature mandated new high school graduation requirements, including minimum coursework in language arts, mathematics, science, and social studies.[14] The 1985 education reform package instituted certification tests of basic skills and subject matter knowledge for prospective teachers, established a state academy for training school administrators, mandated periodic evaluation of teachers and all other certified school personnel, and required school districts to conduct staff development programs. The state moved gradually toward standards-based reform in the 1990s, although the Illinois School Code still contains many provisions (regulations and mandates) that some critics view as impediments to a standards-based, outcomes-focused education system.

Illinois Learning Standards

In July 1997, ISBE adopted new "Illinois Learning Standards," a revised and updated set of expectations for what students should know and be able to do as a consequence of their elementary and secondary schooling. According to ISBE, one of the key reasons for the new learning standards was the need to prepare students for a rapidly changing world of technological breakthroughs, explosion of information, and global economies:

---

[13] See Bakalis, 1986; Sanders, 1986; Sevener, 1991.

[14] See Sevener, 1985.

"To be successful in a world characterized by change, students will need to learn the basics, but the basics of the 1990s and the new century to come go far beyond the basics of the 1960s, 1970s, or 1980s. In addition to basic knowledge and skills, students will need to acquire new ways to learn that will serve them throughout their lives" (ISBE, 1997a, p. iv). The Illinois Learning Standards were used as a guide for redesigning the state assessment program, which includes a new Illinois Standards Achievement Test (ISAT) to replace IGAP, as well as a Prairie State Achievement Examination for graduating high school seniors. ISBE has also encouraged the development of an integrated assessment system in which state assessments are complemented by local assessment programs to monitor student progress.

Professional Standards for Teachers

In November 1996, ISBE adopted a new framework for comprehensive restructuring of the state's system for teacher recruitment, preparation, certification, and continuing professional development. The "Illinois Framework" called for standards-based teacher preparation, a career continuum guided by national standards, advanced certification opportunities for qualified teachers and other educational practitioners, and new standards, strategies, and resources for professional development (ISBE, 1996a).[15] In 1997, the Illinois General Assembly enacted legislation that initiated a new standards-based teacher certification system involving three tiers: a four-year, nonrenewable initial certificate, a five-year standard certificate with continuing education or professional development required for renewal, and a master certificate for those who achieve certification from the National Board for Professional Teaching Standards. The legislation also established alternative routes to certification for teachers, as well as for school superintendents, principals, and other administrators.

---

[15] A subsequent report contained more detailed recommendations for moving toward implementation of the framework (ISBE, 1997c).

Performance and Accountability

The state has begun to implement a new performance-based accountability system linked to student achievement and focused on low-performing schools. In September 1997, ISBE released its first "Academic Early Warning List," consisting of 125 schools (including 93 schools in Chicago) that had not met minimum state standards on IGAP tests over the previous two years or had shown significant declines over the previous three years. Members of ISBE staff were appointed to work with the schools on strategies to improve student learning.[16]   Schools on the Warning List must produce a revised school improvement plan, are subject to external review every two years to gauge their progress, and are eligible for targeted school improvement funds. Schools that fail to improve their performance for two consecutive years while on the Warning List are to be placed on an "Academic Watch List." State law mandates that if a school remains on the Watch List for another two years, ISBE must either authorize removal of the local school board and replace it with an independent authority or dissolve the school district and reassign pupils to another district.

Another element of the state's emerging accountability system has been a new Quality Assurance and Improvement Planning Process initiated in January 1997. The program has three major components: school improvement planning (which has been required of all public schools since 1991); internal review of existing school policies and practices; and external review by a team of educators, parents, and community members from outside the local school district. External review teams focus on three key areas: teaching and learning; student learning, progress, and achievement; and the school-based learning community (ISBE, 1997d, 1999).

State legislation enacted in December 1997 mandated performance-based contracts for superintendents, principals, and other local school administrators, as well as for the state superintendent of education. These performance-based contracts are to include goals and indicators of student performance and academic improvement. The same legislation also prohibited the practice of "social promotion," that is, promoting students to

---

[16] In Chicago, school probation managers served as ISBE contacts.

the next grade level without regard to their academic performance. School districts are required to provide remedial programs (e.g., "summer bridge" programs) for students who are not eligible for promotion.[17]

School Finance

Public school finance in Illinois has been the subject of intense and prolonged debate, usually overshadowing other education policy issues. Critics have contended that high reliance on local property taxes and erosion of the state share of education funding have produced huge fiscal disparities among school districts.[18] In December 1997, the Illinois General Assembly broke many years of political deadlock and enacted some significant changes in state aid for elementary and secondary education. The "foundation level"—the per-pupil funding amount guaranteed from state and local sources—was increased to $4,225 for the 1998-99 school year, with a three-year continuing appropriation for the new school aid formula. The legislation also revised the method for providing additional funds for serving students from low-income families. The major beneficiaries of these changes in state funding were, for the most part, poorer elementary school districts.[19]

Proponents praised the legislation for providing more resources for the poorest school districts and for setting a specific foundation level by statute, rather than allowing state funding to be contingent on the available appropriation in any given year. Some critics maintained that the legislation did not change the basic structure of school finance and the reliance on property taxes as the primary source of education funding in Illinois; others contended that the school finance reform goals

---

[17] Social promotion had already been eliminated in the Chicago public schools.

[18] See, e.g., Hess, 2001; Wong, 1996; Chicago Assembly, 1994.

[19] Grade-weighting of pupil counts for general state aid, which had especially benefited high schools, was eliminated. The adverse impact of the new law on high school districts was mitigated by a "hold harmless" provision that guaranteed each district the same level of funding that it had previously received.

of equity for students and equity for taxpayers had been replaced by minimal adequacy of funding.[20]

CHICAGO SCHOOL REFORM

Education reform efforts in Chicago have involved both bottom-up and top-down strategies for improving school performance and accountability. In 1988, the General Assembly passed the Chicago School Reform Act, which radically decentralized the city's school system. Local school councils (LSCs) consisting of parents, community residents, and teachers were given substantial responsibilities, including hiring and firing principals, creating and approving school improvement plans, and helping to create and approve school budgets. State compensatory education funds previously controlled by central administration were reallocated to schools on a per-pupil basis. In addition to these structural changes in school governance, the 1988 reforms also set systemwide performance goals (e.g., 50% of students in each school were to reach national norms within five years) and required schools to develop three-year improvement plans that would be updated and evaluated on an annual basis.[21]

The Chicago School Reform Amendatory Act of 1995 reorganized and consolidated the central administration of the school system. The city's mayor was given the authority to appoint a new Chicago School Reform Board of Trustees, as well as fill the new position of chief executive officer (CEO).[22] The 1995 legislation also established the Chicago Academic Accountability Council and gave the CEO and the Board stronger

---

[20] For a range of different views, see ISBE, 1997e; Dye, Goldstein, and McGuire, 1998; Hess and Braskamp, 1998; D. Meyer, 2001.

[21] See Bryk, Kerbow, and Rollow, 1997; Hess, 2001; Lewis, 2001. The 1988 legislation also created a new 15-member Board of Education and a School Board Nominating Commission, which screened candidates and provided the mayor with a list from which to appoint board members. The mayor's choices then went to the City Council for final approval.

[22] Starting in 1999, the mayor appointed a seven-member board, with staggered, four-year terms.

tools for intervention in low-performing schools. These new options included disbanding LSCs, removing principals, and revoking teacher tenure.[23]

The system's new leadership instituted an accountability system with three levels of intervention for low-performing schools: remediation, probation, and reconstitution. In fall 1996, 109 of the system's 557 public schools were put on academic probation, and another 31 were given remediation status. Schools were placed on probation if less than 15 percent of their students were performing at grade level on reading achievement tests. These schools were assigned external partners and probation managers to provide technical assistance and to monitor improvement efforts. In June 1997, seven Chicago high schools faced reconstitution, under which principals were subject to removal and staff were required to reapply for their positions or seek employment elsewhere in the school system. These schools had been placed on probation the previous September and had failed to demonstrate significant improvement in test scores, attendance, graduation rates, and overall performance. Five of the seven principals and about 30 percent of the teachers at the reconstituted schools were replaced.[24]

In May 1997, the Chicago School Reform Board of Trustees adopted its own Chicago Academic Standards to complement state learning standards. The new standards, which were formulated in collaboration with the Chicago Teachers Union (CTU) Quest Center, will be the basis for a new assessment system for the Chicago public schools.

STUDENT ACHIEVEMENT TRENDS

Since the mid-1980s, much of the education policy focus in Illinois, as well as in other states, has been on raising standardized test scores as a way of promoting school improvement. Student achievement results in reading and mathematics have exhibited

---

[23] See Bryk, Kerbow, and Rollow, 1997; Hess, 2001; Wong, 2001.

[24] See Hess, 2001; Easton and Storey, 2001. "Re-engineering," a sanction more severe than probation but less severe than reconstitution, was introduced in 1999-2000. "Intervention," a modified version of reconstitution, was introduced in 2000-2001.

similar trends at the national, state, and local levels. Average achievement scores in mathematics have been rising consistently at most grade levels, while reading scores have been relatively flat or declining. These trends have been evident in nationwide results from the National Assessment of Educational Progress (NAEP) since the 1980s, statewide IGAP tests in Illinois in the 1990s, and the performance of Chicago public school students on the Iowa Tests of Basic Skills (ITBS) and the Tests of Achievement and Proficiency (TAP) in the 1990s.[25]

There has also been substantial progress in reducing student achievement gaps among racial and ethnic groups. For both African-Americans and Hispanics, NAEP reading and mathematics scores at most grade levels showed significant improvement in the 1970s and 1980s. This progress, however, showed some signs of slowing down in the 1990s, and average test scores for both African-American and Hispanic students remain substantially behind those of their White counterparts.[26]

Finally, national data indicate much more progress in raising the minimum level of basic skills in both reading and mathematics than in raising the proportion of students who demonstrate higher levels of achievement for their grade. Similarly, in the Chicago public schools, some progress has been made in reducing the proportion of students in the early grades who score in the bottom national quartile in reading achievement, but there has been little or no improvement in the proportion of students reaching the top quartile.[27]

STUDENT ENROLLMENT TRENDS

The six-county Chicago metropolitan area has nearly 300 public school districts and more than 1.29 million students (64% of statewide enrollment). In fall 1999, student enrollment in the

---

[25] See Roderick, 2001, Tables 7-9; Bryk, Kerbow, and Rollow, 1997; Easton and Storey, 2001. Reading achievement trends in Chicago present a mixed picture, with some improvement in ITBS results in the elementary grades.

[26] See Roderick, 2001, Table 9.

[27] See Roderick, 2001, Tables 10-11.

region was about evenly divided among Chicago (33%), suburban Cook County (28%), and the five collar counties (39%). Chicago is by far the region's largest school district, with over 430,000 students in some 550 schools.[28] As of fall 1999, the Chicago public schools enrolled two-thirds of Black students, 54 percent of Hispanic students, and 70 percent of all low income students in the metropolitan area (see Tables 1-2).[29]

Although the region's racial minorities are heavily concentrated in Chicago, there have been some significant changes in student demographics across the six-county metro area. The most notable trend has been the burgeoning numbers of Hispanic students, who accounted for nearly 75 percent of public school enrollment growth in the region between 1984 and 1999. Within the Chicago school system, both White enrollment and Black enrollment have been declining, while Hispanic enrollment has been rapidly growing (see Table 3).

In suburban Cook County, White enrollment has fallen, while both Black and Hispanic enrollments have increased; Hispanic enrollment more than tripled between 1984 and 1999. African-Americans are primarily concentrated in south suburban school districts, as well as in some western suburbs. Many of these districts have student populations that are 85-95 percent Black. Hispanic students are more widely dispersed, with substantial enrollment in various west suburban and northwest suburban school districts. In the collar counties, there has been enrollment growth for all major racial groups, with marked increases among Hispanics. Both Black and Hispanic students have a significant presence in larger communities such as Aurora, Elgin, Joliet, and Waukegan (see Tables 3-4).

---

[28] The second largest district, Unit District 46 in Elgin, has only about 35,000 students. Some school districts in the metropolitan area consist of only one school.

[29] "Low-income" students include children eligible for free or reduced school lunches, children in families receiving public aid, and children in substitute care.

TABLE 1: Public School Enrollment in Metropolitan Chicago, Fall 1999

	Total enrollment	Pct. distr.	White	Pct. distr.	Black	Pct. distr.	Hispanic	Pct. distr.	Asian	Pct. distr.
Metro area	1,295,004	100.0	622,980	100.0	338,731	100.0	272,413	100.0	58,666	100.0
Chicago	431,750	33.3	42,970	6.9	226,611	66.9	147,705	54.2	13,731	23.4
Suburban Cook	368,661	28.5	215,303	34.6	74,885	22.1	56,631	20.8	21,313	36.3
DuPage County	153,564	11.9	119,342	19.2	6,816	2.0	14,034	5.2	13,104	22.3
Kane County	97,518	7.5	62,508	10.0	7,456	2.2	24,083	8.8	3,265	5.6
Lake County	122,741	9.5	87,226	14.0	10,903	3.2	19,108	7.0	5,254	9.0
McHenry County	43,121	3.3	39,026	6.3	289	0.1	3,192	1.2	544	0.9
Will County	77,649	6.0	56,605	9.1	11,771	3.5	7,660	2.8	1,455	2.5

Source: ISBE, 2000.

TABLE 2: Public School Enrollment of Students from Low-Income Households, Metropolitan Chicago, Fall 1999

	Low-income enrollment	Pct. distr.	Pct. low-income
Metro area	517,914	100.0	40.0
Chicago	366,057	70.7	84.8
Suburban Cook	83,707	16.2	22.7
DuPage County	9,035	1.7	5.9
Kane County	21,749	4.2	22.3
Lake County	20,322	3.9	16.6
McHenry County	3,138	0.6	7.3
Will County	13,906	2.7	17.9

Source: ISBE, 2000.

TABLE 3: Changes in Public School Enrollment in Metropolitan Chicago, 1984 to 1999

	Fall 1984	Pct. distr.	Fall 1999	Pct distr.	Change 1984-99	Pct. change
Chicago	431,226	100.0	431,750	100.0	524	0.1
White	63,430	14.7	42,970	10.0	-20,460	-32.3
Black	261,386	60.6	226,611	52.5	-34,775	-13.3
Hispanic	94,246	21.9	147,705	34.2	53,459	56.7
Asian	11,421	2.6	13,731	3.2	2,310	20.2
Suburban Cook	322,181	100.0	368,661	100.0	46,480	14.4
White	249,495	77.4	215,303	58.4	-34,192	-13.7
Black	44,856	13.9	74,885	20.3	30,029	66.9
Hispanic	16,101	5.0	56,631	15.4	40,530	251.7
Asian	11,315	3.5	21,313	5.8	9,998	88.4

TABLE 3 (continued)

	Fall 1984	Pct. distr.	Fall 1999	Pct distr.	Change 1984-99	Pct. change
DuPage County	111,678	100.0	153,564	100.0	41,886	37.5
White	100,107	89.6	119,342	77.7	19,235	19.2
Black	2,367	2.1	6,816	4.4	4,449	188.0
Hispanic	3,346	3.0	14,034	9.1	10,688	319.4
Asian	5,660	5.1	13,104	8.5	7,444	131.5
Kane County	67,264	100.0	97,518	100.0	30,254	45.0
White	52,068	77.4	62,508	64.1	10,440	20.1
Black	5,368	8.0	7,456	7.6	2,088	38.9
Hispanic	8,121	12.1	24,083	24.7	15,962	196.6
Asian	1,636	2.4	3,265	3.3	1,629	99.6
Lake County	82,473	100.0	122,741	100.0	40,268	48.8
White	68,564	83.1	87,226	71.1	18,662	27.2
Black	7,352	8.9	10,903	8.9	3,551	48.3
Hispanic	5,269	6.4	19,108	15.6	13,839	262.6
Asian	1,818	2.2	5,254	4.3	3,436	189.0
McHenry County	26,666	100.0	43,121	100.0	16,455	61.7
White	25,815	96.8	39,026	90.5	13,211	51.2
Black	38	0.1	289	0.7	251	660.5
Hispanic	645	2.4	3,192	7.4	2,547	394.9
Asian	156	0.6	544	1.3	388	248.7
Will County	60,262	100.0	77,649	100.0	17,387	28.9
White	46,754	77.6	56,605	72.9	9,851	21.1
Black	9,240	15.3	11,771	15.2	2,531	27.4
Hispanic	3,194	5.3	7,660	9.9	4,466	139.8
Asian	945	1.6	1,455	1.9	510	54.0
Metro area	1,102,730	100.0	1,295,004	100.0	192,274	17.4
White	606,233	55.0	622,980	48.1	16,747	2.8
Black	330,607	30.0	338,731	26.2	8,124	2.5
Hispanic	130,922	11.9	272,413	21.0	141,491	108.1
Asian	32,951	3.0	58,666	4.5	25,715	78.0

Source: ISBE, 1985, 2000.

TABLE 4: Student Enrollment in Selected Suburban School Districts in Metropolitan Chicago, Fall 1999

	Total	Pct. White	Pct. Black	Pct. Hispanic	Pct. Asian	Pct. low-income
Suburban Cook						
Palatine Community Consolidated School District 15	12,719	71.0	3.7	16.8	8.1	16.0
Wheeling Community Consolidated School District 21	7,199	62.6	3.3	27.2	6.9	27.8
Elk Grove Comm. Consol. School Dist. 59 (Arl. Hts.)	6,557	63.4	3.6	20.3	12.3	22.2
Evanston Community Consolidated School District 65	7,149	42.1	45.5	8.9	3.3	34.1
Mannheim School District 83 (Franklin Park)	2,734	43.5	1.8	51.1	3.5	14.5
Bellwood School District 88	3,171	2.2	66.9	30.2	0.7	48.4
Maywood School District 89	5,686	5.6	63.2	30.8	0.4	55.4
Oak Park Elementary School District 97	5,075	58.8	34.7	3.6	2.6	14.5
Cicero School District 99	11,917	8.0	0.6	90.8	0.5	67.7
Cook County School District 130 (Blue Island)	3,705	35.2	25.8	38.8	0.2	59.3
Prairie Hills Elementary School Dist. 144 (Hazel Crest)	3,011	8.8	87.6	2.7	0.9	75.7
Dolton School District 149	3,941	1.2	96.9	1.7	0.2	55.1
Harvey School District 152	3,438	0.7	89.9	8.9	0.4	82.5
Chicago Heights School District 170	3,350	11.3	52.6	36.1	0.0	77.2
J.S. Morton High School District 201 (Cicero)	6,231	28.6	0.5	69.2	1.5	43.0
Thornton Township High School Dist. 205 (S. Holland)	6,292	6.1	89.4	4.0	0.4	38.0
Proviso Township High School District 209 (Maywood)	4,198	5.9	68.8	23.5	1.8	29.3
Township High School District 214 (Arlington Heights)	11,414	75.0	3.1	12.3	9.3	14.0
Rich Township High School Dist. 227 (Olympia Fields)	3,137	25.1	70.7	2.8	1.3	30.0
Bremen Community High School Dist. 228 (Midlothian)	4,542	57.4	36.2	4.5	1.6	13.2

TABLE 4 (continued)

	Total enrollment	Pct. White	Pct. Black	Pct. Hispanic	Pct. Asian	Pct. low-income
DuPage County						
Addison School District 4	3,877	55.0	2.5	37.2	5.3	20.3
West Chicago School District 33	3,814	45.5	1.7	51.1	1.7	22.6
Kane County						
Elgin Unit School District 46	35,546	57.0	7.5	28.8	6.5	29.7
Aurora West Unit School District 129	10,127	49.5	20.9	27.7	1.9	27.1
Aurora East Unit School District 131	10,482	14.3	15.5	69.1	0.8	49.8
Community Unit School District 300 (Carpentersville)	16,136	75.2	4.4	18.3	1.7	15.2
Lake County						
Waukegan Community Unit School District 60	14,813	14.8	25.9	56.8	2.5	54.9
Round Lake Community Unit School District 116	5,848	53.5	5.2	40.0	0.8	42.1
North Chicago Unit School District 187	4,538	19.7	57.8	19.9	2.3	55.7
Will County						
Joliet School District 86	9,219	29.0	40.3	29.7	1.0	58.3
Crete Monee Community Unit School District 201U	4,249	48.8	47.0	3.3	0.6	24.6
Joliet Township High School District 204	4,271	44.6	31.0	22.2	1.8	51.5

Source: ISBE, 2000.

FINDINGS AND RECOMMENDATIONS

ACHIEVING HIGHER STANDARDS

A central goal of education reform should be to assure that all elementary and secondary school students acquire the basic skills and higher-order skills needed to prepare for the 21st century. The State Board of Education has adopted new Illinois Learning Standards in seven areas: English-language arts, mathematics, science, social science, physical development and health, fine arts, and foreign languages. The new state standards, which include both basic and higher-order skills within each learning area, were broadly accepted by Chicago Assembly participants as a starting point for defining what all students should know and be able to do as a result of public schooling.

Implementing State Learning Standards

State government and local school districts have joint responsibility and complementary roles in assuring that all students progress to the best of their abilities. The state has the responsibility of supplying equitable and adequate resources to establish and implement minimum standards, while local school districts have the responsibility of meeting and exceeding those standards. Priority should be given to school improvement efforts for students and schools most needing to improve their performance.

Some Chicago Assembly participants called attention to differences in the resources and capacities of local school districts to reach the state learning standards. They emphasized the need for minimum state funding consistent with the cost of implementing standards, as well as greater flexibility for spending by local school districts.

Assessing Performance

Both the state and local school districts must assure that we have the appropriate tools to assess the performance of all students in relation to state learning standards. A variety of assessment methods should be used to measure student progress. These include (1) assessment of individual students through a

range of measurements aligned with state standards; (2) assessment of the "value added" by schools in the educational process, thus taking into account the different starting points of
students; and (3) assessment of teacher performance.[30]

Some Chicago Assembly participants warned that standardized test scores should not be the objective of education and
questioned whether we have appropriate tools to assess the
development of children as lifelong learners and productive citizens. They expressed concern that political and financial constraints put pressure on schools to focus on outcomes that can
be standardized and quantified rather than to promote genuine
learning; there is a danger that schools will emphasize "teaching
to the test," while overlooking the different needs, abilities, and
learning styles of students.

Overcoming Disparities

A major obstacle to improving educational outcomes for all students in the Chicago metropolitan area is a "two-tiered" education system. Chicago Assembly participants regard the existence of a two-tiered education system as an unacceptable situation that undermines the political, social, and economic well-
being of the metropolitan region and the state. The two-tiered
system is manifested in a variety of ways, including differences
in student performance, socioeconomic status, race and ethnicity, demographics, and local community resources—all of
which can exist both between and within school districts.
Proper measures must be taken to eliminate such disparities.
Some Chicago Assembly participants argue strongly that most
school improvement efforts should focus on the "bottom tier" of
low-performing schools and school districts that primarily serve
low-income and minority students.

---

[30] The concept of "value added" refers to how much a school
contributes to student learning above and beyond prior student
achievement and the contributions of home and community. See
Easton and Storey, 2001.

ENHANCING ACCOUNTABILITY

Standards-based approaches to school reform have been linked to the idea of holding schools and school systems accountable for student outcomes. Accountability strategies have ranged from strengthening statewide standards for school performance to decentralizing decision-making to the school and community level. Other approaches to accountability have been advanced by proponents of public and private school choice. Educational voucher plans seek to use market-based incentives for improving education. Proponents of charter schools want to introduce competition within the public system through the creation of alternative schools that are given public funding and substantial autonomy in exchange for being held accountable for results.

Shared Responsibility

Education reform for the 21st century requires a strong system of accountability involving multiple stakeholders. Accountability efforts should include students (at appropriate age levels), parents, teachers, principals, schools, and school districts, as well as state government. All of these stakeholders share some degree of responsibility for educational outcomes. Some Chicago Assembly participants advanced the idea of a "hierarchy of responsibility." For example, accountability for students requires that they receive effective classroom instruction, while holding teachers accountable entails providing them with appropriate institutional support. Other participants emphasized that the state should be held accountable for providing funding to assure a minimum adequate education for all students.

Leadership and Accountability at the School Level

A primary focus of accountability should be principals and teachers at the school level. Principals should act as both educational leaders and effective managers who help staff to adapt to new programs. Some Chicago Assembly participants advocated a "team model" of accountability—with principals and teachers working together as a team and students learning together as a team.

Many Chicago Assembly participants stressed the idea of decentralization of decision-making to the school level—sometimes called school-based or site-based management. Accountability requires exercise of authority, flexibility in decision-making, and joint problem-solving. Some participants expressed frustration with state regulations and categorical funding restrictions and called for more flexibility in school-level and district-level spending to reallocate resources and direct them to areas of greatest need.

Incentives for Improved Performance

Effective accountability systems necessarily involve both positive and negative incentives. Participants noted that current accountability measures are most often negative and sometimes punitive; they expressed a desire to put greater emphasis on positive incentives that involve rewards and recognition for improvement, as well as appropriate intervention in and support for low-performing schools.

School Choice Models of Accountability

Chicago Assembly participants did not reach agreement on the issues of school choice and market-based incentives for school improvement. Proponents of school choice contended that the market was the ultimate accountability tool. Critics feared that this approach (especially voucher plans) would exacerbate the existing inequities of a two-tiered education system. Other participants did not endorse school choice but were willing to experiment with various models.

BUILDING CAPACITY FOR REFORM

Education reform for the 21st century must involve building the capacity needed to achieve higher standards. In many states across the nation, policymakers concerned with standards-based reform have begun to pursue strategies to assist schools and educators in developing the knowledge and skills, resources, and organizational capacity to prepare students for the challenges of the next century.[31]   Achieving higher standards also requires that schools make the most effective use of their resources—either existing resources or new resources—to improve student learning.   These challenges are most daunting in troubled inner-city schools that face multiple impediments to change.[32]

Focusing on Teaching

Building the capacity of schools to enhance student performance should focus on improving the quality of teaching.   The National Commission on Teaching and America's Future (NCTAF) has emphasized that what teachers know and can do makes the crucial difference in what children learn (NCTAF, 1996).[33]   The Illinois State Board of Education has adopted a new framework for comprehensive restructuring of the state's system for teacher recruitment, preparation, certification, and continuing professional development.   Some Chicago Assembly participants expressed strong support for these state efforts to move toward a standards-based education system by linking expectations and standards for student learning with professional standards and professional development for educators.

Attracting high-quality teachers: Illinois must attract and retain many more high-quality teachers.   In addition to the difficulties in recruiting highly skilled teachers generally, there is the particular challenge of attracting and retaining teachers in

---

[31] See Massell, 2001; Massell, Kirst, and Hoppe, 1997; Goertz, Floden, and O'Day, 1996.

[32] See Picus, 2001; Payne, 2001.

[33] The NCTAF report includes recommendations regarding higher professional standards for teachers, reinventing teacher preparation and professional development, improving teacher recruitment, and encouraging and rewarding teacher knowledge and skills.   The commission's members included Governor Jim Edgar; Illinois was one of seven states to form partnerships with NCTAF to develop new programs and policies consistent with the report's agenda for quality teaching.

low-performing school districts and in districts with limited financial resources. Chicago Assembly participants offered a range of ideas for attracting talented people to the teaching profession:

• earlier, stronger, and expanded teacher recruitment efforts, especially for the Chicago public schools and other school districts serving large numbers of low-income students;
• alternative certification as a way to draw talented individuals from other professions to the teaching field;
• greater flexibility in salary schedules in order to enable schools to offer competitive salaries in subject areas with teacher shortages;
• incentives to attract highly skilled teachers to low-performing schools and school districts;
• efforts to promote the teaching profession and improve the public perception of teaching.

Strategies for more effective teaching: Participants recommended a number of strategies to encourage excellence in teaching, including strengthening incentives to improve student achievement:

• reward systems based on classroom performance, including outcomes as measured by improvements in student achievement, rather than just seniority and advanced degrees;
• alternative approaches to assessing teacher performance, including peer review, portfolios of teacher work, and student and parent evaluation of teachers;
• encouraging teaching excellence by recognizing lead teachers or master teachers;
• establishing mentoring programs to provide support for beginning teachers, as well as to enhance the professional growth of experienced teachers;
• strengthening the ability of principals to make personnel decisions.

Professional development: Building capacity for education reform requires investment in professional development opportunities for teachers and other educational practitioners, as well as institutional and collegial support for improved teaching. Traditional approaches to teacher professional development have been criticized as involving short-term, passive activities with limited follow-up.[34] Tools and strategies for more effective professional development should include site-based, team-oriented activities that are an integral part of school operations, that reduce the professional isolation of teachers through collaboration and mutual support among peers, and that promote the development of the school as a learning community.[35]

Educational Partnerships

Active, involved communities and partnerships with a wide variety of stakeholders are crucial to capacity-building. Effective educational partnerships can be important tools for expanding resources and building long-term support for school reform. Such partnerships can take many forms and focus on a range of different activities, including curriculum development, student support services, school-to-work transition, and community involvement.[36]

Framing effective education policy at the community level requires creating and sustaining trust in relationships among stakeholders, including board members, administrators, teachers, and parents. Collaboration with the broader community should also involve other educators, local businesses, colleges and universities, government agencies, adult learners, senior citizens, and community and civic organizations, among others. To be sustained, collaboration with this "mosaic of partners" should be integrated into the life of the school, rather than compartmentalized into a separate program.

School partnerships with business can be an important vehicle for mobilizing expertise and other resources. Some Chicago Assembly participants emphasized that partnerships with business should involve more effective utilization of efforts and

---

[34] See Payne, 2001, p. 247.

[35] See NGA, 1994; ISBE, 1996a.

[36] See Goertz, Floden, and O'Day, 1996; Danzberger, Bodinger-deUriarte, and Clark, 1996.

resources that are matched with specific school needs. Others proposed enlisting the business community in efforts to address the needs of the rapidly growing population of Latino students.

Collaboration with institutions of higher education has been a notable element of school reform initiatives in Chicago. Some participants advocated expanded involvement of colleges and universities in public school improvement efforts, drawing on the expertise of scientists, mathematicians, computer specialists, historians, writers, and other faculty, as well as from those in schools and departments of education.

Other Capacity-Building Initiatives

Chicago Assembly participants cited a variety of other examples of capacity-building efforts that should be encouraged or expanded. Broader collaborative approaches to capacity-building include cross-district partnerships and regional support networks. Regional offices of education and intermediate service centers, which serve as links between the State Board of Education and local school districts (outside Chicago), offer professional development and training programs, technical assistance, and other resources in areas such as standards and assessment, school improvement and quality review, and learning technologies.

The Illinois Learning Partnership, a statewide coalition of major stakeholders in education reform, supports the development of "regional learning networks" in different parts of the state. These networks are collaborative groups of school leadership teams—comprised of school personnel, parents, teachers, community members, and board members—working to develop strategies to enhance student achievement and effect systemic change in their local schools.[37]

The Illinois Right to Read Initiative is a five-year effort, launched by ISBE in fall 1997, to improve reading and literacy. The initiative is designed to disseminate and share information on effective, research-based reading instruction; strengthen the

---

[37] Members of the Illinois Learning Partnership include the Chicago Urban League, Illinois Education Association, Illinois Federation of Teachers, Illinois Parent Teacher Association, Illinois State Board of Education, and Voices for Illinois Children.

ability of educators to teach children to read; mobilize resources and expertise through a Reading Education Partnership Council that includes educators, employers, community and parent organizations, and libraries; and provide schools with targeted resources for reading improvement (ISBE, 1997b).

Preparing students for the 21st century will require building capacity for making the most effective use of new educational technologies. Many schools in metropolitan Chicago and across the state are beginning to use technology to enhance the learning process. The State Board of Education has adopted an information technology plan that calls for expanding student access to technological resources, enabling teachers to effectively utilize technologies as learning tools in the classroom, and developing capacity for educational technology at the school and community levels (ISBE, 1996b).

CHALLENGES FOR THE FUTURE

The idea of systemic, standards-based education reform presents an ambitious policy agenda. State and local education policy in Illinois has been moving incrementally toward a standards-based model in designing and implementing of challenging learning standards, reliable assessment tools to measure student progress, and effective performance-based accountability systems. Continuing policy challenges include aligning and coordinating various state and local initiatives while maintaining local control, building capacity for standards-based reform at the school level, and developing strategies that move beyond school-by-school improvement to broader systemic change. As we move into the 21st century, public schools in metropolitan Chicago (and elsewhere in Illinois) face additional policy challenges regarding early childhood education, postsecondary education, and issues of diversity and equity.

Early Childhood Education

A significant trend in education for younger children has been rising expectations for what constitutes "readiness" for school, as well as growing participation in preschool programs. A key provision of Illinois school reform legislation in 1985 was funding for the expansion of prekindergarten programs for low-income children in public schools.   In fall 1999, over 46,000 children were enrolled in public prekindergarten programs in Illinois, nearly four times the enrollment in fall 1984.   Nonetheless, national data show that preschool participation rates for disadvantaged children—especially Hispanic children—are substantially lower than for children from more affluent and highly educated families.[38]

The widening gap in preschool enrollment suggests that those children who could benefit most from preschool are least likely to attend and thereby risk falling further behind their more advantaged counterparts.   In view of the widely documented benefits of early childhood education, expanding access to and improving the quality of preschool programs should be a high priority.   Some Chicago Assembly participants maintain that the initial focus should be programs for at-risk children, in a range of different settings, with links to current welfare-to-work initiatives.   There should also be efforts to integrate day care programs and prekindergarten programs.

Postsecondary Education

One of the most striking trends in the U.S. economy involves the link between educational attainment (i.e., years of schooling) and economic success.   Income disparities between workers with high levels and low levels of educational attainment have grown dramatically.   The increasing economic importance of postsecondary education has been accompanied by wider racial disparities in college completion.   Among 25-to-29-year-old high school graduates in 1999, 36 percent of Whites had completed four years of college, compared with only 17 percent of African-Americans and 14 percent of Hispanics.[39]

Policy strategies to enable more students to attend and succeed in college should be developed at both the state level and the community level.   Building stronger bridges to postsecondary education will require concerted efforts to improve the performance of high schools, which have been characterized as the

---

[38] See Roderick, 2001, Tables 5-6.

[39] See Roderick, 2001, Table 13.

weakest link in the public educational system.[40] In addition, proponents of "K-16 reform" contend that significant progress at the elementary and secondary levels will require closer collaboration with institutions of higher education. Emerging K-16 strategies include aligning college admissions with standards-based reform and improving teacher preparation for K-12 education.[41]

Diversity and Equity

According to the State Board of Education, Illinois Learning Standards are meant to provide the basis for other reforms to improve teaching and learning and are "part of meeting Illinois's obligation to provide fair and equitable educational opportunities for all students" (ISBE, 1997a, p. iv). For many school districts across the Chicago metropolitan area, the changing demographics of student enrollment are highlighting issues of diversity and equity. New policy challenges include closing racial and ethnic gaps in student achievement, educating a rapidly growing Latino student population in the context of a shortage of Latino teachers, and conceptualizing methods of using racial and cultural diversity as an educational resource. Improving learning opportunities and achieving higher standards for all students in all schools is the most critical task on the agenda of education reform for the 21st century.

REFERENCES

AFT (1997). *Making Standards Matter, 1997: An Annual Fifty-State Report on Efforts to Raise Academic Standards*. Washington, D.C.: American Federation of Teachers.
Bakalis, Michael J. (1986). "Illinois School Reform: After the Cheering Stopped," *Illinois Issues*, May 1986, pp. 15-17.
Barnett, W. Steven (1996). "Economics of School Reform: Three Promising Models." In Helen F. Ladd, ed., *Holding*

---

[40] See Roderick, 2001. In 1998-99, 41 out of 87 schools on the state's Academic Early Warning List were high schools.

[41] See Haycock, 1997.

*Schools Accountable: Performance-Based Reform in Educa-
tion.* Washington, D.C.: Brookings Institution.
Bryk, Anthony S., David Kerbow, and Sharon Rollow (1997).
"Chicago School Reform." In Diane Ravitch and Joseph P.
Viteritti, eds., *New Schools for a New Century: The Rede-
sign of Urban Education.* New Haven: Yale University
Press.
Bryk, Anthony S., Yeow Men Thum, John Q. Easton, and Stu-
art Luppescu (1998). *Academic Productivity of Chicago
Public Schools.* Chicago: Consortium on Chicago School
Research, University of Chicago.
CCSSO (1997). *Status Report: State Systemic Education
Improvements.* Washington, D.C.: Council of Chief State
School Officers.
Chicago Assembly (1994). *Paying for State and Local Govern-
ment; Report of the Chicago Assembly.* Chicago: Center for
Urban Research and Policy Studies, University of Chicago,
and Metropolitan Planning Council.
CPRE (1998). *States and Districts and Comprehensive School
Reform.* CPRE Policy Brief. Philadelphia: Consortium for
Policy Research in Education, Graduate School of Educa-
tion, University of Pennsylvania.
Danzberger, Jacqueline, Cristine Bodinger-deUriarte, and Mi-
chele Clark (1996). *A Guide to Promising Practices in
Educational Partnerships.* Washington, D.C.: Office of
Educational Research and Improvement, U.S. Department of
Education.
Dye, Richard F., Scott Goldstein, and Therese McGuire (1998).
An Evaluation of Illinois' 1997 School Reforms. Chicago:
Institute of Government and Public Affairs, University of
Illinois, and Metropolitan Planning Council.
Easton, John Q., and Sandra L. Storey (2001). "Standards and
Assessment in School Accountability Systems in Illinois."
In this volume.
Elmore, Richard F., and Associates (1990). *Restructuring
Schools: The Next Generation of Educational Reform.* San
Francisco: Jossey-Bass.
Elmore, Richard F., and Susan H. Fuhrman (1995). "Opportu-
nity-to-Learn Standards and the State Role in Education,
Teachers College Record, vol. 96, no. 3 (Spring 1995),
pp. 432-457.
Goertz, Margaret E., Robert E. Floden, and Jennifer O'Day
(1996). *Systemic Reform.* Washington, D.C.: Office of

Educational Research and Improvement, U.S. Department of Education.

Haycock, Kati (1997). "K-16 Reform: What's In It for Schools? What's In It for Universities?" *Thinking K-16*, Fall 1997. Washington, D.C.: The Education Trust.

Hess, G. Alfred, Jr. (2001). "Education Reform Policy in Illinois: Problems, Conundrums, and Strategies." In this volume.

Hess, G. Alfred, Jr., and David Braskamp (1998). "The 1997 Illinois School Finance Revisions: Less than Meets the Eye." Evanston: Center for Urban School Policy, Northwestern University.

ISBE (1985). "1984-1985 Public School Fall Enrollment and Housing Report." Springfield: Illinois State Board of Education.

_____ (1996a). *Illinois Framework for Restructuring the Recruitment, Preparation, Licensure, and Continuing Professional Development of Teachers.* Springfield: Illinois State Board of Education, November 1996.

_____ (1996b). *K-12 Information Technology Plan.* Springfield: Illinois State Board of Education.

_____ (1997a). *Illinois Learning Standards.* Springfield: Illinois State Board of Education, July 1997.

_____ (1997b). *The Illinois Right to Read Initiative.* Springfield: Illinois State Board of Education, September 1997.

_____ (1997c). *Preparing Educators for the 21st Century.* Springfield: Illinois State Board of Education, November 1997.

_____ (1997d). "Quality Assurance and Improvement Planning Process: An Overview," *Superintendent's Policy Bulletin 97P-07*, April 15, 1997.

_____ (1997e). *Superintendent's Bulletin*, Special Edition, December 9, 1997. Springfield: Illinois State Board of Education.

_____ (1999). "Guidelines for Internal and External Review." Springfield: Center for Accountability and Quality Assurance, Illinois State Board of Education, May 1999.

_____ (2000). "1999-2000 Public School Fall Enrollment and Housing Report." Springfield: Illinois State Board of Education.

Ladd, Helen F., ed. (1996). *Holding Schools Accountable: Performance-Based Reform in Education.* Washington, D.C.: Brookings Institution.

Lewis, Dan A. (2001). "Lessons of Chicago School Reform: From Radical Decentralization to Administrative Pragmatism." In this volume.

Massell, Diane (2001). "Standards-Based Reform in the States: Progress and Challenges." In this volume.

Massell, Diane, Michael Kirst, and Margaret Hoppe (1997). *Persistence and Change: Standards-Based Systemic Reform in Nine States.* CPRE Policy Brief. Philadelphia: Consortium for Policy Research in Education, Graduate School of Education, University of Pennsylvania.

McLaughlin, Milbrey W., and Lorrie A. Shepard, with Jennifer O'Day (1995). *Improving Education through Standards-Based Reform: A Report of the National Academy of Education Panel on Standards-Based Education Reform.* Stanford, Calif.: National Academy of Education.

Meyer, Dea (2001). "Comments: Education Funding in Illinois." In this volume.

Meyer, Robert H. (1996). "Comments on Chapters Two, Three, and Four." In Helen F. Ladd, ed., *Holding Schools Accountable: Performance-Based Reform in Education.* Washington, D.C.: Brookings Institution.

Murnane, Richard J., and Frank Levy (1992). "Education and Training." In Henry J. Aaron and Charles L. Schultze, eds., *Setting Domestic Priorities: What Can Government Do?* Washington, D.C.: Brookings Institution.

NCEE (1983). *A Nation at Risk: The Imperative for Educational Reform.* Report of the National Commission on Excellence in Education. Washington, D.C.: U.S. Department of Education.

NCEST (1992). *Raising Standards for American Education: A Report to Congress, the Secretary of Education, the National Education Goals Panel, and the American People.* Washington, D.C.: National Council on Education Standards and Testing.

NCTAF (1996). *What Matters Most: Teaching for America's Future.* Report of the National Commission on Teaching and America's Future. New York: Teachers College, Columbia University.

Newmann, Fred W. (1993). "What Is a Restructured School?" *Principal*, January 1993, pp. 5-8.

NGA (1994). *Professional Development for Educators: A Priority for Reaching High Standards.* Washington, D.C.: National Governors' Association.

O'Day, Jennifer A., and Marshall S. Smith (1993). "Systemic Reform and Educational Opportunity." In Susan H. Fuhrman, ed. *Designing Coherent Education Policy: Improving the System.* San Francisco: Jossey-Bass.

Payne, Charles M. (2001). "So Much Reform, So Little Change: Building-Level Obstacles to Urban School Reform." In this volume.

Picus, Lawrence O. (2001). "Improving Student Learning: How Does Money Matter?" In this volume.

Porter, Andrew (1995). "The Uses and Misuses of Opportunity-to-Learn Standards," *Educational Researcher*, January-February 1995, pp. 21-27.

Ravitch, Diane (1995). *National Standards in American Education: A Citizen's Guide.* Washington, D.C.: Brookings Institution Press.

Roderick, Melissa (2001). "Educational Trends and Issues in the Region, the State, and the Nation." In this volume.

Sanders, Ted (1986). "Illinois Educational Reform: A Thoughtful Response to Crisis," *Illinois Issues*, May 1986, pp. 17-19.

Sevener, Donald (1985). "Education at Fork in the Road: Mandates or Outcomes," *Illinois Issues*, April 1985, pp. 18-23.

_____ (1991). "Revisiting the 1985 Education Reforms: Is the 'Old School Bus' Running Better?" *Illinois Issues*, May 1991, pp. 14-16.

Smith, Marshall S., and Jennifer O'Day (1991). "Systemic School Reform." In Susan H. Fuhrman and Betty Malen, eds., *The Politics of Curriculum and Testing. The 1990 Yearbook of the Politics of Education Association.* New York: The Falmer Press.

U.S. Department of Education (1996). *Goals 2000: Increasing Student Achievement Through State and Local Initiatives.* Report to the Congress. Washington, D.C.: U.S. Department of Education.

Wohlstetter, Priscilla, Susan Albers Mohrman, and Peter J. Robertson (1997). "Successful School-Based Management: A Lesson for Restructuring Urban Schools." In Diane Ravitch and Joseph P. Viteritti, eds., *New Schools for a New Century: The Redesign of Urban Education.* New Haven: Yale University Press.

Wong, Kenneth K. (1996). "Toward Fiscal Responsibility in Illinois Public Education." In Lawrence B. Joseph, ed., *Dilemmas of Fiscal Reform: Paying for State and Local Gov-*

ernment in Illinois. A Chicago Assembly Book. Chicago: Center for Urban Research and Policy Studies, University of Chicago; distributed by University of Illinois Press.
_____ (2001). "Comments: Integrated Governance." In this volume.

CHICAGO ASSEMBLY PARTICIPANTS
"EDUCATION REFORM FOR THE 21ST CENTURY"
JANUARY 26-27, 1998

Rosa Abreu
Education Staff Attorney
Mexican American Legal Defense
  and Educational Fund
(Chicago)

Mark Angelini
Vice President
The Shaw Company
(Chicago)

John Ayers
Executive Director
Leadership for Quality Education
(Chicago)

Suzanne Bassi
Former Chair
Education Research Development
(ED-RED)
(Palatine)

Larry Bennett
Professor of Political Science
DePaul University
(Chicago)

Heidi Biederman
Executive Director
Large Unit District Association
(Elgin)

Joyce Bristow
Executive Assistant to the
  Chief Education Officer
Chicago Public Schools

Barbara Buell
Executive Director
Chicago Panel on School Policy

Karen Carlson
Executive Director
Chicago Academic Accountability
  Council

Sheila Castillo
Director
Chicago Association of
  Local School Councils

Louise E. Coleman
Superintendent
Joliet School District 86
(Joliet)

Victoria Davis
Executive Director
Illinois Learning Partnership
(Naperville)

Antonio Delgado
Senior Advocate
Latino Institute
(Chicago)

Rolanda H. Derderian
Vice President
Prime Group Realty Trust
(Chicago)

John Q. Easton
Deputy Director
Consortium on Chicago School
  Research
University of Chicago

Lauren Beth Gash
State Representative, 60th District
(Deerfield)

Ed Geppert, Jr.
Secretary-Treasurer
Illinois Federation of Teachers
(Oakbrook)

Sharon Gist Gilliam
Board Member
Illinois State Board of Education
(Chicago)

G. Alfred Hess, Jr.
Research Professor, School of
    Education and Social Policy
Northwestern University
(Evanston)

Doris Holleb
Professorial Lecturer
Social Sciences Collegiate Division
University of Chicago

Joyce Hollingsworth
Executive Director
Government Assistance Program
(Chicago)

Hattie Jackson
Director, Education Department
Chicago Urban League

Richard Laine
Associate Superintendent
Illinois State Board of Education
(Springfield)

Elliot Lehman
Co-Chairman, Emeritus
Fel-Pro, Inc.
(Skokie)

Dan A. Lewis
Professor, School of Education
    and Social Policy
Northwestern University
(Evanston)

James Lewis
Vice President for Research
    and Planning
Chicago Urban League

Vivian Loseth
Director, Chicago Comer Project
Youth Guidance
(Chicago)

Clayton Marquardt
Executive Director
Illinois Education Association
(Springfield)

Jeff Mays
Executive Vice President
Illinois State Chamber of Commerce
(Chicago)

Marilyn McConachie
Board Member
Illinois State Board of Education
(Northbrook)

Dea Meyer
Vice President
Civic Committee of the
    Commercial Club
(Chicago)

Michael H. Moskow
President
Federal Reserve Bank of Chicago

Clyde E. Murphy
Executive Director
Chicago Lawyers' Committee for
    Civil Rights Under Law

Diana Nelson
Director of Public Affairs
Union League Club of Chicago

Carolyn D. Nordstrom
President
Chicago United, Inc.

Jeri Nowakowski
Executive Director
North Central Regional
    Educational Laboratory
(Oak Brook)

James Nowlan
Senior Fellow, Institute of
    Government and Public Affairs
University of Illinois

Raymond P. O'Connell
Vice President, Public Relations
AT&T
(Chicago)

Renae Ogletree
Executive Director
Chicago Youth Agency Partnership

Alice J. Palmer
College of Education
University of Illinois at Chicago

Natalye Paquin
Senior Assistant to the President
Chicago School Reform Board
 of Trustees

Charles Payne
Professor, Department of
 African-American Studies
Northwestern University
(Evanston)

Sylvia Puente
Director of Public Policy
 and Advocacy
Latino Institute
(Chicago)

Steven Rauschenberger
State Senator, 33rd District
(Elgin)

Elizabeth Perriello Rice
Program Officer
Prince Charitable Trusts
(Chicago)

Cindy Richards
Editorial Page Deputy Editor
Chicago Sun-Times

Melissa Roderick
Associate Professor, School of
 Social Service Administration
University of Chicago

Ken Rolling
Executive Director
Chicago Annenberg Challenge

Patrick G. Ryan, Jr.
President
Ryan Enterprises
(Chicago)

Jeffery Schoenberg
State Representative, 58th District
(Wilmette)

Chris Slowik
Organizational Director
South Cooperative Organization
 for Public Education (SCOPE)
(Blue Island)

Jerome Stermer
President
Voices for Illinois Children
(Chicago)

Nancy Stevenson
Public Affairs Representative
Voices for Illinois Children
(Chicago)

Elizabeth Tisdahl
Chair, Education Research
 Development (ED-RED)
(Evanston)

Beverly Tunney
President
Chicago Principals and
 Administrators Association

Anna M. Weselak
President
Illinois PTA
(Lombard)

Norman Wetzel
Superintendent
Community Unit School District 300
(Carpentersville)

Wim Wiewel
Dean, College of Urban Planning
 and Public Affairs
University of Illinois at Chicago

Julie Woestehoff
Executive Director
Parents United for Responsible
 Education (PURE)
(Chicago)

Bonnie J. Wood
Executive Director
East West Corporate Corridor
 Association
(Lombard)

Observers

M. Margaret Blandford
Executive Director
W. P. and H. B. White Foundation
(Chicago)

Janet Hansen
Study Director
Committee on Education Finance
National Academy of Sciences
(Washington, D.C.)

Kent Lawrence
President and Executive Director
M. R. Bauer Foundation
(Chicago)

Linda Lenz
Editor and Publisher
Catalyst: Voices of Chicago
   School Reform
(Chicago)

Debra D. Schwartz
Senior Associate
Office of the President
John D. and Catherine T.
   MacArthur Foundation
(Chicago)

Project Director

Laurence E. Lynn, Jr.
Director, Center for Urban
   Research and Policy Studies
Irving B. Harris Graduate School
   of Public Policy Studies
The University of Chicago

Program Director

Lawrence B. Joseph
Associate Director, Center for
   Urban Research and Policy
   Studies
Irving B. Harris Graduate School
   of Public Policy Studies
The University of Chicago

Project Associate

MarySue Barrett
President
Metropolitan Planning Council

Staff

Scott Goldstein
Regional Development Director
Metropolitan Planning Council

Erin Krasik
Irving B. Harris Graduate School
  of Public Policy Studies
The University of Chicago

Jennifer Matjasko
Irving B. Harris Graduate School
  of Public Policy Studies
The University of Chicago

Audra Millen
Irving B. Harris Graduate School
  of Public Policy Studies
The University of Chicago

Reva Nelson
School of Social Service
  Administration
The University of Chicago

Martha Ross
School of Social Service
  Administration
The University of Chicago

Jodie Zalk
Irving B. Harris Graduate School
  of Public Policy Studies
The University of Chicago

Drafting Committee

John Ayers**
Suzanne Bassi**
Larry Bennett*
Ed Geppert
Joyce Hollingsworth*
James Lewis
Marilyn McConachie
Clyde Murphy
Diana Nelson
Carolyn Nordstrom
James Nowlan*
Raymond O'Connell
Renae Ogletree**
Sylvia Puente**
Patrick Ryan
Norman Wetzel
Wim Wiewel*

* Facilitator
** Recorder

CHICAGO ASSEMBLY PROGRAM COMMITTEE*
"EDUCATION REFORM FOR THE 21ST CENTURY"

John Ayers
Executive Director
Leadership for Quality Education

MarySue Barrett
President
Metropolitan Planning Council

Suzanne Bassi
Former Chairperson
Education Research Development
(ED-RED)

Heidi Biederman
Executive Director
Large Unit District Association

Sharon Gist Gilliam
Board Member
Illinois State Board of Education

Richard Laine
Associate Superintendent for
   Policy, Planning, and Resource
   Management
Illinois State Board of Education

Dan Lewis
Professor, School of Education
   and Social Policy
Northwestern University

James Lewis
Vice President, Research
   and Planning
Chicago Urban League

Diana Nelson
Director of Public Affairs
Union League Club of Chicago

Alexander Polikoff
Executive Director
Business and Professional People
   for the Public Interest

Sylvia Puente
Director of Public Policy
   and Advocacy
Latino Institute

Melissa Roderick
Associate Professor
School of Social Service
   Administration
University of Chicago

Jerome Stermer
President
Voices for Illinois Children

Wim Wiewel
Dean, College of Urban Planning
   and Public Affairs
University of Illinois at Chicago

Ex officio

Lawrence B. Joseph
Associate Director
Center for Urban Research
   and Policy Studies
Irving B. Harris Graduate School
   of Public Policy Studies
The University of Chicago

* Titles and affiliations as of January 1998.

CHICAGO ASSEMBLY ADVISORY BOARD*

Mark A. Angelini
Vice President
The Shaw Company

MarySue Barrett
President
Metropolitan Planning Council

Larry Bennett
Professor of Political Science
DePaul University

Pastora San Juan Cafferty
Professor, School of Social
    Service Administration
The University of Chicago

Eduardo Camacho
Assistant Vice President
St. Paul Federal Bank

P. Lindsay Chase-Lansdale
Professor, School of Education
    and Social Policy
Northwestern University

Barbara Flynn Currie
State Representative
26th District

Sharon Gist Gilliam
Executive Vice President
Unison Consulting Group

Donald Haider
Professor, J. L. Kellogg Graduate
    School of Management
Northwestern University

Doris B. Holleb
Professorial Lecturer
Social Sciences Collegiate Division
University of Chicago

James Lewis
Executive Director
Institute for Metropolitan Affairs
Roosevelt University

Dea Meyer
Vice President
Civic Committee of the Commercial
    Club of Chicago

Robert T. Michael
Dean, Irving B. Harris Graduate
    School of Public Policy Studies
The University of Chicago

Michael Newman
Assistant Director
AFSCME, Council 31

Philip Nyden
Director, Center for Urban
    Research and Learning
Loyola University Chicago

Elizabeth S. Ruyle
Executive Director
South Suburban Mayors and
    Managers Association

Kenneth B. Smith
Senior Fellow
The Chicago Community Trust

Jerome Stermer
President
Voices for Illinois Children

Carole J. Travis
Director, Illinois State Council
Service Employees International
    Union

Wim Wiewel
Dean, College of Business
    Administration
University of Illinois at Chicago

* As of December 2000.

Ex officio

Laurence E. Lynn, Jr.
Director
Center for Urban Research
  and Policy Studies
Irving B. Harris Graduate School
  of Public Policy Studies
The University of Chicago

Lawrence B. Joseph
Associate Director
Center for Urban Research
  and Policy Studies
Irving B. Harris Graduate School
  of Public Policy Studies
The University of Chicago